UNDERSTANDING MENTAL HEALTH

EDUCATING AND CREATING MENTAL HEALTH AWARENESS

Vuyo Nyeli

Vuyo Nyeli Publishers

Copyright © 2022 Vuyo Nyeli

All rights reserved. In terms of Copyright Act 98 of 1978, no part of this book may be reproduced, scanned, or distributed in any printed or electronic form without permission. Please do not participate in or encourage piracy of copyrighted materials in violation of the author's rights. Purchase only authorized editions.

Vuyo Nyeli has asserted her right to be identified as the author of this book in accordance with the Copyright Act No 98 of 1978
While the author has made every effort to provide accurate telephone numbers and up-to-date information from the best and most reliable sources at the time of publication, neither the publisher nor the author assumes any responsibility for errors or for changes that occur after publication. Further, the publisher does not have any control over and does not assume any responsibility for author or third-party websites or their content.

ISBN: 9798374338256

Cover design by: KDP images

DISCLAIMER: The information in this book is true and correct to the best of the author's knowledge. The book is intended only as a general guide to specific types of mental disorders and is not intended as a replacement for sound medical advice or services from the individual reader's personal physician. All recommendations herein are made without guarantees by the author or publisher. The author and the publisher disclaim all liability, direct or consequential, in connection with the use of any information or suggestion in this book.

*To my son Liwa.
I love you with my whole heart.*

"Mental illnesses, unlike broken bones, are invisible to everyone but those experiencing them. But their reality is no different and no less painful. Many will suffer in silence"

PROF SWARAN SINGH (HEAD OF MENTAL & WELLBEING, UNIVERSITY OF WARWICK)

CONTENTS

Title Page
Copyright
Dedication
Epigraph
Foreword
Introduction

Chapter I	1
What is mental wellness?	2
Chapter II	11
Chapter III	16
Chapter IV	26
Chapter V	29
Chapter VI	43
- Attention deficit/hyperactivity disorder (ADHD)	63
- Schizophrenia	75
- Schizoaffective disorder	87
- Delusional disorder	96
Types of depression	129
Other disorders that cause depression symptoms	131
- Male depression: Understanding the issues	143
- Postpartum/Postnatal depression	147
Postpartum depression in new fathers	150
Postpartum psychosis	156
- Nervous breakdown: What does it mean?	161

- Generalized anxiety disorder 163
- Panic disorder 174
- Obsessive-compulsive disorder (OCD) 183
- Post-traumatic stress disorder 194
- Social anxiety disorder 206
- Dissociative amnesia 225
- Dissociative identity disorder 226
- Depersonalization-derealization disorder 227
- Anorexia nervosa 242
- Bulimia Nervosa 255
- Binge-eating disorder 265
- Pica eating disorder 274
- Rumination eating disorder 284
- Enuresis 290
- Encopresis 291
- Insomnia 298
- Sleep apnea 313

Central sleep apnea 315

- Restless legs syndrome 327
- Narcolepsy 334
- Oppositional defiant disorder 359
- Intermittent explosive disorder 371

Part of your treatment may include: 377

- Conduct disorder 382
- Pyromania 388
- Kleptomania 391
- Compulsive gambling/gambling disorder 432
- Delirium 443

Delirium and dementia	446
- Alzheimer's disease	455
- Traumatic brain injury	476
- Dementia	494
Other disorders linked to dementia	498
Dementia-like conditions that can be reversed	499
Risk factors that can't be changed	501
Risk factors you can change	502
Cluster A personality disorders	516
Cluster B personality disorders	518
Cluster C personality disorders	520
- Sexual sadism disorder	532
- Voyeuristic disorder	537
- Pedophilic disorder	542
Chapter VII	545
Chapter VIII	549
Chapter IX	558
Chapter X	571
About The Author	577
References	579
Note to reader	581
Conclusion	583
Acknowledgement	585

FOREWORD

I have always had a desire to make a difference in other's lives. When Vuyo asked me to assist her in starting a podcast about creating mental health awareness. I was honoured. The success of the podcast created a bigger sense of inspiration and opened the door of this book. I have known Vuyo since 2019, our relationship began with friendship and now she is like an older sister to me. I always regard her as an insipratonal individual, survivor and a fighter. The biggest lesson I have learned from her is, "never take your eyes off the bigger picture, despite what you're going through in life".

Personally, I am honoured to have been appointed by Vuyo to proofread this book. I believe this book will make a difference and educate the readers about mental health as well as how to apply the knowledge gained in their own lives. I would also like to acknowledge the hard work and effort you have made in writing this book. I love how the book explains the subject of mental health as a whole, and the emphasis it has on how important our mental health is. I believe everyone should read this book, and I am certain that there's a lot to learn, from basic to advanced knowledge. Most importantly, the book completely brings clarity and changes the generalised perception about mental health issues and illnesses.

I, Phumulani Sgudla the founder of Visionary Designs. I am a professional designer, business consultant in digital marketing as well as in web development.

INTRODUCTION

Mental health determines and affects how we think, feel and act. Mental health includes our emotional, psychological and social well-being. It also helps us determine how we handle stress, relate to others and healthy life choices and decisions. Mental health is important at every life stage, from childhood, adolescence and through adulthood.

The World Health Organization (WHO) defined mental health to be 'a state of well-being in which the individual realizes his or her own abilities, can cope with the normal stresses of life, can work productively and fruitfully, and is able to make a contribution to his or her community' (WHO, 2014)

CHAPTER I

Defining Mental Wellness

Mental wellness is a term that is increasingly used in the popular lexicon, but it is vague and not well-understood. People associate mental wellness with many different types of activities: meditating, listening to music, talking to a friend, taking a walk-in nature, taking a vacation, getting a massage, taking a bubble bath, squeezing a stress ball, or just carving out some time for peace and quiet in daily life. When we talk about mental wellness, we are not just focusing on our mental or cognitive functioning, but also our emotions; our social relationships; our ability to function in daily life; and even our spiritual, religious, or existential state. Most people would agree that mental wellness is different than happiness, but very few could elaborate precisely how the two are different. Sometimes the term mental wellness is used synonymously with mental health or mental well-being, two terms that are also not well-defined. A simple and concise definition for mental wellness and summary of related terminologies and definitions (for mental illness, mental health, mental well-being, and happiness) is provided below.

WHAT IS MENTAL WELLNESS?

Mental wellness is an internal resource that helps us think, feel, connect, and function; it is an active process that helps us to build resilience, grow, and flourish. This definition characterizes mental wellness as a dynamic, renewable, and positive resource, and as an active process that requires initiative and conscious action. It recognizes mental wellness as an internal experience that encompasses multiple dimensions:

- *Mental:* How we think; how we process, understand, and use information.
- *Emotional:* How we feel; how we manage and express our emotions.
- *Social:* How we connect; our relationships with others.
- *Psychological:* How we act or function, or how we "put the pieces together;" taking external inputs along with our internal capacity and then making decisions or doing things.

This new definition of mental wellness distills the concepts included in many existing definitions, notably from the World Health Organization (WHO) and the U.S. Surgeon General, to align with current practices and understanding. Key concepts included in those definitions are: feeling good, being resilient and functional, enjoying positive relationships, contributing to society or community, realizing potential, and having a sense of fulfilment or coherence. Mental wellness is sometimes associated with the concept of psychological well-being, which includes self-acceptance, growth, purpose, autonomy, environmental mastery, and positive relationships. Mental wellness has been described as a process, a resource, a state of being, or a balance point between resources and challenges. This definition builds upon well-established (but not widely known) theories from psychology and academic literature, and it frames them in a language that is more understandable to consumers, businesspeople, and policymakers.

Five key things everyone should know about mental wellness:

1. Mental wellness is more than just the absence of mental illness

There is a tendency to think of mental wellness and mental illness as a simple continuum, with severe and chronic mental disorders on one end, happiness and flourishing on the other end, and varying degrees of resilience or coping with mental and emotional disturbances in the middle. This view does not accurately reflect the nuanced and dynamic relationship between mental illness and mental wellness. The complex relationship between mental illness and mental wellness is best understood by envisioning them sitting on two separate continuums.

- **The horizontal axis measures mental illness from high to low.** This axis measures the presence or absence of diagnosable mental disorders (e.g., depression, anxiety, personality disorders, etc.), based upon the Diagnostic and Statistical Manual of Mental Disorders, 5th Edition (DSM-5). Treatment of mental illness typically takes a clinical or pathogenic approach, which focuses on diagnosing a problem, treating the symptoms, and bringing a person back to "normal." Care is typically delivered by trained mental health professionals (e.g., psychiatrists, psychologists, social workers, etc.).

- **The vertical axis measures mental wellness from languishing to flourishing.** This axis captures the many factors that shape our overall mental health and well-being, but are not clinical conditions – e.g., stress, worry, loneliness, or sadness at the negative end, and happiness, life satisfaction, strong relationships, or personal growth at the positive end. Mental wellness offers a salutogenic approach that focuses on positive human functioning: preventing illness, maintaining good mental health, and pursuing optimal mental well-being. Mental wellness is self-directed, personal, and subjective; it typically relies on self-care and personal agency to cope with everyday challenges and proactively pursue a higher level of happiness and well-being. Mental wellness can be empowering because it acknowledges the universal desire for peace, joy, happiness, meaning, and purpose.

Subsequent research over the last two decades has supported the dual continuum model, which captures several important concepts about mental wellness and mental illness:

- A lack of mental illness does not equate to mental wellness. About 15% of the world's population suffers from a diagnosed mental or substance use disorder, but that does not mean that the other 85% of the population is "mentally well" or leading healthy, happy, productive, and satisfied lives. Many people who do not have a mental illness still "do not feel healthy or function well," because of pervasive stress, worry, loneliness, and other challenges. Those who are "languishing" rather than "flourishing" (even when free of a diagnosed mental illness) tend to do worse in terms of "physical health outcomes, healthcare utilization, missed days of work, and psychosocial functioning." Low mental wellness ("languishing") can be debilitating; it is more common than depression and is associated with emotional and psychosocial impairment comparable to that of a depressive episode.

- Mental wellness can co-exist with mental illness. Research on the dual continuum model shows that the presence of mental illness does not necessarily imply an absence of mental wellness, and vice versa. For example, a person with obsessive compulsive disorder, attention deficit disorder, or mild depression can still demonstrate moderate or positive mental wellness (e.g., having good relationships, feeling happy, or functioning well at a job). Corey Keyes' study of Americans ages 25-74 found that 70% of those with a diagnosed mental illness had a "moderate" or "flourishing" level of mental wellness. Meanwhile, among those free of mental illness in the previous year, only 20% were "flourishing" in their mental wellness.

- Mental wellness can mitigate and prevent mental illness. Increasing our level of mental wellness can protect us against developing mental illness and can also mitigate the symptoms of these illnesses. Keyes' studies showed that those who are "flourishing" function better than those with moderate or "languishing" mental wellness, regardless of whether a person has a diagnosed mental illness or not. People whose level of mental wellness declined from flourishing to moderate were over 3.5 times more likely to develop mental illness than those who stayed flourishing, while people whose mental wellness declined from moderate to languishing were 86% more likely to develop mental illness. Meanwhile, Keyes' research also showed that improving one's mental wellness from languishing to moderate reduced the risk of future mental illness by nearly half. We are not suggesting here that mental wellness can solve or cure mental illness, but that the practices that support and improve our mental wellness (e.g., good sleep, good nutrition, exercise, meaningful relationships, reducing stress, meditation) are increasingly recognized as protective factors for our mental health, as well as helping reduce the severity and symptoms of mental illness (alongside conventional treatment regimens).

2. Mental wellness is an active process of moving from languishing to resilience, to flourishing

Our mental wellness is not a static state of being. Mental wellness is a lifelong process and a proactive strategy to strengthen our mental, emotional, social, and psychological resources. On one level, mental wellness is about prevention;

coping with life's adversity; and being resilient when we face stress, worry, loneliness, anger, and sadness. On another level, mental wellness moves us toward a deeper, richer, and more meaningful human experience, which is often described as flourishing. The notion of flourishing as the peak mental state has been shaped by developments in the psychology field during the 20th century, including Abraham Maslow's hierarchy of needs, Carl Rogers and humanistic psychology (a holistic approach of self-exploration and working toward full human potential), and Martin Seligman's positive psychology (emphasizing eudaimonia and human flourishing). Concepts of self-actualization, the pursuit of fulfillment, and the untapped potential that lies in all people were disseminated and popularized by the Human Potential Movement in the 1960s-1970s.

The psychology field has explored various methods of measuring individuals' mental wellness, but these tools depend upon self-reporting and are inherently subjective. Flourishing is a personal experience. For some people, it may mean functioning at the top of their game on a daily basis – staying engaged, sharp, and focused; and achieving their life goals and vision. For others, flourishing could mean moving toward self-transcendence – going beyond the "self" to associate with a higher purpose; living in truth, unity, and harmony with the universal order; and developing a sense of peace and joy that is independent of external circumstances or events. This concept of mental wellness is often associated with the realms of human consciousness, spiritual practices, and religious devotion. Our definition of what it means to flourish is also shaped by culture. For example, in some cultures people put the highest value on individual balance and inner harmony for living a thriving and happy life. Other cultures may take a more collectivist view, placing high value on peace, family relationships, and social harmony. The important point is that flourishing (as a peak level of mental wellness) is different for different people, depending on their values, beliefs, culture, and personal journey.

3. Mental wellness helps to shift the perspective away from stigma to shared humanity and shared responsibility

Even though the mental health field has done a lot of work to mitigate the stigma surrounding mental illness, a sense of shame, denial, and secrecy continues to afflict people in communities and cultures around the world. Mental wellness can help shift our focus toward a more positive and empowering approach (how we can feel, think, connect, and function better), rather than just avoiding or coping with illness. Importantly, mental wellness emphasizes our capacity to build resilience; to reduce suffering; to find inner peace, joy, and fulfilment; to seek purpose, meaning, and happiness; and to connect to others. By acknowledging this as a universal condition and longing shared by all people, there is no need to feel shame or to feel that we are alone in this endeavor.

During the last century, modern psychology and its approaches to treating mental illness have tended to focus on individual behavior and individual-level interventions, such as talk therapy and drugs. Mental wellness favors a more holistic approach that encompasses personal agency alongside social and environmental dimensions (e.g., family, friends, community connections, living environments). In doing so, mental wellness helps shift our perspective toward a sense of shared humanity and shared responsibility, while also bringing attention to the many external forces that deeply influence our overall mental health and well-being – including socioeconomic status, culture and values, built environment, technology, and much more.

This approach does not ignore or refute the immense need for more resources and better methods to address and treat mental illness. Rather, it emphasizes that the promotion of mental wellness is an equally important (yet often overlooked) approach that can address a multitude of individual and societal problems (such as loneliness and stress), while also complementing approaches to mental illness and even helping to prevent mental illness and reduce its associated costs.

4. Mental wellness grows out of a grassroots, consumer-driven movement

There is a huge global need to address mental illness and to help people in mental distress who are vulnerable to developing a full-blown mental disorder. The needs are vast, and resources are scarce, and the "talk and pills" approach does not work for everyone. Meanwhile, people with poor mental wellness ("languishing") desperately need non-clinical, non-pathologizing strategies and tools to cope. As discussed above, evidence shows that improving our mental wellness can even reduce our risk of developing mental illness. And yet, not enough attention is paid globally to mental illness prevention and mental wellness promotion, and mental health has never been well-integrated into public health structures.

Our healthcare systems (including mental health) are not set up to help the spiraling number of people who are facing everyday mental and emotional challenges like stress, burnout, loneliness, or sadness. In response to these immense gaps, mental wellness has grown out of a grassroots, consumer-led movement that seeks self-directed, alternative solutions outside of the established fields of medicine, psychiatry, and psychology. Mental wellness encompasses many natural and complementary modalities that have been around for millennia, and that have operated on the fringes of modern psychology and medicine for decades. It embraces a holistic approach that recognizes the mind-body connection, and therefore extends to lifestyle strategies such as nutrition and exercise. Mental wellness modalities mostly exist outside of healthcare systems and reimbursement schemes. Presently, many of these modalities lack the validation of clinical evidence and double-blind studies that are required for approval of medical treatment protocols and pharmaceuticals.

5. Mental wellness is multi-dimensional, holistic, and personal

Mental wellness recognizes the integrated and holistic nature of our health and well-being. The state of our mind affects our body, and vice versa. Our mental wellness is also connected to our beliefs and values, to other people, to nature, and even to the realms of consciousness and spirituality. The approaches for improving our mental wellness are diverse and inclusive, and they are enriched by cultural, social, and religious traditions and contexts. The numerous pathways toward mental wellness have been extensively catalogued in GWI's 2018 Mental Wellness Initiative white paper and in a recently published chapter in the Oxford Research Encyclopedia of Global Public Health.

CHAPTER II

The Importance Of Mental Health

Without mental wellness or good mental health, we will not be able to fulfil our full potential or play an active part in everyday life. Maintaining a positive mental health and treating any mental health condition is crucial in stabilizing constructive behaviors, emotions and thoughts. Nurturing mental health doesn't just improve our day-to-day functioning, but it helps us control or at least combat some of the physical problems directly linked to mental health conditions. For instance, heart disease and stress are related, so managing stress might have a positive outcome on heart disease. Good mental health is more important than ever before as it impacts every area of our lives. Its importance ripples into everything we do, think or say. So, focusing on mental health care can increase productivity, enhance our self-image and improve relationships.

Let us understand in detail why is mental health important and what we can do to keep it intact:

1. Mental health plays a crucial role in relationships

The link between mental health and relationships is one of the most compelling reasons for its importance. Mental Illness might have an impact on how we interact with our friends and family. Mental illnesses frequently result in passive-aggressiveness, hostility, and the incapacity to participate in social activities. This may result in conflicts with our friends and family. Mental illness has the potential to compel us to overthrow our loved ones for no apparent reason. Self-care for mental health and, if necessary, medication can help us live a mentally stable existence while also maintaining our relationships.

2. Mental health affects physical health

There's a link between our mental health and our physical health. Mental illness can induce stress and have an effect on our immune systems. As a result, our bodies ability to cope with illness may be jeopardized. A sick mind can lead to anxiety and sadness, both of which can make it difficult to move about and stay active. The mind-body connection is well-established, which is why mental health awareness is so crucial.

3. Mental health is related to emotional well-being

Every day, how you feel on the inside is just as important as how physically healthy you are. Mental health advice demonstrates how a negative mind can make you feel down, irritated, or disturbed. Taking care of our emotional well-being can help us be more productive and effective at work and in our daily activities. To maintain track of our emotional and overall well-being, we can seek mental health advice from friends, family, and a psychologist or psychotherapist.

4. Mental health awareness can help in curbing suicide rates

According to South African Depression and Anxiety Group (SADAG), South Africa sees an estimated 23 suicides and 460 attempted suicides a day. The youngest suicide case in South Africa was a 6-year-old child. Men in South Africa are four times more likely to die by suicide than women. Chambers said it is normally a combination of issues that pushes someone to end their life. "It is never just one thing or reason that causes someone to end life. They have found that the main factors include undiagnosed or untreated depression, relationship issues, financial issues, and trauma," she explained. This demonstrates the link between mental health and suicide, as well as how early medical intervention and self-care can help minimize the number of suicide deaths. It is critical to follow suggestions to maintain our mental health and to be aware of the mental health of those around us at all times.

5. Mental health is linked with crime and victimization

As per some studies, poor mental health puts one at an increased risk of committing violent crimes. It also leads to self-victimization and abuse. This risk is further substantiated if the individual consumes drugs and alcohol and is averse to taking medication. In most cases, crimes by mentally unfit persons are committed against family members or those within their close circles. Seeking tips for mental health from a medical professional and understanding why mental health is important can help in avoiding such scenarios.

6. Mental health is connected to productivity and financial stability

One of the many reasons why it's crucial to look after your mental health is that it boosts your overall productivity and financial security. According to research published in the American Journal of Psychiatry, those with serious mental diseases earn 40% less than those in good mental health. According to the World Health Organization, almost 200 million workdays are lost each year owing to depression alone. It is widely known that poor mental health causes a drop in productivity, which has an impact on financial stability. It is critical that we do the appropriate things for mental health in order to secure strong work performance and financial security.

7. Mental health is linked to societal factors

As previously stated, poor mental health can lead to an increase in crime and violence. Children of adults with mental problems, on the other hand, are more likely to experience abuse, neglect, and behavioral issues. They are likely to grow up to be complex human beings who struggle to find societal acceptance and support. It has also been noted that people who are having mental difficulties become socially isolated and find it difficult to maintain a healthy social life. In conclusion, mental health problems can have a significant societal impact. As a result, it's critical to learn how to maintain excellent mental health and seek medical advice on the subject.

8. Mental health affects the quality of life

From the above discussion, it is clear why it is important to take care of your mental health. An unhealthy mind can cause us to lose interest in the things we once enjoyed. It can lead to ups and downs and overwhelm us to a point where we cannot carry on with even the most basic tasks. Untreated mental health is often identified with a sense of hopelessness, sadness, worthlessness, feelings of guilt, anxiety, fear, and a perceived loss of control. It is important to recognize these symptoms and seek tips for mental health from a certified professional before it is too late.

9. Mental health awareness can help in ending stigma

While many people suffer from mental illness, only a small

percentage seek treatment because of the stigma associated with it. This is why it is critical to raise mental health awareness. The stigma associated with mental health has an impact not only on the number of persons seeking therapy but also on the resources available for effective treatment. For those suffering from underlying mental illnesses, these may be insurmountable difficulties. Individuals can be encouraged to identify their symptoms, practice self-care, and seek therapy or medical support if necessary by spreading the word about mental health tips.

10. Mental health awareness enables community building

We can establish better support facilities for those suffering from mental illnesses if we actively campaign for why mental health awareness is crucial. It would have the potential to generate a more tolerant and kind global society, and hence increase the chances of recovery in situations of mental illness. Learning about mental health and teaching others about it will help us bring about a much-needed change and heal the planet — one person at a time!

CHAPTER III

The Benefits Of Good Mental Health

Just as physical fitness helps our bodies to stay strong, mental fitness helps us to achieve and sustain a state of good mental health. When we are mentally healthy, we enjoy our life and environment, and the people in it. We can be creative, learn, try new things, and take risks. We are better able to cope with difficult times in our personal and professional lives. We feel the sadness and anger that can come with the death of a loved one, a job loss or relationship problems and other difficult events, but in time, we are able to get on with and enjoy our lives once again.

Chances are, you are already taking steps to sustain your mental health, as well as your physical health – you just might not realize it.

Three important ways to improve your mental fitness are to get physical, eat right, and take control of stress:

1. Get Physical

We've known for a long time about the benefits of exercise as a proactive way to enhance our physical condition and combat disease; now, exercise is recognized as an essential element in building and maintaining mental fitness.

So, if you already do exercise of some kind, give yourself two pats on the back – you're improving your physical and mental fitness.

Exercise has many psychological benefits. For example:

- Physical activity is increasingly becoming part of the prescription for the treatment of depression and anxiety. Exercise alone is not a cure, but it does

have a positive impact.
- Research has found that regular physical activity appears as effective as psychotherapy for treating mild to moderate depression. Therapists also report that patients who exercise regularly simply feel better and are less likely to overeat or abuse alcohol and drugs.
- Exercise can reduce anxiety. Many studies have come to this conclusion. People who exercise report feeling less stressed or nervous. Even five minutes of aerobic exercise (exercise which requires oxygen, such as a step class, swimming, walking) can stimulate anti-anxiety effects.
- Physical exercise helps to counteract the withdrawal, inactivity and feelings of hopelessness that characterize depression. Studies show that both aerobic and anaerobic exercise (exercise which does not require oxygen, such as weightlifting) have anti-depressive effects.
- Moods such as tension, fatigue, anger and vigor are all positively affected by exercise.
- Exercising can improve the way you perceive your physical condition, athletic abilities and body image. Enhanced self-esteem is another benefit.
- Last, but not least, exercise brings you into contact with other people in a non-clinical, positive environment. For the length of your walk or workout or aqua-fit class, you engage with people who share your interest in that activity.

Feel the Rush

We may not realize what caused it, but most of us have felt it. Whether we're engaged in a leisurely swim or an adrenaline-charged rock climb, there is that moment when suddenly pain or discomfort drops away and we are filled with a sense of euphoria. We have endorphins to thank for these moments of bliss. Endorphins are chemicals produced in the brain, which bind to neuro-receptors to give relief from pain. Discovered in 1975, the role of endorphins is still being studied. They are believed to: relieve pain; enhance the immune system; reduce stress; and delay the aging process. Exercise stimulates the release of endorphins, sending these depression-fighting, contentment-building chemicals throughout the body. No wonder we feel good after a workout or brisk walk.

Endorphin release varies from person to person; some people will feel an endorphin rush, or second wind, after jogging for 10 minutes. Others will jog for half an hour before their second wind kicks in.

You don't have to exercise vigorously to stimulate endorphin release: meditation, acupuncture, massage therapy, even eating spicy food or breathing deeply – these all cause your body to produce endorphins naturally.

So, enjoy some moderate exercise and feel the endorphin rush!

2. Eat Right

Here's some food for thought – Making the right nutritional choices can affect more than the fit of our clothes; it can have an impact on our mental health. A new study by the UK's Mental Health Foundation suggests that poor diet has played a role in the significant increase in mental health problems over the past 50 years. The trend away from eating less fresh produce and consuming more saturated fats and sugars, including substances like pesticides, additives and trans-fats, can prevent the brain from functioning properly, says the Feeding Minds study. It makes a persuasive link between changing food fads and increases in Attention Deficit Hyperactivity Disorder, Alzheimer's disease and schizophrenia.

The message is not a new one, but it is perhaps the most forceful argument yet for paying more attention to the nutrition-mental health connection. What we put on our plates becomes the raw material for our brains to manufacture hormones and neurotransmitters – chemical substances that control our sleep, mood and behavior. If we shortchange the brain, we also shortchange our intellectual and emotional potential. Our diet also supplies the vitamins which our bodies cannot create, and which we need to help speed up the chemical processes that we need for survival and brain function. Vitamin deficiencies sometimes manifest themselves as depression and can cause mood swings, anxiety and agitation, as well as a host of physical problems.

Mental health professionals point out that good eating habits are vital for people wanting to optimize the effectiveness of and cope with possible side effects of medications used to treat mental illnesses.

Clearly, selecting which foods to eat has consequences beyond immediate taste bud satisfaction. To optimize our brain function, we need to eat a balanced diet of:

- Fresh fruits and vegetables
- Foods high in omega-3 fatty acids, such as fish, nuts, seeds and eggs
- Protein
- Whole grains

3. Take Control of Stress

Stress is a fact of life. No matter how much we might long for a stress-free existence, the fact is, stress is actually necessary. It's how we respond to stress that can negatively affect our lives. Stress is defined as any change that we have to adapt to. This includes difficult life events (bereavement, illness) and positive ones. Getting a new job or going on vacation are certainly perceived to be happy occurrences, but they, too, are changes, also known as stress, that require some adaptation. Learning to effectively cope with stress can ease our bodies and our minds. Meditation and other relaxation methods, exercise, visualization are all helpful techniques for reducing the negative impact of stress.

Stress can be beneficial – in moderation. That's because short episodes of stress trigger chemicals that improve memory, increase energy levels and enhance alertness and productivity. But chronic stress has debilitating effects on our overall health. Physically, it can contribute to migraines, ulcers, muscle tension and fatigue. Canadian researchers found that chronic stress more than doubled the risk of heart attacks.

Persistent stress also affects us emotionally and intellectually, and can cause:

- Decreased concentration and memory
- Confusion
- Loss of sense of humor
- Anxiety
- Anger
- Irritability
- Fear

The link between stress and mental illness has yet to be fully understood, but it is known that stress can negatively affect an episode of mental illness.

Managing Stress

First, it's important to recognize the source(s) of your stress. Events such as the death of a loved one, starting a new job or moving house are certainly stressful. However, much of our stress comes from within us. How we interpret things – a conversation, a performance review, even a look –

determines whether something becomes a stressor. Negative self-talk, where we focus on self-criticism and pessimistic over-analysis, can turn an innocent remark into a major source of stress.

Understanding where your stress originates can help you decide on a course of action. External stressors, like bereavement or career changes, can be managed over time and with the support of family and friends. Internal stressors, caused by our own negative interpretation, require changes in attitude and behavior. The goal of managing stress is to cue the "relaxation response". This is the physiological and psychological calming process our body goes through when we perceive that the danger, or stressful event, has passed.

Here are some tips for triggering the relaxation response:

- **Learn relaxation techniques** – Practicing meditation or breathing awareness every day can relieve chronic stress and realign your outlook in a more positive way. Good breathing habits alone can improve both your psychological and physical well-being.
- **Set realistic goals** – Learning to say no is essential for some people. Assess your schedule and identify tasks or activities that you can or should let go. Don't automatically volunteer to do something until you've considered whether it is feasible and healthy for you to do so.
- **Exercise** – You don't have to train for a marathon, but regular, moderate exercise helps ease tension, improves sleep and self-esteem. Making exercise a habit is key.
- **Enjoy yourself** – Taking the time for a favorite hobby is a great way of connecting with and nurturing your creative self.
- **Visualization** – Athletes achieve results by

picturing themselves crossing the finish line first. Use the same technique to practice "seeing" yourself succeed in whatever situation is uppermost in your mind.
- **Maintain a healthy lifestyle** – A good diet is often the first thing to go when we're feeling stressed. Making a meal instead of buying one ready-made may seem like a challenge, but it will be probably cheaper and certainly better for you and the simple action of doing something good for yourself can soothe stressful feelings.
- **Talk about it** – Sharing your troubles with a friend may help you to put things in perspective and to feel that you're not alone. You may also learn some other ways to manage stress effectively.

Other benefits of mental health include, but aren't limited to:

- Reduction in anxiety.
- Improved moods.
- Clearer thinking.
- A greater sense of calm or inner peace.
- Increased self-esteem.
- Reduced risk of depression.
- Improvements in relationships.

The development of practical coping skills has never been more necessitated in this ever-changing world. Rather than continuing to simply soldier on, a focus on thriving through adversity is where mental health benefits can be achieved. Improved mental health has been well documented with the introduction of improved levels of physical fitness. The fitness industry has decades of research showing the benefits of taking special and intentional care of one's body. The concept of being mentally healthy is not necessarily new, but it certainly has more areas of growth in scientific research.

This is likely because historically, medicine has studied what was wrong so that it could be cured.

A more recent approach to physical and mental wellbeing has been prevention. Exercise is a preventative activity for both physical and mental health. When you strengthen your body, there is less pain in aging. The same can be said for strengthening our mental health.

Benefits of mental health through physical fitness include, but aren't limited to:

- Sharper memory.
- Clarity in thinking.
- Higher self-esteem.
- Better sleep.
- Increased energy.
- Stronger resilience.
- Increased BDNF (Brain-Derived Neurotrophic Factor), which improves neurotransmission.

Counselling has, unfortunately, had a stigma attached. The medical model was developed to fix what was "broken." People receiving counselling are not broken. Human beings are malleable and can rewire themselves. A professional counsellor can help with this plasticity by allowing the release of painful or unhelpful thoughts and behaviors.

Potential Benefits of Counseling:

- Improvement in communication and interpersonal skills.
- Greater self-acceptance.
- Increased self-esteem.
- Improved self-expression and management of emotions.
- Relief from depression, anxiety, and other mental health conditions.

- Clarity.

Coaching is another area where practitioners can increase the benefits of mental health. While coaching is not therapy, it can be very therapeutic. Having a trained coach can create areas of growth that clear the way for massive personal improvement.

Potential Benefits of Coaching:

- Learning acceptance and self-appreciation
- Improved connection with self and others
- Simplifying life
- Reduced stress
- Harmony and peace
- Increased self-awareness
- Reduction in isolation
- Improvements in relationships
- Improved communication
- Overcoming procrastination
- Gaining work and or life satisfaction
- Increased self-reliance
- Improved decision making
- Mindset shifts
- Increased self-worth
- Improved time management skills

A look at the research

Exercise may be one of the most underused treatments for improving mental health. Research has shown that patients suffering from depressive or anxiety sensitive disorders benefit significantly from increased exercise interventions

(Smits et al., 2008). The Center for Disease Control recommends 150 minutes of moderate activity or 75 minutes of vigorous activity to reduce the risk of premature death. Astonishingly, most of the population fails to come close to meeting the guidelines to improve their wellbeing. The research has not determined which type of exercise is the most beneficial for mental health. Aerobic exercise strengthens the cardiovascular system but also releases serotonin to improve mood. However, weight training and mind spirit practices like yoga show great benefits as well.

Journaling is a powerful tool used as an intervention in many different areas of wellbeing. The benefits can be seen not only in mental, but also physical wellness. Research has shown improvement in breast cancer patient recovery through the use of journaling.

Adolescent use of reflective journaling has shown increases in self-efficacy, self-regulation, and self-motivation. Reflective journaling has also been used to the great benefit of those working to overcome addiction. The use of a journal offers a space to release inner fears and stress as a reflective process. The reduction of stress and unwanted negative thoughts are benefits that are seen through consistent practice. Journaling has also been proven to improve critical thinking skills.

CHAPTER IV

What Is A Mental Health Problem?

Mental health problems are struggles and difficulties that affect everyone from time to time. Everyone experiences mental health problems at some point and these problems can affect your ability to handle day-to-day situation and enjoy life. Approximately one in four adults and one in six children (5 – 16-year-olds) will experience a mental health problem in any given year. Common mental health problems include Depression and Anxiety, while rarer problems include Schizophrenia, Personality Disorder, Eating Disorder and Bipolar Disorder. Mental health problems can affect the way you think, feel and behave. They can affect anyone regardless of *age, race, religion or income.*

These types of problems do not always require medical treatment. They are however, usually diagnosed by a doctor or mental health specialist. Having a diagnosis does not necessarily mean you are unwell right now. You could have a diagnosis of a mental health problem but, at the moment, be able to manage it and function well at work and at home. Equally, you might not have a diagnosis, but still be finding things very difficult. Everyone's experience is different and can change at different times. Some people recover from their mental health problems with self-help and support from others; others require professional help.

Associated with mental health problems are:
- Low self-esteem
- Frustration or anger
- Behavior problems
- School learning problems

- Feeling stressed
- Worry
- Sleeping problems

What causes mental health problems?

Mental health problems can have a wide range of causes. It is likely that many people experience a combination of causes – although some people may be more deeply affected by certain factors than others.

The following factors could potentially result in a period of poor mental health:

- Past trauma, abuse or neglect
- Domestic violence, bullying or other abuse as an adult
- Social isolation or loneliness
- Experiencing discrimination and stigma, including racism
- Social disadvantage, poverty or debt
- Bereavement (losing someone close to you)
- Severe or long-term stress
- Having a long-term physical health condition
- Unemployment or losing your job
- Homelessness or poor housing
- Being a long-term care for someone
- Drug and alcohol misuse
- A breakup or divorce
- Dysfunctional family life
- being a long-term carer for someone
- drug and alcohol misuse
- significant trauma as an adult, such as military combat, being involved in a serious incident in which you feared for your life, or being the victim of a violent crime
- physical causes – for example, a head injury or a

neurological condition such as epilepsy can have an impact on your behavior and mood. (It's important to rule out potential physical causes before seeking further treatment for a mental health problem).

Although lifestyle factors including work, diet, drugs and lack of sleep can all affect your mental health, if you experience a mental health problem there are usually other factors as well.

CHAPTER V

What Is A Mental Illness?

Mental illness, also called mental health disorders, refers to a wide range of mental health conditions — disorders that affect your mood, thinking and behavior. Examples of mental illness include depression, anxiety disorders, schizophrenia, eating disorders and addictive behaviors. Many people have mental health concerns from time to time. But a mental health concern becomes a mental illness when ongoing signs and symptoms cause frequent stress and affect your ability to function.

A mental illness can make you miserable and can cause problems in your daily life, such as at school or work or in relationships. In most cases, symptoms can be managed with a combination of medications and talk therapy (psychotherapy).

Symptoms

Signs and symptoms of mental illness can vary, depending on the disorder, circumstances and other factors. Mental illness symptoms can affect emotions, thoughts and behaviors.

Examples of signs and symptoms include:

- Feeling sad or down
- Confused thinking or reduced ability to concentrate
- Excessive fears or worries, or extreme feelings of guilt
- Extreme mood changes of highs and lows
- Withdrawal from friends and activities

- Significant tiredness, low energy or problems sleeping
- Detachment from reality (delusions), paranoia or hallucinations
- Inability to cope with daily problems or stress
- Trouble understanding and relating to situations and to people
- Problems with alcohol or drug use
- Major changes in eating habits
- Sex drive changes
- Excessive anger, hostility or violence
- Suicidal thinking

Sometimes symptoms of a mental health disorder appear as physical problems, such as stomach pain, back pain, headaches, or other unexplained aches and pains.

When to see a doctor

If you have any signs or symptoms of a mental illness, see your primary care provider or a mental health professional. Most mental illnesses don't improve on their own, and if untreated, a mental illness may get worse over time and cause serious problems.

If you have suicidal thoughts

Suicidal thoughts and behavior are common with some mental illnesses. If you think you may hurt yourself or attempt suicide, get help right away:

- Call *10111 or 10177* immediately.
- Call your mental health specialist.
- Call a suicide hotline number — *0800 567 567, 24hr helpline 0800 12 13 14, SMS 31393* (a SADAG counsellor will call you back).
- Seek help from your primary care provider.
- Reach out to a close friend or loved one.

Suicidal thinking doesn't get better on its own — so get help.

Helping a loved one

If your loved one shows signs of mental illness, have an open and honest discussion with him or her about your concerns. You may not be able to force someone to get professional care, but you can offer encouragement and support. You can also help your loved one find a qualified mental health professional and make an appointment. You may even be able to go along to the appointment.

If your loved one has done self-harm or is considering doing so, take the person to the hospital or call for emergency help.

Causes

Mental illnesses, in general, are thought to be caused by a variety of genetic and environmental factors:

- **Inherited traits.** Mental illness is more common in people whose blood relatives also have a mental illness. Certain genes may increase your risk of developing a mental illness, and your life situation may trigger it.
- **Environmental exposures before birth.** Exposure to environmental stressors, inflammatory conditions, toxins, alcohol or drugs while in the womb can sometimes be linked to mental illness.
- **Brain chemistry.** Neurotransmitters are naturally occurring brain chemicals that carry signals to other parts of your brain and body. When the neural networks involving these chemicals are impaired, the function of nerve receptors and nerve systems change, leading to depression and other emotional disorders.

Risk factors

- Certain factors may increase your risk of developing a mental illness, including:
- A history of mental illness in a blood relative, such as a parent or sibling
- Stressful life situations, such as financial problems, a loved one's death or a divorce
- An ongoing (chronic) medical condition, such as diabetes
- Brain damage as a result of a serious injury (traumatic brain injury), such as a violent blow to the head
- Traumatic experiences, such as military combat or assault
- Use of alcohol or recreational drugs
- A childhood history of abuse or neglect
- Few friends or few healthy relationships
- A previous mental illness

Mental illness is common. About 1 in 5 adults has a mental illness in any given year. Mental illness can begin at any age, from childhood through later adult years, but most cases begin earlier in life.

The effects of mental illness can be temporary or long lasting. You also can have more than one mental health disorder at the same time. For example, you may have depression and a substance use disorder.

Complications

Mental illness is a leading cause of disability. Untreated mental illness can cause severe emotional, behavioral and physical health problems. Complications sometimes linked to mental illness include:

- Unhappiness and decreased enjoyment of life
- Family conflicts
- Relationship difficulties

- Social isolation
- Problems with tobacco, alcohol and other drugs
- Missed work or school, or other problems related to work or school
- Legal and financial problems
- Poverty and homelessness
- Self-harm and harm to others, including suicide or homicide
- Weakened immune system, so your body has a hard time resisting infections
- Heart disease and other medical conditions

Prevention

There's no sure way to prevent mental illness. However, if you have a mental illness, taking steps to control stress, to increase your resilience and to boost low self-esteem may help keep your symptoms under control. Follow these steps:

- **Pay attention to warning signs.** Work with your doctor or therapist to learn what might trigger your symptoms. Make a plan so that you know what to do if symptoms return. Contact your doctor or therapist if you notice any changes in symptoms or how you feel. Consider involving family members or friends to watch for warning signs.
- **Get routine medical care.** Don't neglect checkups or skip visits to your primary care provider, especially if you aren't feeling well. You may have a new health problem that needs to be treated, or you may be experiencing side effects of medication.
- **Get help when you need it.** Mental health conditions can be harder to treat if you wait until symptoms get bad. Long-term maintenance treatment also may help prevent a relapse of symptoms.
- **Take good care of yourself.** Sufficient sleep, healthy

eating and regular physical activity are important. Try to maintain a regular schedule. Talk to your primary care provider if you have trouble sleeping or if you have questions about diet and physical activity.

Diagnosis

To determine a diagnosis and check for related complications, you may have:

- **A physical exam.** Your doctor will try to rule out physical problems that could cause your symptoms.
- **Lab tests.** These may include, for example, a check of your thyroid function or a screening for alcohol and drugs.
- **A psychological evaluation.** A doctor or mental health professional talks to you about your symptoms, thoughts, feelings and behavior patterns. You may be asked to fill out a questionnaire to help answer these questions.

Determining which mental illness you have

Sometimes it's difficult to find out which mental illness may be causing your symptoms. But taking the time and effort to get an accurate diagnosis will help determine the appropriate treatment. The more information you have, the more you will be prepared to work with your mental health professional in understanding what your symptoms may represent.

The defining symptoms for each mental illness are detailed in the Diagnostic and Statistical Manual of Mental Disorders (DSM-5), published by the American Psychiatric Association. This manual is used by mental health professionals to diagnose mental conditions and by insurance companies to reimburse for treatment.

Treatment

Your treatment depends on the type of mental illness you have, its severity and what works best for you. In many cases, a combination of treatments works best.

If you have a mild mental illness with well-controlled symptoms, treatment from your primary care provider may be sufficient. However, often a team approach is appropriate to make sure all your psychiatric, medical and social needs are met. This is especially important for severe mental illnesses, such as schizophrenia.

Your treatment team

Your treatment team may include your:
- Family or primary care doctor
- Nurse practitioner
- Physician assistant
- Psychiatrist, a medical doctor who diagnoses and treats mental illnesses
- Psychotherapist, such as a psychologist or a licensed counselor
- Pharmacist
- Social worker
- Family members

Medications

Although psychiatric medications don't cure mental illness, they can often significantly improve symptoms. Psychiatric medications can also help make other treatments, such as psychotherapy, more effective. The best medications for you will depend on your particular situation and how your body responds to the medication.

Some of the most commonly used classes of prescription psychiatric medications include:

- **Antidepressants.** Antidepressants are used to treat depression, anxiety and sometimes other conditions. They can help improve symptoms such as sadness, hopelessness, lack of energy, difficulty concentrating and lack of interest in activities. Antidepressants are not addictive and do not cause dependency.
- **Anti-anxiety medications.** These drugs are used to treat anxiety disorders, such as generalized anxiety disorder or panic disorder. They may also help reduce agitation and insomnia. Long-term anti-anxiety drugs typically are antidepressants that also work for anxiety. Fast-acting anti-anxiety drugs help with short-term relief, but they also have the potential to cause dependency, so ideally they'd be used short term.
- **Mood-stabilizing medications.** Mood stabilizers are most commonly used to treat bipolar disorders, which involves alternating episodes of mania and depression. Sometimes mood stabilizers are used with antidepressants to treat depression.
- **Antipsychotic medications.** Antipsychotic drugs are typically used to treat psychotic disorders, such as schizophrenia. Antipsychotic medications may also be used to treat bipolar disorders or used with antidepressants to treat depression.

Psychotherapy

Psychotherapy, also called talk therapy, involves talking about your condition and related issues with a mental health professional. During psychotherapy, you learn about your condition and your moods, feelings, thoughts and behavior. With the insights and knowledge you gain, you can learn coping and stress management skills. There are many types of psychotherapy, each with its own approach to improving your mental well-being. Psychotherapy often can be successfully completed in a few months, but in some cases, long-term treatment may be needed. It can take place one-on-one, in a group or with family members.

When choosing a therapist, you should feel comfortable and be confident that he or she is capable of listening and hearing what you have to say. Also, it's important that your therapist understands the life journey that has helped shape who you are and how you live in the world.

Brain-stimulation treatments

Brain-stimulation treatments are sometimes used for depression and other mental health disorders. They're generally reserved for situations in which medications and psychotherapy haven't worked. They include electroconvulsive therapy, repetitive transcranial magnetic stimulation, deep brain stimulation and vagus nerve stimulation.

Make sure you understand all the risks and benefits of any recommended treatment.

Hospital and residential treatment programs

Sometimes mental illness becomes so severe that you need care in a psychiatric hospital. This is generally recommended when you can't care for yourself properly or when you're in immediate danger of harming yourself or someone else.

Options include 24-hour inpatient care, partial or day hospitalization, or residential treatment, which offers a temporary supportive place to live. Another option may be intensive outpatient treatment.

Substance misuse treatment

Problems with substance use commonly occur along with mental illness. Often it interferes with treatment and worsens mental illness. If you can't stop using drugs or alcohol on your own, you need treatment. Talk to your doctor about treatment options.

Participating in your own care

Working together, you and your primary care provider or mental health professional can decide which treatment may be best, depending on your symptoms and their severity, your personal preferences, medication side effects, and other factors. In some cases, a mental illness may be so severe that a doctor or loved one may need to guide your care until you're well enough to participate in decision-making.

Lifestyle and home remedies

In most cases, a mental illness won't get better if you try to treat it on your own without professional care. But you can do some things for yourself that will build on your treatment plan:

- **Stick to your treatment plan.** Don't skip therapy sessions. Even if you're feeling better, don't skip your medications. If you stop, symptoms may come back. And you could have withdrawal-like symptoms if you stop a medication too suddenly. If you have bothersome drug side effects or other problems with treatment, talk to your doctor before making changes.
- **Avoid alcohol and drug use.** Using alcohol or recreational drugs can make it difficult to treat a mental illness. If you're addicted, quitting can be a real challenge. If you can't quit on your own, see

your doctor or find a support group to help you.
- **Stay active.** Exercise can help you manage symptoms of depression, stress and anxiety. Physical activity can also counteract the effects of some psychiatric medications that may cause weight gain. Consider walking, swimming, gardening or any form of physical activity that you enjoy. Even light physical activity can make a difference.
- **Make healthy choices.** Maintaining a regular schedule that includes sufficient sleep, healthy eating and regular physical activity are important to your mental health.
- **Don't make important decisions when your symptoms are severe.** Avoid decision-making when you're in the depth of mental illness symptoms, since you may not be thinking clearly.
- **Determine priorities.** You may reduce the impact of your mental illness by managing time and energy. Cut back on obligations when necessary and set reasonable goals. Give yourself permission to do less when symptoms are worse. You may find it helpful to make a list of daily tasks or use a planner to structure your time and stay organized.
- **Learn to adopt a positive attitude.** Focusing on the positive things in your life can make your life better and may even improve your health. Try to accept changes when they occur, and keep problems in perspective. Stress management techniques, including relaxation methods, may help.

Coping and support

Coping with a mental illness is challenging. Talk to your doctor or therapist about improving your coping skills, and consider these tips:

- **Learn about your mental illness.** Your doctor or therapist can provide you with information or may recommend classes, books or websites. Include your family, too — this can help the people who care about you understand what you're going through and learn how they can help.
- **Join a support group.** Connecting with others facing similar challenges may help you cope. Support groups for mental illness are available in many communities and online. One good place to start is the National Alliance on Mental Illness.
- **Stay connected with friends and family.** Try to participate in social activities, and get together with family or friends regularly. Ask for help when you need it, and be upfront with your loved ones about how you're doing.
- **Keep a journal.** Or jot down brief thoughts or record symptoms on a smartphone app. Keeping track of your personal life and sharing information with your therapist can help you identify what triggers or improves your symptoms. It's also a healthy way to explore and express pain, anger, fear and other emotions.

Preparing for your appointment

Whether you schedule an appointment with your primary care provider to talk about mental health concerns or you're referred to a mental health professional, such as a psychiatrist or psychologist or , take steps to prepare for your appointment.

If possible, take a family member or friend along. Someone who has known you for a long time may be able to share important information, with your permission.

What you can do

Before your appointment, make a list of:

- **Any symptoms you or people close to you have noticed,** and for how long
- **Key personal information,** including traumatic events in your past and any current, major stressors
- **Your medical information,** including other physical or mental health conditions
- **Any medications,** vitamins, herbal products or other supplements you take, and their dosages
- **Questions to ask** your doctor or mental health professional

Questions to ask may include:

- What type of mental illness might I have?
- Why can't I get over mental illness on my own?
- How do you treat my type of mental illness?
- Will talk therapy help?
- Are there medications that might help?
- How long will treatment take?
- What can I do to help myself?
- Do you have any brochures or other printed material that I can have?
- What websites do you recommend?

Don't hesitate to ask any other questions during your appointment.

What to expect from your doctor

During your appointment, your doctor or mental health professional is likely to ask you questions about your mood, thoughts and behavior, such as:

- When did you first notice symptoms?
- How is your daily life affected by your symptoms?
- What treatment, if any, have you had for mental illness?

- What have you tried on your own to feel better or control your symptoms?
- What things make you feel worse?
- Have family members or friends commented on your mood or behavior?
- Do you have blood relatives with a mental illness?
- What do you hope to gain from treatment?
- What medications or over-the-counter herbs and supplements do you take?
- Do you drink alcohol or use recreational drugs?

Your doctor or mental health professional will ask additional questions based on your responses, symptoms and needs. Preparing and anticipating questions will help you make the most of your time with the doctor.

CHAPTER VI
CLASSES OF MENTAL ILLNESSES
The main classes of mental illness are:
1. **Neurodevelopmental disorders.** This class covers a wide range of problems that usually begin in infancy or childhood, often before the child begins grade school. Examples include autism spectrum disorder, attention-deficit/hyperactivity disorder (ADHD) and learning disorders.
2. **Schizophrenia spectrum and other psychotic disorders.** Psychotic disorders cause detachment from reality — such as delusions, hallucinations, and disorganized thinking and speech. The most notable example is schizophrenia, although other classes of disorders can be associated with detachment from reality at times.
3. **Bipolar and related disorders.** This class includes disorders with alternating episodes of mania — periods of excessive activity, energy and excitement — and depression.
4. **Depressive disorders.** These include disorders that affect how you feel emotionally, such as the level of sadness and happiness, and they can disrupt your ability to function. Examples include major depressive disorder and premenstrual dysphoric disorder.
5. **Anxiety disorders.** Anxiety is an emotion characterized by the anticipation of future danger or misfortune, along with excessive worrying. It can include behavior aimed at avoiding situations that cause anxiety. This class includes generalized anxiety disorder, panic disorder, obsessive-

compulsive disorders (OCD) and post-traumatic disorder (PTSD)
6. **Dissociative disorders.** These are disorders in which your sense of self is disrupted, such as with dissociative identity disorder and dissociative amnesia.
7. **Somatic symptom and related disorders.** A person with one of these disorders may have physical symptoms that cause major emotional distress and problems functioning. There may or may not be another diagnosed medical condition associated with these symptoms, but the reaction to the symptoms is not normal. The disorders include somatic symptom disorder, illness anxiety disorder and factitious disorder.
8. **Eating disorders.** These disorders include disturbances related to eating that impact nutrition and health, such as anorexia nervosa and binge-eating disorder.
9. **Elimination disorders.** These disorders relate to the inappropriate elimination of urine or stool by accident or on purpose. Bed-wetting (enuresis) is an example.
10. **Sleep-wake disorders.** These are disorders of sleep severe enough to require clinical attention, such as insomnia, sleep apnea and restless legs syndrome.
11. **Sexual dysfunctions.** These include disorders of sexual response, such as premature ejaculation and orgasm disorders.
12. **Gender dysphoria.** This refers to the distress that accompanies a person's stated desire to be another gender.
13. **Disruptive, impulse-control and conduct disorders.** These disorders include problems with emotional and behavioral self-control, such as kleptomania or intermittent explosive disorder.

14. **Substance-related and addictive disorders.** These include problems associated with the excessive use of alcohol, caffeine, tobacco and drugs. This class also includes gambling disorder.
15. **Neurocognitive disorders.** Neurocognitive disorders affect your ability to think and reason. These acquired (rather than developmental) cognitive problems include delirium, as well as neurocognitive disorders due to conditions or diseases such as traumatic brain injury or Alzheimer's disease.
16. **Personality disorders.** A personality disorder involves a lasting pattern of emotional instability and unhealthy behavior that causes problems in your life and relationships. Examples include borderline, antisocial and narcissistic personality disorders.
17. **Paraphilic disorders.** These disorders include sexual interest that causes personal distress or impairment or causes potential or actual harm to another person. Examples are sexual sadism disorder, voyeuristic disorder and pedophilic disorder.

1. **Neurodevelopmental disorders:**

- Autism spectrum disorder

Autism spectrum disorder is a condition related to brain development that impacts how a person perceives and socializes with others, causing problems in social interaction and communication. The disorder also includes limited and repetitive patterns of behavior. The term "spectrum" in autism spectrum disorder refers to the wide range of symptoms and severity. Autism spectrum disorder includes conditions that were previously considered separate — autism, Asperger's syndrome, childhood disintegrative disorder and an unspecified form of pervasive developmental disorder. Some people still use the term "Asperger's syndrome," which is generally thought to be at the mild end of autism spectrum disorder.

Autism spectrum disorder begins in early childhood and eventually causes problems functioning in society — socially, in school and at work, for example. Often children show symptoms of autism within the first year. A small number of children appear to develop normally in the first year, and then go through a period of regression between 18 and 24 months of age when they develop autism symptoms.

While there is no cure for autism spectrum disorder, intensive, early treatment can make a big difference in the lives of many children.

Symptoms

Some children show signs of autism spectrum disorder in early infancy, such as reduced eye contact, lack of response to their name or indifference to caregivers. Other children may develop normally for the first few months or years of life, but then suddenly become withdrawn or aggressive or lose language skills they've already acquired. Signs usually are seen by age 2 years. Each child with autism spectrum disorder is likely to have a unique pattern of behavior and level of severity — from low functioning to high functioning.

Some children with autism spectrum disorder have difficulty learning, and some have signs of lower than normal intelligence. Other children with the disorder have normal to high intelligence — they learn quickly, yet have trouble communicating and applying what they know in everyday life and adjusting to social situations. Because of the unique mixture of symptoms in each child, severity can sometimes be difficult to determine. It's generally based on the level of impairments and how they impact the ability to function.

Below are some common signs shown by people who have autism spectrum disorder.

Social communication and interaction

A child or adult with autism spectrum disorder may have problems with social interaction and communication skills, including any of these signs:

- Fails to respond to his or her name or appears not to hear you at times
- Resists cuddling and holding, and seems to prefer playing alone, retreating into his or her own world
- Has poor eye contact and lacks facial expression
- Doesn't speak or has delayed speech, or loses previous ability to say words or sentences
- Can't start a conversation or keep one going, or only starts one to make requests or label items
- Speaks with an abnormal tone or rhythm and may use a singsong voice or robot-like speech
- Repeats words or phrases verbatim, but doesn't understand how to use them
- Doesn't appear to understand simple questions or directions
- Doesn't express emotions or feelings and appears unaware of others' feelings
- Doesn't point at or bring objects to share interest
- Inappropriately approaches a social interaction by being passive, aggressive or disruptive
- Has difficulty recognizing nonverbal cues, such as interpreting other people's facial expressions, body postures or tone of voice

Patterns of behavior

A child or adult with autism spectrum disorder may have limited, repetitive patterns of behavior, interests or activities, including any of these signs:

- Performs repetitive movements, such as rocking, spinning or hand flapping
- Performs activities that could cause self-harm, such as biting or head-banging
- Develops specific routines or rituals and becomes disturbed at the slightest change
- Has problems with coordination or has odd movement patterns, such as clumsiness or walking on toes, and has odd, stiff or exaggerated body language
- Is fascinated by details of an object, such as the spinning wheels of a toy car, but doesn't understand the overall purpose or function of the object
- Is unusually sensitive to light, sound or touch, yet may be indifferent to pain or temperature
- Doesn't engage in imitative or make-believe play
- Fixates on an object or activity with abnormal intensity or focus
- Has specific food preferences, such as eating only a few foods, or refusing foods with a certain texture

As they mature, some children with autism spectrum disorder become more engaged with others and show fewer disturbances in behavior. Some, usually those with the least severe problems, eventually may lead normal or near-normal lives. Others, however, continue to have difficulty with language or social skills, and the teen years can bring worse behavioral and emotional problems.

When to see a doctor

Babies develop at their own pace, and many don't follow exact timelines found in some parenting books. But children with autism spectrum disorder usually show some signs of delayed development before age 2 years. If you're concerned about your child's development or you suspect that your child may have autism spectrum disorder, discuss your concerns with your doctor. The symptoms associated with the disorder can also be linked with other developmental disorders.

Signs of autism spectrum disorder often appear early in development when there are obvious delays in language skills and social interactions. Your doctor may recommend developmental tests to identify if your child has delays in cognitive, language and social skills, if your child:

- Doesn't respond with a smile or happy expression by 6 months
- Doesn't mimic sounds or facial expressions by 9 months
- Doesn't babble or coo by 12 months
- Doesn't gesture — such as point or wave — by 14 months
- Doesn't say single words by 16 months
- Doesn't play "make-believe" or pretend by 18 months
- Doesn't say two-word phrases by 24 months
- Loses language skills or social skills at any age

Causes

Autism spectrum disorder has no single known cause. Given the complexity of the disorder, and the fact that symptoms and severity vary, there are probably many causes. Both genetics and environment may play a role.

- **Genetics.** Several different genes appear to

be involved in autism spectrum disorder. For some children, autism spectrum disorder can be associated with a genetic disorder, such as Rett syndrome or fragile X syndrome. For other children, genetic changes (mutations) may increase the risk of autism spectrum disorder. Still other genes may affect brain development or the way that brain cells communicate, or they may determine the severity of symptoms. Some genetic mutations seem to be inherited, while others occur spontaneously.
- **Environmental factors.** Researchers are currently exploring whether factors such as viral infections, medications or complications during pregnancy, or air pollutants play a role in triggering autism spectrum disorder.

No link between vaccines and autism spectrum disorder

One of the greatest controversies in autism spectrum disorder centers on whether a link exists between the disorder and childhood vaccines. Despite extensive research, no reliable study has shown a link between autism spectrum disorder and any vaccines. In fact, the original study that ignited the debate years ago has been retracted due to poor design and questionable research methods.

Avoiding childhood vaccinations can place your child and others in danger of catching and spreading serious diseases, including whooping cough (pertussis), measles or mumps.

Risk factors

The number of children diagnosed with autism spectrum disorder is rising. It's not clear whether this is due to better detection and reporting or a real increase in the number of cases, or both.

Autism spectrum disorder affects children of all races and nationalities, but certain factors increase a child's risk. These may include:

- **Your child's sex.** Boys are about four times more likely to develop autism spectrum disorder than girls are.
- **Family history.** Families who have one child with autism spectrum disorder have an increased risk of having another child with the disorder. It's also not uncommon for parents or relatives of a child with autism spectrum disorder to have minor problems with social or communication skills themselves or to engage in certain behaviors typical of the disorder.
- **Other disorders.** Children with certain medical conditions have a higher than normal risk of autism spectrum disorder or autism-like symptoms. Examples include fragile X syndrome, an inherited disorder that causes intellectual problems; tuberous sclerosis, a condition in which benign tumors develop in the brain; and Rett syndrome, a genetic condition occurring almost exclusively in girls, which causes slowing of head growth, intellectual disability and loss of purposeful hand use.
- **Extremely preterm babies.** Babies born before 26 weeks of gestation may have a greater risk of autism spectrum disorder.
- **Parents' ages.** There may be a connection between children born to older parents and autism spectrum disorder, but more research is necessary to establish this link.

Complications

Problems with social interactions, communication and behavior can lead to:

- Problems in school and with successful learning
- Employment problems
- Inability to live independently
- Social isolation
- Stress within the family
- Victimization and being bullied

Prevention

There's no way to prevent autism spectrum disorder, but there are treatment options. Early diagnosis and intervention is most helpful and can improve behavior, skills and language development. However, intervention is helpful at any age. Though children usually don't outgrow autism spectrum disorder symptoms, they may learn to function well.

Diagnosis

Your child's doctor will look for signs of developmental delays at regular checkups. If your child shows any symptoms of autism spectrum disorder, you'll likely be referred to a specialist who treats children with autism spectrum disorder, such as a child psychiatrist or psychologist, pediatric neurologist, or developmental pediatrician, for an evaluation.

Because autism spectrum disorder varies widely in symptoms and severity, making a diagnosis may be difficult. There isn't a specific medical test to determine the disorder. Instead, a specialist may:

- Observe your child and ask how your child's

social interactions, communication skills and behavior have developed and changed over time
- Give your child tests covering hearing, speech, language, developmental level, and social and behavioral issues
- Present structured social and communication interactions to your child and score the performance
- Use the criteria in the Diagnostic and Statistical Manual of Mental Disorders (DSM-5), published by the American Psychiatric Association
- Include other specialists in determining a diagnosis
- Recommend genetic testing to identify whether your child has a genetic disorder such as Rett syndrome or fragile X syndrome

Treatment

No cure exists for autism spectrum disorder, and there is no one-size-fits-all treatment. The goal of treatment is to maximize your child's ability to function by reducing autism spectrum disorder symptoms and supporting development and learning. Early intervention during the preschool years can help your child learn critical social, communication, functional and behavioral skills.

The range of home-based and school-based treatments and interventions for autism spectrum disorder can be overwhelming, and your child's needs may change over time. Your health care provider can recommend options and help identify resources in your area.

If your child is diagnosed with autism spectrum disorder, talk to experts about creating a treatment strategy and build a team of professionals to meet your child's needs.

Treatment options may include:

- **Behavior and communication therapies.** Many programs address the range of social, language and behavioral difficulties associated with autism spectrum disorder. Some programs focus on reducing problem behaviors and teaching new skills. Other programs focus on teaching children how to act in social situations or communicate better with others. Applied behavior analysis (ABA) can help children learn new skills and generalize these skills to multiple situations through a reward-based motivation system.
- **Educational therapies.** Children with autism spectrum disorder often respond well to highly structured educational programs. Successful programs typically include a team of specialists and a variety of activities to improve social skills, communication and behavior. Preschool children who receive intensive, individualized behavioral interventions often show good progress.
- **Family therapies.** Parents and other family members can learn how to play and interact with their children in ways that promote social interaction skills, manage problem behaviors, and teach daily living skills and communication.
- **Other therapies.** Depending on your child's needs, speech therapy to improve communication skills, occupational therapy to teach activities of daily living, and physical therapy to improve movement and balance may be beneficial. A psychologist can recommend ways to address problem behavior.
- **Medications.** No medication can improve the core signs of autism spectrum disorder, but specific medications can help control symptoms. For example, certain medications may be prescribed if your child is hyperactive;

antipsychotic drugs are sometimes used to treat severe behavioral problems; and antidepressants may be prescribed for anxiety. Keep all health care providers updated on any medications or supplements your child is taking. Some medications and supplements can interact, causing dangerous side effects.

Managing other medical and mental health conditions

In addition to autism spectrum disorder, children, teens and adults can also experience:

- **Medical health issues.** Children with autism spectrum disorder may also have medical issues, such as epilepsy, sleep disorders, limited food preferences or stomach problems. Ask your child's doctor how to best manage these conditions together.
- **Problems with transition to adulthood.** Teens and young adults with autism spectrum disorder may have difficulty understanding body changes. Also, social situations become increasingly complex in adolescence, and there may be less tolerance for individual differences. Behavior problems may be challenging during the teen years.
- **Other mental health disorders.** Teens and adults with autism spectrum disorder often experience other mental health disorders, such as anxiety and depression. Your doctor, mental health professional, and community advocacy and service organizations can offer help.

Planning for the future

Children with autism spectrum disorder typically

continue to learn and compensate for problems throughout life, but most will continue to require some level of support. Planning for your child's future opportunities, such as employment, college, living situation, independence and the services required for support can make this process smoother.

Alternative medicine

Because autism spectrum disorder can't be cured, many parents seek alternative or complementary therapies, but these treatments have little or no research to show that they're effective. You could, unintentionally, reinforce negative behaviors. And some alternative treatments are potentially dangerous.

Talk with your child's doctor about the scientific evidence of any therapy that you're considering for your child.

Examples of complementary and alternative therapies that may offer some benefit when used in combination with evidence-based treatments include:

- **Creative therapies.** Some parents choose to supplement educational and medical intervention with art therapy or music therapy, which focuses on reducing a child's sensitivity to touch or sound. These therapies may offer some benefit when used along with other treatments.
- **Sensory-based therapies.** These therapies are based on the unproven theory that people with autism spectrum disorder have a sensory processing disorder that causes problems tolerating or processing sensory information, such as touch, balance and hearing. Therapists use brushes, squeeze toys, trampolines and other materials to stimulate these senses. Research has not shown these therapies to be effective, but it's

possible they may offer some benefit when used along with other treatments.
- **Massage.** While massage may be relaxing, there isn't enough evidence to determine if it improves symptoms of autism spectrum disorder.
- **Pet or horse therapy.** Pets can provide companionship and recreation, but more research is needed to determine whether interaction with animals improves symptoms of autism spectrum disorder.

Some complementary and alternative therapies may not be harmful, but there's no evidence that they're helpful. Some may also include significant financial cost and be difficult to implement. Examples of these therapies include:
- **Special diets.** There's no evidence that special diets are an effective treatment for autism spectrum disorder. And for growing children, restrictive diets can lead to nutritional deficiencies. If you decide to pursue a restrictive diet, work with a registered dietitian to create an appropriate meal plan for your child.
- **Vitamin supplements and probiotics.** Although not harmful when used in normal amounts, there is no evidence they are beneficial for autism spectrum disorder symptoms, and supplements can be expensive. Talk to your doctor about vitamins and other supplements and the appropriate dosage for your child.
- **Acupuncture.** This therapy has been used with the goal of improving autism spectrum disorder symptoms, but the effectiveness of acupuncture is not supported by research.

Some complementary and alternative treatments do not have evidence that they are beneficial and they're potentially dangerous. Examples of complementary and alternative treatments that are not recommended for autism spectrum disorder include:

- **Chelation therapy.** This treatment is said to remove mercury and other heavy metals from the body, but there's no known link with autism spectrum disorder. Chelation therapy for autism spectrum disorder is not supported by research evidence and can be very dangerous. In some cases, children treated with chelation therapy have died.
- **Hyperbaric oxygen treatments.** Hyperbaric oxygen is a treatment that involves breathing oxygen inside a pressurized chamber. This treatment has not been shown to be effective in treating autism spectrum disorder symptoms and is not approved by the Food and Drug Administration (FDA) for this use.
- **Intravenous immunoglobulin (IVIG) infusions.** There is no evidence that using IVIG infusions improves autism spectrum disorder, and the FDA has not approved immunoglobulin products for this use.

Coping and support

Raising a child with autism spectrum disorder can be physically exhausting and emotionally draining. These suggestions may help:

- **Find a team of trusted professionals.** A team, coordinated by your doctor, may include social workers, teachers, therapists, and a case manager or service coordinator. These professionals can help identify and evaluate the resources in your area and explain financial services and state and federal programs for children and adults with

disabilities.
- **Keep records of visits with service providers.** Your child may have visits, evaluations and meetings with many people involved in his or her care. Keep an organized file of these meetings and reports to help you decide about treatment options and monitor progress.
- **Learn about the disorder.** There are many myths and misconceptions about autism spectrum disorder. Learning the truth can help you better understand your child and his or her attempts to communicate.
- **Take time for yourself and other family members.** Caring for a child with autism spectrum disorder can put stress on your personal relationships and your family. To avoid burnout, take time out to relax, exercise or enjoy your favorite activities. Try to schedule one-on-one time with your other children and plan date nights with your spouse or partner — even if it's just watching a movie together after the children go to bed.
- **Seek out other families of children with autism spectrum disorder.** Other families struggling with the challenges of autism spectrum disorder may have useful advice. Some communities have support groups for parents and siblings of children with the disorder.
- **Ask your doctor about new technologies and therapies.** Researchers continue to explore new approaches to help children with autism spectrum disorder. See the Centers for Disease Control and Prevention website on autism spectrum disorders for helpful materials and links to resources.

Preparing for your appointment

Your child's health care provider will look for developmental problems at regular checkups. Mention any concerns you have during your appointment. If your child shows any signs of autism spectrum disorder, you'll likely be referred to a specialist who treats children with the disorder for an evaluation.

Bring a family member or friend with you to the appointment, if possible, to help you remember information and for emotional support.

Here's some information to help you prepare for your appointment.

What you can do

Before your child's appointment, make a list of:

- **Any medications,** including vitamins, herbs and over-the-counter medicines that your child is taking, and their dosages.
- **Any concerns** you have about your child's development and behavior.
- **When your child began talking and reaching developmental milestones.** If your child has siblings, also share information about when they reached their milestones.
- **A description of how your child plays and interacts** with other children, siblings and parents.
- **Questions** to ask your child's doctor to make the most of your time.

In addition, it may be helpful to bring:

- **Notes of any observations from other adults and caregivers,** such as babysitters, relatives

and teachers. If your child has been evaluated by other health care professionals or an early intervention or school program, bring this assessment.
- **A record of developmental milestones for your child,** such as a baby book or baby calendar, if you have one.
- **A video of your child's unusual behaviors or movements,** if you have one.

Questions to ask your child's doctor may include:
- Why do you think my child does (or doesn't) have autism spectrum disorder?
- Is there a way to confirm the diagnosis?
- If my child does have autism spectrum disorder, is there a way to tell how severe it is?
- What changes can I expect to see in my child over time?
- What kind of special therapies or care do children with autism spectrum disorder need?
- How much and what kinds of regular medical care will my child need?
- What kind of support is available to families of children with autism spectrum disorder?
- How can I learn more about autism spectrum disorder?
- Don't hesitate to ask other questions during your appointment.

What to expect from your child's doctor

Your child's doctor is likely to ask you a number of questions. Be ready to answer them to reserve time to go over any points you want to focus on. Your doctor may ask:
- What specific behaviors prompted your visit today?
- When did you first notice these signs in your child?

Have others noticed signs?
- Have these behaviors been continuous or occasional?
- Does your child have any other symptoms that might seem unrelated to autism spectrum disorder, such as stomach problems?
- Does anything seem to improve your child's symptoms?
- What, if anything, appears to worsen symptoms?
- When did your child first crawl? Walk? Say his or her first word?
- What are some of your child's favorite activities?
- How does your child interact with you, siblings and other children? Does your child show interest in others, make eye contact, smile or want to play with others?
- Does your child have a family history of autism spectrum disorder, language delay, Rett syndrome, obsessive-compulsive disorder, or anxiety or other mood disorders?
- What is your child's education plan? What services does he or she receive through school?

- ATTENTION DEFICIT/ HYPERACTIVITY DISORDER (ADHD)

Attention-deficit/hyperactivity disorder (ADHD) is a mental health disorder that includes a combination of persistent problems, such as difficulty paying attention, hyperactivity and impulsive behavior. ADHD can lead to unstable relationships, poor work or school performance, low self-esteem, and other problems. In some cases, ADHD is not recognized or diagnosed until the person is an adult. Adult ADHD symptoms may not be as clear as ADHD symptoms in children. In adults, hyperactivity may decrease, but struggles with impulsiveness, restlessness and difficulty paying attention may continue.

Treatment for adult ADHD is similar to treatment for childhood ADHD. Adult ADHD treatment includes medications, psychological counseling (psychotherapy) and treatment for any mental health conditions that occur along with ADHD.

Symptoms

Some people with ADHD have fewer symptoms as they age, but some adults continue to have major symptoms that interfere with daily functioning. In adults, the main features of ADHD may include difficulty paying attention, impulsiveness and restlessness. Symptoms can range from mild to severe.

Many adults with ADHD aren't aware they have it — they just know that everyday tasks can be a challenge. Adults with ADHD may find it difficult to focus and prioritize, leading to missed deadlines and forgotten meetings or social plans. The inability to control impulses can range from impatience waiting in line or driving in traffic to mood swings and outbursts of anger.

Adult ADHD symptoms may include:

- Impulsiveness
- Disorganization and problems prioritizing
- Poor time management skills
- Problems focusing on a task
- Trouble multitasking
- Excessive activity or restlessness
- Poor planning
- Low frustration tolerance
- Frequent mood swings
- Problems following through and completing tasks
- Hot temper
- Trouble coping with stress

What's typical behavior and what's ADHD?

Almost everyone has some symptoms similar to ADHD at some point in their lives. If your difficulties are recent or occurred only occasionally in the past, you probably don't have ADHD. ADHD is diagnosed only when symptoms are severe enough to cause ongoing problems in more than one area of your life. These persistent and disruptive symptoms can be traced back to early childhood.

Diagnosis of ADHD in adults can be difficult because certain ADHD symptoms are similar to those caused by other conditions, such as anxiety or mood disorders. And many adults with ADHD also have at least one other mental health condition, such as depression or anxiety.

When to see a doctor

If any of the symptoms listed above continually disrupt your life, talk to your doctor about whether you might have ADHD.

Different types of health care professionals may diagnose and supervise treatment for ADHD. Seek a provider who has training and experience in caring for adults with ADHD.

Causes

While the exact cause of ADHD is not clear, research efforts continue. Factors that may be involved in the development of ADHD include:

- **Genetics.** ADHD can run in families, and studies indicate that genes may play a role.
- **Environment.** Certain environmental factors also may increase risk, such as lead exposure as a child.
- **Problems during development.** Problems with the central nervous system at key moments in development may play a role.

Risk factors

Risk of ADHD may increase if:

- You have blood relatives, such as a parent or sibling, with ADHD or another mental health disorder
- Your mother smoked, drank alcohol or used drugs during pregnancy
- As a child, you were exposed to environmental toxins — such as lead, found mainly in paint and pipes in older buildings
- You were born prematurely

Complications

ADHD can make life difficult for you. ADHD has been linked to:

- Poor school or work performance
- Unemployment
- Financial problems

- Trouble with the law
- Alcohol or other substance misuse
- Frequent car accidents or other accidents
- Unstable relationships
- Poor physical and mental health
- Poor self-image
- Suicide attempts

Coexisting conditions

Although ADHD doesn't cause other psychological or developmental problems, other disorders often occur along with ADHD and make treatment more challenging. These include:

- **Mood disorders.** Many adults with ADHD also have depression, bipolar disorder or another mood disorder. While mood problems aren't necessarily due directly to ADHD, a repeated pattern of failures and frustrations due to ADHD can worsen depression.
- **Anxiety disorders.** Anxiety disorders occur fairly often in adults with ADHD. Anxiety disorders may cause overwhelming worry, nervousness and other symptoms. Anxiety can be made worse by the challenges and setbacks caused by ADHD.
- **Other psychiatric disorders.** Adults with ADHD are at increased risk of other psychiatric disorders, such as personality disorders, intermittent explosive disorder and substance use disorders.
- **Learning disabilities.** Adults with ADHD may score lower on academic testing than would be expected for their age, intelligence and education. Learning disabilities can include problems with understanding and communicating.

Diagnosis

Signs and symptoms of ADHD in adults can be hard to spot. However, core symptoms start early in life — before age 12 — and continue into adulthood, creating major problems.

No single test can confirm the diagnosis. Making the diagnosis will likely include:

- **Physical exam,** to help rule out other possible causes for your symptoms
- **Information gathering,** such as asking you questions about any current medical issues, personal and family medical history, and the history of your symptoms
- **ADHD rating scales or psychological tests** to help collect and evaluate information about your symptoms

Other conditions that resemble ADHD

Some medical conditions or treatments may cause signs and symptoms similar to those of ADHD. Examples include:

- **Mental health disorders,** such as depression, anxiety, conduct disorders, learning and language deficits, or other psychiatric disorders
- **Medical problems that can affect thinking or behavior,** such as a developmental disorder, seizure disorder, thyroid problems, sleep disorders, brain injury or low blood sugar (hypoglycemia)
- **Drugs and medications,** such as alcohol or other substance misuse and certain medications

Treatment

Standard treatments for ADHD in adults typically involve medication, education, skills training and psychological counseling. A combination of these is often the most effective treatment. These treatments can help manage many symptoms of ADHD, but they don't cure it. It may take some time to determine what works best for you.

Medications

Talk with your doctor about the benefits and risks of any medications.

- **Stimulants,** such as products that include methylphenidate or amphetamine, are typically the most commonly prescribed medications for ADHD, but other medications may be prescribed. Stimulants appear to boost and balance levels of brain chemicals called neurotransmitters.
- **Other medications** used to treat ADHD include the nonstimulant atomoxetine and certain antidepressants such as bupropion. Atomoxetine and antidepressants work slower than stimulants do, but these may be good options if you can't take stimulants because of health problems or if stimulants cause severe side effects.

The right medication and the right dose vary among individuals, so it may take time to find out what's right for you. Tell your doctor about any side effects.

Psychological counselling

Counseling for ADHD generally includes psychological counselling (psychotherapy), education about the disorder and learning skills to help you be successful.

Psychotherapy may help you:

- Improve your time management and organizational skills
- Learn how to reduce your impulsive behavior
- Develop better problem-solving skills
- Cope with past academic, work or social failures
- Improve your self-esteem

- Learn ways to improve relationships with your family, co-workers and friends
- Develop strategies for controlling your temper

Common types of psychotherapy for ADHD include:

- **Cognitive behavioral therapy.** This structured type of counseling teaches specific skills to manage your behavior and change negative thinking patterns into positive ones. It can help you deal with life challenges, such as school, work or relationship problems, and help address other mental health conditions, such as depression or substance misuse.
- **Marital counseling and family therapy.** This type of therapy can help loved ones cope with the stress of living with someone who has ADHD and learn what they can do to help. Such counseling can improve communication and problem-solving skills

Working on relationships

If you're like many adults with ADHD, you may be unpredictable and forget appointments, miss deadlines, and make impulsive or irrational decisions. These behaviors can strain the patience of the most forgiving co-worker, friend or partner.

Therapy that focuses on these issues and ways to better monitor your behavior can be very helpful. So can classes to improve communication and develop conflict resolution and problem-solving skills. Couples therapy and classes in which family members learn more about ADHD may significantly improve your relationships.

Lifestyle and home remedies

Because ADHD is a complex disorder and each person is unique, it's hard to make recommendations for all adults who have ADHD. But some of these suggestions may help:

- **Make a list of tasks to accomplish each day.** Prioritize the items. Make sure you're not trying to do too much.
- **Break down tasks** into smaller, more manageable steps. Consider using checklists.
- **Use sticky pads** to write notes to yourself. Put them on the fridge, on the bathroom mirror, in the car or in other places where you'll see the reminders.
- **Keep an appointment book** or electronic calendar to track appointments and deadlines.
- **Carry a notebook or electronic device with you** so that you can note ideas or things you'll need to remember.
- **Take time to set up systems to file and organize information,** both on your electronic devices and for paper documents. Get in the habit of using these systems consistently.
- **Follow a routine** that's consistent from day to day and keep items, such as your keys and your wallet, in the same place.
- **Ask for help** from family members or other loved ones.

Alternative medicine

There's little research to indicate that alternative medicine treatments can reduce ADHD symptoms. However, studies indicate that mindfulness meditation may help improve mood and attention in adults who have ADHD, as well as those who don't have ADHD.

Before using alternative interventions for ADHD, talk with your doctor about risks and possible benefits.

Coping and support

While treatment can make a big difference with ADHD, taking other steps can help you understand ADHD and learn to manage it. Some resources that may help you are listed below. Ask your health care team for more advice on resources.

- **Support groups.** Support groups allow you to meet other people with ADHD so that you can share experiences, information and coping strategies. These groups are available in person in many communities and also online.
- **Social support.** Involve your spouse, close relatives and friends in your ADHD treatment. You may feel reluctant to let people know you have ADHD, but letting others know what's going on can help them understand you better and improve your relationships.
- **Co-workers, supervisors and teachers.** ADHD can make work and school a challenge. You may feel embarrassed telling your boss or professor that you have ADHD, but most likely he or she will be willing to make small accommodations to help you succeed. Ask for what you need to improve your performance, such as more in-depth explanations or more time on certain tasks.

Preparing for your appointment

You're likely to start by first talking to your primary care provider. Depending on the results of the initial evaluation, he or she may refer you to a specialist, such as a psychologist, psychiatrist or other mental health professional.

What you can do

To prepare for your appointment, make a list of:

- **Any symptoms you've had and problems they've**

- **caused,** such as trouble at work, at school or in relationships.
- **Key personal information,** including any major stresses or recent life changes you've had.
- **All medications you take,** including any vitamins, herbs or supplements, and the dosages. Also include the amount of caffeine and alcohol you use, and whether you use recreational drugs.
- **Questions to ask** your doctor.

Bring any past evaluations and results of formal testing with you, if you have them.

Basic questions to ask your doctor include:

- What are the possible causes of my symptoms?
- What kinds of tests do I need?
- What treatments are available and which do you recommend?
- What are the alternatives to the primary approach that you're suggesting?
- I have these other health problems. How can I best manage these conditions together?
- Should I see a specialist such as a psychiatrist or psychologist?
- Is there a generic alternative to the medicine you're prescribing?
- What types of side effects can I expect from the medication?
- Are there any printed materials that I can have? What websites do you recommend?

Don't hesitate to ask questions anytime you don't understand something.

What to expect from your doctor

Be ready to answer questions your doctor may ask, such as:

- When do you first remember having problems focusing, paying attention or sitting still?
- Have your symptoms been continuous or occasional?
- Which symptoms bother you most, and what problems do they seem to cause?
- How severe are your symptoms?
- In what settings have you noticed the symptoms: at home, at work or in other situations?
- What was your childhood like? Did you have social problems or trouble in school?
- How is your current and past academic and work performance?
- What are your sleep hours and patterns?
- What, if anything, appears to worsen your symptoms?
- What, if anything, seems to improve your symptoms?
- What medications do you take?
- Do you consume caffeine?
- Do you drink alcohol or use recreational drugs?

Your doctor or mental health professional will ask additional questions based on your responses, symptoms and needs. Preparing and anticipating questions will help you make the most of your time with the doctor.

2. Schizophrenia spectrum and other psychotic disorders:

Psychotic disorders are severe mental illnesses that cause distorted thinking. Individuals under a psychoses episode frequently experience hallucinations or delusions, making them lose touch with reality. When a person loses touch with reality, he/she often start to distrust those around them and make decisions that put themselves or others in danger. As a result, people with psychotic disorders must get medication and treatment.

The most common psychotic disorders are:
- Schizophrenia
- Schizoaffective disorder
- Delusional disorder

SCHIZOPHRENIA

Schizophrenia is a serious mental disorder in which people interpret reality abnormally. Schizophrenia may result in some combination of hallucinations, delusions, and extremely disordered thinking and behavior that impairs daily functioning, and can be disabling.

People with schizophrenia require lifelong treatment. Early treatment may help get symptoms under control before serious complications develop and may help improve the long-term outlook.

Symptoms

Schizophrenia involves a range of problems with thinking (cognition), behavior and emotions. Signs and symptoms may vary, but usually involve delusions, hallucinations or disorganized speech, and reflect an impaired ability to function. Symptoms may include:

- **Delusions.** These are false beliefs that are not based in reality. For example, you think that you're being harmed or harassed; certain gestures or comments are directed at you; you have exceptional ability or fame; another person is in love with you; or a major catastrophe is about to occur. Delusions occur in most people with schizophrenia.
- **Hallucinations.** These usually involve seeing or hearing things that don't exist. Yet for the person with schizophrenia, they have the full force and impact of a normal experience. Hallucinations can be in any of the senses, but hearing voices is the most common hallucination.
- **Disorganized thinking (speech).** Disorganized thinking is inferred from disorganized speech.

Effective communication can be impaired, and answers to questions may be partially or completely unrelated. Rarely, speech may include putting together meaningless words that can't be understood, sometimes known as word salad.
- **Extremely disorganized or abnormal motor behavior.** This may show in a number of ways, from childlike silliness to unpredictable agitation. Behavior isn't focused on a goal, so it's hard to do tasks. Behavior can include resistance to instructions, inappropriate or bizarre posture, a complete lack of response, or useless and excessive movement.
- **Negative symptoms.** This refers to reduced or lack of ability to function normally. For example, the person may neglect personal hygiene or appear to lack emotion (doesn't make eye contact, doesn't change facial expressions or speaks in a monotone). Also, the person may lose interest in everyday activities, socially withdraw or lack the ability to experience pleasure.

Symptoms can vary in type and severity over time, with periods of worsening and remission of symptoms. Some symptoms may always be present.

In men, schizophrenia symptoms typically start in the early to mid-20s. In women, symptoms typically begin in the late 20s. It's uncommon for children to be diagnosed with schizophrenia and rare for those older than age 45.

Symptoms in teenagers

Schizophrenia symptoms in teenagers are similar to those in adults, but the condition may be more difficult to recognize. This may be in part because some of the early symptoms of schizophrenia in teenagers are common for typical

development during teen years, such as:
- Withdrawal from friends and family
- A drop in performance at school
- Trouble sleeping
- Irritability or depressed mood
- Lack of motivation

Also, recreational substance use, such as marijuana, methamphetamines or LSD, can sometimes cause similar signs and symptoms.

Compared with schizophrenia symptoms in adults, teens may be:
- Less likely to have delusions
- More likely to have visual hallucinations

When to see a doctor

People with schizophrenia often lack awareness that their difficulties stem from a mental disorder that requires medical attention. So, it often falls to family or friends to get them help.

Helping someone who may have schizophrenia

If you think someone you know may have symptoms of schizophrenia, talk to him or her about your concerns. Although you can't force someone to seek professional help, you can offer encouragement and support and help your loved one find a qualified doctor or mental health professional.

If your loved one poses a danger to self or others or can't provide his or her own food, clothing, or shelter, you may need to call *10111 or 10177* for help so that your loved one can be evaluated by a mental health professional. In some cases, emergency hospitalization may be needed. *The Mental Health Care Act No 17 of 2022* makes provisions that allow that for those with such impairments, others to act in their best interest and make decisions on their affairs. In this regard, legislation provides for involuntary or compulsory admission to mental health facilities and involuntary treatment.

Suicidal thoughts and behavior

Suicidal thoughts and behavior are common among people with schizophrenia. If you have a loved one who is in danger of attempting suicide or has made a suicide attempt, make sure someone stays with that person. Call *10111 or 10177* immediately. Or, if you think you can do so safely, take the person to the nearest hospital emergency room.

Causes

It's not known what causes schizophrenia, but researchers believe that a combination of genetics, brain chemistry and environment contributes to development of the disorder. Problems with certain naturally occurring brain chemicals, including neurotransmitters called dopamine and glutamate, may contribute to schizophrenia. Neuroimaging studies show differences in the brain structure and central nervous system of people with schizophrenia. While researchers aren't certain about the significance of these changes, they indicate that schizophrenia is a brain disease.

Risk factors

Although the precise cause of schizophrenia isn't known, certain factors seem to increase the risk of developing or triggering schizophrenia, including:
- Having a family history of schizophrenia
- Some pregnancy and birth complications, such as malnutrition or exposure to toxins or viruses that

may impact brain development
- Taking mind-altering (psychoactive or psychotropic) drugs during teen years and young adulthood

Complications

Left untreated, schizophrenia can result in severe problems that affect every area of life. Complications that schizophrenia may cause or be associated with include:

- Suicide, suicide attempts and thoughts of suicide
- Anxiety disorders and obsessive-compulsive disorder (OCD)
- Depression
- Abuse of alcohol or other drugs, including nicotine
- Inability to work or attend school
- Financial problems and homelessness
- Social isolation
- Health and medical problems
- Being victimized
- Aggressive behavior, although it's uncommon

Prevention

There's no sure way to prevent schizophrenia, but sticking with the treatment plan can help prevent relapses or worsening of symptoms. In addition, researchers hope that learning more about risk factors for schizophrenia may lead to earlier diagnosis and treatment.

Diagnosis

Diagnosis of schizophrenia involves ruling out other mental health disorders and determining that symptoms are not due to substance abuse, medication or a medical condition.

Determining a diagnosis of schizophrenia may include:
- **Physical exam.** This may be done to help rule out other problems that could be causing symptoms and to check for any related complications.
- **Tests and screenings.** These may include tests that help rule out conditions with similar symptoms, and screening for alcohol and drugs. The doctor may also request imaging studies, such as an MRI or CT scan.
- **Psychiatric evaluation.** A doctor or mental health professional checks mental status by observing appearance and demeanor and asking about thoughts, moods, delusions, hallucinations, substance use, and potential for violence or suicide. This also includes a discussion of family and personal history.
- **Diagnostic criteria for schizophrenia.** A doctor or mental health professional may use the criteria in the Diagnostic and Statistical Manual of Mental Disorders (DSM-5), published by the American Psychiatric Association.

Treatment

Schizophrenia requires lifelong treatment, even when symptoms have subsided. Treatment with medications and psychosocial therapy can help manage the condition. In some cases, hospitalization may be needed.

A psychiatrist experienced in treating schizophrenia usually guides treatment. The treatment team also may include a psychologist, social worker, psychiatric nurse and possibly a case manager to coordinate care. The full-team approach may be available in clinics with expertise in schizophrenia treatment.

Medications

Medications are the cornerstone of schizophrenia treatment, and antipsychotic medications are the most commonly prescribed drugs. They're thought to control symptoms by affecting the brain neurotransmitter dopamine.

The goal of treatment with antipsychotic medications is to effectively manage signs and symptoms at the lowest possible dose. The psychiatrist may try different drugs, different doses or combinations over time to achieve the desired result. Other medications also may help, such as antidepressants or anti-anxiety drugs. It can take several weeks to notice an improvement in symptoms.

Because medications for schizophrenia can cause serious side effects, people with schizophrenia may be reluctant to take them. Willingness to cooperate with treatment may affect drug choice. For example, someone who is resistant to taking medication consistently may need to be given injections instead of taking a pill.

Ask your doctor about the benefits and side effects of any medication that's prescribed.

First-generation antipsychotics

These first-generation antipsychotics have frequent and potentially significant neurological side effects, including the possibility of developing a movement disorder (tardive dyskinesia) that may or may not be reversible. First-generation antipsychotics include:

- Chlorpromazine
- Fluphenazine
- Haloperidol
- Perphenazine

These antipsychotics are often cheaper than second-generation antipsychotics, especially the generic versions, which can be an important consideration when long-term treatment is necessary.

Second-generation antipsychotics

These newer, second-generation medications are generally preferred because they pose a lower risk of serious side effects than do first-generation antipsychotics. Second-generation antipsychotics include:

- Aripiprazole (Abilify)
- Asenapine (Saphris)
- Brexpiprazole (Rexulti)
- Cariprazine (Vraylar)
- Clozapine (Clozaril, Versacloz)
- Iloperidone (Fanapt)
- Lurasidone (Latuda)
- Olanzapine (Zyprexa)
- Paliperidone (Invega)
- Quetiapine (Seroquel)
- Risperidone (Risperdal)
- Ziprasidone (Geodon)

Long-acting injectable antipsychotics

Some antipsychotics may be given as an intramuscular or subcutaneous injection. They are usually given every two to four weeks, depending on the medication. Ask your doctor about more information on injectable medications. This may be an option if someone has a preference for fewer pills and may help with adherence.

Common medications that are available as an injection include:

- Aripiprazole (Abilify Maintena, Aristada)
- Fluphenazine decanoate
- Haloperidol decanoate
- Paliperidone (Invega Sustenna, Invega Trinza)
- Risperidone (Risperdal Consta, Perseris)

Psychosocial interventions

Once psychosis recedes, in addition to continuing on medication, psychological and social (psychosocial) interventions are important. These may include:

- **Individual therapy.** Psychotherapy may help to normalize thought patterns. Also, learning to cope with stress and identify early warning signs of relapse can help people with schizophrenia manage their illness.
- **Social skills training.** This focuses on improving communication and social interactions and improving the ability to participate in daily activities.
- **Family therapy.** This provides support and education to families dealing with schizophrenia.
- **Vocational rehabilitation and supported employment.** This focuses on helping people with schizophrenia prepare for, find and keep jobs.

Most individuals with schizophrenia require some form of daily living support. Many communities have programs to help people with schizophrenia with jobs, housing, self-help groups and crisis situations. A case manager or someone on the treatment team can help find resources. With appropriate treatment, most people with schizophrenia can manage their illness.

Hospitalization

During crisis periods or times of severe symptoms, hospitalization may be necessary to ensure safety, proper nutrition, adequate sleep and basic hygiene.

Electroconvulsive therapy

For adults with schizophrenia who do not respond to drug therapy, electroconvulsive therapy (ECT) may be considered. ECT may be helpful for someone who also has depression.

Coping and support

Coping with a mental disorder as serious as schizophrenia can be challenging, both for the person with the condition and for friends and family. Here are some ways to cope:

- **Learn about schizophrenia.** Education about the disorder can help the person with schizophrenia understand the importance of sticking to the treatment plan. Education can help friends and family understand the disorder and be more compassionate with the person who has it.
- **Stay focused on goals.** Managing schizophrenia is an ongoing process. Keeping treatment goals in mind can help the person with schizophrenia stay motivated. Help your loved one remember to take responsibility for managing the disorder and working toward goals.
- **Avoid alcohol and drug use.** Using alcohol, nicotine or recreational drugs can make it difficult to treat schizophrenia. If your loved one is addicted, quitting can be a real challenge. Get advice from the health care team on how best to approach this issue.
- **Ask about social services assistance.** These services may be able to assist with affordable housing, transportation and other daily activities.
- **Learn relaxation and stress management.** The person with schizophrenia and loved ones may benefit from stress-reduction techniques such as meditation, yoga or tai chi.

- **Join a support group.** Support groups for people with schizophrenia can help them reach out to others facing similar challenges. Support groups may also help family and friends cope.

Preparing for your appointment

If you're seeking help for someone with schizophrenia, you may start by seeing his or her family doctor or health care professional. However, in some cases when you call to set up an appointment, you may be referred immediately to a psychiatrist

What you can do

To prepare for the appointment, make a list of:

- **Any symptoms your loved one is experiencing,** including any that may seem unrelated to the reason for the appointment
- **Key personal information,** including any major stresses or recent life changes
- **Medications, vitamins,** herbs and other supplements that he or she is taking, including the dosages
- **Questions to ask** the doctor

Go with your loved one to the appointment. Getting the information firsthand will help you know what you're facing and what you need to do for your loved one.

For schizophrenia, some basic questions to ask the doctor include:

- What's likely causing the symptoms or condition?
- What are other possible causes for the symptoms or condition?
- What kinds of tests are needed?
- Is this condition likely temporary or lifelong?

- What's the best treatment?
- What are the alternatives to the primary approach you're suggesting?
- How can I be most helpful and supportive?
- Do you have any brochures or other printed material that I can have?
- What websites do you recommend?

Don't hesitate to ask any other questions during your appointment.

What to expect from your doctor

The doctor is likely to ask you a number of questions. Anticipating some of these questions can help make the discussion productive. Questions may include:

- What are your loved one's symptoms, and when did you first notice them?
- Has anyone else in your family been diagnosed with schizophrenia?
- Have symptoms been continuous or occasional?
- Has your loved one talked about suicide?
- How well does your loved one function in daily life — is he or she eating regularly, going to work or school, bathing regularly?
- Has your loved one been diagnosed with any other medical conditions?
- What medications is your loved one currently taking?

The doctor or mental health professional will ask additional questions based on responses, symptoms and needs.

- SCHIZOAFFECTIVE DISORDER

Schizoaffective disorder is a mental health disorder that is marked by a combination of schizophrenia symptoms, such as hallucinations or delusions, and mood disorder symptoms, such as depression or mania. The two types of schizoaffective disorder — both of which include some symptoms of schizophrenia — are:

- **Bipolar type,** which includes episodes of mania and sometimes major depression
- **Depressive type,** which includes only major depressive episodes

Schizoaffective disorder may run a unique course in each affected person.

Untreated schizoaffective disorder may lead to problems functioning at work, at school and in social situations, causing loneliness and trouble holding down a job or attending school. People with schizoaffective disorder may need assistance and support with daily functioning. Treatment can help manage symptoms and improve quality of life.

Symptoms

Schizoaffective disorder symptoms may vary from person to person. People with the condition experience psychotic symptoms, such as hallucinations or delusions, as well as symptoms of a mood disorder — either bipolar type (episodes of mania and sometimes depression) or depressive type (episodes of depression). Although the development and course of schizoaffective disorder may vary, defining features include a major mood episode (depressed or manic mood) and at least a two-week period of psychotic symptoms when a major mood episode is not present.

Signs and symptoms of schizoaffective disorder depend on the type — bipolar or depressive type — and may include, among others:

- Delusions — having false, fixed beliefs, despite evidence to the contrary
- Hallucinations, such as hearing voices or seeing things that aren't there
- Impaired communication and speech, such as being incoherent
- Bizarre or unusual behavior
- Symptoms of depression, such as feeling empty, sad or worthless
- Periods of manic mood, with an increase in energy and a decreased need for sleep over several days, and behaviors that are out of character
- Impaired occupational, academic and social functioning
- Problems with managing personal care, including cleanliness and physical appearance

When to see a doctor

If you think someone you know may have schizoaffective disorder symptoms, talk to that person about your concerns. Although you can't force someone to seek professional help, you can offer encouragement and support and help find a qualified doctor or mental health professional.

If your loved one can't provide his or her own food, clothing or shelter, or if the safety of your loved one or others is a concern, you may need to call *10111 or 10177* for help so that your loved one can be evaluated by a mental health professional.

Suicidal thoughts or behavior

Talk of suicide or suicidal behavior may occur in someone with schizoaffective disorder. If you have a loved one who is in danger of attempting suicide or has made a suicide attempt, make sure someone stays with that person. Call *10111 or 10177* immediately. Or, if you can do so safely, take the person to the nearest hospital emergency room.

Causes

The exact causes of schizoaffective disorder are still being investigated, but genetics are likely a factor.

Risk factors

Factors that increase the risk of developing schizoaffective disorder include:

- Having a close blood relative — such as a parent or sibling — who has schizoaffective disorder, schizophrenia or bipolar disorder
- Stressful events that may trigger symptoms
- Taking mind-altering drugs, which may worsen symptoms when an underlying disorder is present

Complications

- People with schizoaffective disorder are at an increased risk of:
- Suicide, suicide attempts or suicidal thoughts
- Social isolation
- Family and interpersonal conflicts
- Unemployment
- Anxiety disorders
- Alcohol or other substance use problems
- Significant health problems
- Poverty and homelessness

Diagnosis

Diagnosis of schizoaffective disorder involves ruling out other mental health disorders and concluding that symptoms are not due to substance use, medication or a medical condition. Determining a diagnosis of schizoaffective disorder may include:

- **Physical exam.** This may be done to help rule out other problems that could be causing symptoms and to check for any related complications.
- **Tests and screenings.** These may include tests that help rule out conditions with similar symptoms, and screening for alcohol and drugs. In certain situations, the doctor may also request imaging studies, such as an MRI or CT scan.
- **Psychiatric evaluation.** A doctor or mental health professional checks mental status by observing appearance and demeanor and asking about thoughts, moods, delusions, hallucinations, substance use and potential for suicide. This also includes a discussion of family and personal history.
- **Diagnostic criteria for schizoaffective disorder.** Your doctor or mental health professional may use the criteria in the Diagnostic and Statistical Manual of Mental Disorders DSM-5, published by the American Psychiatric Association.

Treatment

People with schizoaffective disorder generally respond best to a combination of medications, psychotherapy and life skills training. Treatment varies, depending on the type and severity of symptoms and whether the disorder is the depressive or bipolar type. In some cases, hospitalization may be needed. Long-term treatment can help to manage the symptoms.

Medications

In general, doctors prescribe medications for schizoaffective disorder to relieve psychotic symptoms, stabilize mood and treat depression. These medications may include:

- **Antipsychotics.** The only medication approved by the Food and Drug Administration specifically for the treatment of schizoaffective disorder is the antipsychotic drug paliperidone (Invega). However, doctors may prescribe other antipsychotic drugs to help manage psychotic symptoms such as delusions and hallucinations.
- **Mood-stabilizing medications.** When the schizoaffective disorder is bipolar type, mood stabilizers can help level out the mania highs and depression lows.
- **Antidepressants.** When depression is the underlying mood disorder, antidepressants can help manage feelings of sadness, hopelessness, or difficulty with sleep and concentration.

Psychotherapy

In addition to medication, psychotherapy, also called talk therapy, may help. Psychotherapy may include:

- **Individual therapy.** Psychotherapy may help to normalize thought patterns and reduce symptoms. Building a trusting relationship in therapy can help people with schizoaffective disorder better understand their condition and learn to manage symptoms. Effective sessions focus on real-life plans, problems, relationships and coping

strategies.
- **Family or group therapy.** Treatment can be more effective when people with schizoaffective disorder are able to discuss their real-life problems with others. Supportive group settings can also help reduce social isolation, provide a reality check during periods of psychosis, increase appropriate use of medications and develop better social skills.
- **Life skills training.** Learning social and vocational skills can help reduce isolation and improve quality of life.
- **Social skills training.** This focuses on improving communication and social interactions and improving the ability to participate in daily activities. New skills and behaviors specific to settings such as the home or workplace can be practiced.
- **Vocational rehabilitation and supported employment.** This focuses on helping people with schizoaffective disorder prepare for, find and keep jobs.

Hospitalization

During crisis periods or times of severe symptoms, hospitalization may be necessary to ensure safety, proper nutrition, adequate sleep and basic personal care.

Electroconvulsive therapy

For adults with schizoaffective disorder who do not respond to psychotherapy or medications, electroconvulsive therapy (ECT) may be considered.

Coping and support

Schizoaffective disorder requires ongoing treatment and support. People with schizoaffective disorder can benefit from:

- **Learning about the disorder.** Education about schizoaffective disorder may help the person stick to the treatment plan. Education can also help friends and family understand the disorder and be more compassionate.
- **Paying attention to warning signs.** Identify things that may trigger symptoms or interfere with carrying out daily activities. Make a plan for what to do if symptoms return. Contact the doctor or therapist if needed to prevent the situation from worsening.
- **Joining a support group.** Support groups can help make connections with others facing similar challenges. Support groups may also help family and friends cope.
- **Asking about social services assistance.** These services may be able to help with affordable housing, transportation and daily activities.
- **Also, avoid recreational drugs, tobacco and alcohol.** These can worsen schizoaffective symptoms or interfere with medications. If necessary, get appropriate treatment for a substance use problem.

Preparing for your appointment

If you think you may have schizoaffective disorder or that your loved one may have it, take steps to prepare for the appointment, whether it's with a primary care doctor or a mental health professional, such as a psychiatrist.

If the appointment is for a relative or friend, offer to go with him or her. Getting the information firsthand will help you know what you're facing and how you can help your loved one.

What you can do

To prepare for the appointment, make a list of:

- **Any symptoms you've noticed,** including any that may seem unrelated to the reason for the appointment
- **Key personal information,** including any family history of mental health disorders, any major stresses or recent life changes
- **All medications,** vitamins, herbal preparations and any other supplements, and the dosages
- **Questions to ask** the doctor to help you make the most of your time

Some basic questions to ask include:

- What is likely causing the symptoms?
- Are there any other possible causes?
- How will you determine the diagnosis?
- Is this condition likely temporary or long term?
- What treatments do you recommend?
- What are the alternatives to the primary approach you're suggesting?
- What are the side effects of the medication you're prescribing?
- Are there any brochures or other printed material that I can have?
- What websites do you recommend?

Don't hesitate to ask any other questions during the appointment.

- What to expect from your doctor
- Your doctor is likely to ask several questions, such as:
- What symptoms have you noticed?
- When did you start noticing symptoms?
- Have symptoms been continuous or occasional?

- Have you thought about or attempted suicide?
- How are you functioning in daily life — are you eating regularly, bathing regularly, going to work, school or social activities?
- Have other family members or friends expressed concern about your behavior?
- Have you been diagnosed with any other medical conditions?
- Has anyone else in your family been diagnosed with or treated for mental illness?

Be ready to answer these questions so you'll have time to go over any other points you want to focus on.

- DELUSIONAL DISORDER

Delusional disorder is a type of psychotic disorder. Its main symptom is the presence of one or more delusions.

A delusion is an unshakable belief in something that's untrue. The belief isn't a part of the person's culture or subculture, and almost everyone else knows this belief to be false.

People with delusional disorder often experience non-bizarre delusions. Non-bizarre delusions involve situations that could possibly occur in real life, such as being followed, deceived or loved from a distance. These delusions usually involve the misinterpretation of perceptions or experiences. In reality, these situations are either untrue or are highly exaggerated. Non-bizarre delusions are different from bizarre delusions, which include beliefs that are impossible in our reality, such as believing someone has removed an organ from your body without any physical evidence of the procedure.

People with delusional disorder often continue to socialize and function well, apart from the subject of their delusion. Generally, they don't behave in an odd or unusual manner. This is unlike people with other psychotic disorders, who might also have delusions as a symptom. In some cases, however, people with delusional disorder might become so preoccupied with their delusions that their lives are disrupted.

Types of delusional disorder

There are different types of delusional disorder, which are determined based on the main theme of the delusions the person experiences. The types of delusional disorder include:

- **Erotomanic:** People with this type of delusional disorder believe that another person, often someone important or famous, is in love with them. They may attempt to contact the person of the delusion and engage in stalking behavior.
- **Grandiose:** People with this type of delusional disorder have an overinflated sense of self-worth, power, knowledge or identity. They may believe they have a great talent or have made an important discovery.
- **Jealous:** People with this type of delusional disorder believe that their spouse or sexual partner is unfaithful without any concrete evidence.
- **Persecutory:** People with this type of delusional disorder believe someone or something is mistreating, spying on or attempting to harm them (or someone close to them). People with this type of delusional disorder may make repeated complaints to legal authorities.
- **Somatic:** People with this type of delusional disorder believe that they have a physical issue or medical problem, such as a parasite or a bad odor.
- **Mixed:** People with this type of delusional disorder have two or more of the types of delusions listed above.

Difference between delusional disorder and schizophrenia

Schizophrenia is a spectrum (or range) of conditions that involve psychotic symptoms, which include:

- Disorganized speech or behavior
- Negative symptoms (a decrease in emotion in a person's facial expressions and motivation)

Delusional disorder is different from schizophrenia because there aren't any other psychotic symptoms other than delusions.

In addition, in contrast to schizophrenia, delusional disorder is relatively rare, and daily functioning isn't as impaired as it is in schizophrenia.

Who does delusional disorder affect?

Delusional disorder most often occurs in middle to late life, with the average age of onset being 40 years. The persecutory and jealous types of delusional disorder are more common in people assigned male at birth (AMAB), and the erotomanic type is more common in people assigned female at birth (AFAB).

People who tend to be socially isolated are more likely to develop delusional disorder. These populations include:

- Immigrants who have language barriers
- People who are deaf
- People who are visually impaired
- Elderly people

How common is delusional disorder?

Although delusions might be a symptom of more common disorders, such as schizophrenia, delusional disorder itself is rather rare. Approximately 0.05% to 0.1% of the adult population has delusional disorder.

What is the most common type of delusional disorder?

The most common type of delusional disorder is the *persecutory type* — when someone believes others are out to harm them despite evidence to the contrary.

Symptoms

The presence of delusions is the most obvious sign of delusional disorder, which vary based on the type.

Another characteristic of this condition is that the person often lacks self-awareness that their delusions are problematic. They're unable to accept that their delusions are irrational or inaccurate, even if they recognize that other people would describe their delusions this way.

Anger and violent behavior may be present if someone is experiencing persecutory, jealous or erotomanic delusions.

People with delusional disorder may also develop anxiety and/or depression as a result of the delusions.

Early symptoms of delusional disorder may include:
- Feelings of being exploited.
- Preoccupation with the loyalty or trustworthiness of friends.
- A tendency to read threatening meanings into benign remarks or events.
- Persistently holding grudges.
- A readiness to respond and react to perceived slights.

Causes

As with many other psychotic disorders, researchers don't yet know the exact cause of delusional disorder. Researchers are, however, looking at the role of various factors that may contribute to the development of the condition, including:
- **Genetic factors:** The fact that delusional disorder is more common in people who have family members with delusional disorder or schizophrenia suggests there might be a genetic factor involved. Researchers believe that, as with other mental disorders, a tendency to develop delusional disorder might be passed on from parents to their

biological children.
- **Biological factors:** Researchers are studying how abnormalities of certain areas of your brain might be involved in the development of delusional disorder. An imbalance of certain chemicals in your brain, called neurotransmitters, has been linked to the formation of delusional symptoms.
- **Environmental and psychological factors:** Evidence suggests that delusional disorder can be triggered by stress. Alcohol use disorder and substance use disorder might contribute to the condition. Hypersensitivity and ego defense mechanisms like reaction formation, projection and denial are some psychodynamic theories for the development of delusional disorder. Social isolation, envy, distrust, suspicion and low self-esteem are also some psychological factors that may lead to a person seeking an explanation for these feelings and, thus, forming a delusion as a solution.

Diagnosis

How is delusional disorder diagnosed?

Healthcare providers — mainly mental health professionals — diagnose delusional disorder when a person has one or more delusions for one month or more that can't be explained by any other condition. The person must also not have the characteristic symptoms of other psychotic disorders, such as schizophrenia. If someone is experiencing signs and symptoms of delusional disorder, a healthcare provider will perform a complete medical history and physical examination. Although there aren't any laboratory tests to diagnose delusional disorder, their healthcare provider might use various diagnostic tests — such as imaging tests, a urine drug screen and blood tests — to rule out any physical conditions, medications or substances that could be causing the symptoms. If their healthcare provider finds no physical reason for the symptoms, a consultation with a psychiatrist or psychologist will likely be made. Psychiatrists and psychologists use specially designed interview and assessment tools to evaluate a person for a psychotic disorder. They'll ask questions about the delusions and assess the person's mental status. The psychiatrist or psychologist may also interview family members and friends so they can provide further details about the person's delusions and a timeline of the symptoms.

As other mental health conditions can cause delusions, mental health professionals carefully assess the person for other symptoms. Delusional disorder can be misdiagnosed as any of the following conditions:

- Obsessive-compulsive disorder.
- Schizophrenia.
- Delirium/major neurocognitive disorder.
- Bipolar disorder.
- Personality disorders, especially borderline personality disorder and paranoid personality disorder.

Treatment

Treatment for delusional disorder most often includes psychotherapy (talk therapy) and medication, but delusional disorder is highly resistant to treatment with medication alone. People with delusional disorder often don't seek treatment for the condition on their own because most people with delusional disorder don't realize their delusions are problematic or incorrect. It's more likely they'll seek help due to other mental health conditions such as depression or anxiety.

People with severe symptoms or who are at risk of hurting themselves or others might need to be admitted to the hospital until the condition is stabilized.

Psychotherapy for delusional disorder

Psychotherapy is a term for a variety of treatment techniques that aim to help people identify and change troubling emotions, thoughts and behaviors. Working with a mental health professional, such as a psychologist or psychiatrist, can provide support, education and guidance to the person and their family.

Through therapy, people with delusional disorder can learn to manage their symptoms, identify early warning signs of relapse and develop relapse prevention plans. Types of psychotherapy include:

- **Individual psychotherapy:** This type of therapy can help a person recognize and correct the underlying thinking that has become distorted.
- **Cognitive behavioral therapy (CBT):** This is a structured, goal-oriented type of therapy. A mental health professional helps people take a close look at their thoughts and emotions. They'll come to understand how their thoughts affect their actions. Through CBT, they can unlearn negative thoughts and behaviors and learn to adopt healthier thinking patterns and habits.
- **Family-focused therapy:** This therapy can help people with delusional disorder and their families. This treatment involves psychoeducation regarding delusional disorder, communication improvement training and problem-solving skills training.

Medications for delusional disorder

The primary medications used to help treat delusional disorder are called antipsychotics (neuroleptics). Medications include the following:

- **First-generation ("typical") antipsychotics:** Healthcare providers have used these medications to treat mental health conditions since the mid-1950s. These medicines work by blocking dopamine receptors in your brain. Dopamine is a neurotransmitter believed to be involved in the development of delusions. First-generation antipsychotics include:
    - chlorpromazine (Thorazine)
    - fluphenazine (Prolixin)
    - haloperidol (Haldol)
    - thiothixene (Navane)
    - trifluoperazine (Stelazine)
    - perphenazine (Trilafon)
    - thioridazine (Mellaril)
- **Second-generation ("atypical") antipsychotics:** These newer antipsychotics are also effective in treating the symptoms of delusional disorder. They work by blocking dopamine and serotonin receptors in your brain. These drugs include:
    - risperidone (Risperdal)
    - clozapine (Clozaril)
    - quetiapine (Seroquel)
    - ziprasidone (Geodon)
    - olanzapine (Zyprexa)

These medications are usually better tolerated than first-generation antipsychotics.

Other medications that healthcare providers might prescribe

to treat delusional disorder include anxiolytics and antidepressants. Anxiolytics might help if the person has a very high level of anxiety and/or problems sleeping. Antidepressants can help treat depression, which often occurs in people with delusional disorder.

Prevention

There's no known way to prevent delusional disorder. However, early diagnosis and treatment can help decrease the disruption to the person's life, family and friendships.

Prognosis

What is the prognosis (outlook) for delusional disorder?

The prognosis (outlook) for people with delusional disorder varies depending on a few factors, including:

- The type of delusional disorder.
- The severity of the delusions.
- The person's life circumstances, including the availability of support and a willingness to stick with treatment.

Delusional disorder doesn't usually significantly affect a person's daily functioning, but the severity of the delusion may gradually get worse. Most people with delusional disorder can remain employed as long as their work doesn't involve things related to their delusions.

The prognosis of delusional disorder is better if the person sticks to their treatment plan. Almost 50% of people have a full recovery, more than 20% of people report a decrease in symptoms and less than 20% of people report minimal to no change in symptoms.

Unfortunately, many people with this condition don't seek help. It's often difficult for people with mental health conditions to recognize they're not well. They also might be too embarrassed or afraid to seek treatment. Without treatment, delusional disorder can be a life-long condition.

Complications

If left untreated, delusional disorder might lead to:
- Depression, often as a consequence of difficulties associated with the delusions.
- Social isolation.
- Legal issues — for example, stalking or harassing the person involved with the delusion could lead to arrest.
- Self-harm or harm to others. This is more common in the jealous and persecutory types.

Coping and support

If you know someone with delusional disorder, you can help by providing support and encouragement for them to seek help and treatment. People with delusional disorder who feel pressured or repeatedly criticized by others will likely experience stress, which may worsen their symptoms. Because of this, a positive approach may be more helpful and effective. The friends and family members of people with delusional disorder often experience stress, depression, grief and isolation. It's important to take care of your mental health and seek help if you're experiencing these symptoms

3. **Bipolar and related disorders**

- Bipolar disorder

Bipolar disorder, formerly called manic depression, is a mental health condition that causes extreme mood swings that include emotional highs (mania or hypomania) and lows (depression). When you become depressed, you may feel sad or hopeless and lose interest or pleasure in most activities. When your mood shifts to mania or hypomania (less extreme than mania), you may feel euphoric, full of energy or unusually irritable. These mood swings can affect sleep, energy, activity, judgment, behavior and the ability to think clearly. Episodes of mood swings may occur rarely or multiple times a year. While most people will experience some emotional symptoms between episodes, some may not experience any.

Although bipolar disorder is a lifelong condition, you can manage your mood swings and other symptoms by following a treatment plan. In most cases, bipolar disorder is treated with medications and psychological counseling (psychotherapy).

Symptoms

There are several types of bipolar and related disorders. They may include mania or hypomania and depression. Symptoms can cause unpredictable changes in mood and behavior, resulting in significant distress and difficulty in life.

- **Bipolar I disorder.** You've had at least one manic episode that may be preceded or followed by hypomanic or major depressive episodes. In some cases, mania may trigger a break from reality (psychosis).
- **Bipolar II disorder.** You've had at least one major depressive episode and at least one hypomanic episode, but you've never had a manic episode.
- **Cyclothymic disorder.** You've had at least two years — or one year in children and teenagers — of many periods of hypomania symptoms and periods

of depressive symptoms (though less severe than major depression).
- **Other types.** These include, for example, bipolar and related disorders induced by certain drugs or alcohol or due to a medical condition, such as Cushing's disease, multiple sclerosis or stroke.
- **Bipolar II disorder is not a milder form of bipolar I disorder,** but a separate diagnosis. While the manic episodes of bipolar I disorder can be severe and dangerous, individuals with bipolar II disorder can be depressed for longer periods, which can cause significant impairment.

Although bipolar disorder can occur at any age, typically it's diagnosed in the teenage years or early 20s. Symptoms can vary from person to person, and symptoms may vary over time.

Mania and hypomania

Mania and hypomania are two distinct types of episodes, but they have the same symptoms. Mania is more severe than hypomania and causes more noticeable problems at work, school and social activities, as well as relationship difficulties. Mania may also trigger a break from reality (psychosis) and require hospitalization.

Both a manic and a hypomanic episode include three or more of these symptoms:
- Abnormally upbeat, jumpy or wired
- Increased activity, energy or agitation
- Exaggerated sense of well-being and self-confidence (euphoria)
- Decreased need for sleep
- Unusual talkativeness
- Racing thoughts
- Distractibility

- Poor decision-making — for example, going on buying sprees, taking sexual risks or making foolish investments

Major depressive episode

A major depressive episode includes symptoms that are severe enough to cause noticeable difficulty in day-to-day activities, such as work, school, social activities or relationships. An episode includes five or more of these symptoms:

- Depressed mood, such as feeling sad, empty, hopeless or tearful (in children and teens, depressed mood can appear as irritability)
- Marked loss of interest or feeling no pleasure in all — or almost all — activities
- Significant weight loss when not dieting, weight gain, or decrease or increase in appetite (in children, failure to gain weight as expected can be a sign of depression)
- Either insomnia or sleeping too much
- Either restlessness or slowed behavior
- Fatigue or loss of energy
- Feelings of worthlessness or excessive or inappropriate guilt
- Decreased ability to think or concentrate, or indecisiveness
- Thinking about, planning or attempting suicide

Other features of bipolar disorder

Signs and symptoms of bipolar I and bipolar II disorders may include other features, such as anxious distress, melancholy, psychosis or others. The timing of symptoms may include diagnostic labels such as mixed or rapid cycling. In addition, bipolar symptoms may occur during pregnancy or change with the seasons.

Symptoms in children and teens

Symptoms of bipolar disorder can be difficult to identify in children and teens. It's often hard to tell whether these are normal ups and downs, the results of stress or trauma, or signs of a mental health problem other than bipolar disorder. Children and teens may have distinct major depressive or manic or hypomanic episodes, but the pattern can vary from that of adults with bipolar disorder. And moods can rapidly shift during episodes. Some children may have periods without mood symptoms between episodes.

The most prominent signs of bipolar disorder in children and teenagers may include severe mood swings that are different from their usual mood swings.

When to see a doctor

Despite the mood extremes, people with bipolar disorder often don't recognize how much their emotional instability disrupts their lives and the lives of their loved ones and don't get the treatment they need. And if you're like some people with bipolar disorder, you may enjoy the feelings of euphoria and cycles of being more productive. However, this euphoria is always followed by an emotional crash that can leave you depressed, worn out — and perhaps in financial, legal or relationship trouble.

If you have any symptoms of depression or mania, see your doctor or mental health professional. Bipolar disorder doesn't get better on its own. Getting treatment from a mental health professional with experience in bipolar disorder can help you get your symptoms under control.

Causes

The exact cause of bipolar disorder is unknown, but several

factors may be involved, such as:

- **Biological differences.** People with bipolar disorder appear to have physical changes in their brains. The significance of these changes is still uncertain but may eventually help pinpoint causes.
- **Genetics.** Bipolar disorder is more common in people who have a first-degree relative, such as a sibling or parent, with the condition. Researchers are trying to find genes that may be involved in causing bipolar disorder.

Risk factors

Factors that may increase the risk of developing bipolar disorder or act as a trigger for the first episode include:

- Having a first-degree relative, such as a parent or sibling, with bipolar disorder
- Periods of high stress, such as the death of a loved one or other traumatic event
- Drug or alcohol abuse

Complications

Left untreated, bipolar disorder can result in serious problems that affect every area of your life, such as:

- Problems related to drug and alcohol use
- Suicide or suicide attempts
- Legal or financial problems
- Damaged relationships
- Poor work or school performance

Co-occurring conditions

If you have bipolar disorder, you may also have another health condition that needs to be treated along with bipolar disorder. Some conditions can worsen bipolar disorder symptoms or make treatment less successful. Examples include:

- Anxiety disorders
- Eating disorders
- Attention-deficit/hyperactivity disorder (ADHD)
- Alcohol or drug problems
- Physical health problems, such as heart disease, thyroid problems, headaches or obesity

Prevention

There's no sure way to prevent bipolar disorder. However, getting treatment at the earliest sign of a mental health disorder can help prevent bipolar disorder or other mental health conditions from worsening.

If you've been diagnosed with bipolar disorder, some strategies can help prevent minor symptoms from becoming full-blown episodes of mania or depression:

- **Pay attention to warning signs.** Addressing symptoms early on can prevent episodes from getting worse. You may have identified a pattern to your bipolar episodes and what triggers them. Call your doctor if you feel you're falling into an episode of depression or mania. Involve family members or friends in watching for warning signs.
- **Avoid drugs and alcohol.** Using alcohol or recreational drugs can worsen your symptoms and make them more likely to come back.
- **Take your medications exactly as directed.** You may be tempted to stop treatment — but don't. Stopping your medication or reducing your dose on your own may cause withdrawal effects or your symptoms may worsen or return.

Diagnosis

To determine if you have bipolar disorder, your evaluation may include:

- **Physical exam.** Your doctor may do a physical exam and lab tests to identify any medical problems that could be causing your symptoms.
- **Psychiatric assessment.** Your doctor may refer you to a psychiatrist, who will talk to you about your thoughts, feelings and behavior patterns. You may also fill out a psychological self-assessment or questionnaire. With your permission, family members or close friends may be asked to provide information about your symptoms.
- **Mood charting.** You may be asked to keep a daily record of your moods, sleep patterns or other factors that could help with diagnosis and finding the right treatment.
- **Criteria for bipolar disorder.** Your psychiatrist may compare your symptoms with the criteria for bipolar and related disorders in the Diagnostic and Statistical Manual of Mental Disorders (DSM-5), published by the American Psychiatric Association.

Diagnosis in children

Although diagnosis of children and teenagers with bipolar disorder includes the same criteria that are used for adults, symptoms in children and teens often have different patterns and may not fit neatly into the diagnostic categories.

Also, children who have bipolar disorder are frequently also diagnosed with other mental health conditions such as attention-deficit/hyperactivity disorder (ADHD) or behavior problems, which can make diagnosis more complicated. Referral to a child psychiatrist with experience in bipolar disorder is recommended.

Treatment

Treatment is best guided by a medical doctor who specializes in diagnosing and treating mental health conditions (psychiatrist) who is skilled in treating bipolar and related disorders. You may have a treatment team that also includes a psychologist, social worker and psychiatric nurse.

Bipolar disorder is a lifelong condition. Treatment is directed at managing symptoms. Depending on your needs, treatment may include:

- **Medications.** Often, you'll need to start taking medications to balance your moods right away.
- **Continued treatment.** Bipolar disorder requires lifelong treatment with medications, even during periods when you feel better. People who skip maintenance treatment are at high risk of a relapse of symptoms or having minor mood changes turn into full-blown mania or depression.
- **Day treatment programs.** Your doctor may recommend a day treatment program. These programs provide the support and counseling you need while you get symptoms under control.
- **Substance abuse treatment.** If you have problems with alcohol or drugs, you'll also need substance abuse treatment. Otherwise, it can be very difficult to manage bipolar disorder.
- **Hospitalization.** Your doctor may recommend hospitalization if you're behaving dangerously, you feel suicidal or you become detached from reality (psychotic). Getting psychiatric treatment at a hospital can help keep you calm and safe and stabilize your mood, whether you're having a manic or major depressive episode.

The primary treatments for bipolar disorder include

medications and psychological counselling (psychotherapy) to control symptoms, and also may include education and support groups.

Medications

A number of medications are used to treat bipolar disorder. The types and doses of medications prescribed are based on your particular symptoms.

Medications may include:

- **Mood stabilizers.** You'll typically need mood-stabilizing medication to control manic or hypomanic episodes. Examples of mood stabilizers include lithium (Lithobid), valproic acid (Depakene), divalproex sodium (Depakote), carbamazepine (Tegretol, Equetro, others) and lamotrigine (Lamictal).
- **Antipsychotics.** If symptoms of depression or mania persist in spite of treatment with other medications, adding an antipsychotic drug such as olanzapine (Zyprexa), risperidone (Risperdal), quetiapine (Seroquel), aripiprazole (Abilify), ziprasidone (Geodon), lurasidone (Latuda) or asenapine (Saphris) may help. Your doctor may prescribe some of these medications alone or along with a mood stabilizer.
- **Antidepressants.** Your doctor may add an antidepressant to help manage depression. Because an antidepressant can sometimes trigger a manic episode, it's usually prescribed along with a mood stabilizer or antipsychotic.
- **Antidepressant-antipsychotic.** The medication Symbyax combines the antidepressant fluoxetine and the antipsychotic olanzapine. It works as a depression treatment and a mood stabilizer.

- **Anti-anxiety medications.** Benzodiazepines may help with anxiety and improve sleep, but are usually used on a short-term basis.

Finding the right medication

Finding the right medication or medications for you will likely take some trial and error. If one doesn't work well for you, there are several others to try. This process requires patience, as some medications need weeks to months to take full effect. Generally, only one medication is changed at a time so that your doctor can identify which medications work to relieve your symptoms with the least bothersome side effects. Medications also may need to be adjusted as your symptoms change.

Side effects

Mild side effects often improve as you find the right medications and doses that work for you, and your body adjusts to the medications. Talk to your doctor or mental health professional if you have bothersome side effects. Don't make changes or stop taking your medications. If you stop your medication, you may experience withdrawal effects or your symptoms may worsen or return. You may become very depressed, feel suicidal, or go into a manic or hypomanic episode. If you think you need to make a change, call your doctor.

Medications and pregnancy

A number of medications for bipolar disorder can be associated with birth defects and can pass through breast milk to your baby. Certain medications, such as valproic acid and divalproex sodium, should not be used during pregnancy. Also, birth control medications may lose effectiveness when taken along with certain bipolar disorder medications.

Discuss treatment options with your doctor before you become pregnant, if possible. If you're taking medication to treat your bipolar disorder and think you may be pregnant, talk to your doctor right away.

Psychotherapy

Psychotherapy is a vital part of bipolar disorder treatment and can be provided in individual, family or group settings. Several types of therapy may be helpful. These include:

- **Interpersonal and social rhythm therapy (IPSRT).** IPSRT focuses on the stabilization of daily rhythms, such as sleeping, waking and mealtimes. A consistent routine allows for better mood management. People with bipolar disorder may benefit from establishing a daily routine for sleep, diet and exercise.
- **Cognitive behavioral therapy (CBT).** The focus is identifying unhealthy, negative beliefs and behaviors and replacing them with healthy, positive ones. CBT can help identify what triggers your bipolar episodes. You also learn effective strategies to manage stress and to cope with upsetting situations.
- **Psychoeducation.** Learning about bipolar disorder (psychoeducation) can help you and your loved ones understand the condition. Knowing what's going on can help you get the best support, identify issues, make a plan to prevent relapse and stick with treatment.
- **Family-focused therapy.** Family support and communication can help you stick with your treatment plan and help you and your loved ones recognize and manage warning signs of mood

swings.

Other treatment options

Depending on your needs, other treatments may be added to your depression therapy.

During electroconvulsive therapy (ECT), electrical currents are passed through the brain, intentionally triggering a brief seizure. ECT seems to cause changes in brain chemistry that can reverse symptoms of certain mental illnesses. ECT may be an option for bipolar treatment if you don't get better with medications, can't take antidepressants for health reasons such as pregnancy or are at high risk of suicide.

Transcranial magnetic stimulation (TMS) is being investigated as an option for those who haven't responded to antidepressants.

Treatment in children and teenagers

Treatments for children and teenagers are generally decided on a case-by-case basis, depending on symptoms, medication side effects and other factors. Generally, treatment includes:

- **Medications.** Children and teens with bipolar disorder are often prescribed the same types of medications as those used in adults. There's less research on the safety and effectiveness of bipolar medications in children than in adults, so treatment decisions are often based on adult research.
- **Psychotherapy.** Initial and long-term therapy can help keep symptoms from returning. Psychotherapy can help children and teens manage their routines, develop coping skills, address learning difficulties, resolve social problems, and help strengthen family bonds and communication.

And, if needed, it can help treat substance abuse problems common in older children and teens with bipolar disorder.
- **Psychoeducation.** Psychoeducation can include learning the symptoms of bipolar disorder and how they differ from behavior related to your child's developmental age, the situation and appropriate cultural behavior. Understanding about bipolar disorder can also help you support your child.
- **Support.** Working with teachers and school counselors and encouraging support from family and friends can help identify services and encourage success.

Lifestyle and home remedies

You'll probably need to make lifestyle changes to stop cycles of behavior that worsen your bipolar disorder. Here are some steps to take:

- **Quit drinking or using recreational drugs.** One of the biggest concerns with bipolar disorder is the negative consequences of risk-taking behavior and drug or alcohol abuse. Get help if you have trouble quitting on your own.
- **Form healthy relationships.** Surround yourself with people who are a positive influence. Friends and family members can provide support and help you watch for warning signs of mood shifts.
- **Create a healthy routine.** Having a regular routine for sleeping, eating and physical activity can help balance your moods. Check with your doctor before starting any exercise program. Eat a healthy diet. If you take lithium, talk with your doctor about appropriate fluid and salt intake. If you have trouble sleeping, talk to your doctor or mental health

professional about what you can do.
- **Check first before taking other medications.** Call the doctor who's treating you for bipolar disorder before you take medications prescribed by another doctor or any over-the-counter supplements or medications. Sometimes other medications trigger episodes of depression or mania or may interfere with medications you're taking for bipolar disorder.
- **Consider keeping a mood chart.** Keeping a record of your daily moods, treatments, sleep, activities and feelings may help identify triggers, effective treatment options and when treatment needs to be adjusted.

Alternative medicine

There isn't much research on alternative or complementary medicine — sometimes called integrative medicine — and bipolar disorder. Most of the studies are on major depression, so it isn't clear how these nontraditional approaches work for bipolar disorder.

If you choose to use alternative or complementary medicine in addition to your physician-recommended treatment, take some precautions first:

- **Don't stop taking your prescribed medications or skip therapy sessions.** Alternative or complementary medicine is not a substitute for regular medical care when it comes to treating bipolar disorder.
- **Be honest with your doctors and mental health professionals.** Tell them exactly which alternative or complementary treatments you use or would like to try.
- **Be aware of potential dangers.** Alternative and complementary products aren't regulated the way

prescription drugs are. Just because it's natural doesn't mean it's safe. Before using alternative or complementary medicine, talk to your doctor about the risks, including possible serious interactions with medications.

Coping and support

Coping with bipolar disorder can be challenging. Here are some strategies that can help:

- **Learn about bipolar disorder.** Education about your condition can empower you and motivate you to stick to your treatment plan and recognize mood changes. Help educate your family and friends about what you're going through.
- **Stay focused on your goals.** Learning to manage bipolar disorder can take time. Stay motivated by keeping your goals in mind and reminding yourself that you can work to repair damaged relationships and other problems caused by your mood swings.
- **Join a support group.** Support groups for people with bipolar disorder can help you connect to others facing similar challenges and share experiences.
- **Find healthy outlets.** Explore healthy ways to channel your energy, such as hobbies, exercise and recreational activities.
- **Learn ways to relax and manage stress.** Yoga, tai chi, massage, meditation or other relaxation techniques can be helpful.

Preparing for your appointment

You may start by seeing your primary care doctor or a psychiatrist. You may want to take a family member or friend along to your appointment, if possible, for support and to help remember information.

What you can do

Before your appointment, make a list of:

- **Any symptoms you've had,** including any that may seem unrelated to the reason for the appointment
- **Key personal information,** including any major stresses or recent life changes
- **All medications, vitamins,** herbs or other supplements you're taking, and the dosages
- **Questions to ask** your doctor

Some questions to ask your doctor may include:

- Do I have bipolar disorder?
- Are there any other possible causes for my symptoms?
- What kinds of tests will I need?
- What treatments are available? Which do you recommend for me?
- What side effects are possible with that treatment?
- What are the alternatives to the primary approach that you're suggesting?
- I have these other health conditions. How can I best manage these conditions together?
- Should I see a psychiatrist or other mental health professional?
- Is there a generic alternative to the medicine you're prescribing?
- Are there any brochures or other printed material that I can have?
- What websites do you recommend?

Don't hesitate to ask other questions during your appointment.

What to expect from your doctor

Your doctor will likely ask you a number of questions. Be ready to answer them to reserve time to go over any points you want to focus on. Your doctor may ask:

- When did you or your loved ones first begin noticing your symptoms?
- How frequently do your moods change?
- Do you ever have suicidal thoughts when you're feeling down?
- Do your symptoms interfere with your daily life or relationships?
- Do you have any blood relatives with bipolar disorder or depression?
- What other mental or physical health conditions do you have?
- Do you drink alcohol, smoke cigarettes or use recreational drugs?
- How much do you sleep at night? Does it change over time?
- Do you go through periods when you take risks that you wouldn't normally take, such as unsafe sex or unwise, spontaneous financial decisions?
- What, if anything, seems to improve your symptoms?
- What, if anything, appears to worsen your symptoms?

4. Depressive disorders

- Depression

Depression is a mood disorder that causes a persistent feeling of sadness and loss of interest. Also called major depressive disorder or clinical depression, it affects how you feel, think and behave and can lead to a variety of emotional and physical problems. You may have trouble doing normal day-to-day activities, and sometimes you may feel as if life isn't worth living.

More than just a bout of the blues, depression isn't a weakness and you can't simply "snap out" of it. Depression may require long-term treatment. But don't get discouraged. Most people with depression feel better with medication, psychotherapy or both.

Symptoms

Although depression may occur only once during your life, people typically have multiple episodes. During these episodes, symptoms occur most of the day, nearly every day and may include:

- Feelings of sadness, tearfulness, emptiness or hopelessness
- Angry outbursts, irritability or frustration, even over small matters
- Loss of interest or pleasure in most or all normal activities, such as sex, hobbies or sports
- Sleep disturbances, including insomnia or sleeping too much
- Tiredness and lack of energy, so even small tasks take extra effort
- Reduced appetite and weight loss or increased cravings for food and weight gain
- Anxiety, agitation or restlessness
- Slowed thinking, speaking or body movements
- Feelings of worthlessness or guilt, fixating on past failures or self-blame
- Trouble thinking, concentrating, making decisions and remembering things
- Frequent or recurrent thoughts of death, suicidal thoughts, suicide attempts or suicide

- Unexplained physical problems, such as back pain or headaches

For many people with depression, symptoms usually are severe enough to cause noticeable problems in day-to-day activities, such as work, school, social activities or relationships with others. Some people may feel generally miserable or unhappy without really knowing why.

Depression symptoms in children and teens

Common signs and symptoms of depression in children and teenagers are similar to those of adults, but there can be some differences.

In younger children, symptoms of depression may include sadness, irritability, clinginess, worry, aches and pains, refusing to go to school, or being underweight.

In teens, symptoms may include sadness, irritability, feeling negative and worthless, anger, poor performance or poor attendance at school, feeling misunderstood and extremely sensitive, using recreational drugs or alcohol, eating or sleeping too much, self-harm, loss of interest in normal activities, and avoidance of social interaction.

Depression symptoms in older adults

Depression is not a normal part of growing older, and it should never be taken lightly. Unfortunately, depression often goes undiagnosed and untreated in older adults, and they may feel reluctant to seek help. Symptoms of depression may be different or less obvious in older adults, such as:

- Memory difficulties or personality changes
- Physical aches or pain
- Fatigue, loss of appetite, sleep problems or loss of interest in sex — not caused by a medical condition or medication

- Often wanting to stay at home, rather than going out to socialize or doing new things
- Suicidal thinking or feelings, especially in older men

When to see a doctor

If you feel depressed, make an appointment to see your doctor or mental health professional as soon as you can. If you're reluctant to seek treatment, talk to a friend or loved one, any health care professional, a faith leader, or someone else you trust.

Causes

It's not known exactly what causes depression. As with many mental disorders, a variety of factors may be involved, such as:

- **Biological differences.** People with depression appear to have physical changes in their brains. The significance of these changes is still uncertain, but may eventually help pinpoint causes.
- **Brain chemistry.** Neurotransmitters are naturally occurring brain chemicals that likely play a role in depression. Recent research indicates that changes in the function and effect of these neurotransmitters and how they interact with neurocircuits involved in maintaining mood stability may play a significant role in depression and its treatment.
- **Hormones.** Changes in the body's balance of hormones may be involved in causing or triggering depression. Hormone changes can result with pregnancy and during the weeks or months after delivery (postpartum) and from thyroid problems, menopause or a number of other conditions.

- **Hereditary factors.** Depression is more common in people whose blood relatives also have this condition. Researchers are trying to find genes that may be involved in causing depression.

Risk factors

Depression often begins in the teens, 20s or 30s, but it can happen at any age. More women than men are diagnosed with depression, but this may be due in part because women are more likely to seek treatment.

Factors that seem to increase the risk of developing or triggering depression include:

- Certain personality traits, such as low self-esteem and being too dependent, self-critical or pessimistic
- Traumatic or stressful events, such as physical or sexual abuse, the death or loss of a loved one, a difficult relationship, or financial problems
- Blood relatives with a history of depression, bipolar disorder, alcoholism or suicide
- Being lesbian, gay, bisexual or transgender, or having variations in the development of genital organs that aren't clearly male or female (intersex) in an unsupportive situation
- History of other mental health disorders, such as anxiety disorder, eating disorders or post-traumatic stress disorder
- Abuse of alcohol or recreational drugs
- Serious or chronic illness, including cancer, stroke, chronic pain or heart disease
- Certain medications, such as some high blood pressure medications or sleeping pills (talk to your doctor before stopping any medication)

Complications

Depression is a serious disorder that can take a terrible toll on you and your family. Depression often gets worse if it isn't treated, resulting in emotional, behavioral and health problems that affect every area of your life.

Examples of complications associated with depression include:

- Excess weight or obesity, which can lead to heart disease and diabetes
- Pain or physical illness
- Alcohol or drug misuse
- Anxiety, panic disorder or social phobia
- Family conflicts, relationship difficulties, and work or school problems
- Social isolation
- Suicidal feelings, suicide attempts or suicide
- Self-mutilation, such as cutting
- Premature death from medical conditions

Prevention

There's no sure way to prevent depression. However, these strategies may help.

- Take steps to control stress, to increase your resilience and boost your self-esteem.
- Reach out to family and friends, especially in times of crisis, to help you weather rough spells.
- Get treatment at the earliest sign of a problem to help prevent depression from worsening.
- Consider getting long-term maintenance treatment to help prevent a relapse of symptoms.

Diagnosis

Your doctor may determine a diagnosis of depression based on:

- **Physical exam.** Your doctor may do a physical exam and ask questions about your health. In some cases, depression may be linked to an underlying physical health problem.
- **Lab tests.** For example, your doctor may do a blood test called a full blood count or test your thyroid to make sure it's functioning properly.
- **Psychiatric evaluation.** Your mental health professional asks about your symptoms, thoughts, feelings and behavior patterns. You may be asked to fill out a questionnaire to help answer these questions.
- **DSM-5.** Your mental health professional may use the criteria for depression listed in the Diagnostic and Statistical Manual of Mental Disorders (DSM-5), published by the American Psychiatric Association.

TYPES OF DEPRESSION

Symptoms caused by major depression can vary from person to person. To clarify the type of depression you have, your doctor may add one or more specifiers. A specifier means that you have depression with specific features, such as:

- **Anxious distress** — depression with unusual restlessness or worry about possible events or loss of control
- **Mixed features** — simultaneous depression and mania, which includes elevated self-esteem, talking too much and increased energy
- **Melancholic features** — severe depression with lack of response to something that used to bring pleasure and associated with early morning awakening, worsened mood in the morning, major changes in appetite, and feelings of guilt, agitation or sluggishness
- **Atypical features** — depression that includes the ability to temporarily be cheered by happy events, increased appetite, excessive need for sleep, sensitivity to rejection, and a heavy feeling in the arms or legs
- **Psychotic features** — depression accompanied by delusions or hallucinations, which may involve personal inadequacy or other negative themes
- **Catatonia** — depression that includes motor activity that involves either uncontrollable and purposeless movement or fixed and inflexible posture
- **Peripartum onset** — depression that occurs during pregnancy
- **Postnatal depression** – occurs in the weeks or months after delivery

- **Seasonal pattern** — depression related to changes in seasons and reduced exposure to sunlight

OTHER DISORDERS THAT CAUSE DEPRESSION SYMPTOMS

Several other disorders, such as those below, include depression as a symptom. It's important to get an accurate diagnosis, so you can get appropriate treatment.

- **Bipolar I and II disorders.** These mood disorders include mood swings that range from highs (mania) to lows (depression). It's sometimes difficult to distinguish between bipolar disorder and depression.
- **Cyclothymic disorder.** Cyclothymic (sy-kloe-THIE-mik) disorder involves highs and lows that are milder than those of bipolar disorder.
- **Disruptive mood dysregulation disorder.** This mood disorder in children includes chronic and severe irritability and anger with frequent extreme temper outbursts. This disorder typically develops into depressive disorder or anxiety disorder during the teen years or adulthood.
- **Persistent depressive disorder.** Sometimes called dysthymia (dis-THIE-me-uh), this is a less severe but more chronic form of depression. While it's usually not disabling, persistent depressive disorder can prevent you from functioning normally in your daily routine and from living life to its fullest.
- **Premenstrual dysphoric disorder.** This involves depression symptoms associated with hormone changes that begin a week before and improve within a few days after the onset of your period, and are minimal or gone after completion of your period.
- **Other depression disorders.** This includes

depression that's caused by the use of recreational drugs, some prescribed medications or another medical condition.

Treatment

Medications and psychotherapy are effective for most people with depression. Your primary care doctor or psychiatrist can prescribe medications to relieve symptoms. However, many people with depression also benefit from seeing a psychiatrist, psychologist or other mental health professional.

If you have severe depression, you may need a hospital stay, or you may need to participate in an outpatient treatment program until your symptoms improve.

Here's a closer look at depression treatment options.

Medications

Many types of antidepressants are available, including those below. Be sure to discuss possible major side effects with your doctor or pharmacist.

- **Selective serotonin reuptake inhibitors (SSRIs).** Doctors often start by prescribing an SSRI. These drugs are considered safer and generally cause fewer bothersome side effects than other types of antidepressants. SSRIs include citalopram (Celexa), escitalopram (Lexapro), fluoxetine (Prozac), paroxetine (Paxil, Pexeva), sertraline (Zoloft) and vilazodone (Viibryd).
- **Serotonin-norepinephrine reuptake inhibitors (SNRIs).** Examples of SNRIs include duloxetine (Cymbalta), venlafaxine (Effexor XR), desvenlafaxine (Pristiq, Khedezla) and levomilnacipran (Fetzima).
- **Atypical antidepressants.** These medications don't

fit neatly into any of the other antidepressant categories. They include bupropion (Wellbutrin XL, Wellbutrin SR, Aplenzin, Forfivo XL), mirtazapine (Remeron), nefazodone, trazodone and vortioxetine (Trintellix).
- **Tricyclic antidepressants.** These drugs — such as imipramine (Tofranil), nortriptyline (Pamelor), amitriptyline, doxepin, trimipramine (Surmontil), desipramine (Norpramin) and protriptyline (Vivactil) — can be very effective, but tend to cause more-severe side effects than newer antidepressants. So, tricyclics generally aren't prescribed unless you've tried an SSRI first without improvement.
- **Monoamine oxidase inhibitors (MAOIs).** MAOIs — such as tranylcypromine (Parnate), phenelzine (Nardil) and isocarboxazid (Marplan) — may be prescribed, typically when other drugs haven't worked, because they can have serious side effects. Using MAOIs requires a strict diet because of dangerous (or even deadly) interactions with foods — such as certain cheeses, pickles and wines — and some medications and herbal supplements. Selegiline (Emsam), a newer MAOI that sticks on the skin as a patch, may cause fewer side effects than other MAOIs do. These medications can't be combined with SSRIs.
- **Other medications.** Other medications may be added to an antidepressant to enhance antidepressant effects. Your doctor may recommend combining two antidepressants or adding medications such as mood stabilizers or antipsychotics. Anti-anxiety and stimulant medications also may be added for short-term use.

Finding the right medication

If a family member has responded well to an antidepressant, it may be one that could help you. Or you may need to try several medications or a combination of medications before you find one that works. This requires patience, as some medications need several weeks or longer to take full effect and for side effects to ease as your body adjusts.

Inherited traits play a role in how antidepressants affect you. In some cases, where available, results of genetic tests (done by a blood test or cheek swab) may offer clues about how your body may respond to a particular antidepressant. However, other variables besides genetics can affect your response to medication.

Risks of abruptly stopping medication

Don't stop taking an antidepressant without talking to your doctor first. Antidepressants aren't considered addictive, but sometimes physical dependence (which is different from addiction) can occur.

Stopping treatment abruptly or missing several doses can cause withdrawal-like symptoms, and quitting suddenly may cause a sudden worsening of depression. Work with your doctor to gradually and safely decrease your dose.

Antidepressants and pregnancy

If you're pregnant or breast-feeding, some antidepressants may pose an increased health risk to your unborn child or nursing child. Talk with your doctor if you become pregnant or you're planning to become pregnant.

Antidepressants and increased suicide risk

Most antidepressants are generally safe, but the Food and Drug Administration (FDA) requires all antidepressants to carry a black box warning, the strictest warning for prescriptions. In some cases, children, teenagers and young adults under age 25 may have an increase in suicidal thoughts or behavior when taking antidepressants, especially in the first few weeks after starting or when the dose is changed.

Anyone taking an antidepressant should be watched closely for worsening depression or unusual behavior, especially when starting a new medication or with a change in dosage. If you or someone you know has suicidal thoughts when taking an antidepressant, immediately contact a doctor or get emergency help.

Keep in mind that antidepressants are more likely to reduce suicide risk in the long run by improving mood.

Psychotherapy

Psychotherapy is a general term for treating depression by talking about your condition and related issues with a mental health professional. Psychotherapy is also known as talk therapy or psychological therapy.

Different types of psychotherapy can be effective for depression, such as cognitive behavioral therapy or interpersonal therapy. Your mental health professional may also recommend other types of therapies. Psychotherapy can help you:

- Adjust to a crisis or other current difficulty
- Identify negative beliefs and behaviors and replace them with healthy, positive ones
- Explore relationships and experiences, and develop positive interactions with others
- Find better ways to cope and solve problems
- Identify issues that contribute to your depression and change behaviors that make it worse
- Regain a sense of satisfaction and control in your life and help ease depression symptoms, such as

hopelessness and anger
- Learn to set realistic goals for your life
- Develop the ability to tolerate and accept distress using healthier behaviors

Alternate formats for therapy

Formats for depression therapy as an alternative to face-to-face office sessions are available and may be an effective option for some people. Therapy can be provided, for example, as a computer program, by online sessions, or using videos or workbooks. Programs can be guided by a therapist or be partially or totally independent.

Before you choose one of these options, discuss these formats with your therapist to determine if they may be helpful for you. Also, ask your therapist if he or she can recommend a trusted source or program. Some may not be covered by your insurance or medical aid and not all developers and online therapists have the proper credentials or training.

Smartphones and tablets that offer mobile health apps, such as support and general education about depression, are not a substitute for seeing your doctor or therapist.

Hospital and residential treatment

In some people, depression is so severe that a hospital stay is needed. This may be necessary if you can't care for yourself properly or when you're in immediate danger of harming yourself or someone else. Psychiatric treatment at a hospital can help keep you calm and safe until your mood improves.

Partial hospitalization or day treatment programs also may help some people. These programs provide the outpatient support and counseling needed to get symptoms under control.

Other treatment options

For some people, other procedures, sometimes called brain stimulation therapies, may be suggested:

- **Electroconvulsive therapy (ECT).** In ECT, electrical currents are passed through the brain to impact the function and effect of neurotransmitters in your brain to relieve depression. ECT is usually used for people who don't get better with medications, can't take antidepressants for health reasons or are at high risk of suicide.
- **Transcranial magnetic stimulation (TMS).** TMS may be an option for those who haven't responded to antidepressants. During TMS, a treatment coil placed against your scalp sends brief magnetic pulses to stimulate nerve cells in your brain that are involved in mood regulation and depression.

Lifestyle and home remedies

Depression generally isn't a disorder that you can treat on your own. But in addition to professional treatment, these self-care steps can help:

- **Stick to your treatment plan.** Don't skip psychotherapy sessions or appointments. Even if you're feeling well, don't skip your medications. If you stop, depression symptoms may come back, and you could also experience withdrawal-like symptoms. Recognize that it will take time to feel better.
- **Learn about depression.** Education about your condition can empower you and motivate you to stick to your treatment plan. Encourage your family to learn about depression to help them understand and support you.

- **Pay attention to warning signs.** Work with your doctor or therapist to learn what might trigger your depression symptoms. Make a plan so that you know what to do if your symptoms get worse. Contact your doctor or therapist if you notice any changes in symptoms or how you feel. Ask relatives or friends to help watch for warning signs.
- **Avoid alcohol and recreational drugs.** It may seem like alcohol or drugs lessen depression symptoms, but in the long run they generally worsen symptoms and make depression harder to treat. Talk with your doctor or therapist if you need help with alcohol or substance use.
- **Take care of yourself.** Eat healthy, be physically active and get plenty of sleep. Consider walking, jogging, swimming, gardening or another activity that you enjoy. Sleeping well is important for both your physical and mental well-being. If you're having trouble sleeping, talk to your doctor about what you can do.

Alternative medicine

Alternative medicine is the use of a nonconventional approach instead of conventional medicine. Complementary medicine is a nonconventional approach used along with conventional medicine — sometimes called integrative medicine.

Make sure you understand the risks as well as possible benefits if you pursue alternative or complementary therapy. Don't replace conventional medical treatment or psychotherapy with alternative medicine. When it comes to depression, alternative treatments aren't a substitute for medical care.

Supplements

Examples of supplements that are sometimes used for depression include:

- Omega-3 fatty acids. These healthy fats are found in cold-water fish, flaxseed, flax oil, walnuts and some other foods. Omega-3 supplements are being studied as a possible treatment for depression. While considered generally safe, in high doses, omega-3 supplements may interact with other medications. More research is needed to determine if eating foods with omega-3 fatty acids can help relieve depression.

Nutritional and dietary products aren't monitored by the FDA the same way medications are. You can't always be certain of what you're getting and whether it's safe. Also, because some herbal and dietary supplements can interfere with prescription medications or cause dangerous interactions, talk to your doctor or pharmacist before taking any supplements.

Mind-body connections

Integrative medicine practitioners believe the mind and body must be in harmony for you to stay healthy. Examples of mind-body techniques that may be helpful for depression include:

- Acupuncture
- Relaxation techniques such as yoga or tai chi
- Meditation
- Guided imagery
- Massage therapy
- Music or art therapy
- Spirituality
- Aerobic exercise

Relying solely on these therapies is generally not enough to treat depression. They may be helpful when used in addition to medication and psychotherapy.

Coping and support

Talk with your doctor or therapist about improving your coping skills, and try these tips:

- **Simplify your life.** Cut back on obligations when possible, and set reasonable goals for yourself. Give yourself permission to do less when you feel down.
- **Write in a journal.** Journaling, as part of your treatment, may improve mood by allowing you to express pain, anger, fear or other emotions.
- **Read reputable self-help books and websites.** Your doctor or therapist may be able to recommend books or websites to read.
- **Locate helpful groups.** Many organizations and podcasts, such as *Vuyo Nyeli Wellness Services and The Mental Health Podcast with Vuyo Nyeli*, offer education, awareness, counselling, and other resources to help with depression. Employee assistance programs also may offer help for mental health concerns.
- **Don't become isolated.** Try to participate in social activities, and get together with family or friends regularly. Support groups for people with depression can help you connect to others facing similar challenges and share experiences.
- **Learn ways to relax and manage your stress.** Examples include meditation, progressive muscle relaxation, yoga and tai chi.
- **Structure your time. Plan your day.** You may find it helps to make a list of daily tasks, use sticky notes as reminders or use a planner to stay organized.
- **Don't make important decisions when you're**

down. Avoid decision-making when you're feeling depressed, since you may not be thinking clearly.

What you can do

Before your appointment, make a list of:
- **Any symptoms you've had,** including any that may seem unrelated to the reason for your appointment
- **Key personal information,** including any major stresses or recent life changes
- **All medications, vitamins** or other supplements that you're taking, including dosages
- **Questions to ask** your doctor or mental health professional

Take a family member or friend along, if possible, to help you remember all of the information provided during the appointment.

Some basic questions to ask your doctor include:
- Is depression the most likely cause of my symptoms?
- What are other possible causes for my symptoms?
- What kinds of tests will I need?
- What treatment is likely to work best for me?
- What are the alternatives to the primary approach that you're suggesting?
- I have these other health conditions. How can I best manage them together?
- Are there any restrictions that I need to follow?
- Should I see a psychiatrist or other mental health professional?
- What are the main side effects of the medications you're recommending?
- Is there a generic alternative to the medicine you're prescribing?

- Are there any brochures or other printed material that I can have? What websites do you recommend?

Don't hesitate to ask other questions during your appointment.

What to expect from your doctor

Your doctor will likely ask you a number of questions. Be ready to answer them to reserve time to go over any points you want to focus on. Your doctor may ask:

- When did you or your loved ones first notice your symptoms of depression?
- How long have you felt depressed? Do you generally always feel down, or does your mood fluctuate?
- Does your mood ever swing from feeling down to feeling intensely happy (euphoric) and full of energy?
- Do you ever have suicidal thoughts when you're feeling down?
- Do your symptoms interfere with your daily life or relationships?
- Do you have any blood relatives with depression or another mood disorder?
- What other mental or physical health conditions do you have?
- Do you drink alcohol or use recreational drugs?
- How much do you sleep at night? Does it change over time?
- What, if anything, seems to improve your symptoms?
- What, if anything, appears to worsen your symptoms?

- MALE DEPRESSION: UNDERSTANDING THE ISSUES

Male depression is a serious medical condition, but many men try to ignore it or refuse treatment. Learn the signs and symptoms — and what to do.

Do you feel irritable, isolated or withdrawn? Do you find yourself working all the time? Drinking too much? These unhealthy coping strategies may be clues that you have male depression.

Depression can affect men and women differently. When depression occurs in men, it may be masked by unhealthy coping behavior. For a number of reasons, male depression often goes undiagnosed and can have devastating consequences when it goes untreated. But male depression usually gets better with treatment.

Male depression signs and symptoms

Depression signs and symptoms can differ in men and women. Men also tend to use different coping skills — both healthy and unhealthy — than women do. It isn't clear why men and women may experience depression differently. It likely involves a number of factors, including brain chemistry, hormones and life experiences.

Like women with depression, men with depression may:

- Feel sad, hopeless or empty
- Feel extremely tired
- Have difficulty sleeping or sleep too much
- Not get pleasure from activities usually enjoyed

Other behaviors in men that could be signs of depression — but not recognized as such — include:

- Escapist behavior, such as spending a lot of time at work or on sports
- Physical symptoms, such as headaches, digestive problems and pain
- Problems with alcohol or drug use
- Controlling, violent or abusive behavior
- Irritability or inappropriate anger
- Risky behavior, such as reckless driving

Because these behaviors could be signs of or might overlap with other mental health issues, or may be associated with medical conditions, professional help is the key to an accurate diagnosis and appropriate treatment.

Male depression often goes undiagnosed

Men with depression often aren't diagnosed for several reasons, including:

- **Failure to recognize depression.** You may think that feeling sad or emotional is always the main symptom of depression. But for many men, that isn't the primary symptom. For example, headaches, digestive problems, tiredness, irritability or long-term pain can sometimes indicate depression. So can feeling isolated and seeking distraction to avoid dealing with feelings or relationships.
- **Downplaying signs and symptoms.** You may not recognize how much your symptoms affect you, or you may not want to admit to yourself or to anyone else that you're depressed. But ignoring, suppressing or masking depression with unhealthy behavior will only worsen the negative emotions.
- **Reluctance to discuss depression symptoms.** You may not be open to talking about your feelings with family or friends, let alone with a doctor or mental

health professional. Like many men, you may have learned to emphasize self-control. You may think it's not manly to express feelings and emotions associated with depression, and you try to suppress them.
- **Resisting mental health treatment.** Even if you suspect you have depression, you may avoid diagnosis or refuse treatment. You may avoid getting help because you're worried that the stigma of depression could damage your career or cause family and friends to lose respect for you.

Male depression and suicide

Although women attempt suicide more often than men do, men are more likely to complete suicide. That's because men:

- Use methods that are more likely to cause death, such as guns
- May act more impulsively on suicidal thoughts
- Show fewer warning signs, such as talking about suicide

Male depression and coping skills

Treatment, including psychotherapy, with a mental health professional can help you learn healthy coping skills. These may include:

- **Goals.** Set realistic goals and prioritize tasks.
- **Support.** Seek out emotional support from a partner or family or friends. Learn strategies for making social connections so that you can get involved in social activities.
- **Coping.** Learn ways to manage stress, such as meditation and mindfulness, and develop problem-solving skills.
- **Decisions.** Delay making important decisions, such

as changing jobs, until your depression symptoms improve.
- **Activities.** Engage in activities you typically enjoy, such as ball games, fishing or a hobby.
- **Health.** Try to stick to a regular schedule and make healthy lifestyle choices, including healthy eating and regular physical activity, to help promote better mental health.

Many effective treatments are available for depression. So don't try to tough out male depression on your own — the consequences could be devastating.

Get help when you need it

Asking for help can be hard for men. But without treatment, depression is unlikely to go away, and it may get worse. Untreated depression can make you and the people close to you miserable. It can cause problems in every aspect of your life, including your health, career, relationships and personal safety.

Depression, even if it's severe, usually improves with medications or psychological counseling (psychotherapy) or both. If you or someone close to you thinks you may be depressed, talk to your doctor or a mental health professional. It's a sign of strength to ask for advice or seek help when you need it.

- POSTPARTUM/ POSTNATAL DEPRESSION

The birth of a baby can trigger a jumble of powerful emotions, from excitement and joy to fear and anxiety. But it can also result in something you might not expect — depression. Most new moms experience postpartum "baby blues" after childbirth, which commonly include mood swings, crying spells, anxiety and difficulty sleeping. Baby blues typically begin within the first two to three days after delivery, and may last for up to two weeks. But some new moms experience a more severe, long-lasting form of depression known as postpartum depression. Rarely, an extreme mood disorder called postpartum psychosis also may develop after childbirth.

Postpartum depression isn't a character flaw or a weakness. Sometimes it's simply a complication of giving birth. If you have postpartum depression, prompt treatment can help you manage your symptoms and help you bond with your baby.

Symptoms

Signs and symptoms of depression after childbirth vary, and they can range from mild to severe.

Baby blues symptoms

Signs and symptoms of baby blues — which last only a few days to a week or two after your baby is born — may include:

- Mood swings
- Anxiety
- Sadness
- Irritability
- Feeling overwhelmed

- Crying
- Reduced concentration
- Appetite problems
- Trouble sleeping

Postpartum depression symptoms

Postpartum depression may be mistaken for baby blues at first — but the signs and symptoms are more intense and last longer, and may eventually interfere with your ability to care for your baby and handle other daily tasks. Symptoms usually develop within the first few weeks after giving birth, but may begin earlier — during pregnancy — or later — up to a year after birth.

Postpartum depression signs and symptoms may include:

- Depressed mood or severe mood swings
- Excessive crying
- Difficulty bonding with your baby
- Withdrawing from family and friends
- Loss of appetite or eating much more than usual
- Inability to sleep (insomnia) or sleeping too much
- Overwhelming fatigue or loss of energy
- Reduced interest and pleasure in activities you used to enjoy
- Intense irritability and anger
- Fear that you're not a good mother
- Hopelessness
- Feelings of worthlessness, shame, guilt or inadequacy
- Diminished ability to think clearly, concentrate or make decisions
- Restlessness
- Severe anxiety and panic attacks
- Thoughts of harming yourself or your baby
- Recurrent thoughts of death or suicide

Untreated, postpartum depression may last for many months or longer.

Postpartum psychosis

With postpartum psychosis — a rare condition that typically develops within the first week after delivery — the signs and symptoms are severe. Signs and symptoms may include:

- Confusion and disorientation
- Obsessive thoughts about your baby
- Hallucinations and delusions
- Sleep disturbances
- Excessive energy and agitation
- Paranoia
- Attempts to harm yourself or your baby

Postpartum psychosis may lead to life-threatening thoughts or behaviors and requires immediate treatment.

POSTPARTUM DEPRESSION IN NEW FATHERS

New fathers can experience postpartum depression, too. They may feel sad or fatigued, be overwhelmed, experience anxiety, or have changes in their usual eating and sleeping patterns — the same symptoms mothers with postpartum depression experience.

Fathers who are young, have a history of depression, experience relationship problems or are struggling financially are most at risk of postpartum depression. Postpartum depression in fathers — sometimes called paternal postpartum depression — can have the same negative effect on partner relationships and child development as postpartum depression in mothers can.

If you're a new father and are experiencing symptoms of depression or anxiety during your partner's pregnancy or in the first year after your child's birth, talk to your health care professional. Similar treatments and supports provided to mothers with postpartum depression can be beneficial in treating postpartum depression in fathers.

When to see a doctor

If you're feeling depressed after your baby's birth, you may be reluctant or embarrassed to admit it. But if you experience any symptoms of postpartum baby blues or postpartum depression, call your doctor and schedule an appointment. If you have symptoms that suggest you may have postpartum psychosis, get help immediately.

It's important to call your doctor as soon as possible if the signs and symptoms of depression have any of these features:

- Don't fade after two weeks
- Are getting worse
- Make it hard for you to care for your baby
- Make it hard to complete everyday tasks
- Include thoughts of harming yourself or your baby

Helping a friend or loved one

People with depression may not recognize or acknowledge that they're depressed. They may not be aware of signs and symptoms of depression. If you suspect that a friend or loved one has postpartum depression or is developing postpartum psychosis, help them seek medical attention immediately. Don't wait and hope for improvement.

Causes

There's no single cause of postpartum depression, but physical and emotional issues may play a role.

- **Physical changes.** After childbirth, a dramatic drop in hormones (oestrogen and progesterone) in your body may contribute to postpartum depression. Other hormones produced by your thyroid gland also may drop sharply — which can leave you feeling tired, sluggish and depressed.
- **Emotional issues.** When you're sleep deprived and overwhelmed, you may have trouble handling even minor problems. You may be anxious about your ability to care for a newborn. You may feel less attractive, struggle with your sense of identity or feel that you've lost control over your life. Any of these issues can contribute to postpartum depression.

Risk factors

Any new mom can experience postpartum depression and

it can develop after the birth of any child, not just the first. However, your risk increases if:

- You have a history of depression, either during pregnancy or at other times
- You have bipolar disorder
- You had postpartum depression after a previous pregnancy
- You have family members who've had depression or other mood disorders
- You've experienced stressful events during the past year, such as pregnancy complications, illness or job loss
- Your baby has health problems or other special needs
- You have twins, triplets or other multiple births
- You have difficulty breast-feeding
- You're having problems in your relationship with your spouse or significant other
- You have a weak support system
- You have financial problems
- The pregnancy was unplanned or unwanted

Complications

Left untreated, postpartum depression can interfere with mother-child bonding and cause family problems.

- **For mothers.** Untreated postpartum depression can last for months or longer, sometimes becoming a chronic depressive disorder. Even when treated, postpartum depression increases a woman's risk of future episodes of major depression.
- **For fathers.** Postpartum depression can have a ripple effect, causing emotional strain for everyone close to a new baby. When a new mother is depressed, the risk of depression in the baby's father may also increase. And new dads are already

at increased risk of depression, whether or not their partner is affected.
- **For children.** Children of mothers who have untreated postpartum depression are more likely to have emotional and behavioral problems, such as sleeping and eating difficulties, excessive crying, and delays in language development.

Prevention

If you have a history of depression — especially postpartum depression — tell your doctor if you're planning on becoming pregnant or as soon as you find out you're pregnant.

- **During pregnancy,** your doctor can monitor you closely for signs and symptoms of depression. He or she may have you complete a depression-screening questionnaire during your pregnancy and after delivery. Sometimes mild depression can be managed with support groups, counseling or other therapies. In other cases, antidepressants may be recommended — even during pregnancy.
- **After your baby is born,** your doctor may recommend an early postpartum checkup to screen for signs and symptoms of postpartum depression. The earlier it's detected, the earlier treatment can begin. If you have a history of postpartum depression, your doctor may recommend antidepressant treatment or psychotherapy immediately after delivery.

Diagnosis

Your doctor will usually talk with you about your feelings, thoughts and mental health to distinguish between a short-term case of postpartum baby blues and a more severe form of depression. Don't be embarrassed — postpartum depression is common. Share your symptoms with your doctor so that a useful treatment plan can be created for you.

As part of your evaluation, your doctor may:
- Do a depression screening that may include having you fill out a questionnaire
- Order blood tests to determine whether an underactive thyroid is contributing to your signs and symptoms
- Order other tests, if warranted, to rule out other causes for your symptoms

Treatment

Treatment and recovery time vary, depending on the severity of your depression and your individual needs. If you have an underactive thyroid or an underlying illness, your doctor may treat those conditions or refer you to the appropriate specialist. Your doctor may also refer you to a mental health professional.

Baby blues

The baby blues usually fade on their own within a few days to one to two weeks. In the meantime:
- Get as much rest as you can.
- Accept help from family and friends.
- Connect with other new moms.
- Create time to take care of yourself.
- Avoid alcohol and recreational drugs, which can make mood swings worse.

Postpartum depression

Postpartum depression is often treated with psychotherapy (also called talk therapy or mental health counseling), medication or both.

- **Psychotherapy.** It may help to talk through your

concerns with a psychiatrist, psychologist or other mental health professional. Through therapy, you can find better ways to cope with your feelings, solve problems, set realistic goals and respond to situations in a positive way. Sometimes family or relationship therapy also helps.
- **Antidepressants.** Your doctor may recommend an antidepressant. If you're breast-feeding, any medication you take will enter your breast milk. However, most antidepressants can be used during breast-feeding with little risk of side effects for your baby. Work with your doctor to weigh the potential risks and benefits of specific antidepressants.

With appropriate treatment, postpartum depression symptoms usually improve. In some cases, postpartum depression can continue, becoming chronic depression. It's important to continue treatment after you begin to feel better. Stopping treatment too early may lead to a relapse.

POSTPARTUM PSYCHOSIS

Postpartum psychosis requires immediate treatment, usually in the hospital. Treatment may include:

- **Medication.** Treatment may require a combination of medications — such as antipsychotic medications, mood stabilizers and benzodiazepines — to control your signs and symptoms.
- **Electroconvulsive therapy (ECT).** If your postpartum depression is severe and you experience postpartum psychosis, ECT may be recommended if symptoms do not respond to medication. ECT is a procedure in which small electrical currents are passed through the brain, intentionally triggering a brief seizure. ECT seems to cause changes in brain chemistry that can reduce the symptoms of psychosis and depression, especially when other treatments have been unsuccessful.

Treatment for postpartum psychosis can challenge a mother's ability to breast-feed. Separation from the baby makes breast-feeding difficult, and some medications used to treat postpartum psychosis aren't recommended for women who are breast-feeding. If you're experiencing postpartum psychosis, your doctor can help you work through these challenges.

Lifestyle and home remedies

In addition to professional treatment, you can do some things for yourself that build on your treatment plan and help speed recovery.

UNDERSTANDING MENTAL HEALTH

- **Make healthy lifestyle choices.** Include physical activity, such as a walk with your baby, and other forms of exercise in your daily routine. Try to get adequate rest. Eat healthy foods and avoid alcohol.
- **Set realistic expectations.** Don't pressure yourself to do everything. Scale back your expectations for the perfect household. Do what you can and leave the rest.
- **Make time for yourself.** Take some time for yourself and get out of the house. That may mean asking a partner to take care of the baby or arranging for a sitter. Do something you enjoy, such as a hobby or some form of entertainment. You might also schedule some time alone with your partner or friends.
- **Avoid isolation.** Talk with your partner, family and friends about how you're feeling. Ask other mothers about their experiences. Breaking the isolation may help you feel human again.
- **Ask for help.** Try to open up to the people close to you and let them know you need help. If someone offers to baby-sit, take them up on it. If you can sleep, take a nap, or maybe you can catch a movie or meet for coffee with friends. You may also benefit from asking for help with parenting skills that can include caregiving techniques to improve your baby's sleep and soothe fussing and crying.

Remember, taking care of your baby includes taking care of yourself.

Coping and support

The already stressful, exhausting period following a baby's birth is more difficult when depression occurs. But remember, postpartum depression is never anyone's fault. It's a common medical condition that needs treatment.

So, if you're having trouble coping with postpartum depression, talk with a therapist. Ask your doctor or therapist about local support groups for new moms or women who have postpartum depression.

The sooner you get help, the sooner you'll be fully equipped to cope with depression and enjoy your new baby.

Preparing for your appointment

After your first appointment, your doctor may refer you to a mental health professional who can create the right treatment plan for you. You may want to find a trusted family member or friend to join you for your appointment to help you remember all of the information discussed.

What you can do

Before your appointment, make a list of:

- **Any symptoms you've been experiencing** and for how long
- **All of your medical issues,** including physical conditions or mental health disorders, such as depression
- **All the medications you take,** including prescription and over-the-counter medications as well as vitamins, herbs and other supplements, and the dosages
- **Questions to ask** your doctor

Questions to ask your doctor include:

- What is my diagnosis?
- What treatments are likely to help me?
- What are the possible side effects of the treatments you're proposing?

- How much and how soon do you expect my symptoms to improve with treatment?
- Is the medication you're prescribing safe to take while breast-feeding?
- How long will I need to be treated?
- What lifestyle changes can help me manage my symptoms?
- How often should I be seen for follow-up visits?
- Am I at increased risk of other mental health problems?
- Am I at risk of this condition recurring if I have another baby?
- Is there any way to prevent a recurrence if I have another baby?
- Are there any printed materials that I can have? What websites do you recommend?

Don't hesitate to ask any other questions during your appointment.

What to expect from your doctor

A doctor or mental health professional who sees you for possible postpartum depression may ask:

- What are your symptoms, and when did they start?
- Have your symptoms been getting better or worse over time?
- Are your symptoms affecting your ability to care for your baby?
- Do you feel as bonded to your baby as you expected?
- Are you able to sleep when you have the chance and get out of bed when it's time to wake up?
- How would you describe your energy level?
- Has your appetite changed?
- How often would you say you feel anxious, irritable or angry?

- Have you had any thoughts of harming yourself or your baby?
- How much support do you have in caring for your baby?
- Are there other significant stressors in your life, such as financial or relationship problems?
- Have you been diagnosed with any other medical conditions?
- Have you ever been diagnosed with any mental health conditions, such as depression or bipolar disorder? If so, what type of treatment helped the most?

Your primary care provider or mental health professional will ask additional questions based on your responses, symptoms and needs. Preparing for and anticipating questions will help you make the most of your appointment time.

- NERVOUS BREAKDOWN: WHAT DOES IT MEAN?

What does it mean to have a nervous breakdown?

The term "nervous breakdown" is sometimes used by people to describe a stressful situation in which they're temporarily unable to function normally in day-to-day life. It's commonly understood to occur when life's demands become physically and emotionally overwhelming. The term was frequently used in the past to cover a variety of mental disorders, but it's no longer used by mental health professionals today.

Nervous breakdown isn't a medical term, nor does it indicate a specific mental illness. But that doesn't mean it's a normal or a healthy response to stress. What some people call a nervous breakdown may indicate an underlying mental health problem that needs attention, such as depression or anxiety.

Signs of a so-called nervous breakdown vary from person to person and depend on the underlying cause. Exactly what constitutes a nervous breakdown also varies from one culture to another. Generally, it's understood to mean that a person is no longer able to function normally. For example, he or she may:

- Call in sick to work for days or longer
- Avoid social engagements and miss appointments
- Have trouble following healthy patterns of eating, sleeping and hygiene

A number of other unusual or dysfunctional behaviors may be considered signs and symptoms of a nervous breakdown.

If you feel that you're experiencing a nervous breakdown, get help. If you have a primary care provider, talk to him or her about your signs and symptoms or seek help from a mental health professional.

5. Anxiety disorders:

- Anxiety disorder

Anxiety disorder is a mental health disorder characterized by feelings of worry, anxiety or fear that are strong enough to interfere with one's daily activities. Many people experience some anxiety in their lives, but they find it comes and goes. Symptoms include stress that's out of proportion to the impact of the event, inability to set aside a worry and restlessness. Without treatment, an anxiety can progress to the point that the individual feels anxious all the time. Anxiety disorders are a common mental illness in South Africa. *Approximately 1 in 5 South Africans are affected each year*, according to the South African Depression and Anxiety Group (SADAG).

Anxiety disorders can be treated with psychotherapy or medication – or a combination of the two. Therapy will help the individual identify when they feel anxiety and utilize coping mechanisms to reduce the anxious feelings.

There are many types of anxiety disorders, but some common ones include:
- Generalized anxiety disorder
- Panic disorder
- Obsessive-compulsive disorder (OCD)
- Post-traumatic stress disorder (PTSD)
- Social anxiety disorder

- GENERALIZED ANXIETY DISORDER

It's normal to feel anxious from time to time, especially if your life is stressful. However, excessive, ongoing anxiety and worry that are difficult to control and interfere with day-to-day activities may be a sign of generalized anxiety disorder. It's possible to develop generalized anxiety disorder as a child or an adult. Generalized anxiety disorder has symptoms that are similar to panic disorder, obsessive-compulsive disorder and other types of anxiety, but they're all different conditions.

Living with generalized anxiety disorder can be a long-term challenge. In many cases, it occurs along with other anxiety or mood disorders. In most cases, generalized anxiety disorder improves with psychotherapy or medications. Making lifestyle changes, learning coping skills and using relaxation techniques also can help.

Symptoms

Generalized anxiety disorder symptoms can vary. They may include:

- Persistent worrying or anxiety about a number of areas that are out of proportion to the impact of the events
- Overthinking plans and solutions to all possible worst-case outcomes
- Perceiving situations and events as threatening, even when they aren't
- Difficulty handling uncertainty
- Indecisiveness and fear of making the wrong decision
- Inability to set aside or let go of a worry
- Inability to relax, feeling restless, and feeling keyed

- up or on edge
- Difficulty concentrating, or the feeling that your mind "goes blank"

Physical signs and symptoms may include:
- Fatigue
- Trouble sleeping
- Muscle tension or muscle aches
- Trembling, feeling twitchy
- Nervousness or being easily startled
- Sweating
- Nausea, diarrhoea or irritable bowel syndrome
- Irritability

There may be times when your worries don't completely consume you, but you still feel anxious even when there's no apparent reason. For example, you may feel intense worry about your safety or that of your loved ones, or you may have a general sense that something bad is about to happen.

Your anxiety, worry or physical symptoms cause you significant distress in social, work or other areas of your life. Worries can shift from one concern to another and may change with time and age.

Symptoms in children and teenagers

Children and teenagers may have similar worries to adults, but also may have excessive worries about:
- Performance at school or sporting events
- Family members' safety
- Being on time (punctuality)
- Earthquakes, nuclear war or other catastrophic events

A child or teen with excessive worry may:

- Feel overly anxious to fit in
- Be a perfectionist
- Redo tasks because they aren't perfect the first time
- Spend excessive time doing homework
- Lack confidence
- Strive for approval
- Require a lot of reassurance about performance
- Have frequent stomachaches or other physical complaints
- Avoid going to school or avoid social situations

When to see a doctor

Some anxiety is normal, but see your doctor if:

- You feel like you're worrying too much, and it's interfering with your work, relationships or other parts of your life
- You feel depressed or irritable, have trouble with drinking or drugs, or you have other mental health concerns along with anxiety
- You have suicidal thoughts or behaviors — seek emergency treatment immediately

Your worries are unlikely to simply go away on their own, and they may actually get worse over time. Try to seek professional help before your anxiety becomes severe — it may be easier to treat early on.

Causes

As with many mental health conditions, the cause of generalized anxiety disorder likely arises from a complex interaction of biological and environmental factors, which may include:

- Differences in brain chemistry and function
- Genetics
- Differences in the way threats are perceived

- Development and personality

Risk factors

Women are diagnosed with generalized anxiety disorder somewhat more often than men are. The following factors may increase the risk of developing generalized anxiety disorder:

- **Personality.** A person whose temperament is timid or negative or who avoids anything dangerous may be more prone to generalized anxiety disorder than others are.
- **Genetics.** Generalized anxiety disorder may run in families.
- **Experiences.** People with generalized anxiety disorder may have a history of significant life changes, traumatic or negative experiences during childhood, or a recent traumatic or negative event. Chronic medical illnesses or other mental health disorders may increase risk.

Complications

Having generalized anxiety disorder can be disabling. It can:

- Impair your ability to perform tasks quickly and efficiently because you have trouble concentrating
- Take your time and focus from other activities
- Sap your energy
- Increase your risk of depression

Generalized anxiety disorder can also lead to or worsen other physical health conditions, such as:

- Digestive or bowel problems, such as irritable bowel syndrome or ulcers
- Headaches and migraines
- Chronic pain and illness
- Sleep problems and insomnia

- Heart-health issues

Generalized anxiety disorder often occurs along with other mental health problems, which can make diagnosis and treatment more challenging. Some mental health disorders that commonly occur with generalized anxiety disorder include:

- Phobias
- Panic disorder
- Post-traumatic stress disorder (PTSD)
- Obsessive-compulsive disorder (OCD)
- Depression
- Suicidal thoughts or suicide
- Substance abuse

Prevention

There's no way to predict for certain what will cause someone to develop generalized anxiety disorder, but you can take steps to reduce the impact of symptoms if you experience anxiety:

- **Get help early.** Anxiety, like many other mental health conditions, can be harder to treat if you wait.
- **Keep a journal.** Keeping track of your personal life can help you and your mental health professional identify what's causing you stress and what seems to help you feel better.
- **Prioritize issues in your life.** You can reduce anxiety by carefully managing your time and energy.
- **Avoid unhealthy substance use.** Alcohol and drug use and even nicotine or caffeine use can cause or worsen anxiety. If you're addicted to any of these substances, quitting can make you anxious. If you can't quit on your own, see your doctor or find a treatment program or support group

or organizations like Alcoholics Anonymous South Africa.

Diagnosis

To help diagnose generalized anxiety disorder, your doctor or mental health professional may:

- Do a physical exam to look for signs that your anxiety might be linked to medications or an underlying medical condition
- Order blood or urine tests or other tests, if a medical condition is suspected
- Ask detailed questions about your symptoms and medical history
- Use psychological questionnaires to help determine a diagnosis
- Use the criteria listed in the Diagnostic and Statistical Manual of Mental Disorders (DSM-5), published by the American Psychiatric Association

Treatment

Treatment decisions are based on how significantly generalized anxiety disorder is affecting your ability to function in your daily life. The two main treatments for generalized anxiety disorder are psychotherapy and medications. You may benefit most from a combination of the two. It may take some trial and error to discover which treatments work best for you.

Psychotherapy

Also known as talk therapy or psychological counseling, psychotherapy involves working with a therapist to reduce your anxiety symptoms. Cognitive behavioral therapy is the most effective form of psychotherapy for generalized anxiety disorder.

Generally, a short-term treatment, cognitive behavioral

therapy focuses on teaching you specific skills to directly manage your worries and help you gradually return to the activities you've avoided because of anxiety. Through this process, your symptoms improve as you build on your initial success.

Medications

Several types of medications are used to treat generalized anxiety disorder, including those below. Talk with your doctor about benefits, risks and possible side effects.

- **Antidepressants.** Antidepressants, including medications in the selective serotonin reuptake inhibitor (SSRI) and serotonin and norepinephrine reuptake inhibitor (SNRI) classes, are the first line medication treatments. Examples of antidepressants used to treat generalized anxiety disorder include escitalopram (Lexapro), duloxetine (Cymbalta), venlafaxine (Effexor XR) and paroxetine (Paxil, Pexeva). Your doctor also may recommend other antidepressants.
- **Buspirone.** An anti-anxiety medication called buspirone may be used on an ongoing basis. As with most antidepressants, it typically takes up to several weeks to become fully effective.
- **Benzodiazepines.** In limited circumstances, your doctor may prescribe a benzodiazepine for relief of anxiety symptoms. These sedatives are generally used only for relieving acute anxiety on a short-term basis. Because they can be habit-forming, these medications aren't a good choice if you have or had problems with alcohol or drug abuse.

Lifestyle and home remedies

While most people with anxiety disorders need

psychotherapy or medications to get anxiety under control, lifestyle changes also can make a difference. Here's what you can do:

- **Keep physically active.** Develop a routine so that you're physically active most days of the week. Exercise is a powerful stress reducer. It may improve your mood and help you stay healthy. Start out slowly and gradually increase the amount and intensity of your activities.
- **Make sleep a priority.** Do what you can to make sure you're getting enough sleep to feel rested. If you aren't sleeping well, see your doctor.
- **Use relaxation techniques.** Visualization techniques, meditation and yoga are examples of relaxation techniques that can ease anxiety.
- **Eat healthy.** Healthy eating — such as focusing on vegetables, fruits, whole grains and fish — may be linked to reduced anxiety, but more research is needed.
- **Avoid alcohol and recreational drugs.** These substances can worsen anxiety.
- **Quit smoking and cut back or quit drinking coffee.** Both nicotine and caffeine can worsen anxiety.

Alternative medicine

Several herbal remedies have been studied as treatments for anxiety. Results tend to be mixed, and in several studies people report no benefits from their use. More research is needed to fully understand the risks and benefits. Some herbal supplements, such as kava and valerian, increase the risk of serious liver damage. Other supplements, such as passionflower or theanine, may have a calming effect, but they're often combined with other products so it's hard to tell whether they help with symptoms of anxiety.

Before taking any herbal remedies or supplements, talk with

your doctor to make sure they're safe and won't interact with any medications you take.

Coping and support

To cope with generalized anxiety disorder, here's what you can do:

- Stick to your treatment plan.
- Take medications as directed.
- Keep therapy appointments.
- Practice the skills you learn in psychotherapy.

Consistency can make a big difference, especially when it comes to taking your medication.

Take action. Work with your mental health professional to figure out what's making you anxious and address it.

- **Let it go.** Don't dwell on past concerns. Change what you can in the present moment and let the rest take its course.
- **Break the cycle.** When you feel anxious, take a brisk walk or delve into a hobby to refocus your mind away from your worries.
- **Socialize.** Don't let worries isolate you from loved ones or enjoyable activities. Social interaction and caring relationships can lessen your worries.
- **Join a support group for people with anxiety.** Here, you can find compassion, understanding and shared experiences. You may find support groups in your community or on the internet, for example, South African Depression Group (SADAG)

Preparing for your appointment

You may see your primary care doctor, or your doctor may refer you to a mental health professional. Here's some information to help you get ready for your appointment.

What you can do

Before your appointment, make a list of:

- **Any symptoms you've been experiencing**, including when they occur, what seems to make them better or worse, and how much they affect your day-to-day activities, such as work, school or relationships
- **Key personal information**, including major life changes or stressful events you've dealt with recently and any traumatic experiences you've had in the past
- **Medical information**, including other physical or mental health conditions with which you've been diagnosed
- **Any medications**, vitamins, herbs or other supplements you're taking, including the dosages
- **Questions** to ask your doctor or mental health professional

Some questions to ask your doctor may include:

- What's the most likely cause of my symptoms?
- Are there other possible issues or physical health problems that could be causing or worsening my anxiety?
- Do I need any tests?
- What treatment do you recommend?
- Should I see a psychiatrist, psychologist or other mental health professional?
- Would medication help? If so, is there a generic alternative to the medicine you're prescribing?
- Are there any brochures or other printed material that I can have? What websites do you recommend?

Don't hesitate to ask other questions during your appointment.

What to expect from your doctor

Your doctor or mental health professional will likely ask you a number of questions. Be ready to answer them to reserve time to go over any points you want to focus on. Questions may include:

- What are your symptoms?
- What things do you tend to worry about?
- Do your symptoms interfere with your daily activities?
- Do you avoid anything because of your anxiety?
- Have your feelings of anxiety been occasional or continuous?
- When did you first begin noticing your anxiety?
- Does anything in particular seem to trigger your anxiety or make it worse?
- What, if anything, seems to improve your feelings of anxiety?
- What, if any, physical or mental health conditions do you have?
- What traumatic experiences have you had recently or in the past?
- Do you regularly drink alcohol or use recreational drugs?
- Do you have any blood relatives with anxiety or other mental health conditions, such as depression?

- PANIC DISORDER

A panic attack is a sudden episode of intense fear that triggers severe physical reactions when there is no real danger or apparent cause. Panic attacks can be very frightening. When panic attacks occur, you might think you're losing control, having a heart attack or even dying. Many people have just one or two panic attacks in their lifetimes, and the problem goes away, perhaps when a stressful situation ends. But if you've had recurrent, unexpected panic attacks and spent long periods in constant fear of another attack, you may have a condition called panic disorder.

Although panic attacks themselves aren't life-threatening, they can be frightening and significantly affect your quality of life. But treatment can be very effective.

Symptoms

Panic attacks typically begin suddenly, without warning. They can strike at any time — when you're driving a car, at the mall, sound asleep or in the middle of a business meeting. You may have occasional panic attacks, or they may occur frequently.

Panic attacks have many variations, but symptoms usually peak within minutes. You may feel fatigued and worn out after a panic attack subsides.

Panic attacks typically include some of these signs or symptoms:

- Sense of impending doom or danger
- Fear of loss of control or death
- Rapid, pounding heart rate
- Sweating

- Trembling or shaking
- Shortness of breath or tightness in your throat
- Chills
- Hot flashes
- Nausea
- Abdominal cramping
- Chest pain
- Headache
- Dizziness, lightheadedness or faintness
- Numbness or tingling sensation
- Feeling of unreality or detachment

One of the worst things about panic attacks is the intense fear that you'll have another one. You may fear having panic attacks so much that you avoid certain situations where they may occur.

When to see a doctor

If you have panic attack symptoms, seek medical help as soon as possible. Panic attacks, while intensely uncomfortable, are not dangerous. But panic attacks are hard to manage on your own, and they may get worse without treatment.

Panic attack symptoms can also resemble symptoms of other serious health problems, such as a heart attack, so it's important to get evaluated by your primary care provider if you aren't sure what's causing your symptoms.

Diagnosis

Your primary care provider will determine if you have panic attacks, panic disorder or another condition, such as heart or thyroid problems, with symptoms that resemble panic attacks.

To help pinpoint a diagnosis, you may have:

- A complete physical exam
- Blood tests to check your thyroid and other possible conditions and tests on your heart, such as an electrocardiogram (ECG or EKG)
- A psychological evaluation to talk about your symptoms, fears or concerns, stressful situations, relationship problems, situations you may be avoiding, and family history

You may fill out a psychological self-assessment or questionnaire. You also may be asked about alcohol or other substance use.

Causes

It's not known what causes panic attacks or panic disorder, but these factors may play a role:

- Genetics
- Major stress
- Temperament that is more sensitive to stress or prone to negative emotions
- Certain changes in the way parts of your brain function

Panic attacks may come on suddenly and without warning at first, but over time, they're usually triggered by certain situations.

Some research suggests that your body's natural fight-or-flight response to danger is involved in panic attacks. For example, if a grizzly bear came after you, your body would react instinctively. Your heart rate and breathing would speed up as your body prepared for a life-threatening situation. Many of the same reactions occur in a panic attack. But it's unknown why a panic attack occurs when there's no obvious danger present.

Risk factors

Symptoms of panic disorder often start in the late teens or early adulthood and affect more women than men.

Factors that may increase the risk of developing panic attacks or panic disorder include:

- Family history of panic attacks or panic disorder
- Major life stress, such as the death or serious illness of a loved one
- A traumatic event, such as sexual assault or a serious accident
- Major changes in your life, such as a divorce or the addition of a baby
- Smoking or excessive caffeine intake
- History of childhood physical or sexual abuse

Complications

Left untreated, panic attacks and panic disorder can affect almost every area of your life. You may be so afraid of having more panic attacks that you live in a constant state of fear, ruining your quality of life.

Complications that panic attacks may cause or be linked to include:

- Development of specific phobias, such as fear of driving or leaving your home
- Frequent medical care for health concerns and other medical conditions
- Avoidance of social situations
- Problems at work or school
- Depression, anxiety disorders and other psychiatric disorders

- Increased risk of suicide or suicidal thoughts
- Alcohol or other substance misuse
- Financial problems

For some people, panic disorder may include agoraphobia — avoiding places or situations that cause you anxiety because you fear being unable to escape or get help if you have a panic attack. Or you may become reliant on others to be with you in order to leave your home.

Prevention

There's no sure way to prevent panic attacks or panic disorder. However, these recommendations may help.

- **Get treatment for panic attacks** as soon as possible to help stop them from getting worse or becoming more frequent.
- **Stick with your treatment plan** to help prevent relapses or worsening of panic attack symptoms.
- **Get regular physical activity,** which may play a role in protecting against anxiety.

Diagnosis

Your primary care provider will determine if you have panic attacks, panic disorder or another condition, such as heart or thyroid problems, with symptoms that resemble panic attacks.

To help pinpoint a diagnosis, you may have:

- A complete physical exam
- Blood tests to check your thyroid and other possible conditions and tests on your heart, such as an electrocardiogram (ECG or EKG)
- A psychological evaluation to talk about your symptoms, fears or concerns, stressful situations, relationship problems, situations you may be

avoiding, and family history

You may fill out a psychological self-assessment or questionnaire. You also may be asked about alcohol or other substance use.

Criteria for diagnosis of panic disorder

Not everyone who has panic attacks has panic disorder. For a diagnosis of panic disorder, the Diagnostic and Statistical Manual of Mental Disorders (DSM-5), published by the American Psychiatric Association, lists these points:

- You have frequent, unexpected panic attacks.
- At least one of your attacks has been followed by one month or more of ongoing worry about having another attack; continued fear of the consequences of an attack, such as losing control, having a heart attack or "going crazy"; or significant changes in your behavior, such as avoiding situations that you think may trigger a panic attack.
- Your panic attacks aren't caused by drugs or other substance use, a medical condition, or another mental health condition, such as social phobia or obsessive-compulsive disorder.

If you have panic attacks but not a diagnosed panic disorder, you can still benefit from treatment. If panic attacks aren't treated, they can get worse and develop into panic disorder or phobias.

Treatment

Treatment can help reduce the intensity and frequency of your panic attacks and improve your function in daily life. The main treatment options are psychotherapy and medications. One or both types of treatment may be recommended, depending on your preference, your history, the severity of your panic disorder and whether you have access to therapists who have special training in treating panic disorders.

Psychotherapy

Psychotherapy, also called talk therapy, is considered an effective first choice treatment for panic attacks and panic disorder. Psychotherapy can help you understand panic attacks and panic disorder and learn how to cope with them. A form of psychotherapy called cognitive behavioral therapy can help you learn, through your own experience, that panic symptoms are not dangerous. Your therapist will help you gradually re-create the symptoms of a panic attack in a safe, repetitive manner. Once the physical sensations of panic no longer feel threatening, the attacks begin to resolve. Successful treatment can also help you overcome fears of situations that you've avoided because of panic attacks.

Seeing results from treatment can take time and effort. You may start to see panic attack symptoms reduce within several weeks, and often symptoms decrease significantly or go away within several months. You may schedule occasional maintenance visits to help ensure that your panic attacks remain under control or to treat recurrences.

Medications

Medications can help reduce symptoms associated with panic attacks as well as depression if that's an issue for you. Several types of medication have been shown to be effective in managing symptoms of panic attacks, including:

- **Selective serotonin reuptake inhibitors (SSRIs).** Generally safe with a low risk of serious side effects, SSRI antidepressants are typically recommended as the first choice of medications to treat panic attacks. SSRIs approved by the Food and Drug

Administration (FDA) for the treatment of panic disorder include fluoxetine (Prozac), paroxetine (Paxil, Pexeva) and sertraline (Zoloft).
- **Serotonin and norepinephrine reuptake inhibitors (SNRIs).** These medications are another class of antidepressants. The SNRI venlafaxine (Effexor XR) is FDA approved for the treatment of panic disorder.
- **Benzodiazepines.** These sedatives are central nervous system depressants. Benzodiazepines approved by the FDA for the treatment of panic disorder include alprazolam (Xanax) and clonazepam (Klonopin). Benzodiazepines are generally used only on a short-term basis because they can be habit-forming, causing mental or physical dependence. These medications are not a good choice if you've had problems with alcohol or drug use. They can also interact with other drugs, causing dangerous side effects.

If one medication doesn't work well for you, your doctor may recommend switching to another or combining certain medications to boost effectiveness. Keep in mind that it can take several weeks after first starting a medication to notice an improvement in symptoms.

All medications have a risk of side effects, and some may not be recommended in certain situations, such as pregnancy. Talk with your doctor about possible side effects and risks.

Lifestyle and home remedies

While panic attacks and panic disorder benefit from professional treatment, these self-care steps can help you manage symptoms:
- **Stick to your treatment plan.** Facing your fears can be difficult, but treatment can help you feel like you're not a hostage in your own home.

- **Join a support group.** Joining a group for people with panic attacks or anxiety disorders can connect you with others facing the same problems.
- **Avoid caffeine, alcohol, smoking and recreational drugs.** All of these can trigger or worsen panic attacks.
- **Practice stress management and relaxation techniques.** For example, yoga, deep breathing and progressive muscle relaxation — tensing one muscle at a time, and then completely releasing the tension until every muscle in the body is relaxed — also may be helpful.
- **Get physically active.** Aerobic activity may have a calming effect on your mood.
- **Get sufficient sleep.** Get enough sleep so that you don't feel drowsy during the day.

- OBSESSIVE-COMPULSIVE DISORDER (OCD)

Obsessive-compulsive disorder (OCD) features a pattern of unwanted thoughts and fears (obsessions) that lead you to do repetitive behaviors (compulsions). These obsessions and compulsions interfere with daily activities and cause significant distress. You may try to ignore or stop your obsessions, but that only increases your distress and anxiety. Ultimately, you feel driven to perform compulsive acts to try to ease your stress. Despite efforts to ignore or get rid of bothersome thoughts or urges, they keep coming back. This leads to more ritualistic behavior — the vicious cycle of OCD. OCD often centers around certain themes — for example, an excessive fear of getting contaminated by germs. To ease your contamination fears, you may compulsively wash your hands until they're sore and chapped.

If you have OCD, you may be ashamed and embarrassed about the condition, but treatment can be effective.

Symptoms

Obsessive-compulsive disorder usually includes both obsessions and compulsions. But it's also possible to have only obsession symptoms or only compulsion symptoms. You may or may not realize that your obsessions and compulsions are excessive or unreasonable, but they take up a great deal of time and interfere with your daily routine and social, school or work functioning.

Obsession symptoms

OCD obsessions are repeated, persistent and unwanted thoughts, urges or images that are intrusive and cause distress or anxiety. You might try to ignore them or get rid of them by performing a compulsive behavior or ritual. These obsessions typically intrude when you're trying to think of or do other things.

Obsessions often have themes to them, such as:

- Fear of contamination or dirt
- Doubting and having difficulty tolerating uncertainty
- Needing things orderly and symmetrical
- Aggressive or horrific thoughts about losing control and harming yourself or others
- Unwanted thoughts, including aggression, or sexual or religious subjects

Examples of obsession signs and symptoms include:

- Fear of being contaminated by touching objects others have touched
- Doubts that you've locked the door or turned off the stove
- Intense stress when objects aren't orderly or facing a certain way
- Images of driving your car into a crowd of people
- Thoughts about shouting obscenities or acting inappropriately in public
- Unpleasant sexual images
- Avoidance of situations that can trigger obsessions, such as shaking hands

Compulsion symptoms

OCD compulsions are repetitive behaviors that you feel driven to perform. These repetitive behaviors or mental acts are meant to reduce anxiety related to your obsessions or prevent something bad from happening. However, engaging in the compulsions brings no pleasure and may offer only a temporary relief from anxiety.

You may make up rules or rituals to follow that help control your anxiety when you're having obsessive thoughts. These compulsions are excessive and often are not realistically related to the problem they're intended to fix.

As with obsessions, compulsions typically have themes, such as:

- Washing and cleaning
- Checking
- Counting
- Orderliness
- Following a strict routine
- Demanding reassurance

Examples of compulsion signs and symptoms include:

- Hand-washing until your skin becomes raw
- Checking doors repeatedly to make sure they're locked
- Checking the stove repeatedly to make sure it's off
- Counting in certain patterns
- Silently repeating a prayer, word or phrase
- Arranging your canned goods to face the same way

Severity varies

OCD usually begins in the teen or young adult years, but it can start in childhood. Symptoms usually begin gradually and tend to vary in severity throughout life. The types of obsessions and compulsions you experience can also change over time. Symptoms generally worsen when you experience greater stress. OCD, usually considered a lifelong disorder, can have mild to moderate symptoms or be so severe and time-consuming that it becomes disabling.

When to see a doctor

There's a difference between being a perfectionist — someone who requires flawless results or performance, for example — and having OCD. OCD thoughts aren't simply excessive worries about real problems in your life or liking to have things clean or arranged in a specific way.

If your obsessions and compulsions are affecting your quality of life, see your doctor or mental health professional.

Causes

The cause of obsessive-compulsive disorder isn't fully understood. Main theories include:

- **Biology.** OCD may be a result of changes in your body's own natural chemistry or brain functions.
- **Genetics.** OCD may have a genetic component, but specific genes have yet to be identified.
- **Learning.** Obsessive fears and compulsive behaviors can be learned from watching family members or gradually learned over time.

Risk factors

Factors that may increase the risk of developing or triggering obsessive-compulsive disorder include:

- **Family history.** Having parents or other family members with the disorder can increase your risk of developing OCD.
- **Stressful life events.** If you've experienced traumatic or stressful events, your risk may increase. This reaction may, for some reason, trigger the intrusive thoughts, rituals and emotional distress characteristic of OCD.
- **Other mental health disorders.** OCD may be related to other mental health disorders, such as anxiety disorders, depression, substance abuse or tic disorders.

Complications

Problems resulting from obsessive-compulsive disorder may include, among others:

- Excessive time spent engaging in ritualistic behaviors
- Health issues, such as contact dermatitis from frequent hand-washing
- Difficulty attending work, school or social activities
- Troubled relationships
- Overall poor quality of life
- Suicidal thoughts and behavior

Prevention

There's no sure way to prevent obsessive-compulsive disorder. However, getting treatment as soon as possible may help prevent OCD from worsening and disrupting activities and your daily routine.

Diagnosis

Steps to help diagnose obsessive-compulsive disorder may include:

- **Psychological evaluation.** This includes discussing your thoughts, feelings, symptoms and behavior patterns to determine if you have obsessions or compulsive behaviors that interfere with your quality of life. With your permission, this may include talking to your family or friends.
- **Diagnostic criteria for OCD.** Your doctor may use criteria in the Diagnostic and Statistical Manual of Mental Disorders (DSM-5), published by the American Psychiatric Association.
- **Physical exam.** This may be done to help rule out other problems that could be causing

your symptoms and to check for any related complications.

Diagnostic challenges

It's sometimes difficult to diagnose OCD because symptoms can be similar to those of obsessive-compulsive personality disorder, anxiety disorders, depression, schizophrenia or other mental health disorders. And it's possible to have both OCD and another mental health disorder. Work with your doctor so that you can get the appropriate diagnosis and treatment.

Treatment

Obsessive-compulsive disorder treatment may not result in a cure, but it can help bring symptoms under control so that they don't rule your daily life. Depending on the severity of OCD, some people may need long-term, ongoing or more intensive treatment.

The two main treatments for OCD are psychotherapy and medications. Often, treatment is most effective with a combination of these.

Psychotherapy

Cognitive behavioral therapy (CBT), a type of psychotherapy, is effective for many people with OCD. Exposure and response prevention (ERP), a component of CBT therapy, involves gradually exposing you to a feared object or obsession, such as dirt, and having you learn ways to resist the urge to do your compulsive rituals. ERP takes effort and practice, but you may enjoy a better quality of life once you learn to manage your obsessions and compulsions.

Medications

Certain psychiatric medications can help control the

obsessions and compulsions of OCD. Most commonly, antidepressants are tried first.

Antidepressants approved by the U.S. Food and Drug Administration (FDA) to treat OCD include:

- Clomipramine (Anafranil) for adults and children 10 years and older
- Fluoxetine (Prozac) for adults and children 7 years and older
- Fluvoxamine for adults and children 8 years and older
- Paroxetine (Paxil, Pexeva) for adults only
- Sertraline (Zoloft) for adults and children 6 years and older

However, your doctor may prescribe other antidepressants and psychiatric medications.

Medications: What to consider

Here are some issues to discuss with your doctor about medications for OCD:

- **Choosing a medication.** In general, the goal is to effectively control symptoms at the lowest possible dosage. It's not unusual to try several drugs before finding one that works well. Your doctor might recommend more than one medication to effectively manage your symptoms. It can take weeks to months after starting a medication to notice an improvement in symptoms.
- **Side effects.** All psychiatric medications have potential side effects. Talk to your doctor about possible side effects and about any health monitoring needed while taking psychiatric drugs. And let your doctor know if you experience troubling side effects.
- **Suicide risk.** Most antidepressants are generally safe, but the FDA requires that all antidepressants

carry black box warnings, the strictest warnings for prescriptions. In some cases, children, teenagers and young adults under 25 may have an increase in suicidal thoughts or behavior when taking antidepressants, especially in the first few weeks after starting or when the dose is changed. If suicidal thoughts occur, immediately contact your doctor or get emergency help. Keep in mind that antidepressants are more likely to reduce suicide risk in the long run by improving mood.
- **Interactions with other substances.** When taking an antidepressant, tell your doctor about any other prescription or over-the-counter medications, herbs or other supplements you take. Some antidepressants can make some other medications less effective and cause dangerous reactions when combined with certain medications or herbal supplements.
- **Stopping antidepressants.** Antidepressants aren't considered addictive, but sometimes physical dependence (which is different from addiction) can occur. So stopping treatment abruptly or missing several doses can cause withdrawal-like symptoms, sometimes called discontinuation syndrome. Don't stop taking your medication without talking to your doctor, even if you're feeling better — you may have a relapse of OCD symptoms. Work with your doctor to gradually and safely decrease your dose.

Talk to your doctor about the risks and benefits of using specific medications.

Other treatment

Sometimes, psychotherapy and medications aren't effective enough to control OCD symptoms. In treatment-resistant cases, other options may be offered:

- **Intensive outpatient and residential treatment programs.** Comprehensive treatment programs that emphasize ERP therapy principles may be helpful for people with OCD who struggle with being able to function because of the severity of their symptoms. These programs typically last several weeks.
- **Deep brain stimulation (DBS).** DBS is approved by the FDA to treat OCD in adults age 18 years and older who don't respond to traditional treatment approaches. DBS involves implanting electrodes within certain areas of your brain. These electrodes produce electrical impulses that may help regulate abnormal impulses.
- **Transcranial magnetic stimulation (TMS).** The FDA approved a specific device (BrainsWay Deep Transcranial Magnetic Stimulation) to treat OCD in adults ages 22 to 68 years, when traditional treatment approaches have not been effective. TMS is a noninvasive procedure that uses magnetic fields to stimulate nerve cells in the brain to improve symptoms of OCD. During a TMS session, an electromagnetic coil is placed against your scalp near your forehead. The electromagnet delivers a magnetic pulse that stimulates nerve cells in your brain.

Talk to your doctor to make sure you understand all the pros and cons and possible health risks of DBS and TMS if you're considering one of these procedures.

Lifestyle and home remedies

Obsessive-compulsive disorder is a chronic condition, which means it may always be part of your life. While OCD warrants treatment by a professional, you can do some things for yourself to build on your treatment plan:

- **Practice what you learn.** Work with your mental health professional to identify techniques and skills that help manage symptoms, and practice these regularly.
- **Take your medications as directed.** Even if you're feeling well, resist any temptation to skip your medications. If you stop, OCD symptoms are likely to return.
- **Pay attention to warning signs.** You and your doctor may have identified issues that can trigger your OCD symptoms. Make a plan so that you know what to do if symptoms return. Contact your doctor or therapist if you notice any changes in symptoms or how you feel.
- **Check first before taking other medications.** Contact the doctor who's treating you for OCD before you take medications prescribed by another doctor or before taking any over-the-counter medications, vitamins, herbal remedies or other supplements to avoid possible interactions.

Coping and support

Coping with obsessive-compulsive disorder can be challenging. Medications can have unwanted side effects, and you may feel embarrassed or angry about having a condition that requires long-term treatment. Here are some ways to help cope with OCD:

- **Learn about OCD.** Learning about your condition can empower you and motivate you to stick to your treatment plan.
- **Stay focused on your goals.** Keep your recovery goals in mind and remember that recovery from OCD is an ongoing process.
- **Join a support group.** Reaching out to others facing similar challenges can provide you with support

and help you cope with challenges.
- **Find healthy outlets.** Explore healthy ways to channel your energy, such as hobbies and recreational activities. Exercise regularly, eat a healthy diet and get adequate sleep.
- **Learn relaxation and stress management.** In addition to professional treatment, stress management techniques such as meditation, visualization, muscle relaxation, massage, deep breathing, yoga or tai chi may help ease stress and anxiety.
- **Stick with your regular activities.** Try not to avoid meaningful activities. Go to work or school as you usually would. Spend time with family and friends. Don't let OCD get in the way of your life.

- POST-TRAUMATIC STRESS DISORDER

Post-traumatic stress disorder (PTSD) is a mental health condition that's triggered by a terrifying event — either experiencing it or witnessing it. Symptoms may include flashbacks, nightmares and severe anxiety, as well as uncontrollable thoughts about the event. Most people who go through traumatic events may have temporary difficulty adjusting and coping, but with time and good self-care, they usually get better. If the symptoms get worse, last for months or even years, and interfere with your day-to-day functioning, you may have PTSD.

Getting effective treatment after PTSD symptoms develop can be critical to reduce symptoms and improve function.

Symptoms

Post-traumatic stress disorder symptoms may start within one month of a traumatic event, but sometimes symptoms may not appear until years after the event. These symptoms cause significant problems in social or work situations and in relationships. They can also interfere with your ability to go about your normal daily tasks.

PTSD symptoms are generally grouped into four types: intrusive memories, avoidance, negative changes in thinking and mood, and changes in physical and emotional reactions. Symptoms can vary over time or vary from person to person.

Intrusive memories

- Symptoms of intrusive memories may include:
- Recurrent, unwanted distressing memories of the traumatic event
- Reliving the traumatic event as if it were happening again (flashbacks)

- Upsetting dreams or nightmares about the traumatic event
- Severe emotional distress or physical reactions to something that reminds you of the traumatic event

Avoidance

Symptoms of avoidance may include:

- Trying to avoid thinking or talking about the traumatic event
- Avoiding places, activities or people that remind you of the traumatic event
- Negative changes in thinking and mood

Symptoms of negative changes in thinking and mood may include:

- Negative thoughts about yourself, other people or the world
- Hopelessness about the future
- Memory problems, including not remembering important aspects of the traumatic event
- Difficulty maintaining close relationships
- Feeling detached from family and friends
- Lack of interest in activities you once enjoyed
- Difficulty experiencing positive emotions
- Feeling emotionally numb

Changes in physical and emotional reactions

Symptoms of changes in physical and emotional reactions (also called arousal symptoms) may include:

- Being easily startled or frightened
- Always being on guard for danger
- Self-destructive behavior, such as drinking too much or driving too fast
- Trouble sleeping
- Trouble concentrating

- Irritability, angry outbursts or aggressive behavior
- Overwhelming guilt or shame

For children 6 years old and younger, signs and symptoms may also include:

- Re-enacting the traumatic event or aspects of the traumatic event through play
- Frightening dreams that may or may not include aspects of the traumatic event

Intensity of symptoms

PTSD symptoms can vary in intensity over time. You may have more PTSD symptoms when you're stressed in general, or when you come across reminders of what you went through. For example, you may hear a car backfire and relive combat experiences. Or you may see a report on the news about a sexual assault and feel overcome by memories of your own assault.

When to see a doctor

If you have disturbing thoughts and feelings about a traumatic event for more than a month, if they're severe, or if you feel you're having trouble getting your life back under control, talk to your doctor or a mental health professional. Getting treatment as soon as possible can help prevent PTSD symptoms from getting worse.

If you have suicidal thoughts

If you or someone you know has suicidal thoughts, get help right away through one or more of these resources:

- Reach out to a close friend or loved one.
- Call a suicide hotline number — *0800 567 567, 24hr helpline 0800 12 13 14, SMS 31393* (a SADAG counsellor will call you back)

- Make an appointment with your doctor or a mental health professional.

When to get emergency help

If you think you may hurt yourself or attempt suicide, call *10111 or 10177* immediately.

If you know someone who's in danger of attempting suicide or has made a suicide attempt, make sure someone stays with that person to keep him or her safe. Call *10111 or 10177* immediately. Or, if you can do so safely, take the person to the nearest hospital emergency room.

Diagnosis

To diagnose post-traumatic stress disorder, your doctor will likely:

- **Perform a physical exam** to check for medical problems that may be causing your symptoms
- **Do a psychological evaluation** that includes a discussion of your signs and symptoms and the event or events that led up to them
- **Use the criteria in the Diagnostic and Statistical Manual of Mental Disorders (DSM-5),** published by the American Psychiatric Association

Diagnosis of PTSD requires exposure to an event that involved the actual or possible threat of death, violence or serious injury. Your exposure can happen in one or more of these ways:

- You directly experienced the traumatic event
- You witnessed, in person, the traumatic event occurring to others
- You learned someone close to you experienced or was threatened by the traumatic event
- You are repeatedly exposed to graphic details of

traumatic events (for example, if you are a first responder to the scene of traumatic events)

You may have PTSD if the problems you experience after this exposure continue for more than a month and cause significant problems in your ability to function in social and work settings and negatively impact relationships.

Treatment

Post-traumatic stress disorder treatment can help you regain a sense of control over your life. The primary treatment is psychotherapy, but can also include medication. Combining these treatments can help improve your symptoms by:

- Teaching you skills to address your symptoms
- Helping you think better about yourself, others and the world
- Learning ways to cope if any symptoms arise again
- Treating other problems often related to traumatic experiences, such as depression, anxiety, or misuse of alcohol or drugs

You don't have to try to handle the burden of PTSD on your own.

Psychotherapy

Several types of psychotherapy, also called talk therapy, may be used to treat children and adults with PTSD. Some types of psychotherapy used in PTSD treatment include:

- **Cognitive therapy.** This type of talk therapy helps you recognize the ways of thinking (cognitive patterns) that are keeping you stuck — for example, negative beliefs about yourself and the risk of traumatic things happening again. For PTSD, cognitive therapy often is used along with exposure therapy.

- **Exposure therapy.** This behavioral therapy helps you safely face both situations and memories that you find frightening so that you can learn to cope with them effectively. Exposure therapy can be particularly helpful for flashbacks and nightmares. One approach uses virtual reality programs that allow you to re-enter the setting in which you experienced trauma.
- **Eye movement desensitization and reprocessing (EMDR).** EMDR combines exposure therapy with a series of guided eye movements that help you process traumatic memories and change how you react to them.

Your therapist can help you develop stress management skills to help you better handle stressful situations and cope with stress in your life. All these approaches can help you gain control of lasting fear after a traumatic event. You and your mental health professional can discuss what type of therapy or combination of therapies may best meet your needs.

You may try individual therapy, group therapy or both. Group therapy can offer a way to connect with others going through similar experiences.

Medications

Several types of medications can help improve symptoms of PTSD:

- **Antidepressants.** These medications can help symptoms of depression and anxiety. They can also help improve sleep problems and concentration. The selective serotonin reuptake inhibitor (SSRI) medications sertraline (Zoloft) and paroxetine (Paxil) are approved by the Food and Drug Administration (FDA) for PTSD treatment.

- **Anti-anxiety medications.** These drugs can relieve severe anxiety and related problems. Some anti-anxiety medications have the potential for abuse, so they are generally used only for a short time.
- **Prazosin.** While several studies indicated that prazosin (Minipress) may reduce or suppress nightmares in some people with PTSD, a more recent study showed no benefit over placebo. But participants in the recent study differed from others in ways that potentially could impact the results. Individuals who are considering prazosin should speak with a doctor to determine whether or not their particular situation might merit a trial of this drug.

You and your doctor can work together to figure out the best medication, with the fewest side effects, for your symptoms and situation. You may see an improvement in your mood and other symptoms within a few weeks.

Tell your doctor about any side effects or problems with medications. You may need to try more than one or a combination of medications, or your doctor may need to adjust your dosage or medication schedule before finding the right fit for you.

Coping and support

If stress and other problems caused by a traumatic event affect your life, see your doctor or mental health professional. You can also take these actions as you continue with treatment for post-traumatic stress disorder:

- **Follow your treatment plan.** Although it may take a while to feel benefits from therapy or medications, treatment can be effective, and most people do recover. Remind yourself that it takes time. Following your treatment plan and

routinely communicating with your mental health professional will help move you forward.
- **Learn about PTSD.** This knowledge can help you understand what you're feeling, and then you can develop coping strategies to help you respond effectively.
- **Take care of yourself.** Get enough rest, eat a healthy diet, exercise and take time to relax. Try to reduce or avoid caffeine and nicotine, which can worsen anxiety.
- **Don't self-medicate.** Turning to alcohol or drugs to numb your feelings isn't healthy, even though it may be a tempting way to cope. It can lead to more problems down the road, interfere with effective treatments and prevent real healing.
- **Break the cycle.** When you feel anxious, take a brisk walk or jump into a hobby to re-focus.
- **Stay connected.** Spend time with supportive and caring people — family, friends, faith leaders or others. You don't have to talk about what happened if you don't want to. Just sharing time with loved ones can offer healing and comfort.
- **Consider a support group.** Ask your mental health professional for help finding a support group or contact veterans' organizations or your community's social services system. Or look for local support groups in an online directory.

When someone you love has PTSD

The person you love may seem like a different person than you knew before the trauma — angry and irritable, for example, or withdrawn and depressed. PTSD can significantly strain the emotional and mental health of loved ones and friends. Hearing about the trauma that led to your loved one's PTSD may be painful for you and even cause you to relive difficult events. You may find yourself avoiding his or her attempts to talk about the trauma or feeling hopeless that your loved one will get better. At the same time, you may feel guilty that you can't fix your loved one or hurry up the process of healing.

Remember that you can't change someone. However, you can:

- **Learn about PTSD.** This can help you understand what your loved one is going through.
- **Recognize that avoidance and withdrawal are part of the disorder.** If your loved one resists your help, allow space and let your loved one know that you're available when he or she is ready to accept your help.
- **Offer to attend medical appointments.** If your loved one is willing, attending appointments can help you understand and assist with treatment.
- **Be willing to listen.** Let your loved one know you're willing to listen, but you understand if he or she doesn't want to talk. Try not to force your loved one to talk about the trauma until he or she is ready.
- **Encourage participation.** Plan opportunities for activities with family and friends. Celebrate good events.
- **Make your own health a priority.** Take care of yourself by eating healthy, being physically active and getting enough rest. Take time alone or with friends, doing activities that help you recharge.
- **Seek help if you need it.** If you have difficulty coping, talk with your doctor. He or she may refer you to a therapist who can help you work through your stress.
- **Stay safe.** Plan a safe place for yourself and your children if your loved one becomes violent or abusive.

Preparing for your appointment

If you think you may have post-traumatic stress disorder, make an appointment with your doctor or a mental health professional. Here's some information to help you prepare for your appointment, and what to expect.

Take a trusted family member or friend along, if possible. Sometimes it can be difficult to remember all the information provided to you.

What you can do

Before your appointment, make a list of:

- **Any symptoms you've been experiencing,** and for how long.
- **Key personal information,** especially events or experiences — even in your distant past — that have made you feel intense fear, helplessness or horror. It will help your doctor to know if there are memories you can't directly access without feeling an overwhelming need to push them out of your mind.
- **Things you have stopped doing or are avoiding** because of your stress.
- **Your medical information,** including other physical or mental health conditions with which you've been diagnosed. Also include any medications or supplements you're taking, and the dosages.
- **Questions to ask** so that you can make the most of your appointment.

Some basic questions to ask your doctor or mental health professional may include:

- What do you believe is causing my symptoms?
- Are there any other possible causes?
- How will you determine my diagnosis?
- Is my condition likely temporary or long term?
- What treatments do you recommend for this disorder?
- I have other health problems. How best can I manage these together with PTSD?
- How soon do you expect my symptoms to improve?
- Does PTSD increase my risk of other mental health problems?
- Do you recommend any changes at home, work or school to encourage recovery?
- Would it help my recovery to tell my teachers or co-workers about my diagnosis?
- Are there any printed materials on PTSD that I can have? What websites do you recommend?

Don't hesitate to ask any other questions during your appointment.

What to expect from your doctor

Your doctor is likely to ask you a number of questions. Be ready to answer them to reserve time to go over any points you want to focus on. Your doctor may ask:

- What symptoms are concerning to you or your loved ones?
- When did you or your loved ones first notice your symptoms?
- Have you ever experienced or witnessed a traumatic event?
- Do you have disturbing thoughts, memories or nightmares of the trauma you experienced?
- Do you avoid certain people, places or situations that remind you of the traumatic experience?

- Have you been having any problems at school, work or in your personal relationships?
- Have you ever thought about harming yourself or others?
- Do you drink alcohol or use recreational drugs? How often?
- Have you been treated for other psychiatric symptoms or mental illness in the past? If yes, what type of therapy was most helpful?

- SOCIAL ANXIETY DISORDER

It's normal to feel nervous in some social situations. For example, going on a date or giving a presentation may cause that feeling of butterflies in your stomach. But in social anxiety disorder, also called social phobia, everyday interactions cause significant anxiety, self-consciousness and embarrassment because you fear being scrutinized or judged negatively by others. In social anxiety disorder, fear and anxiety lead to avoidance that can disrupt your life. Severe stress can affect your relationships, daily routines, work, school or other activities.

Social anxiety disorder can be a chronic mental health condition, but learning coping skills in psychotherapy and taking medications can help you gain confidence and improve your ability to interact with others.

Symptoms

Feelings of shyness or discomfort in certain situations aren't necessarily signs of social anxiety disorder, particularly in children. Comfort levels in social situations vary, depending on personality traits and life experiences. Some people are naturally reserved and others are more outgoing.

In contrast to everyday nervousness, social anxiety disorder includes fear, anxiety and avoidance that interfere with relationships, daily routines, work, school or other activities. Social anxiety disorder typically begins in the early to mid-teens, though it can sometimes start in younger children or in adults.

Emotional and behavioral symptoms

- Signs and symptoms of social anxiety disorder can include constant:

- Fear of situations in which you may be judged negatively
- Worry about embarrassing or humiliating yourself
- Intense fear of interacting or talking with strangers
- Fear that others will notice that you look anxious
- Fear of physical symptoms that may cause you embarrassment, such as blushing, sweating, trembling or having a shaky voice
- Avoidance of doing things or speaking to people out of fear of embarrassment
- Avoidance of situations where you might be the center of attention
- Anxiety in anticipation of a feared activity or event
- Intense fear or anxiety during social situations
- Analysis of your performance and identification of flaws in your interactions after a social situation
- Expectation of the worst possible consequences from a negative experience during a social situation

For children, anxiety about interacting with adults or peers may be shown by crying, having temper tantrums, clinging to parents or refusing to speak in social situations.

Performance type of social anxiety disorder is when you experience intense fear and anxiety during speaking or performing in public but not in other types of more general social situations.

Physical symptoms

Physical signs and symptoms can sometimes accompany social anxiety disorder and may include:

- Blushing
- Fast heartbeat
- Trembling
- Sweating
- Upset stomach or nausea

- Trouble catching your breath
- Dizziness or lightheadedness
- Feeling that your mind has gone blank
- Muscle tension

Avoiding common social situations

Common, everyday experiences may be hard to endure when you have social anxiety disorder, including:

- Interacting with unfamiliar people or strangers
- Attending parties or social gatherings
- Going to work or school
- Starting conversations
- Making eye contact
- Dating
- Entering a room in which people are already seated
- Returning items to a store
- Eating in front of others
- Using a public restroom

Social anxiety disorder symptoms can change over time. They may flare up if you're facing a lot of changes, stress or demands in your life. Although avoiding situations that produce anxiety may make you feel better in the short term, your anxiety is likely to continue over the long term if you don't get treatment.

When to see a doctor

See your doctor or a mental health professional if you fear and avoid normal social situations because they cause embarrassment, worry or panic.

Causes

Like many other mental health conditions, social anxiety disorder likely arises from a complex interaction of biological and environmental factors. Possible causes include:

- **Inherited traits.** Anxiety disorders tend to run in families. However, it isn't entirely clear how much of this may be due to genetics and how much is due to learned behavior.
- **Brain structure.** A structure in the brain called the amygdala (uh-MIG-duh-luh) may play a role in controlling the fear response. People who have an overactive amygdala may have a heightened fear response, causing increased anxiety in social situations.
- **Environment.** Social anxiety disorder may be a learned behavior — some people may develop significant anxiety after an unpleasant or embarrassing social situation. Also, there may be an association between social anxiety disorder and parents who either model anxious behavior in social situations or are more controlling or overprotective of their children.

Risk factors

Several factors can increase the risk of developing social anxiety disorder, including:

- **Family history.** You're more likely to develop social anxiety disorder if your biological parents or siblings have the condition.
- **Negative experiences.** Children who experience teasing, bullying, rejection, ridicule or humiliation may be more prone to social anxiety disorder. In addition, other negative events in life, such as family conflict, trauma or abuse, may be associated with this disorder.
- **Temperament.** Children who are shy, timid, withdrawn or restrained when facing new situations or people may be at greater risk.
- **New social or work demands.** Social anxiety

disorder symptoms typically start in the teenage years, but meeting new people, giving a speech in public or making an important work presentation may trigger symptoms for the first time.
- **Having an appearance or condition that draws attention.** For example, facial disfigurement, stuttering or tremors due to Parkinson's disease can increase feelings of self-consciousness and may trigger social anxiety disorder in some people.

Complications

Left untreated, social anxiety disorder can control your life. Anxieties can interfere with work, school, relationships or enjoyment of life. This disorder can cause:

- Low self-esteem
- Trouble being assertive
- Negative self-talk
- Hypersensitivity to criticism
- Poor social skills
- Isolation and difficult social relationships
- Low academic and employment achievement
- Substance abuse, such as drinking too much alcohol
- Suicide or suicide attempts

Other anxiety disorders and certain other mental health disorders, particularly major depressive disorder and substance abuse problems, often occur with social anxiety disorder.

Prevention

There's no way to predict what will cause someone to develop an anxiety disorder, but you can take steps to reduce the impact of symptoms if you're anxious:

- **Get help early.** Anxiety, like many other mental

health conditions, can be harder to treat if you wait.
- **Keep a journal.** Keeping track of your personal life can help you and your mental health professional identify what's causing you stress and what seems to help you feel better.
- **Set priorities in your life.** You can reduce anxiety by carefully managing your time and energy. Make sure that you spend time doing things you enjoy.
- **Avoid unhealthy substance use.** Alcohol and drug use and even caffeine or nicotine use can cause or worsen anxiety. If you're addicted to any of these substances, quitting can make you anxious. If you can't quit on your own, see your health care provider or find a treatment program or support group to help you.

Diagnosis

- Your health care provider will want to determine whether other conditions may be causing your anxiety or if you have social anxiety disorder along with another physical or mental health disorder.
- Your health care provider may determine a diagnosis based on:
- Physical exam to help assess whether any medical condition or medication may trigger symptoms of anxiety
- Discussion of your symptoms, how often they occur and in what situations
- Review of a list of situations to see if they make you anxious
- Self-report questionnaires about symptoms of social anxiety
- Criteria listed in the Diagnostic and Statistical Manual of Mental Disorders (DSM-5), published by the American Psychiatric Association

DSM-5 criteria for social anxiety disorder include:
- Persistent, intense fear or anxiety about specific social situations because you believe you may be judged negatively, embarrassed or humiliated
- Avoidance of anxiety-producing social situations or enduring them with intense fear or anxiety
- Excessive anxiety that's out of proportion to the situation
- Anxiety or distress that interferes with your daily living
- Fear or anxiety that is not better explained by a medical condition, medication or substance abuse

Treatment

Treatment depends on how much social anxiety disorder affects your ability to function in daily life. The most common treatment for social anxiety disorder includes psychotherapy (also called psychological counseling or talk therapy) or medications or both.

Psychotherapy

Psychotherapy improves symptoms in most people with social anxiety disorder. In therapy, you learn how to recognize and change negative thoughts about yourself and develop skills to help you gain confidence in social situations.

Cognitive behavioral therapy (CBT) is the most effective type of psychotherapy for anxiety, and it can be equally effective when conducted individually or in groups.

In exposure-based CBT, you gradually work up to facing the situations you fear most. This can improve your coping skills and help you develop the confidence to deal with anxiety-inducing situations. You may also participate in skills training or role-playing to practice your social skills and gain comfort and confidence relating to others. Practicing exposures to social situations is particularly helpful to challenge your worries.

First choices in medications

Though several types of medications are available, selective serotonin reuptake inhibitors (SSRIs) are often the first type of drug tried for persistent symptoms of social anxiety. Your health care provider may prescribe paroxetine (Paxil) or sertraline (Zoloft). The serotonin and norepinephrine reuptake inhibitor (SNRI) venlafaxine (Effexor XR) also may be an option for social anxiety disorder. To reduce the risk of side effects, your health care provider may start you at a low dose of medication and gradually increase your prescription to a full dose. It may take several weeks to several months of treatment for your symptoms to noticeably improve.

Other medications

Your health care provider may also prescribe other medications for symptoms of social anxiety, such as:

- **Other antidepressants.** You may have to try several different antidepressants to find the one that's most effective for you with the fewest side effects.
- **Anti-anxiety medications.** Benzodiazepines (ben-zoe-die-AZ-uh-peens) may reduce your level of anxiety. Although they often work quickly, they can be habit-forming and sedating, so they're typically prescribed for only short-term use.
- **Beta blockers.** These medications work by blocking the stimulating effect of epinephrine (adrenaline). They may reduce heart rate, blood pressure, pounding of the heart, and shaking voice and limbs. Because of that, they may work best when used

infrequently to control symptoms for a particular situation, such as giving a speech. They're not recommended for general treatment of social anxiety disorder.

Stick with it

Don't give up if treatment doesn't work quickly. You can continue to make strides in psychotherapy over several weeks or months. Learning new skills to help manage your anxiety takes time. And finding the right medication for your situation can take some trial and error. For some people, the symptoms of social anxiety disorder may fade over time, and medication can be discontinued. Others may need to take medication for years to prevent a relapse.

To make the most of treatment, keep your medical or therapy appointments, challenge yourself by setting goals to approach social situations that cause you anxiety, take medications as directed, and talk to your health care provider about any changes in your condition.

Lifestyle and home remedies

Although social anxiety disorder generally requires help from a medical expert or qualified psychotherapist, you can try some of these techniques to handle situations that are likely to trigger symptoms:

- Learn stress-reduction skills.
- Get physical exercise or be physically active on a regular basis.
- Get enough sleep.
- Eat a healthy, well-balanced diet.
- Avoid alcohol.
- Limit or avoid caffeine.
- Participate in social situations by reaching out to people with whom you feel comfortable.

Practice in small steps

First, consider your fears to identify what situations cause the most anxiety. Then gradually practice these activities until they cause you less anxiety. Begin with small steps by setting daily or weekly goals in situations that aren't overwhelming. The more you practice, the less anxious you'll feel.

Consider practicing these situations:

- Eat with a close relative, friend or acquaintance in a public setting.
- Purposefully make eye contact and return greetings from others or be the first to say hello.
- Give someone a compliment.
- Ask a retail clerk to help you find an item.
- Get directions from a stranger.
- Show an interest in others — ask about their homes, children, grandchildren, hobbies or travels, for instance.
- Call a friend to make plans.

Prepare for social situations

At first, being social when you're feeling anxious is challenging. As difficult or painful as it may seem initially, don't avoid situations that trigger your symptoms. By regularly facing these kinds of situations, you'll continue to build and reinforce your coping skills.

These strategies can help you begin to face situations that make you nervous:

- Prepare for conversation, for example, by reading about current events to identify interesting stories you can talk about.
- Focus on personal qualities you like about yourself.
- Practice relaxation exercises.

- Learn stress management techniques.
- Set realistic social goals.
- Pay attention to how often the embarrassing situations you're afraid of actually take place. You may notice that the scenarios you fear usually don't come to pass.
- When embarrassing situations do happen, remind yourself that your feelings will pass and you can handle them until they do. Most people around you either don't notice or don't care as much as you think, or they're more forgiving than you assume.

Avoid using alcohol to calm your nerves. It may seem like it helps temporarily, but in the long term it can make you feel even more anxious.

Coping and support

These coping methods may help ease your anxiety:
- Routinely reach out to friends and family members.
- Join a local or reputable internet-based support group.
- Join a group that offers opportunities to improve communication and public speaking skills, such as Toastmasters International.
- Do pleasurable or relaxing activities, such as hobbies, when you feel anxious.

Over time, these coping methods can help control your symptoms and prevent a relapse. Remind yourself that you can get through anxious moments, that your anxiety is short-lived and that the negative consequences you worry about so much rarely come to pass.

Preparing for your appointment

You may see your primary care provider, or your provider may refer you to a mental health professional. Here's some information to help you get ready for your appointment.

What you can do

Before your appointment, make a list of:

- **Situations you've been avoiding**, especially those that are important to your functioning
- Any symptoms you've been experiencing, and for how long, including any symptoms that may seem unrelated to the reason for your appointment
- **Key personal information**, especially any significant events or changes in your life shortly before your symptoms appeared
- **Medical information**, including other physical or mental health conditions with which you've been diagnosed
- **Any medications**, vitamins, herbs or other supplements you're taking, including dosages
- **Questions** to ask your health care provider or a mental health professional

You may want to ask a trusted family member or friend to go with you to your appointment, if possible, to help you remember key information.

Some questions to ask your health care provider may include:

- What do you believe is causing my symptoms?
- Are there any other possible causes?
- How will you determine my diagnosis?
- Should I see a mental health specialist?
- Is my condition likely temporary or chronic?
- Are effective treatments available for this condition?
- With treatment, could I eventually be comfortable in the situations that make me so anxious now?
- Am I at increased risk of other mental health

problems?
- Are there any brochures or other printed material that I can have? What websites do you recommend?

Don't hesitate to ask other questions during your appointment.

What to expect from your health care provider

Your health care provider or a mental health professional will likely ask you a number of questions. Be ready to answer them to reserve time to go over any points you want to focus on. Your health care provider may ask:

- Does fear of embarrassment cause you to avoid doing certain activities or speaking to people?
- Do you avoid activities in which you're the center of attention?
- Would you say that being embarrassed or looking stupid is among your worst fears?
- When did you first notice these symptoms?
- When are your symptoms most likely to occur?
- Does anything seem to make your symptoms better or worse?
- How are your symptoms affecting your life, including work and personal relationships?
- Do you ever have symptoms when you're not being observed by others?
- Have any of your close relatives had similar symptoms?
- Have you been diagnosed with any medical conditions?
- Have you been treated for mental health symptoms or mental illness in the past? If yes, what type of therapy was most beneficial?
- Have you ever thought about harming yourself or others?
- Do you drink alcohol or use recreational drugs? If

so, how often?

6. Dissociative disorders

Dissociative disorders are mental disorders that involve experiencing a disconnection and lack of continuity between thoughts, memories, surroundings, actions and identity. People with dissociative disorders escape reality in ways that are involuntary and unhealthy and cause problems with functioning in everyday life.

Dissociative disorders usually develop as a reaction to trauma and help keep difficult memories at bay. Symptoms — ranging from amnesia to alternate identities — depend in part on the type of dissociative disorder you have. Times of stress can temporarily worsen symptoms, making them more obvious.

Treatment for dissociative disorders may include talk therapy (psychotherapy) and medication. Although treating dissociative disorders can be difficult, many people learn new ways of coping and lead healthy, productive lives.

Symptoms

Signs and symptoms depend on the type of dissociative disorders you have, but may include:

- Memory loss (amnesia) of certain time periods, events, people and personal information
- A sense of being detached from yourself and your emotions
- A perception of the people and things around you as distorted and unreal
- A blurred sense of identity
- Significant stress or problems in your relationships, work or other important areas of your life
- Inability to cope well with emotional or

professional stress
- Mental health problems, such as depression, anxiety, and suicidal thoughts and behaviors

There are three major dissociative disorders defined in the Diagnostic and Statistical Manual of Mental Disorders (DSM-5), published by the American Psychiatric Association:

- **Dissociative amnesia.** The main symptom is memory loss that's more severe than normal forgetfulness and that can't be explained by a medical condition. You can't recall information about yourself or events and people in your life, especially from a traumatic time. Dissociative amnesia can be specific to events in a certain time, such as intense combat, or more rarely, can involve complete loss of memory about yourself. It may sometimes involve travel or confused wandering away from your life (dissociative fugue). An episode of amnesia usually occurs suddenly and may last minutes, hours, or rarely, months or years.
- **Dissociative identity disorder.** Formerly known as multiple personality disorder, this disorder is characterized by "switching" to alternate identities. You may feel the presence of two or more people talking or living inside your head, and you may feel as though you're possessed by other identities. Each identity may have a unique name, personal history and characteristics, including obvious differences in voice, gender, mannerisms and even such physical qualities as the need for eyeglasses. There also are differences in how familiar each identity is with the others. People with dissociative identity disorder typically also have dissociative amnesia and often have dissociative fugue.
- **Depersonalization-derealization disorder.** This involves an ongoing or episodic sense of

detachment or being outside yourself — observing your actions, feelings, thoughts and self from a distance as though watching a movie (depersonalization). Other people and things around you may feel detached and foggy or dreamlike, time may be slowed down or sped up, and the world may seem unreal (derealization). You may experience depersonalization, derealization or both. Symptoms, which can be profoundly distressing, may last only a few moments or come and go over many years.

When to see a doctor

Some people with dissociative disorders present in a crisis with traumatic flashbacks that are overwhelming or associated with unsafe behavior. People with these symptoms should be seen in an emergency room.

If you or a loved one has less urgent symptoms that may indicate a dissociative disorder, call your doctor.

Suicidal thoughts or behavior

If you have thoughts of hurting yourself or someone else, call *10111 or 10177* number immediately, go to an emergency room, or confide in a trusted relative or friend. Or call a suicide hotline number — *0800 567 567, 24hr helpline 0800 12 13 14, SMS 31393* (a SADAG counsellor will call you back)

Causes

Dissociative disorders usually develop as a way to cope with trauma. The disorders most often form in children subjected to long-term physical, sexual or emotional abuse or, less often, a home environment that's frightening or highly unpredictable. The stress of war or natural disasters also can bring on dissociative disorders. Personal identity is still forming during childhood. So a child is more able than an adult to step outside of himself or herself and observe trauma as though it's happening to a different person. A child who learns to dissociate in order to endure a traumatic experience may use this coping mechanism in response to stressful situations throughout life.

Risk factors

People who experience long-term physical, sexual or emotional abuse during childhood are at greatest risk of developing dissociative disorders.

Children and adults who experience other traumatic events, such as war, natural disasters, kidnapping, torture, or extended, traumatic, early-life medical procedures, also may develop these conditions.

Complications

People with dissociative disorders are at increased risk of complications and associated disorders, such as:

- Self-harm or mutilation
- Suicidal thoughts and behavior
- Sexual dysfunction
- Alcoholism and drug use disorders
- Depression and anxiety disorders
- Post-traumatic stress disorder
- Personality disorders
- Sleep disorders, including nightmares, insomnia and sleepwalking
- Eating disorders
- Physical symptoms such as lightheadedness or non-epileptic seizures
- Major difficulties in personal relationships and at work

Prevention

Children who are physically, emotionally or sexually abused are at increased risk of developing mental health disorders, such as dissociative disorders. If stress or other personal issues are affecting the way you treat your child, seek help. Talk to a trusted person such as a friend, your doctor or a leader in your faith community. Ask for help locating resources such as parenting support groups and family therapists.

If your child has been abused or has experienced another traumatic event, see a doctor immediately. Your doctor can refer you to a mental health professional who can help your child recover and adopt healthy coping skills.

Diagnosis

Diagnosis usually involves assessment of symptoms and ruling out any medical condition that could cause the symptoms. Testing and diagnosis often involves a referral to a mental health professional to determine your diagnosis.

Evaluation may include:

- **Physical exam.** Your doctor examines you, asks in-depth questions, and reviews your symptoms and personal history. Certain tests may eliminate physical conditions — for example, head injury, certain brain diseases, sleep deprivation or intoxication — that can cause symptoms such as memory loss and a sense of unreality.
- **Psychiatric exam.** Your mental health professional asks questions about your thoughts, feelings, and behavior and discusses your symptoms. With your permission, information from family members or others may be helpful.

- **Diagnostic criteria in the DSM-5.** Your mental health professional may compare your symptoms to the criteria for diagnosis in the Diagnostic and Statistical Manual of Mental Disorders (DSM-5), published by the American Psychiatric Association.

For diagnosis of dissociative disorders, the DSM-5 lists these criteria.

- DISSOCIATIVE AMNESIA

For dissociative amnesia:

- You've had one or more episodes in which you couldn't remember important personal information — usually something traumatic or stressful — or you can't remember your identity or life history. This memory loss is too extensive to be explained by ordinary forgetfulness.
- Your episodes of memory loss don't occur only during the course of another mental health disorder, such as post-traumatic stress disorder. Also, your symptoms are not due to alcohol or other drugs, and they're not caused by a neurological or other medical condition, such as amnesia related to head trauma.
- You may also experience dissociative fugue, where you purposefully travel or experience confused wandering that involves amnesia — inability to remember your identity or other important personal information.
- Your symptoms cause you significant stress or problems in your relationships, work or other important areas of your life.

- DISSOCIATIVE IDENTITY DISORDER

For dissociative identity disorder:

- You display, or others observe, two or more distinct identities or personalities, which may be described in some cultures as possession that is unwanted and involuntary. Each identity has its own pattern of perceiving, relating to and thinking about yourself and the world.
- You have recurrent gaps in memory for everyday events, skills, important personal information and traumatic events that are too extensive to be explained by ordinary forgetfulness.
- Your symptoms are not a part of broadly accepted cultural or religious practice.
- Your symptoms are not due to alcohol or other drugs, or a medical condition. In children, symptoms are not due to imaginary playmates or other fantasy play.
- Your symptoms cause you significant stress or problems in your relationships, work or other important areas of your life.

DEPERSONALIZATION-DEREALIZATION DISORDER

For depersonalization-derealization disorder:

- You have persistent or recurrent experiences of feeling detached from yourself, as if you're an outside observer of your thoughts, sensations, actions or your body (depersonalization). Or you feel detached or experience a lack of reality for your surroundings as if you're in a dream or the world is distorted (derealization).
- While you're experiencing an episode of depersonalization or derealization, you're aware the experience is not reality.
- Your symptoms do not occur only during the course of another mental disorder, such as schizophrenia or panic disorder, or during another dissociative disorder. Your symptoms are also not explained by the direct effects of alcohol or other drugs, or a medical condition, such as temporal lobe epilepsy.
- Your symptoms cause you significant stress or problems in your relationships, work or other important areas of your life.

Treatment

Dissociative disorders treatment may vary based on the type of disorder you have, but generally include psychotherapy and medication.

Psychotherapy

Psychotherapy is the primary treatment for dissociative disorders. This form of therapy, also known as talk therapy, counseling or psychosocial therapy, involves talking about your disorder and related issues with a mental health professional. Look for a therapist with advanced training or experience in working with people who have experienced trauma.

Your therapist will work to help you understand the cause of your condition and to form new ways of coping with stressful circumstances. Over time, your therapist may help you talk more about the trauma you experienced, but generally only when you have the coping skills and relationship with your therapist to safely have these conversations.

Medication

Although there are no medications that specifically treat dissociative disorders, your doctor may prescribe antidepressants, anti-anxiety medications or antipsychotic drugs to help control the mental health symptoms associated with dissociative disorders.

Preparing for your appointment

As a first step, your doctor may ask you to come in for a thorough exam to rule out possible physical causes of your symptoms. However, in some cases you may be referred immediately to a psychiatrist. You may want to take a family member or friend along, if possible, to help you remember information.

Here's some information to help you prepare for your appointment, and what to expect from your doctor.

What you can do

Before your appointment, make a list of:

- **Any symptoms you're experiencing,** including any recent behavior that caused confusion or concern for you or your loved ones.

- **Key personal information,** including any major stresses or recent life changes. Also note events from your past, including your childhood, that caused physical or emotional trauma. If you can't recall some periods of your life, note the time frame and anything you can remember about the period leading up to your amnesia.
- **Your medical information,** including other physical or mental health conditions you have. Include any medications, vitamins, herbs or other supplements you're taking, and the dosages.
- **Questions to ask your doctor** to make the most of your time together

Some questions to ask your doctor may include:

- What's likely causing my symptoms or condition?
- What are other possible causes?
- How will you determine my diagnosis?
- Is my condition likely temporary or long term (chronic)?
- What treatments do you recommend for this disorder?
- How much can I expect my symptoms to improve with treatment?
- How will you monitor my progress?
- I have these other health conditions. How can I best manage them together?
- Should I see a specialist?
- Are there any brochures or other printed material that I can have?
- What websites do you recommend?

Don't hesitate to ask other questions during your appointment.

What to expect from your doctor

Your doctor is likely to ask you a number of questions. Be ready to answer them to reserve time to go over any points you want to focus on. Your doctor may ask:
- What symptoms concern you or your loved ones?
- When did you or your loved ones first notice your symptoms?
- Are there periods of time in your life that you don't remember?
- Have you ever found yourself some distance away from your home or work, and not known how you got there?
- Do you ever feel as if you're outside of your body, observing yourself?
- Do you feel as though there is more than one person, or maybe many people, living inside your head?
- What other symptoms or behaviors are causing you or your loved ones distress?
- How often do you feel anxious or depressed?
- Have your symptoms caused problems in your work or your personal relationships?
- Have you ever thought about harming yourself or others?
- Do you drink alcohol or use recreational drugs?
- Do you now or have you ever served in the military?
- Have you ever been touched against your will?
- Were you physically abused or neglected as a child?
- Was anyone in your family abused during your childhood?
- Are you currently being treated for any other medical conditions, including mental health disorders?

7. **Somatic symptom and related disorders:**

- Somatic symptom disorder

Somatic symptom disorder is characterized by an extreme focus on physical symptoms — such as pain or fatigue — that causes major emotional distress and problems functioning. You may or may not have another diagnosed medical condition associated with these symptoms, but your reaction to the symptoms is not normal.

You often think the worst about your symptoms and frequently seek medical care, continuing to search for an explanation even when other serious conditions have been excluded. Health concerns may become such a central focus of your life that it's hard to function, sometimes leading to disability.

If you have somatic symptom disorder, you may experience significant emotional and physical distress. Treatment can help ease symptoms, help you cope and improve your quality of life.

Symptoms

Symptoms of somatic symptom disorder may be:
- Specific sensations, such as pain or shortness of breath, or more general symptoms, such as fatigue or weakness
- Unrelated to any medical cause that can be identified, or related to a medical condition such as cancer or heart disease, but more significant than what's usually expected
- A single symptom, multiple symptoms or varying symptoms
- Mild, moderate or severe

Pain is the most common symptom, but whatever

your symptoms, you have excessive thoughts, feelings or behaviors related to those symptoms, which cause significant problems, make it difficult to function and sometimes can be disabling.

These thoughts, feelings and behaviors can include:
- Constant worry about potential illness
- Viewing normal physical sensations as a sign of severe physical illness
- Fearing that symptoms are serious, even when there is no evidence
- Thinking that physical sensations are threatening or harmful
- Feeling that medical evaluation and treatment have not been adequate
- Fearing that physical activity may cause damage to your body
- Repeatedly checking your body for abnormalities
- Frequent health care visits that don't relieve your concerns or that make them worse
- Being unresponsive to medical treatment or unusually sensitive to medication side effects
- Having a more severe impairment than is usually expected from a medical condition

For somatic symptom disorder, more important than the specific physical symptoms you experience is the way you interpret and react to the symptoms and how they impact your daily life.

When to see a doctor

Because physical symptoms can be related to medical problems, it's important to be evaluated by your primary care provider if you aren't sure what's causing your symptoms. If your primary care provider believes that you may have somatic symptom disorder, he or she can refer you to a mental health professional.

Caring for a loved one

When physical symptoms considered to be somatic symptom disorder occur, it can be difficult to accept that a life-threatening illness has been eliminated as the cause. Symptoms cause very real distress for the person and reassurance isn't always helpful. Encourage your loved one to consider the possibility of a mental health referral to learn ways to cope with the reaction to symptoms and any disability it causes.

Physical disability may cause the person to be dependent and need extra physical care and emotional support that can exhaust caregivers and cause stress on families and relationships. If you feel overwhelmed by your role as caregiver, you may want to talk to a mental health professional to address your own needs.

Causes

The exact cause of somatic symptom disorder isn't clear, but any of these factors may play a role:

- **Genetic and biological factors,** such as an increased sensitivity to pain
- Family influence, which may be genetic or environmental, or both
- **Personality trait of negativity,** which can impact how you identify and perceive illness and bodily symptoms
- **Decreased awareness of or problems processing emotions,** causing physical symptoms to become the focus rather than the emotional issues
- **Learned behavior** — for example, the attention or other benefits gained from having an illness; or

"pain behaviors" in response to symptoms, such as excessive avoidance of activity, which can increase your level of disability

Risk factors

Risk factors for somatic symptom disorder include:
- Having anxiety or depression
- Having a medical condition or recovering from one
- Being at risk of developing a medical condition, such as having a strong family history of a disease
- Experiencing stressful life events, trauma or violence
- Having experienced past trauma, such as childhood sexual abuse
- Having a lower level of education and socio-economic status

Complications

Somatic symptom disorder can be associated with:
- Poor health
- Problems functioning in daily life, including physical disability
- Problems with relationships
- Problems at work or unemployment
- Other mental health disorders, such as anxiety, depression and personality disorders
- Increased suicide risk related to depression
- Financial problems due to excessive health care visits

Prevention

Little is known about how to prevent somatic symptom disorder. However, these recommendations may help.
- **If you have problems with anxiety or depression,**

- **seek professional help** as soon as possible.
- **Learn to recognize when you're stressed** and how this affects your body — and regularly practice stress management and relaxation techniques.
- **If you think you have somatic symptom disorder, get treatment early** to help stop symptoms from getting worse and impairing your quality of life.
- **Stick with your treatment plan** to help prevent relapses or worsening of symptoms.

Diagnosis

To determine a diagnosis, you'll likely have a physical exam and any tests your doctor recommends. Your doctor or other health care provider can help determine if you have any health conditions that need treatment.

Your medical care provider may also refer you to a mental health professional, who may:

- Conduct a psychological evaluation to talk about your symptoms, fears or concerns, stressful situations, relationship problems, situations you may be avoiding, and family history
- Have you fill out a psychological self-assessment or questionnaire
- Ask you about alcohol, drug or other substance use

Criteria for diagnosis

The Diagnostic and Statistical Manual of Mental Disorders (DSM-5), published by the American Psychiatric Association, emphasizes these points in the diagnosis of somatic symptom disorder:

- You have one or more somatic symptoms — for example, pain or fatigue — that are distressing or

cause problems in your daily life
- You have excessive and persistent thoughts about the seriousness of your symptoms, you have a persistently high level of anxiety about your health or symptoms, or you devote too much time and energy to your symptoms or health concerns
- You continue to have symptoms that concern you, typically for more than six months, even though the symptoms may vary

Treatment

The goal of treatment is to improve your symptoms and your ability to function in daily life. Psychotherapy, also called talk therapy, can be helpful for somatic symptom disorder. Sometimes medications may be added, especially if you're struggling with feeling depressed.

Psychotherapy

Because physical symptoms can be related to psychological distress and a high level of health anxiety, psychotherapy — specifically, cognitive behavioral therapy (CBT) — can help improve physical symptoms.

CBT can help you:
- Examine and adapt your beliefs and expectations about health and physical symptoms
- Learn how to reduce stress
- Learn how to cope with physical symptoms
- Reduce preoccupation with symptoms
- Reduce avoidance of situations and activities due to uncomfortable physical sensations
- Improve daily functioning at home, at work, in relationships and in social situations
- Address depression and other mental health disorders

- Family therapy may also be helpful by examining family relationships and improving family support and functioning.

Medications

Antidepressant medication can help reduce symptoms associated with depression and pain that often occur with somatic symptom disorder.

If one medication doesn't work well for you, your doctor may recommend switching to another or combining certain medications to boost effectiveness. Keep in mind that it can take several weeks after first starting a medication to notice an improvement in symptoms.

Talk with your doctor about medication options and the possible side effects and risks.

Lifestyle and home remedies

While somatic symptom disorder benefits from professional treatment, you can take some lifestyle and self-care steps, including these:

- **Work with your care providers.** Work with your medical care provider and mental health professional to determine a regular schedule for visits to discuss your concerns and build a trusting relationship. Also discuss setting reasonable limits on tests, evaluations and specialist referrals. Avoid seeking advice from multiple doctors or emergency room visits that can make your care more difficult to coordinate and may subject you to duplicate testing.
- **Practice stress management and relaxation techniques.** Learning stress management and relaxation techniques, such as progressive muscle

relaxation, may help improve symptoms.
- **Get physically active.** A graduated activity program may have a calming effect on your mood, improve your physical symptoms and help improve your physical function.
- **Participate in activities.** Stay involved in your work and in social and family activities. Don't wait until your symptoms are resolved to participate.
- **Avoid alcohol and recreational drugs.** Substance use can make your care more difficult. Talk to your health care provider if you need help quitting.

Preparing for your appointment

In addition to a medical evaluation, your primary care provider may refer you to a psychiatrist or psychologist for evaluation and treatment.

What you can do

Before your appointment, make a list of:
- **Your symptoms,** including when they first occurred and how they impact your daily life
- **Key personal information,** including traumatic events in your past and any stressful, major events
- **Medical information,** including other physical or mental health conditions that you have
- **Medications, vitamins,** herbs and other supplements, and the dosages
- **Questions** to ask your medical care provider or mental health professional

Ask a trusted family member or friend to go with you to your appointment, if possible, to lend support and help you remember information.

Questions to ask may include:
- Do I have somatic symptom disorder?

- What treatment approach do you recommend?
- Would therapy be helpful in my case?
- If you're recommending therapy, how often will I need it and for how long?
- If you're recommending medications, are there any possible side effects?
- For how long will I need to take medication?
- How will you monitor whether my treatment is working?
- Are there any self-care steps I can take to help manage my condition?
- Are there any brochures or other printed material that I can have?
- What websites do you recommend?

Don't hesitate to ask any other questions.

What to expect from your doctor

Your medical care provider or mental health professional may ask you questions, such as:

- What are your symptoms, and when did they first occur?
- How do your symptoms affect your life, such as at school, at work and in personal relationships?
- Have you or any of your close relatives been diagnosed with a mental health disorder?
- Have you been diagnosed with any medical conditions?
- Do you use alcohol or recreational drugs? How often?
- Do you get regular physical activity?

Your medical care provider or mental health professional will ask additional questions based on your responses, symptoms and needs. Preparing and anticipating questions will help you make the most of your appointment time..

8. Eating Disorders:

Eating disorders are serious conditions related to persistent eating behaviors that negatively impact your health, your emotions and your ability to function in important areas of life. The most common eating disorders are anorexia nervosa, bulimia nervosa and binge-eating disorder. Most eating disorders involve focusing too much on your weight, body shape and food, leading to dangerous eating behaviors. These behaviors can significantly impact your body's ability to get appropriate nutrition. Eating disorders can harm the heart, digestive system, bones, and teeth and mouth, and lead to other diseases.

Eating disorders often develop in the teen and young adult years, although they can develop at other ages. With treatment, you can return to healthier eating habits and sometimes reverse serious complications caused by the eating disorder.

Some common eating disorders include:

- Anorexia nervosa
- Bulimia nervosa
- Binge eating disorder
- Pica eating disorder
- Rumination disorder

It is estimated that *9% of the global population* has some form of an eating disorder. Anorexia nervosa and bulimia nervosa are the two major eating disorders described in the DSM-IV. International studies suggest that the prevalence of eating disorders is increasing, and that between *1 and 4% of young women* may be affected by these disorders (American Psychiatric Association 1993). Eating disorders would be expected to occur at similar rates among South Africans who espouse Western values. Persons with anorexia nervosa tend to present during their teenage years, while bulimia nervosa presents in late adolescence and in early adulthood. Bulimia is more common than anorexia nervosa. High-risk groups for eating disorders include *ballet dancers, models and gymnasts*. In the past, persons with eating disorders have tended to come from affluent Western caucasian populations, but knowledge that is accumulating both locally and internationally suggests that other ethnic groups, social classes, and age groups are also at risk (Szabo et al 1995). The female to male ratio for the occurrence of these disorders is estimated to be 10 to 1.

ANOREXIA NERVOSA

Anorexia (an-o-REK-see-uh) nervosa — often simply called anorexia — is an eating disorder characterized by an abnormally low body weight, an intense fear of gaining weight and a distorted perception of weight. People with anorexia place a high value on controlling their weight and shape, using extreme efforts that tend to significantly interfere with their lives.

To prevent weight gain or to continue losing weight, people with anorexia usually severely restrict the amount of food they eat. They may control calorie intake by vomiting after eating or by misusing laxatives, diet aids, diuretics or enemas. They may also try to lose weight by exercising excessively. No matter how much weight is lost, the person continues to fear weight gain. Anorexia isn't really about food. It's an extremely unhealthy and sometimes life-threatening way to try to cope with emotional problems. When you have anorexia, you often equate thinness with self-worth.

Anorexia, like other eating disorders, can take over your life and can be very difficult to overcome. But with treatment, you can gain a better sense of who you are, return to healthier eating habits and reverse some of anorexia's serious complications.

Symptoms

The physical signs and symptoms of anorexia nervosa are related to starvation. Anorexia also includes emotional and behavioral issues involving an unrealistic perception of body weight and an extremely strong fear of gaining weight or becoming fat.

It may be difficult to notice signs and symptoms because what is considered a low body weight is different for each person, and some individuals may not appear extremely thin. Also, people with anorexia often disguise their thinness, eating habits or physical problems.

Physical symptoms

Physical signs and symptoms of anorexia may include:

- Extreme weight loss or not making expected developmental weight gains
- Thin appearance
- Abnormal blood counts
- Fatigue
- Insomnia
- Dizziness or fainting
- Bluish discoloration of the fingers
- Hair that thins, breaks or falls out
- Soft, downy hair covering the body
- Absence of menstruation
- Constipation and abdominal pain
- Dry or yellowish skin
- Intolerance of cold
- Irregular heart rhythms
- Low blood pressure
- Dehydration
- Swelling of arms or legs
- Eroded teeth and calluses on the knuckles from induced vomiting

Some people who have anorexia binge and purge, similar to individuals who have bulimia. But people with anorexia generally struggle with an abnormally low body weight, while individuals with bulimia typically are normal to above normal weight.

Emotional and behavioral symptoms

Behavioral symptoms of anorexia may include attempts to lose weight by:

- Severely restricting food intake through dieting or fasting
- Exercising excessively
- Bingeing and self-induced vomiting to get rid of food, which may include the use of laxatives, enemas, diet aids or herbal products

Emotional and behavioral signs and symptoms may include:

- Preoccupation with food, which sometimes includes cooking elaborate meals for others but not eating them
- Frequently skipping meals or refusing to eat
- Denial of hunger or making excuses for not eating
- Eating only a few certain "safe" foods, usually those low in fat and calories
- Adopting rigid meal or eating rituals, such as spitting food out after chewing
- Not wanting to eat in public
- Lying about how much food has been eaten
- Fear of gaining weight that may include repeated weighing or measuring the body
- Frequent checking in the mirror for perceived flaws
- Complaining about being fat or having parts of the body that are fat
- Covering up in layers of clothing
- Flat mood (lack of emotion)
- Social withdrawal
- Irritability
- Insomnia
- Reduced interest in sex

When to see a doctor

Unfortunately, many people with anorexia don't want treatment, at least initially. Their desire to remain thin overrides concerns about their health. If you have a loved one you're worried about, urge her or him to talk to a doctor.

If you're experiencing any of the problems listed above, or if you think you may have an eating disorder, get help. If you're hiding your anorexia from loved ones, try to find a person you trust to talk to about what's going on.

Causes

The exact cause of anorexia is unknown. As with many diseases, it's probably a combination of biological, psychological and environmental factors.

- **Biological.** Although it's not yet clear which genes are involved, there may be genetic changes that make some people at higher risk of developing anorexia. Some people may have a genetic tendency toward perfectionism, sensitivity and perseverance — all traits associated with anorexia.
- **Psychological.** Some people with anorexia may have obsessive-compulsive personality traits that make it easier to stick to strict diets and forgo food despite being hungry. They may have an extreme drive for perfectionism, which causes them to think they're never thin enough. And they may have high levels of anxiety and engage in restrictive eating to reduce it.
- **Environmental.** Modern Western culture emphasizes thinness. Success and worth are often equated with being thin. Peer pressure may help fuel the desire to be thin, particularly among young girls.

Risk factors

Anorexia is more common in girls and women. However, boys and men have increasingly developed eating disorders, possibly related to growing social pressures.

Anorexia is also more common among teenagers. Still, people of any age can develop this eating disorder, though it's rare in those over 40. Teens may be more at risk because of all the changes their bodies go through during puberty. They may also face increased peer pressure and be more sensitive to criticism or even casual comments about weight or body shape.

Certain factors increase the risk of anorexia, including:

- **Genetics.** Changes in specific genes may put certain people at higher risk of anorexia. Those with a first-degree relative — a parent, sibling or child — who had the disorder have a much higher risk of anorexia.
- Dieting and starvation. Dieting is a risk factor for developing an eating disorder. There is strong evidence that many of the symptoms of anorexia are actually symptoms of starvation. Starvation affects the brain and influences mood changes, rigidity in thinking, anxiety and reduction in appetite. Starvation and weight loss may change the way the brain works in vulnerable individuals, which may perpetuate restrictive eating behaviors and make it difficult to return to normal eating habits.
- **Transitions.** Whether it's a new school, home or job; a relationship breakup; or the death or illness of a loved one, change can bring emotional stress and increase the risk of anorexia.

Complications

Anorexia can have numerous complications. At its most severe, it can be fatal. Death may occur suddenly — even when someone is not severely underweight. This may result from abnormal heart rhythms (arrhythmias) or an imbalance of electrolytes — minerals such as sodium, potassium and calcium that maintain the balance of fluids in your body.

Other complications of anorexia include:

Anaemia

- Heart problems, such as mitral valve prolapse, abnormal heart rhythms or heart failure
- Bone loss (osteoporosis), increasing the risk of fractures
- Loss of muscle
- In females, absence of a period
- In males, decreased testosterone
- Gastrointestinal problems, such as constipation, bloating or nausea
- Electrolyte abnormalities, such as low blood potassium, sodium and chloride
- Kidney problems

If a person with anorexia becomes severely malnourished, every organ in the body can be damaged, including the brain, heart and kidneys. This damage may not be fully reversible, even when the anorexia is under control.

In addition to the host of physical complications, people with anorexia also commonly have other mental health disorders as well. They may include:

- Depression, anxiety and other mood disorders
- Personality disorders
- Obsessive-compulsive disorders

- Alcohol and substance misuse
- Self-injury, suicidal thoughts or suicide attempts

Prevention

There's no guaranteed way to prevent anorexia nervosa. Primary care physicians (pediatricians, family physicians and internists) may be in a good position to identify early indicators of anorexia and prevent the development of full-blown illness. For instance, they can ask questions about eating habits and satisfaction with appearance during routine medical appointments.

If you notice that a family member or friend has low self-esteem, severe dieting habits and dissatisfaction with appearance, consider talking to him or her about these issues. Although you may not be able to prevent an eating disorder from developing, you can talk about healthier behavior or treatment options.

Diagnosis

If your doctor suspects that you have anorexia nervosa, he or she will typically do several tests and exams to help pinpoint a diagnosis, rule out medical causes for the weight loss, and check for any related complications.

These exams and tests generally include:

- **Physical exam.** This may include measuring your height and weight; checking your vital signs, such as heart rate, blood pressure and temperature; checking your skin and nails for problems; listening to your heart and lungs; and examining your abdomen.
- **Lab tests.** These may include a complete blood count (CBC) and more-specialized blood tests to check electrolytes and protein as well as functioning of your liver, kidney and thyroid. A

urinalysis also may be done.
- **Psychological evaluation.** A doctor or mental health professional will likely ask about your thoughts, feelings and eating habits. You may also be asked to complete psychological self-assessment questionnaires.
- **Other studies.** X-rays may be taken to check your bone density, check for stress fractures or broken bones, or check for pneumonia or heart problems. Electrocardiograms may be done to look for heart irregularities.

Your mental health professional also may use the diagnostic criteria for anorexia in the Diagnostic and Statistical Manual of Mental Disorders (DSM-5), published by the American Psychiatric Association.

Treatment

Treatment for anorexia is generally done using a team approach, which includes doctors, mental health professionals and dietitians, all with experience in eating disorders. Ongoing therapy and nutrition education are highly important to continued recovery.

Here's a look at what's commonly involved in treating people with anorexia.

Hospitalization and other programs

If your life is in immediate danger, you may need treatment in a hospital emergency room for such issues as a heart rhythm disturbance, dehydration, electrolyte imbalances or a psychiatric emergency. Hospitalization may be required for medical complications, severe psychiatric problems, severe malnutrition or continued refusal to eat.

Medical care

Because of the host of complications anorexia causes, you may need frequent monitoring of vital signs, hydration level and electrolytes, as well as related physical conditions. In severe cases, people with anorexia may initially require feeding through a tube that's placed in their nose and goes to the stomach (nasogastric tube).

Care is usually coordinated by a primary care doctor or a mental health professional, with other professionals involved.

Restoring a healthy weight

The first goal of treatment is getting back to a healthy weight. You can't recover from anorexia without returning to a healthy weight and learning proper nutrition. Those involved in this process may include:

- **Your primary care doctor,** who can provide medical care and supervise your calorie needs and weight gain
- **A psychologist or other mental health professional,** who can work with you to develop behavioral strategies to help you return to a healthy weight
- **A dietitian,** who can offer guidance getting back to regular patterns of eating, including providing specific meal plans and calorie requirements that help you meet your weight goals
- **Your family,** who will likely be involved in helping you maintain normal eating habits

Psychotherapy

These types of therapy may be beneficial for anorexia:

- **Family-based therapy.** This is the only evidence-based treatment for teenagers with anorexia.

Because the teenager with anorexia is unable to make good choices about eating and health while in the grips of this serious condition, this therapy mobilizes parents to help their child with re-feeding and weight restoration until the child can make good choices about health.
- **Individual therapy.** For adults, cognitive behavioral therapy — specifically enhanced cognitive behavioral therapy — has been shown to help. The main goal is to normalize eating patterns and behaviors to support weight gain. The second goal is to help change distorted beliefs and thoughts that maintain restrictive eating.

Medications

No medications are approved to treat anorexia because none has been found to work very well. However, antidepressants or other psychiatric medications can help treat other mental health disorders you may also have, such as depression or anxiety.

Treatment challenges in anorexia

One of the biggest challenges in treating anorexia is that people may not want treatment. Barriers to treatment may include:

- Thinking you don't need treatment
- Fearing weight gain
- Not seeing anorexia as an illness but rather a lifestyle choice

People with anorexia can recover. However, they're at increased risk of relapse during periods of high stress or during triggering situations. Ongoing therapy or periodic appointments during times of stress may help you stay healthy.

Lifestyle and home remedies

When you have anorexia, it can be difficult to take care of yourself properly. In addition to professional treatment, follow these steps:

- **Stick to your treatment plan.** Don't skip therapy sessions and try not to stray from meal plans, even if they make you uncomfortable.
- **Talk to your doctor about appropriate vitamin and mineral supplements.** If you're not eating well, chances are your body isn't getting all of the nutrients it needs, such as Vitamin D or iron. However, getting most of your vitamins and minerals from food is typically recommended.
- **Don't isolate yourself** from caring family members and friends who want to see you get healthy. Understand that they have your best interests at heart.
- **Resist urges to weigh yourself** or check yourself in the mirror frequently. These may do nothing but fuel your drive to maintain unhealthy habits.

Alternative medicine

Dietary supplements and herbal products designed to suppress the appetite or aid in weight loss may be abused by people with anorexia. Weight-loss supplements or herbs can have serious side effects and dangerously interact with other medications. These products do not go through a rigorous review process and may have ingredients that are not posted on the bottle.

Keep in mind that natural doesn't always mean safe. If you use dietary supplements or herbs, discuss the potential risks with your doctor.

Anxiety-reducing approaches that complement anorexia

treatment may increase the sense of well-being and promote relaxation. Examples of these approaches include massage, yoga and meditation.

Coping and support

You may find it difficult to cope with anorexia when you're hit with mixed messages by the media, culture, and perhaps your own family or friends. You may even have heard people joke that they wish they could have anorexia for a while so that they could lose weight.

Whether you have anorexia or your loved one has anorexia, ask your doctor or mental health professional for advice on coping strategies and emotional support. Learning effective coping strategies and getting the support you need from family and friends are vital to successful treatment.

What you can do

Before your appointment, make a list of:

- **Any symptoms you're experiencing,** including any that may seem unrelated to the reason for the appointment. Try to recall when your symptoms began.
- **Key personal information,** including any major stresses or recent life changes.
- **All medications,** vitamins, herbal products, over-the-counter medications and other supplements that you're taking, and their dosages.
- **Questions** to ask your doctor so that you'll remember to cover everything you wanted to.

Some questions you might want to ask your doctor or mental health professional include:

- What kinds of tests do I need? Do these tests require any special preparation?

- Is this condition temporary or long lasting?
- What treatments are available, and which do you recommend?
- Is there a generic alternative to the medicine you're prescribing?
- Are there any brochures or other printed material that I can have? What websites do you recommend?

Don't hesitate to ask other questions during your appointment.

What to expect from your doctor

Your doctor or mental health professional is likely to ask you a number of questions, including:

- How long have you been worried about your weight?
- Do you exercise? How often?
- What ways have you used to lose weight?
- Are you having any physical symptoms?
- Have you ever vomited because you were uncomfortably full?
- Have others expressed concern that you're too thin?
- Do you think about food often?
- Do you ever eat in secret?
- Have any of your family members ever had symptoms of an eating disorder or been diagnosed with an eating disorder?

Be ready to answer these questions to reserve time to go over any points you want to focus on.

BULIMIA NERVOSA

Bulimia (boo-LEE-me-uh) nervosa, commonly called bulimia, is a serious, potentially life-threatening eating disorder. People with bulimia may secretly binge — eating large amounts of food with a loss of control over the eating — and then purge, trying to get rid of the extra calories in an unhealthy way.

To get rid of calories and prevent weight gain, people with bulimia may use different methods. For example, you may regularly self-induce vomiting or misuse laxatives, weight-loss supplements, diuretics or enemas after bingeing. Or you may use other ways to rid yourself of calories and prevent weight gain, such as fasting, strict dieting or excessive exercise.

If you have bulimia, you're probably preoccupied with your weight and body shape. You may judge yourself severely and harshly for your self-perceived flaws. Because it's related to self-image — and not just about food — bulimia can be hard to overcome. But effective treatment can help you feel better about yourself, adopt healthier eating patterns and reverse serious complications.

Symptoms

Bulimia signs and symptoms may include:

- Being preoccupied with your body shape and weight
- Living in fear of gaining weight
- Repeated episodes of eating abnormally large amounts of food in one sitting
- Feeling a loss of control during bingeing — like you can't stop eating or can't control what you eat

- Forcing yourself to vomit or exercising too much to keep from gaining weight after bingeing
- Using laxatives, diuretics or enemas after eating when they're not needed
- Fasting, restricting calories or avoiding certain foods between binges
- Using dietary supplements or herbal products excessively for weight loss

The severity of bulimia is determined by the number of times a week that you purge, usually at least once a week for at least three months.

Helping a loved one with bulimia symptoms

If you think a loved one may have symptoms of bulimia, have an open and honest discussion about your concerns. You can't force someone to seek professional care, but you can offer encouragement and support. You can also help find a qualified doctor or mental health professional, make an appointment, and even offer to go along.

Because most people with bulimia are usually normal weight or slightly overweight, it may not be apparent to others that something is wrong. Red flags that family and friends may notice include:

- Constantly worrying or complaining about being fat
- Having a distorted, excessively negative body image
- Repeatedly eating unusually large quantities of food in one sitting, especially foods the person would normally avoid
- Strict dieting or fasting after binge eating
- Not wanting to eat in public or in front of others
- Going to the bathroom right after eating, during meals or for long periods of time
- Exercising too much

- Having sores, scars or calluses on the knuckles or hands
- Having damaged teeth and gums
- Changing weight
- Swelling in the hands and feet
- Facial and cheek swelling from enlarged glands

Causes

The exact cause of bulimia is unknown. Many factors could play a role in the development of eating disorders, including genetics, biology, emotional health, societal expectations and other issues.

Risk factors

Girls and women are more likely to have bulimia than boys and men are. Bulimia often begins in the late teens or early adulthood.

Factors that increase your risk of bulimia may include:

- **Biology.** People with first-degree relatives (siblings, parents or children) with an eating disorder may be more likely to develop an eating disorder, suggesting a possible genetic link. Being overweight as a child or teen may increase the risk.
- **Psychological and emotional issues.** Psychological and emotional problems, such as depression, anxiety disorders or substance use disorders are closely linked with eating disorders. People with bulimia may feel negatively about themselves. In some cases, traumatic events and environmental stress may be contributing factors.
- **Dieting.** People who diet are at higher risk of developing eating disorders. Many people with bulimia severely restrict calories between binge episodes, which may trigger an urge to again binge

eat and then purge. Other triggers for bingeing can include stress, poor body self-image, food and boredom.

Complications

Bulimia may cause numerous serious and even life-threatening complications. Possible complications include:
- Negative self-esteem and problems with relationships and social functioning
- Dehydration, which can lead to major medical problems, such as kidney failure
- Heart problems, such as an irregular heartbeat or heart failure
- Severe tooth decay and gum disease
- Absent or irregular periods in females
- Digestive problems
- Anxiety, depression, personality disorders or bipolar disorder
- Misuse of alcohol or drugs
- Self-injury, suicidal thoughts or suicide

Prevention

Although there's no sure way to prevent bulimia, you can steer someone toward healthier behavior or professional treatment before the situation worsens. Here's how you can help:
- Foster and reinforce a healthy body image in your children, no matter what their size or shape. Help them build confidence in ways other than their appearance.
- Have regular, enjoyable family meals.
- Avoid talking about weight at home. Focus instead on having a healthy lifestyle.
- Discourage dieting, especially when it involves

unhealthy weight-control behaviors, such as fasting, using weight-loss supplements or laxatives, or self-induced vomiting.
- Talk with your primary care provider. He or she may be in a good position to identify early indicators of an eating disorder and help prevent its development.
- If you notice a relative or friend who seems to have food issues that could lead to or indicate an eating disorder, consider supportively talking to the person about these issues and ask how you can help.

Diagnosis

If your primary care provider suspects you have bulimia, he or she will typically:

- Talk to you about your eating habits, weight-loss methods and physical symptoms
- Do a physical exam
- Request blood and urine tests
- Request a test that can identify problems with your heart (electrocardiogram)
- Perform a psychological evaluation, including a discussion of your attitude toward your body and weight
- Use the criteria for bulimia listed in the Diagnostic and Statistical Manual of Mental Disorders (DSM-5), published by the American Psychiatric Association

Your primary care provider may also request additional tests to help pinpoint a diagnosis, rule out medical causes for weight changes and check for any related complications.

Treatment

When you have bulimia, you may need several types of treatment, although combining psychotherapy with antidepressants may be the most effective for overcoming the disorder.

Treatment generally involves a team approach that includes you, your family, your primary care provider, a mental health professional and a dietitian experienced in treating eating disorders. You may have a case manager to coordinate your care.

Psychotherapy

Psychotherapy, also known as talk therapy or psychological counseling, involves discussing your bulimia and related issues with a mental health professional. Evidence indicates that these types of psychotherapy help improve symptoms of bulimia:

- **Cognitive behavioral therapy** to help you normalize your eating patterns and identify unhealthy, negative beliefs and behaviors and replace them with healthy, positive ones
- **Family-based treatment** to help parents intervene to stop their teenager's unhealthy eating behaviors, to help the teen regain control over his or her eating, and to help the family deal with problems that bulimia can have on the teen's development and the family
- **Interpersonal psychotherapy,** which addresses difficulties in your close relationships, helping to improve your communication and problem-solving skill

Medications

Antidepressants may help reduce the symptoms of bulimia when used along with psychotherapy. The only antidepressant specifically approved by the Food and Drug Administration to treat bulimia is fluoxetine (Prozac), a type of selective serotonin reuptake inhibitor (SSRI), which may help even if you're not depressed.

Nutrition education

Dietitians can design an eating plan to help you achieve healthy eating habits to avoid hunger and cravings and to provide good nutrition. Eating regularly and not restricting your food intake is important in overcoming bulimia.

Hospitalization

Bulimia can usually be treated outside of the hospital. But if symptoms are severe, with serious health complications, you may need treatment in a hospital. Some eating disorder programs may offer day treatment rather than inpatient hospitalization.

Treatment challenges in bulimia

Although most people with bulimia do recover, some find that symptoms don't go away entirely. Periods of bingeing and purging may come and go through the years, depending on your life circumstances, such as recurrence during times of high stress. If you find yourself back in the binge-purge cycle, follow-up sessions with your primary care provider, dietitian and/or mental health professional may help you weather the crisis before your eating disorder spirals out of control again. Learning positive ways to cope, creating healthy relationships and managing stress can help prevent a relapse.

If you've had an eating disorder in the past and you notice your symptoms returning, seek help from your medical team immediately.

Lifestyle and home remedies

In addition to professional treatment, follow these self-care tips:

- **Stick to your treatment plan.** Don't skip therapy sessions and try not to stray from meal plans, even if they make you uncomfortable.
- **Learn about bulimia.** Education about your condition can empower you and motivate you to stick to your treatment plan.
- **Get the right nutrition.** If you aren't eating well or you're frequently purging, it's likely your body isn't getting all of the nutrients it needs. Talk to your primary care provider or dietitian about appropriate vitamin and mineral supplements. However, getting most of your vitamins and minerals from food is typically recommended.
- **Stay in touch.** Don't isolate yourself from caring family members and friends who want to see you get healthy. Understand that they have your best interests at heart and that nurturing, caring relationships are healthy for you.
- **Be kind to yourself.** Resist urges to weigh yourself or check yourself in the mirror frequently. These may do nothing but fuel your drive to maintain unhealthy habits.
- **Be cautious with exercise.** Talk to your primary care provider about what kind of physical activity, if any, is appropriate for you, especially if you exercise excessively to burn off post-binge calories.

Alternative medicine

Dietary supplements and herbal products designed to suppress the appetite or aid in weight loss may be abused by people with eating disorders. Weight-loss supplements or herbs can have serious side effects and dangerously interact with other medications.

Weight-loss and other dietary supplements don't need approval by the Food and Drug Administration (FDA) to go on the market. And natural doesn't always mean safe. If you choose to use dietary supplements or herbs, discuss the potential risks with your primary care provider.

Coping and support

You may find it difficult to cope with bulimia when you're hit with mixed messages by the media, culture, coaches, family, and maybe your own friends or peers. So how do you cope with a disease that can be deadly when you're also getting messages that being thin is a sign of success?

- Remind yourself what a healthy weight is for your body.
- Resist the urge to diet or skip meals, which can trigger binge eating.
- Don't visit websites that advocate or glorify eating disorders.
- Identify troublesome situations that trigger thoughts or behaviors that may contribute to your bulimia, and develop a plan to deal with them.
- Have a plan in place to cope with the emotional distress of setbacks.
- Look for positive role models who can help boost your self-esteem.
- Find pleasurable activities and hobbies that can help distract you from thoughts about bingeing and purging.
- Build up your self-esteem by forgiving yourself, focusing on the positive, and giving yourself credit and encouragement.

Coping advice for parents

If you're the parent of someone with bulimia, you may blame yourself for your child's eating disorder. But eating disorders have many causes, and parenting style is not considered a cause. It's best to focus on how you can help your child now.

Here are some suggestions:

- Ask your child what you can do to help. For example, ask if your teenager would like you to plan family activities after meals to reduce the temptation to purge.
- Listen. Allow your child to express feelings.
- Schedule regular family mealtimes. Eating at routine times is important to help reduce binge eating.
- Let your teenager know any concerns you have. But do this without placing blame.

Remember that eating disorders affect the whole family, and you need to take care of yourself, too. If you feel that you aren't coping well with your teen's bulimia, you might benefit from professional counselling. Or ask your child's primary care provider about support groups for parents of children with eating disorders.

- BINGE-EATING DISORDER

Binge-eating disorder is a serious eating disorder in which you frequently consume unusually large amounts of food and feel unable to stop eating. Almost everyone overeats on occasion, such as having seconds or thirds of a holiday meal. But for some people, excessive overeating that feels out of control and becomes a regular occurrence crosses the line to binge-eating disorder.

When you have binge-eating disorder, you may be embarrassed about overeating and vow to stop. But you feel such a compulsion that you can't resist the urges and continue binge eating. If you have binge-eating disorder, treatment can help.

Symptoms

Most people with binge-eating disorder are overweight or obese, but you may be at a normal weight. Behavioral and emotional signs and symptoms of binge-eating disorder include:

- Eating unusually large amounts of food in a specific amount of time, such as over a two-hour period
- Feeling that your eating behavior is out of control
- Eating even when you're full or not hungry
- Eating rapidly during binge episodes
- Eating until you're uncomfortably full
- Frequently eating alone or in secret
- Feeling depressed, disgusted, ashamed, guilty or upset about your eating
- Frequently dieting, possibly without weight loss

Unlike a person with bulimia, after a binge, you don't regularly compensate for extra calories eaten by vomiting, using laxatives or exercising excessively. You may try to diet or eat normal meals. But restricting your diet may simply lead to more binge eating.

The severity of binge-eating disorder is determined by how often episodes of bingeing occur during a week.

When to see a doctor

If you have any symptoms of binge-eating disorder, seek medical help as soon as possible. Binge-eating problems can vary in their course from short-lived to recurrent or they may persist for years if left untreated.

Talk to your medical care provider or a mental health professional about your binge-eating symptoms and feelings. If you're reluctant to seek treatment, talk to someone you trust about what you're going through. A friend, loved one, teacher or faith leader can help you take the first steps to successful treatment of binge-eating disorder.

Helping a loved one who has symptoms

A person with binge-eating disorder may become an expert at hiding behavior, making it hard for others to detect the problem. If you have a loved one you think may have symptoms of binge-eating disorder, have an open and honest discussion about your concerns.

Provide encouragement and support. Offer to help your loved one find a qualified medical care provider or mental health professional and make an appointment. You might even offer to go along.

Causes

The causes of binge-eating disorder are unknown. But genetics, biological factors, long-term dieting and psychological issues increase your risk.

Risk factors

Binge-eating disorder is more common in women than in men. Although people of any age can have binge-eating disorder, it often begins in the late teens or early 20s.

Factors that can increase your risk of developing binge-eating disorder include:

- **Family history.** You're much more likely to have an eating disorder if your parents or siblings have (or had) an eating disorder. This may indicate that inherited genes increase the risk of developing an eating disorder.
- **Dieting.** Many people with binge-eating disorder have a history of dieting. Dieting or restricting calories during the day may trigger an urge to binge eat, especially if you have symptoms of depression.
- **Psychological issues.** Many people who have binge-eating disorder feel negatively about themselves and their skills and accomplishments. Triggers for bingeing can include stress, poor body self-image and the availability of preferred binge foods.

Complications

You may develop psychological and physical problems related to binge eating.

Complications that may be caused by binge-eating disorder include:

- Poor quality of life
- Problems functioning at work, with your personal life or in social situations

- Social isolation
- Obesity
- Medical conditions related to obesity, such as joint problems, heart disease, type 2 diabetes, gastroesophageal reflux disease (GERD) and some sleep-related breathing disorders

Psychiatric disorders that are often linked with binge-eating disorder include:

- Depression
- Bipolar disorder
- Anxiety
- Substance use disorders

Prevention

Although there's no sure way to prevent binge-eating disorder, if you have symptoms of binge eating, seek professional help. Your medical care provider can advise you on where to get help.

If you think a friend or loved one has a binge-eating problem, steer her or him toward healthier behavior and professional treatment before the situation worsens. If you have a child:

- **Foster and reinforce a healthy body image,** regardless of body shape or size
- **Discuss any concerns with your child's primary care provider,** who may be in a good position to identify early indicators of an eating disorder and help prevent its development

Diagnosis

To diagnose binge-eating disorder, your medical care

provider may recommend a psychological evaluation, including discussion of your eating habits.

Your medical care provider also may want you to have other tests to check for health consequences of binge-eating disorder, such as high cholesterol, high blood pressure, heart problems, diabetes, GERD and some sleep-related breathing disorders. These tests may include:

- A physical exam
- Blood and urine tests
- A sleep disorder center consultation

Treatment

The goals for treatment of binge-eating disorder are to reduce eating binges and achieve healthy eating habits. Because binge eating can be so entwined with shame, poor self-image and other negative emotions, treatment may also address these and any other mental health issues, such as depression. By getting help for binge eating, you can learn how to feel more in control of your eating.

Psychotherapy

Whether in individual or group sessions, psychotherapy (also called talk therapy) can help teach you how to exchange unhealthy habits for healthy ones and reduce bingeing episodes. Examples of psychotherapy include:

- **Cognitive behavioral therapy (CBT).** CBT may help you cope better with issues that can trigger binge-eating episodes, such as negative feelings about your body or a depressed mood. It may also give you a better sense of control over your behavior and help you regulate eating patterns.
- **Interpersonal psychotherapy.** This type of therapy focuses on your relationships with other people.

The goal is to improve your interpersonal skills — how you relate to others, including family, friends and co-workers. This may help reduce binge eating that's triggered by problematic relationships and unhealthy communication skills.
- **Dialectical behavior therapy.** This form of therapy can help you learn behavioral skills to help you tolerate stress, regulate your emotions and improve your relationships with others, all of which can reduce the desire to binge eat.

Medications

Lisdexamfetamine dimesylate (Vyvanse), a drug for attention-deficit hyperactivity disorder, is the first FDA-approved medication to treat moderate to severe binge-eating disorder in adults. A stimulant, Vyvanse can be habit-forming and abused. Common side effects include a dry mouth and insomnia, but more-serious side effects can occur.

Several other types of medication may help reduce symptoms. Examples include:
- **Topiramate (Topamax), an anticonvulsant.** Normally used to control seizures, topiramate has also been found to reduce binge-eating episodes. However, there are side effects, such as dizziness, nervousness, sleepiness and trouble concentrating, so discuss the risks and benefits with your medical care provider.
- **Antidepressants.** Antidepressants may reduce binge-eating. It's not clear how these can reduce binge eating, but it may relate to how they affect certain brain chemicals associated with mood.

While these medications can be helpful in controlling binge-eating episodes, they may not have much impact on weight reduction.

Behavioral weight-loss programs

Many people with binge-eating disorder have a history of failed attempts to lose weight on their own. However, weight-loss programs typically aren't recommended until the binge-eating disorder is treated, because dieting may trigger more binge-eating episodes, making weight loss less successful.

When appropriate, weight-loss programs are generally done under medical supervision to ensure that your nutritional requirements are met. Weight-loss programs that address binge triggers can be especially helpful when you're also getting cognitive behavioral therapy.

Lifestyle and home remedies

Typically, treating binge-eating disorder on your own isn't effective. But in addition to professional help, you can take these self-care steps to reinforce your treatment plan:

- **Stick to your treatment.** Don't skip therapy sessions. If you have a meal plan, do your best to stick to it and don't let setbacks derail your overall efforts.
- **Avoid dieting, unless it's supervised.** Trying to diet can trigger more binge episodes, leading to a vicious cycle that's hard to break. Talk with your medical care provider about appropriate weight management strategies for you — don't diet unless it's recommended for your eating disorder treatment and supervised by your medical care provider.
- **Eat breakfast.** Many people with binge-eating disorder skip breakfast. But, if you eat breakfast,

you may be less prone to eating higher calorie meals later in the day.
- **Arrange your environment.** Availability of certain foods can trigger binges for some people. Keep tempting binge foods out of your home or limit your exposure to those foods as best you can.
- **Get the right nutrients.** Just because you may be eating a lot during binges doesn't mean you're eating the kinds of food that supply all the essential nutrients. Ask your medical care provider if you need to adjust your diet to provide essential vitamins and minerals.
- **Stay connected.** Don't isolate yourself from caring family members and friends who want to see you get healthy. Understand that they have your best interests at heart.
- **Get active.** Ask your medical care provider what kind of physical activity is appropriate for you, especially if you have health problems related to being overweight.

Alternative medicine

Most dietary supplements and herbal products designed to suppress the appetite or aid in weight loss are ineffective and may be misused by people with eating disorders. And natural doesn't always mean safe. Weight-loss supplements or herbs can have serious side effects and dangerously interact with other medications.

If you use dietary supplements or herbs, discuss the potential risks with your medical care provider.

Coping and support

Living with an eating disorder is especially difficult because you have to deal with food on a daily basis. Here are some tips to help you cope:

- **Ease up on yourself.** Don't buy into your own self-criticism.
- **Identify situations that may trigger destructive eating behavior** so you can develop a plan of action to deal with them.
- **Look for positive role models who can help lift your self-esteem.** Remind yourself that the ultrathin models or actresses showcased in women's magazines often don't represent healthy, realistic bodies.
- **Try to find a trusted relative or friend** whom you can talk with about what's going on.
- **Try to find someone who can be your partner** in the battle against binge eating — someone you can call on for support instead of bingeing.
- **Find healthy ways to nurture yourself** by doing something just for fun or to relax, such as yoga, meditation or simply a walk.
- **Consider journaling about your feelings and behaviors.** Journaling can make you more aware of your feelings and actions, and how they're related.

- PICA EATING DISORDER

Pica is an eating disorder where a person compulsively eats things that aren't food and don't have any nutritional value or purpose. Depending on when and why a person does this, pica can be normal, expected and harmless. However, it can cause major problems if a person with this condition eats something toxic or dangerous.

Pronounced "PIKE-ah," pica gets its name from a bird species, the Eurasian magpie (the formal Latin name for that species is Pica pica). This bird has a reputation for eating unusual objects.

Who does pica affect?

Pica can happen to anyone at any age but tends to happen in three specific groups of people:

- Young children, especially those under 6 years old.
- People who are pregnant.
- People with certain mental health conditions, especially autism spectrum disorder, intellectual disabilities or schizophrenia.

How common is pica?

Pica is a relatively common condition, but experts aren't sure exactly how common it is. That's partly because research studies often don't use the same definition for this condition.

It's also common for healthcare providers to miss the condition entirely. This can happen when people don't tell their doctor about it or don't report signs of it in their children.

Yet another reason is that infants and young children often put things in their mouths, which is part of their normal development. This kind of pica usually goes away on its own very quickly.

How does this condition affect my body?

Pica is a condition where a person compulsively eats things that aren't food and don't have any nutritional value. Because it's compulsive, people with this condition have a very hard time controlling the urge on their own. Pica can have a wide range of effects depending on what non-food item(s) a person eats. For people who eat things like ice — a common behavior for someone who is pregnant — pica is harmless. For others, it can lead to eating dangerous or toxic items. Depending on what you eat, pica can damage your teeth. It can also lead to dangerous problems even when you eat things that aren't toxic. An example is when people eat hair *(known as trichophagia)*, which can get stuck in their digestive tract, causing blockages, tearing or other damage.

Parasites that live in the soil can also infect people who eat dirt or clay *(geophagia)*. People can also contract illnesses from eating faeces (poop), especially pet feces that might contain parasites or other germs.

Symptoms

The sole symptom of pica is compulsively eating things that aren't food or have no nutritional value or benefit. Most people with this condition prefer a single type of non-food item they eat.

However, pica can cause other conditions or issues, which have their own sets of symptoms. Other conditions that can happen because of pica include:

- Anaemia (low iron)
- Ascariasis (roundworm infection)
- Constipation.
- Electrolyte imbalance.

- Irregular heart rhythms (arrhythmias)
- Lead poisoning
- Small intestine and large intestine obstruction/blockage

Common non-food items eaten

People with pica often eat the following:

- Ash
- Baby or talcum powder
- Chalk
- Charcoal
- Clay, dirt or soil
- Coffee grounds
- Eggshells
- Faeces (poop) of any kind.
- Hair, string or thread.
- Ice
- Laundry starch
- Paint chips
- Paper
- Pebbles
- Pet food
- Soap
- Wool or cloth

Causes

Experts don't know exactly why pica happens. However, researchers know certain factors increase the risk of developing it.

- **Cultural or learned behaviors.** Certain types of pica are common, socially accepted behaviors in certain cultures and religions.
- **Stress or anxiety.** Pica might be an outlet or coping mechanism for people with these issues.

- **Negative conditions during childhood.** Pica is more common in children living in low socioeconomic situations (such as poverty), but why this happens is unknown. Some possible explanations include that pica is a coping mechanism for children to deal with situations of abuse or neglect. It also might be attention-seeking behavior, especially when one or both parents are absent for any reason.
- **Nutritional deficiencies.** People who show signs of pica often have mineral or other deficiencies in their diet. Iron (anaemia), calcium and zinc deficiencies are some of the most common reasons people show these signs.
- **Mental health conditions.** These include conditions that a person might develop spontaneously, conditions they had at birth because of disruptions in how they developed in the womb and genetic disorders they inherited from their parents.
- **Medical conditions.** Pregnancy and sickle cell anemia are two conditions that have connections to pica.
- **Certain medications** increase the risk of someone developing pica or similar behaviors. But it's unknown if these medications actually cause people to develop pica.

Diagnosis

Diagnosing pica requires four criteria (with the mentioned exceptions explained after the list):

- **Time.** The diagnosis requires persistent eating items or substances with no food or nutrition value for at least one month.

- **Mental development.** This means a person has developed past a certain point mentally and should know not to eat things that aren't food or have no nutritional value.
- **No social and cultural factors.** This means the person doesn't have social or cultural background reasons to explain the behavior.
- **No medical or mental health conditions.** This means pica isn't happening because of any other conditions.

Reasons to not diagnose pica

While pica is an extremely common behavior for several reasons, many of those also disqualify diagnosing it. These include:

- **Cultural or social practices.** True pica is a compulsive behavior that you can't control. People with pica behaviors for cultural or social reasons have control of their actions.
- **Nutritional deficiencies.** People who have low iron or calcium deficiencies often try to compensate for these by eating non-food items. This is actually why pica is acceptable behavior in some cultures. People in certain places around the world eat clay or soil to make up for a lack of iron, calcium or other vitamins and minerals in their diet.
- **Other medical or mental health conditions.** The criteria for diagnosing pica make exceptions for when it happens because of medical and mental health conditions. The only reason to diagnose pica in those circumstances is when it's severe enough to cause health problems or need specific care.

Tests

Most of the tests for pica are looking for problems that

happen because of this condition. These can include a variety of lab, diagnostic and imaging tests, such as:

- **Blood, urine (pee) and stool (poop) tests.** These look for signs of infections, poisoning and electrolyte imbalances.
- **Imaging tests.** These are looking for any signs of blockage or internal damage from this condition. These can include X-rays, computerized tomography (CT) scans, magnetic resonance imaging (MRI), ultrasound and more.
- **Diagnostic tests.** These tests look for indications of serious health problems that can happen with pica. An example of one of these tests is an electrocardiogram (ECG or EKG), which looks for problems with your heart's electrical rhythm that can happen with certain electrolyte imbalances or parasitic infections.

Treatment

Pica in people who are pregnant usually goes away on its own. Children also usually grow out of pica, especially as someone teaches them the difference between edible and non-edible items and objects. For children with intellectual disabilities (or other problems that interfere with learning), removing problematic items and supervision are both very important.

The main form of treatment for pica is therapy, with different therapy methods available depending on the situation and individual needs. A few therapy methods that are possible include:

- **Mild aversive therapy.** This method involves

teaching people to avoid pica behaviors using mild aversions (consequences) to teach people to avoid non-food items and positively reinforcing (rewarding) healthy eating behaviors.
- **Behavioral therapy.** This therapy method involves teaching a person coping mechanisms and strategies to help them change their behavior.
- **Differential reinforcement.** In this method, people learn to avoid pica behaviors by focusing on other behaviors and activities.

Medication

There are very few medications that are likely to help with pica. Antipsychotic medications might help, but the possible side effects usually keep these medications from seeing widespread use.

Taking care of yourself and managing symptoms

Pica is a condition that's usually benign but can become harmful depending on what a person eats. If you have pica, it's important to have an honest discussion with your healthcare provider about it. They can offer guidance and resources to help you or refer you to a healthcare provider who has special training in this condition.

Prevention

Pica happens unpredictably, so there's no way to prevent developing it. There's also no way to reduce your risk of developing this condition.

The only thing you can do that relates to pica is to make sure you eat a balanced diet and don't have any deficiencies in essential vitamins or minerals. While this isn't exactly prevention or reducing risk, because nutritional deficiencies don't count toward a pica diagnosis, this is still important overall.

Prognosis

Pica is a condition that's sometimes dangerous on its own, depending on what non-food items a person eats. The main risks with this condition are when people eat items that are:

- Toxic
- Sharp-edged
- A risk for blocking your digestive tract
- That can cause infections, especially fungi, parasites, bacteria and viruses

How long does this condition last?

Pica is technically a life-long condition because it's not considered curable. People who stop the behavior, either through treatment or who stop on their own, are considered "in remission" as long as they don't resume the behavior.

What's the outlook for pica?

Pica very commonly goes away on its own in children and in people who are pregnant. The condition is usually benign (harmless) for people in these circumstances. The condition itself isn't dangerous, but it can lead to people eating dangerous items. With treatment, this condition can go into remission, and people can live their lives without difficulty from it.

Living with pica

If you have pica, talking to your healthcare provider is an important first step in getting help for it. Their job is to help you while also making sure you feel safe and not judged. They can also help by offering you guidance directly or suggesting an expert who can.

If you have pica and it's causing issues that affect your life,

it's important to keep the following in mind:
- **Be honest with your healthcare provider.** Pica can be a source of embarrassment or shame for many people. That can make it hard for them to talk about how this condition affects their lives. But pica is a mental health condition, meaning it's a medical concern, just like a broken arm or a sinus infection. And, like those conditions, it's good to ask for help and get treatment for this condition.
- **See your healthcare provider as recommended.** Your healthcare provider can set up a schedule of visits as needed. As you progress in treatment, you'll likely need to see them less and less. If this condition starts affecting your life again and you resume pica behaviors, you should return to your healthcare provider and resume treatment.
- **Try to take away items or objects you commonly eat or make it inconvenient to get to them.** One way to prevent or reduce pica behaviors is to remove problematic items or objects as much as possible. If removing them isn't possible, try to make it inconvenient for you to return to pica behaviors.

When should you go to the ER (emergency room)?

Your healthcare provider can guide you in situations where you might need emergency medical care. Overall, you should seek medical attention if you have symptoms of more dangerous conditions, including the following:
- Ascariasis (roundworm infection)
- Electrolyte imbalance
- Irregular heart rhythms (arrhythmias)
- Lead poisoning or other signs of toxic effects
- Small intestine and large intestine obstruction/blockage

You should also seek medical attention for children who swallow any potentially toxic or dangerous items. One example of this is any toy that involves small, magnetic objects, which can easily stick together in the digestive tract and cause life-threatening blockages.

- RUMINATION EATING DISORDER

Rumination syndrome (also known as rumination disorder or merycism) is a feeding and eating disorder in which undigested food comes back up from a person's stomach into his or her mouth (regurgitation). Once the food is back in the mouth, the person may chew it and swallow it again, or spit it out. This behavior usually occurs after every meal, and may appear effortless. Rumination may follow a sensation of burping/belching and typically does not involve nausea or retching. In rumination, the regurgitated food does not tend to taste sour or bitter because it has not had time to fully mix with stomach acid and be digested.

This act of regurgitation is a reflex action that can be a learned and intentional act or can be unintentional. People who have rumination syndrome are not regurgitating food because of a stomach illness or because they feel sick.

Rumination syndrome has been long known to occur in babies and in people with developmental disabilities, but can occur in people of all ages. Children and adults with high levels of stress or anxiety may be at higher risk for rumination syndrome.

Symptoms

The signs and symptoms of rumination syndrome include:
- Regurgitating and re-chewing food on a regular basis
- Digestive problems, such as indigestion and stomach aches
- Dental problems, such as bad breath and tooth decay

- Weight loss
- Chapped lips

Babies who have rumination syndrome may strain or arch their backs (which could also be a sign of gastroesophageal reflux) or make sucking noises with their mouths.

Causes

The exact causes of rumination syndrome are not known. Some people may develop this syndrome if they have emotional problems or if they are undergoing stressful events.

Mechanically, one explanation is that food expands the stomach, which is followed by an increase in abdominal pressure and a relaxation of the lower esophageal sphincter (the juncture where the esophagus [food tube from mouth] meets the stomach). The sequence of events allows stomach contents to be regurgitated.

Diagnosis and Tests

Rumination syndrome can usually be diagnosed based on a medical history and physical exam. In many cases, the patient's symptoms—specifically, the patient has been regurgitating, chewing and swallowing food for at least 3 months, but is not vomiting the food—are enough to make a diagnosis of rumination syndrome.

Officially, according to the Diagnostic and Statistical Manual of Mental Disorders, Fifth Edition, a person must meet the following criteria to be diagnosed with rumination syndrome:

- **Repeated regurgitation of food over a period of at least 1 month.** Regurgitated food may be re-chewed, re-swallowed or spit up.
- **Repeated regurgitation is not due to a**

gastrointestinal or other medical condition (for example, gastroesophageal reflux, pyloric stenosis)
- **The eating disorder must not occur only in the presence of anorexia nervosa, bulimia nervosa, binge eating disorder** or avoidant/restrictive food intake disorder.
- **If the eating disorder occurs together with another mental disorder** (for example, intellectual disability), symptoms must be severe enough and be the main reason for seeking medical care.

Doctors may use tests to rule out other medical issues, such as blockages. These tests may include:

- **Gastric emptying test.** Measures how long it takes for food to move from the stomach to the small intestine.
- **Upper endoscopy.** The doctor examines the esophagus and stomach through an endoscope (a thin tube with a camera on the end) inserted down the throat.
- **X-rays.** Provides doctors with images of the inside of the esophagus and stomach.

Treatment

The main treatment for rumination syndrome is behavioral therapy to stop regurgitation. The behavioral therapy that is usually prescribed for rumination syndrome is diaphragmatic breathing.

The diaphragm is a large, dome-shaped muscle located at the base of the lungs. Diaphragmatic breathing is intended to help you relax the diaphragm and use it correctly while breathing to strengthen it.

To perform diaphragmatic breathing to help control regurgitation:

- Lie on your back on a flat surface or in bed, with your knees bent and your head supported. You can use a pillow under your knees to support your legs. Place one hand on your upper chest and the other just below your rib cage. This will allow you to feel your diaphragm move as you breathe.
- Breathe in slowly through your nose so that your stomach moves out against your hand. Keep the hand on your chest as still as possible. For children, we describe this as "breathing like an opera singer", with the hand on the belly moving out with each slow breath, and moving in with exhalation.
- Tighten your stomach muscles, letting them fall inward as you exhale through pursed lips. Keep the hand on your upper chest as still as possible.

How often should you practice diaphragmatic breathing for rumination syndrome?

Practice this exercise for 5 to 10 minutes, three to four times a day. You can increase the effort of the exercise by placing a book on your abdomen. Individuals can also practice "belly breathing" after each bite or meal, as needed.

Complications

If it is not treated, rumination syndrome can damage the esophagus (the tube leading from the mouth to the stomach). Other complications may include:

- Embarrassment
- Poor nutrition
- Failure to grow
- Electrolyte imbalance
- Dehydration
- Aspiration (inhalation of food into the airway

[trachea/lungs])
- Choking
- Pneumonia
- Death

Prognosis

What is the prognosis (outlook) for people with rumination syndrome?

Many people with rumination syndrome live otherwise healthy lives. Rumination syndrome usually does not affect a person's daily routines.

Living with rumination syndrome

Contact your doctor if you or your child have signs or symptoms of rumination syndrome, especially if you/or your child is regurgitating food on a regular basis.

Prevention

It may be possible to reduce your risk of rumination syndrome by learning more positive coping strategies for stressful situations.

9. Elimination disorders:

Elimination disorders are present in children that urinate or defecate in places other than the toilet. Children with these disorders are usually past the age where such acts are common behavior. This condition is diagnosed in children between the ages of 7 and 12. Elimination disorders primarily fall under enuresis, where urine is passed outside the toilet. Alternately, encopresis is the passage of feces in unsuitable locations away from the toilet. In other cases, it is possible to experience both disorders at the same time.

While some children with these disorders act voluntarily, elimination disorders are frequently characterized by a lack of bowel or bladder control. This means children may urinate or defecate on their beds or clothing without intending to.

Types of Elimination Disorders

Elimination disorders are broadly categorized into enuresis and encopresis.

ENURESIS

This disorder is more commonly known as bedwetting. Children with this condition are unable to control their urine. This usually results in frequent or irregular release on their beds or elsewhere.

In households made up of young children, especially boys —enuresis is a common occurrence. Around 20% of five-year-olds live with this condition. This number goes down to 5%-10% in seven-year-olds. Bedwetting is however more common in the latter age group.

Enuresis may occur in two forms:
1. **Nocturnal only:** Urine is released at night time during sleep
2. **Diurnal only:** Urine incontinence happens during waking hours

Despite taking place during waking hours, diurnal enuresis is involuntary. A child may pass urine where they feel an increased urge to pee.

Other times, this urination is the result of pressure on the abdomen. When children delay urination while in public spaces, this may worsen their chances of involuntary expulsion. Unplanned urination may also take place when laughing.

ENCOPRESIS

As a benchmark, encopresis occurs in children no younger than four years old. This condition is characterized by children passing stool in inappropriate locations like their underwear.

This condition may be voluntary or involuntary, and is a common occurrence in male children. About 4.1% of children between five to six years of age will defecate in unsuitable locations. In 11- to 12-year-olds, this number drops to 1.6%.

Encopresis usually takes place in daytime. This condition may be observed in children that have received, and those that are lacking toilet training.

The disorder is observed in two forms:

1. **Constipation-related encopresis:** In this case, constipation causes stool to be hard and painful to pass. This pain can prevent a child from going to the toilet, leading to greater difficulty in releasing the stool. The strain caused by the feces can weaken colon nerves.3 This can cause liquid or softer stool to leak around the yet-to-be passed stool. The child may also lose control of bowel movements.
2. **Non-retentive fecal incontinence:** this occurs when a child soils their clothing or other inappropriate items without signs of constipation. This child will have bowel movements in unsuitable places or times.

Symptoms

There are notable characteristics of elimination disorders. In either case, the following distinguishing traits are present:

Enuresis

- Repeated bedwetting despite toilet training. This is known as primary enuresis.
- Bedwetting after at least six months of dryness. Otherwise termed secondary enuresis.
- Bedwetting must be frequent for at least two weeks over three consecutive months.

Encopresis

- Stool or liquid stool leakage on underwear
- Constipation
- Straining when stooling
- Dry or hard stool
- Avoiding bowel movements
- Encopretic incidents taking place for at least three months

Diagnosis of Elimination Disorders

Here is how enuresis and encopresis are diagnosed.

Enuresis

To confirm a case of enuresis, other similar disorders should be ruled out. This includes medical conditions such as a UTI, diabetes, seizures, sickle cell, or a sleep disorder.

Likewise, bedwetting could be medication-induced, and not the result of enuresis. SSRIs, antipsychotics, and diuretics may cause incontinence.

When these factors are ruled out, a pediatrician can then determine whether a child is living with enuresis. This may be achieved by examining medical history, or through physical examinations.

Encopresis

When making an encopresis diagnosis, the pediatrician may ask about the child's history of strained bowel movements. This questioning can also require answers about toilet training and diet.

An accurate encopresis diagnosis may also require a rectal examination. The doctor could require an x-ray of the child's abdomen in deciding a diagnosis.

To determine whether encopresis is present, conditions like spinal cord trauma/tumors, cerebral palsy, and diseases of the pelvic muscle and anal sphincter should be assessed.

Causes

Let's take a look a some of the causes behind these two elimination disorders.

Enuresis

There is no precise cause of enuresis. Different factors are however linked to bedwetting, or passing urine in inappropriate places.

For instance, constipation may increase pressure on the bladder, leading to an increased urge to urinate. Deep sleepers who are not easily aroused may also be at higher risk of enuresis.

Where the bladder suffers a delay in maturity, this can affect its capacity to hold urine. Likewise, levels of vasopressin—a hormone that promotes water retention in the kidneys—may decrease. This can impact the chances of holding urine in.

Certain risk factors also increase the chances of enuresis. These include unusual stress in children, growing up in a low socioeconomic environment, divorced parents, the addition of a sibling, or a family history of enuresis.

Encopresis

This condition may result from constipation. A low-fiber diet and poor hydration. Even stress over potty training can contribute to this condition.

Risk factors of encopresis include a low socioeconomic background, fear of using unhygienic toilets, living in a war-torn area, or child hospitalization for another condition. Other contributing factors are bullying and behavioral problems like depression or social anxiety. Poor performance in school could also be a factor.

Treatment of Elimination Disorders

Here are the ways in which these two elimination disorders may be treated:

Enuresis Treatment

There are non-pharmaceutical and pharmaceutical measures available for managing this condition.

Non-Pharmaceutical Management of Enuresis

- **Bell and pad method:** This requires a child to wear a device to sleep. This device contains a sensor that makes a noise when wet to stimulate the child to wake up. The bell and pad method intends to stop the stream, allowing urine to be passed in the toilet instead.
- **Dry Bed Training:** This is another option which combines the bell and pad with behavior treatment for the child with parental support.
- **Nighttime awakenings:** Here, children are woken up at regular hours during the night. This is useful where alarms do not work to alert a child to use the toilet. However, this can lead to sleep problems in the child due to disrupted sleep.

- **Limiting fluid intake:** Children prone to bedwetting can be assisted by restricting their fluid intake before bedtime.
- **Bladder training:** Under this technique, children are taught to hold their urine for longer periods of time. This is useful for diurnal and nocturnal enuresis.
- **Motivational therapy:** The child and their caregivers may receive this therapy to boost morale before beginning any of the methods listed above.

Pharmaceutical Management of Enuresis

Children may be given anti-diuretic hormones (ADH) like desmopressin to manage urine production. Other options include imipramine—a tricyclic antidepressant that helps to relax the bladder, preventing enuretic episodes.

It should be noted that pharmaceutical measures produce higher relapse rates compared to the bell and pad method.

Encopresis Treatment

To manage this condition, a pediatrician may give the affected child a laxative, an enema, or medication to soften the stool. To avoid constipation, parents can encourage a healthy diet high in fiber. Children should also drink more water to alleviate constipation.

Parents can also assist with good bowel habits by planning bathroom time after meals. They may also praise their children for using the toilet. This can encourage regular toilet usage and may prevent excrement on clothing.

10. Sleep-wake disorders:

Sleep disorders are conditions that result in changes in the way that you sleep. A sleep disorder can affect your overall health, safety and quality of life. Sleep deprivation can affect your ability to drive safely and increase your risk of other health problems. Some of the signs and symptoms of sleep disorders include excessive daytime sleepiness, irregular breathing or increased movement during sleep. Other signs and symptoms include an irregular sleep and wake cycle and difficulty falling asleep.

There are many different types of sleep disorders. They're often grouped into categories that explain why they happen or how they affect you. Sleep disorders can also be grouped according to behaviors, problems with your natural sleep-wake cycles, breathing problems, difficulty sleeping or how sleepy you feel during the day.

Some common types of sleep disorders include:

- **Insomnia,** in which you have difficulty falling asleep or staying asleep throughout the night.
- **Sleep apnea,** in which you experience abnormal patterns in breathing while you are asleep. There are several types of sleep apnea.
- **Restless legs syndrome (RLS),** a type of sleep movement disorder. Restless legs syndrome, also called Willis-Ekbom disease, causes an uncomfortable sensation and an urge to move the legs while you try to fall asleep.
- **Narcolepsy,** a condition characterized by extreme sleepiness during the day and falling asleep suddenly during the day.

There are many ways to help diagnose sleep disorders. Doctors can usually treat most sleep disorders effectively once they're correctly diagnosed.

Symptoms

Symptoms of sleep disorders include being very sleepy during the daytime and having trouble falling asleep at night. Some people may fall asleep at inappropriate times, such as while driving. Other symptoms include breathing in an unusual pattern or feeling an uncomfortable urge to move while you are trying to fall asleep. Unusual or bothersome movements or experiences during sleep are also possible. Having an irregular sleep and wake cycle is another symptom of sleep disorders.

- INSOMNIA

Insomnia is a common sleep disorder that can make it hard to fall asleep, hard to stay asleep, or cause you to wake up too early and not be able to get back to sleep. You may still feel tired when you wake up. Insomnia can sap not only your energy level and mood but also your health, work performance and quality of life. How much sleep is enough varies from person to person, but most adults need *seven to eight hours* a night.

At some point, many adults experience short-term (acute) insomnia, which lasts for days or weeks. It's usually the result of stress or a traumatic event. But some people have long-term (chronic) insomnia that lasts for a month or more. Insomnia may be the primary problem, or it may be associated with other medical conditions or medications.

You don't have to put up with sleepless nights. Simple changes in your daily habits can often help.

Symptoms

- Insomnia symptoms may include:
- Difficulty falling asleep at night
- Waking up during the night
- Waking up too early
- Not feeling well-rested after a night's sleep
- Daytime tiredness or sleepiness
- Irritability, depression or anxiety
- Difficulty paying attention, focusing on tasks or remembering
- Increased errors or accidents
- Ongoing worries about sleep

When to see a doctor

If insomnia makes it hard for you to function during the day, see your doctor to identify the cause of your sleep problem and how it can be treated. If your doctor thinks you could have a sleep disorder, you might be referred to a sleep center for special testing.

Causes

Insomnia may be the primary problem, or it may be associated with other conditions.

Chronic insomnia is usually a result of stress, life events or habits that disrupt sleep. Treating the underlying cause can resolve the insomnia, but sometimes it can last for years.

Common causes of chronic insomnia include:

- **Stress.** Concerns about work, school, health, finances or family can keep your mind active at night, making it difficult to sleep. Stressful life events or trauma — such as the death or illness of a loved one, divorce, or a job loss — also may lead to insomnia.
- **Travel or work schedule.** Your circadian rhythms act as an internal clock, guiding such things as your sleep-wake cycle, metabolism and body temperature. Disrupting your body's circadian rhythms can lead to insomnia. Causes include jet lag from traveling across multiple time zones, working a late or early shift, or frequently changing shifts.
- **Poor sleep habits.** Poor sleep habits include an irregular bedtime schedule, naps, stimulating activities before bed, an uncomfortable sleep

environment, and using your bed for work, eating or watching TV. Computers, TVs, video games, smartphones or other screens just before bed can interfere with your sleep cycle.
- **Eating too much late in the evening.** Having a light snack before bedtime is OK, but eating too much may cause you to feel physically uncomfortable while lying down. Many people also experience heartburn, a backflow of acid and food from the stomach into the esophagus after eating, which may keep you awake.

Chronic insomnia may also be associated with medical conditions or the use of certain drugs. Treating the medical condition may help improve sleep, but the insomnia may persist after the medical condition improves.

Additional common causes of insomnia include:
- **Mental health disorders.** Anxiety disorders, such as post-traumatic stress disorder, may disrupt your sleep. Awakening too early can be a sign of depression. Insomnia often occurs with other mental health disorders as well.
- **Medications.** Many prescription drugs can interfere with sleep, such as certain antidepressants and medications for asthma or blood pressure. Many over-the-counter medications — such as some pain medications, allergy and cold medications, and weight-loss products — contain caffeine and other stimulants that can disrupt sleep.
- **Medical conditions.** Examples of conditions linked with insomnia include chronic pain, cancer, diabetes, heart disease, asthma, gastroesophageal reflux disease (GERD), overactive thyroid, Parkinson's disease and Alzheimer's disease.
- **Sleep-related disorders.** Sleep apnea causes you to

stop breathing periodically throughout the night, interrupting your sleep. Restless legs syndrome causes unpleasant sensations in your legs and an almost irresistible desire to move them, which may prevent you from falling asleep.
- **Caffeine, nicotine and alcohol.** Coffee, tea, cola and other caffeinated drinks are stimulants. Drinking them in the late afternoon or evening can keep you from falling asleep at night. Nicotine in tobacco products is another stimulant that can interfere with sleep. Alcohol may help you fall asleep, but it prevents deeper stages of sleep and often causes awakening in the middle of the night.

Insomnia and aging

Insomnia becomes more common with age. As you get older, you may experience:
- **Changes in sleep patterns.** Sleep often becomes less restful as you age, so noise or other changes in your environment are more likely to wake you. With age, your internal clock often advances, so you get tired earlier in the evening and wake up earlier in the morning. But older people generally still need the same amount of sleep as younger people do.
- **Changes in activity.** You may be less physically or socially active. A lack of activity can interfere with a good night's sleep. Also, the less active you are, the more likely you may be to take a daily nap, which can interfere with sleep at night.
- **Changes in health.** Chronic pain from conditions such as arthritis or back problems as well as depression or anxiety can interfere with sleep. Issues that increase the need to urinate during the night —such as prostate or bladder problems — can disrupt sleep. Sleep apnea and restless legs

syndrome become more common with age.
- **More medications.** Older people typically use more prescription drugs than younger people do, which increases the chance of insomnia associated with medications.

Insomnia in children and teens

Sleep problems may be a concern for children and teenagers as well. However, some children and teens simply have trouble getting to sleep or resist a regular bedtime because their internal clocks are more delayed. They want to go to bed later and sleep later in the morning.

Risk factors

Nearly everyone has an occasional sleepless night. But your risk of insomnia is greater if:

- **You're a woman.** Hormonal shifts during the menstrual cycle and in menopause may play a role. During menopause, night sweats and hot flashes often disrupt sleep. Insomnia is also common with pregnancy.
- **You're over age 60.** Because of changes in sleep patterns and health, insomnia increases with age.
- **You have a mental health disorder or physical health condition.** Many issues that impact your mental or physical health can disrupt sleep.
- **You're under a lot of stress.** Stressful times and events can cause temporary insomnia. And major or long-lasting stress can lead to chronic insomnia.
- **You don't have a regular schedule.** For example, changing shifts at work or traveling can disrupt your sleep-wake cycle.

Complications

Sleep is as important to your health as a healthy diet and regular physical activity. Whatever your reason for sleep loss, insomnia can affect you both mentally and physically. People with insomnia report a lower quality of life compared with people who are sleeping well.

Complications of insomnia may include:
- Lower performance on the job or at school
- Slowed reaction time while driving and a higher risk of accidents
- Mental health disorders, such as depression, an anxiety disorder or substance abuse
- Increased risk and severity of long-term diseases or conditions, such as high blood pressure and heart disease

Prevention

Good sleep habits can help prevent insomnia and promote sound sleep:
- Keep your bedtime and wake time consistent from day to day, including weekends.
- Stay active — regular activity helps promote a good night's sleep.
- Check your medications to see if they may contribute to insomnia.
- Avoid or limit naps.
- Avoid or limit caffeine and alcohol, and don't use nicotine.
- Avoid large meals and beverages before bedtime.
- Make your bedroom comfortable for sleep and only use it for sex or sleep.
- Create a relaxing bedtime ritual, such as taking a

warm bath, reading or listening to soft music.

Diagnosis

Depending on your situation, the diagnosis of insomnia and the search for its cause may include:

- **Physical exam.** If the cause of insomnia is unknown, your doctor may do a physical exam to look for signs of medical problems that may be related to insomnia. Occasionally, a blood test may be done to check for thyroid problems or other conditions that may be associated with poor sleep.
- **Sleep habits review.** In addition to asking you sleep-related questions, your doctor may have you complete a questionnaire to determine your sleep-wake pattern and your level of daytime sleepiness. You may also be asked to keep a sleep diary for a couple of weeks.
- **Sleep study.** If the cause of your insomnia isn't clear, or you have signs of another sleep disorder, such as sleep apnea or restless legs syndrome, you may need to spend a night at a sleep center. Tests are done to monitor and record a variety of body activities while you sleep, including brain waves, breathing, heartbeat, eye movements and body movements.

Treatment

Changing your sleep habits and addressing any issues that may be associated with insomnia, such as stress, medical conditions or medications, can restore restful sleep for many people. If these measures don't work, your doctor may recommend cognitive behavioral therapy, medications or both, to help improve relaxation and sleep.

Cognitive behavioral therapy for insomnia

Cognitive behavioral therapy for insomnia (CBT-I) can help you control or eliminate negative thoughts and actions that keep you awake and is generally recommended as the first line of treatment for people with insomnia. Typically, CBT-I is equally or more effective than sleep medications.

The cognitive part of CBT-I teaches you to recognize and change beliefs that affect your ability to sleep. It can help you control or eliminate negative thoughts and worries that keep you awake. It may also involve eliminating the cycle that can develop where you worry so much about getting to sleep that you can't fall asleep.

The behavioral part of CBT-I helps you develop good sleep habits and avoid behaviors that keep you from sleeping well. Strategies include, for example:

- **Stimulus control therapy.** This method helps remove factors that condition your mind to resist sleep. For example, you might be coached to set a consistent bedtime and wake time and avoid naps, use the bed only for sleep and sex, and leave the bedroom if you can't go to sleep within 20 minutes, only returning when you're sleepy.
- **Relaxation techniques.** Progressive muscle relaxation, biofeedback and breathing exercises are ways to reduce anxiety at bedtime. Practicing these techniques can help you control your breathing, heart rate, muscle tension and mood so that you can relax.
- **Sleep restriction.** This therapy decreases the time you spend in bed and avoids daytime naps, causing partial sleep deprivation, which makes you more tired the next night. Once your sleep has improved, your time in bed is gradually increased.

- **Remaining passively awake.** Also called paradoxical intention, this therapy for learned insomnia is aimed at reducing the worry and anxiety about being able to get to sleep by getting in bed and trying to stay awake rather than expecting to fall asleep.
- **Light therapy.** If you fall asleep too early and then awaken too early, you can use light to push back your internal clock. You can go outside during times of the year when it's light outside in the evenings, or you can use a light box. Talk to your doctor about recommendations.

Your doctor may recommend other strategies related to your lifestyle and sleep environment to help you develop habits that promote sound sleep and daytime alertness.

Prescription medications

Prescription sleeping pills can help you get to sleep, stay asleep or both. Doctors generally don't recommend relying on prescription sleeping pills for more than a few weeks, but several medications are approved for long-term use.

Examples include:
- Eszopiclone (Lunesta)
- Ramelteon (Rozerem)
- Zaleplon (Sonata)
- Zolpidem (Ambien, Edluar, Intermezzo, Zolpimist)

Prescription sleeping pills can have side effects, such as causing daytime grogginess and increasing the risk of falling, or they can be habit-forming, so talk to your doctor about these medications and other possible side effects.

Over-the-counter sleep aids

Nonprescription sleep medications contain antihistamines that can make you drowsy, but they're not intended for regular use. Talk to your doctor before you take these, as antihistamines may cause side effects, such as daytime sleepiness, dizziness, confusion, cognitive decline and difficulty urinating, which may be worse in older adults.

Lifestyle and home remedies

No matter what your age, insomnia usually is treatable. The key often lies in changes to your routine during the day and when you go to bed. These tips may help.

Basic tips:

- **Stick to a sleep schedule.** Keep your bedtime and wake time consistent from day to day, including on weekends.
- **Stay active.** Regular activity helps promote a good night's sleep. Schedule exercise at least a few hours before bedtime and avoid stimulating activities before bedtime.
- **Check your medications.** If you take medications regularly, check with your doctor to see if they may be contributing to your insomnia. Also check the labels of OTC products to see if they contain caffeine or other stimulants, such as pseudoephedrine.
- **Avoid or limit naps.** Naps can make it harder to fall asleep at night. If you can't get by without one, try to limit a nap to no more than 30 minutes and don't nap after 3 p.m.
- **Avoid or limit caffeine and alcohol and don't use nicotine.** All of these can make it harder to sleep,

and effects can last for several hours.
- **Don't put up with pain.** If a painful condition bothers you, talk to your doctor about options for pain relievers that are effective enough to control pain while you're sleeping.
- **Avoid large meals and beverages before bed.** A light snack is fine and may help avoid heartburn. Drink less liquid before bedtime so that you won't have to urinate as often.

At bedtime:

- **Make your bedroom comfortable for sleep.** Only use your bedroom for sex or sleep. Keep it dark and quiet, at a comfortable temperature. Hide all clocks in your bedroom, including your wristwatch and cellphone, so you don't worry about what time it is.
- **Find ways to relax.** Try to put your worries and planning aside when you get into bed. A warm bath or a massage before bedtime can help prepare you for sleep. Create a relaxing bedtime ritual, such as taking a hot bath, reading, soft music, breathing exercises, yoga or prayer.
- **Avoid trying too hard to sleep.** The harder you try, the more awake you'll become. Read in another room until you become very drowsy, then go to bed to sleep. Don't go to bed too early, before you're sleepy.
- **Get out of bed when you're not sleeping.** Sleep as much as you need to feel rested, and then get out of bed. Don't stay in bed if you're not sleeping.

Alternative medicine

Many people never visit their doctor for insomnia and try to cope with sleeplessness on their own. Although in many cases safety and effectiveness have not been proved, some people try therapies such as:

- **Melatonin.** This over-the-counter (OTC) supplement is marketed as a way to help overcome insomnia. It's generally considered safe to use melatonin for a few weeks, but no convincing evidence exists to prove that melatonin is an effective treatment for insomnia, and the long-term safety is unknown.
- **Valerian.** This dietary supplement is sold as a sleep aid because it has a mildly sedating effect, although it hasn't been well-studied. Discuss valerian with your doctor before trying it. Some people who have used high doses or used it long term may have had liver damage, although it's not clear if valerian caused the damage.
- **Acupuncture.** There's some evidence that acupuncture may be beneficial for people with insomnia, but more research is needed. If you choose to try acupuncture along with your conventional treatment, ask your doctor how to find a qualified practitioner.
- **Yoga or tai chi.** Some studies suggest that the regular practice of yoga or tai chi can help improve sleep quality.
- **Meditation.** Several small studies suggest that meditation, along with conventional treatment, may help improve sleep and reduce stress.

Caution regarding herbal and dietary sleep aids

Because the Food and Drug Administration does not mandate that manufacturers show proof of effectiveness or safety before marketing dietary supplement sleep aids, talk with your doctor before taking any herbal supplements or other OTC products. Some products can be harmful and some can cause harm if you're taking certain medications.

Preparing for your appointment

If you're having sleep problems, you'll likely start by talking to your primary care doctor. Ask if there's anything you need to do in advance, such as keep a sleep diary. Take your bed partner along, if possible. Your doctor may want to talk to your partner to learn more about how much and how well you're sleeping.

What you can do

Prepare for your appointment by making a list of:

- **Any symptoms you're experiencing,** including any that may seem unrelated to the reason for the appointment.
- **Personal information,** including new or ongoing health problems, major stresses or recent life changes.
- **All medications,** over-the-counter medications, vitamins, and herbal or other supplements that you're taking, including dosages. Let your doctor know about anything you've taken to help you sleep.
- **Questions to ask** your doctor to make the most of your appointment time.

Basic questions to ask your doctor include:

- What is likely causing my insomnia?
- What's the best treatment?
- I have these other health conditions. How can I best manage them together?
- Should I go to a sleep clinic? Will my insurance cover it?
- Are there any brochures or other printed material that I can have?
- What websites do you recommend?

Don't hesitate to ask other questions during your appointment.

What to expect from your doctor

Your doctor may ask you several questions, such as those below.

About your insomnia:

- How often do you have trouble sleeping, and when did the insomnia begin?
- How long does it take you to fall asleep?
- Do you snore or wake up choking for breath?
- How often do you awaken at night, and how long does it take you to fall back to sleep?
- What is your response when you can't sleep?
- What have you tried to improve your sleep?

About your day:

- Do you feel refreshed when you wake up, or are you tired during the day?
- Do you doze off or have trouble staying awake while sitting quietly or driving?
- Do you nap during the day?
- What do you typically eat and drink in the evening?

About your bedtime routine:

- What is your bedtime routine?
- Do you currently take any medications or sleeping pills before bed?
- What time do you go to bed and wake up? Is this different on weekends?
- How many hours a night do you sleep?

About other issues that may affect your sleep:

- Have you experienced any stressful events recently?
- Do you use tobacco or drink alcohol?

- Do you have any family members with sleep problems?
- What medications do you take regularly?

SLEEP APNEA

Sleep apnea is a potentially serious sleep disorder in which breathing repeatedly stops and starts. If you snore loudly and feel tired even after a full night's sleep, you might have sleep apnea.

The main types of sleep apnea are:

- **Obstructive sleep apnea,** the more common form that occurs when throat muscles relax
- **Central sleep apnea,** which occurs when your brain doesn't send proper signals to the muscles that control breathing
- **Complex sleep apnea syndrome**, also known as treatment-emergent central sleep apnea, which occurs when someone has both obstructive sleep apnea and central sleep apnea

If you think you might have sleep apnea, see your doctor. Treatment can ease your symptoms and might help prevent heart problems and other complications.

Symptoms

The signs and symptoms of obstructive and central sleep apneas overlap, sometimes making it difficult to determine which type you have. The most common signs and symptoms of obstructive and central sleep apneas include:

- Loud snoring
- Episodes in which you stop breathing during sleep — which would be reported by another person
- Gasping for air during sleep
- Awakening with a dry mouth
- Morning headache
- Difficulty staying asleep (insomnia)

- Excessive daytime sleepiness (hypersomnia)
- Difficulty paying attention while awake
- Irritability

When to see a doctor

Loud snoring can indicate a potentially serious problem, but not everyone who has sleep apnea snores. Talk to your doctor if you have signs or symptoms of sleep apnea. Ask your doctor about any sleep problem that leaves you fatigued, sleepy and irritable.

Causes

Obstructive sleep apnea

This occurs when the muscles in the back of your throat relax. These muscles support the soft palate, the triangular piece of tissue hanging from the soft palate (uvula), the tonsils, the side walls of the throat and the tongue.

When the muscles relax, your airway narrows or closes as you breathe in. You can't get enough air, which can lower the oxygen level in your blood. Your brain senses your inability to breathe and briefly rouses you from sleep so that you can reopen your airway. This awakening is usually so brief that you don't remember it.

You might snort, choke or gasp. This pattern can repeat itself five to 30 times or more each hour, all night, impairing your ability to reach the deep, restful phases of sleep.

CENTRAL SLEEP APNEA

This less common form of sleep apnea occurs when your brain fails to transmit signals to your breathing muscles. This means that you make no effort to breathe for a short period. You might awaken with shortness of breath or have a difficult time getting to sleep or staying asleep.

Risk factors

Sleep apnea can affect anyone, even children. But certain factors increase your risk.

Obstructive sleep apnea

Factors that increase the risk of this form of sleep apnea include:

- **Excess weight.** Obesity greatly increases the risk of sleep apnea. Fat deposits around your upper airway can obstruct your breathing.
- **Neck circumference.** People with thicker necks might have narrower airways.
- **A narrowed airway.** You might have inherited a narrow throat. Tonsils or adenoids also can enlarge and block the airway, particularly in children.
- **Being male.** Men are two to three times more likely to have sleep apnea than are women. However, women increase their risk if they're overweight, and their risk also appears to rise after menopause.
- **Being older.** Sleep apnea occurs significantly more often in older adults.
- **Family history.** Having family members with sleep apnea might increase your risk.
- **Use of alcohol, sedatives or tranquilizers.** These substances relax the muscles in your throat, which

can worsen obstructive sleep apnea.
- **Smoking.** Smokers are three times more likely to have obstructive sleep apnea than are people who've never smoked. Smoking can increase the amount of inflammation and fluid retention in the upper airway.
- **Nasal congestion.** If you have difficulty breathing through your nose — whether from an anatomical problem or allergies — you're more likely to develop obstructive sleep apnea.
- **Medical conditions.** Congestive heart failure, high blood pressure, type 2 diabetes and Parkinson's disease are some of the conditions that may increase the risk of obstructive sleep apnea. Polycystic ovary syndrome, hormonal disorders, prior stroke and chronic lung diseases such as asthma also can increase risk.

Central sleep apnea

Risk factors for this form of sleep apnea include:

- **Being older.** Middle-aged and older people have a higher risk of central sleep apnea.
- **Being male.** Central sleep apnea is more common in men than it is in women.
- **Heart disorders.** Having congestive heart failure increases the risk.
- **Using narcotic pain medications.** Opioid medications, especially long-acting ones such as methadone, increase the risk of central sleep apnea.
- **Stroke.** Having had a stroke increases your risk of central sleep apnea or treatment-emergent central sleep apnea.

Complications

Sleep apnea is a serious medical condition. Complications

can include:

- **Daytime fatigue.** The repeated awakenings associated with sleep apnea make normal, restorative sleep impossible, making severe daytime drowsiness, fatigue and irritability likely. You might have difficulty concentrating and find yourself falling asleep at work, while watching TV or even when driving. People with sleep apnea have an increased risk of motor vehicle and workplace accidents.

You might also feel quick-tempered, moody or depressed. Children and adolescents with sleep apnea might perform poorly in school or have behavior problems.

- **High blood pressure or heart problems.** Sudden drops in blood oxygen levels that occur during sleep apnea increase blood pressure and strain the cardiovascular system. Having obstructive sleep apnea increases your risk of high blood pressure (hypertension).

Obstructive sleep apnea might also increase your risk of recurrent heart attack, stroke and abnormal heartbeats, such as atrial fibrillation. If you have heart disease, multiple episodes of low blood oxygen (hypoxia or hypoxemia) can lead to sudden death from an irregular heartbeat.

- **Type 2 diabetes.** Having sleep apnea increases your risk of developing insulin resistance and type 2 diabetes.
- **Metabolic syndrome.** This disorder, which includes high blood pressure, abnormal cholesterol levels, high blood sugar and an increased waist circumference, is linked to a higher risk of heart disease.
- **Complications with medications and surgery.**

Obstructive sleep apnea is also a concern with certain medications and general anesthesia. People with sleep apnea might be more likely to have complications after major surgery because they're prone to breathing problems, especially when sedated and lying on their backs.

Before you have surgery, tell your doctor about your sleep apnea and how it's being treated.

- **Liver problems.** People with sleep apnea are more likely to have abnormal results on liver function tests, and their livers are more likely to show signs of scarring (nonalcoholic fatty liver disease).
- **Sleep-deprived partners.** Loud snoring can keep anyone who sleeps near you from getting good rest. It's not uncommon for a partner to have to go to another room, or even to another floor of the house, to be able to sleep.

Diagnosis

Your doctor may make an evaluation based on your signs and symptoms and a sleep history, which you can provide with help from someone who shares your bed or your household, if possible. You're likely to be referred to a sleep disorder center. There, a sleep specialist can help you determine your need for further evaluation.

An evaluation often involves overnight monitoring at a sleep center of your breathing and other body functions during sleep. Home sleep testing also might be an option. Tests to detect sleep apnea include:

- **Nocturnal polysomnography.** During this test, you're hooked up to equipment that monitors your heart, lung and brain activity, breathing patterns, arm and leg movements, and blood oxygen levels

while you sleep.
- **Home sleep tests.** Your doctor might provide you with simplified tests to be used at home to diagnose sleep apnea. These tests usually measure your heart rate, blood oxygen level, airflow and breathing patterns.

If the results are abnormal, your doctor might be able to prescribe a therapy without further testing. Portable monitoring devices don't detect all cases of sleep apnea, however, so your doctor might still recommend polysomnography even if your initial results are normal.

If you have obstructive sleep apnea, your doctor might refer you to an ear, nose and throat doctor to rule out blockage in your nose or throat. An evaluation by a heart doctor (cardiologist) or a doctor who specializes in the nervous system (neurologist) might be necessary to look for causes of central sleep apnea.

Treatment

For milder cases of sleep apnea, your doctor may recommend only lifestyle changes, such as losing weight or quitting smoking. If you have nasal allergies, your doctor will recommend treatment for your allergies. If these measures don't improve your signs and symptoms or if your apnea is moderate to severe, a number of other treatments are available.

Certain devices can help open up a blocked airway. In other cases, surgery might be necessary.

Therapies

- **Continuous positive airway pressure (CPAP).** If you have moderate to severe sleep apnea, you might benefit from using a machine that delivers air pressure through a mask while you sleep. With CPAP (SEE-pap), the air pressure is somewhat greater than that of the surrounding air and is just enough to keep your upper airway passages open, preventing apnea and snoring.

Although CPAP is the most common and reliable method of treating sleep apnea, some people find it cumbersome or uncomfortable. Some people give up on the CPAP machine, but with practice, most people learn to adjust the tension of the straps on the mask to obtain a comfortable and secure fit.

You might need to try more than one type of mask to find one that's comfortable. Don't stop using the CPAP machine if you have problems. Check with your doctor to see what changes can be made to increase your comfort.

Additionally, contact your doctor if you're still snoring or begin snoring again despite treatment. If your weight changes, the pressure settings of the CPAP machine might need to be adjusted.

- **Other airway pressure devices.** If using a CPAP machine continues to be a problem for you, you might be able to use a different type of airway pressure device that automatically adjusts the pressure while you're sleeping (auto-CPAP). Units that supply bilevel positive airway pressure (BPAP) also are available. These provide more pressure when you inhale and less when you exhale.
- **Oral appliances.** Another option is wearing an oral appliance designed to keep your throat open. CPAP is more reliably effective than oral appliances, but oral appliances might be easier to use. Some are designed to open your throat by bringing your jaw forward, which can sometimes relieve snoring and mild obstructive sleep apnea. A number of devices

are available from your dentist. You might need to try different devices before finding one that works for you.

Once you find the right fit, you'll need to follow up with your dentist repeatedly during the first year and then regularly after that to ensure that the fit is still good and to reassess your signs and symptoms.

- **Treatment for associated medical problems.** Possible causes of central sleep apnea include heart or neuromuscular disorders, and treating those conditions might help.
- **Supplemental oxygen.** Using supplemental oxygen while you sleep might help if you have central sleep apnea. Various forms of oxygen are available with devices to deliver oxygen to your lungs.
- **Adaptive servo-ventilation (ASV).** This more recently approved airflow device learns your normal breathing pattern and stores the information in a built-in computer. After you fall asleep, the machine uses pressure to normalize your breathing pattern and prevent pauses in your breathing. ASV appears to be more successful than other forms of positive airway pressure at treating complex sleep apnea in some people. However, it might not be a good choice for people with predominant central sleep apnea and advanced heart failure.

You'll likely read, hear or see TV ads about different treatments for sleep apnea. Talk with your doctor about any treatment before you try it.

Surgery

Surgery is usually only an option after other treatments have failed. Generally, at least a three-month trial of other treatment options is suggested before considering surgery. However, for a small number of people with certain jaw structure problems, it's a good first option.

Surgical options might include:

- **Tissue removal.** During this procedure (uvulopalatopharyngoplasty), your doctor removes tissue from the rear of your mouth and top of your throat. Your tonsils and adenoids usually are removed as well. This type of surgery might be successful in stopping throat structures from vibrating and causing snoring. It's less effective than CPAP and isn't considered a reliable treatment for obstructive sleep apnea.

Removing tissues in the back of your throat with radiofrequency energy (radiofrequency ablation) might be an option if you can't tolerate CPAP or oral appliances.

- **Tissue shrinkage.** Another option is to shrink the tissue at the rear of your mouth and the back of your throat using radiofrequency ablation. This procedure might be used for mild to moderate sleep apnea. One study found this to have effects similar to that of tissue removal, but with fewer surgical risks.
- **Jaw repositioning.** In this procedure, your jaw is moved forward from the remainder of your face bones. This enlarges the space behind the tongue and soft palate, making obstruction less likely. This procedure is known as maxillomandibular advancement.
- **Implants.** Soft rods, usually made of polyester or plastic, are surgically implanted into the soft palate after you've received local anesthetic. More research is needed to determine how well implants work.
- **Nerve stimulation.** This requires surgery to insert a stimulator for the nerve that controls tongue

movement (hypoglossal nerve). The increased stimulation helps keep the tongue in a position that keeps the airway open. More research is needed.
- **Creating a new air passageway (tracheostomy).** You may need this form of surgery if other treatments have failed and you have severe, life-threatening sleep apnea. In this procedure, your surgeon makes an opening in your neck and inserts a metal or plastic tube through which you breathe. You keep the opening covered during the day. But at night you uncover it to allow air to pass in and out of your lungs, bypassing the blocked air passage in your throat.

Other types of surgery may help reduce snoring and contribute to the treatment of sleep apnea by clearing or enlarging air passages:

- Surgery to remove enlarged tonsils or adenoids
- Weight-loss (bariatric) surgery

Lifestyle and home remedies

In some cases, self-care might be a way for you to deal with obstructive sleep apnea and possibly central sleep apnea. Try these tips:

- **Lose excess weight.** Even a slight weight loss might help relieve constriction of your throat. In some cases, sleep apnea can resolve if you return to a healthy weight, but it can recur if you regain the weight.
- **Exercise.** Regular exercise can help ease the symptoms of obstructive sleep apnea even without weight loss. Try to get 30 minutes of moderate activity, such as a brisk walk, most days of the week.
- **Avoid alcohol and certain medications such as**

tranquilizers and sleeping pills. These relax the muscles in the back of your throat, interfering with breathing.
- **Sleep on your side or abdomen rather than on your back.** Sleeping on your back can cause your tongue and soft palate to rest against the back of your throat and block your airway. To keep from rolling onto your back while you sleep, try attaching a tennis ball to the back of your pajama top. There are also commercial devices that vibrate when you roll onto your back in sleep.
- **Don't smoke.** If you're a smoker, look for resources to help you quit.

Preparing for your appointment

If you or your partner suspects that you have sleep apnea, contact your primary care doctor. In some cases, you might be referred immediately to a sleep specialist.

Here's some information to help you get ready for your appointment.

What you can do

When you make the appointment, ask if there's anything you need to do in advance, such as modify your diet or keep a sleep diary.

Make a list of:
- **Your symptoms,** including any that may seem unrelated to the reason for which you scheduled the appointment, and when they began
- **Key personal information,** including family history of a sleep disorder
- **All medications,** vitamins or supplements you take, including doses
- **Questions to ask** your doctor

Take a family member or friend along, if possible, to help you remember the information you receive. Because your bed partner might be more aware of your symptoms than you are, it may help to have him or her along.

For sleep apnea, some questions to ask your doctor include:
- What's the most likely cause of my symptoms?
- What tests do I need? Do these tests require special preparation?
- Is my condition likely temporary or long lasting?
- What treatments are available?
- Which treatment do you think would be best for me?
- I have other health conditions. How can I best manage these conditions together?
- Should I see a specialist?
- Are there brochures or other printed material that I can have? What websites do you recommend?

What to expect from your doctor

Your doctor is likely to ask you questions, including:
- Have your symptoms been continuous, or do they come and go?
- How severe are your symptoms?
- How does your partner describe your symptoms?
- Do you know if you stop breathing during sleep? If so, how many times a night?
- Is there anything that has helped your symptoms?
- Does anything make your symptoms worse, such as sleep position or alcohol consumption?

What you can do in the meantime
- Try to sleep on your side.
- Avoid alcohol for four to six hours before bed.

- Don't take drugs that make you sleepy.
- If you're drowsy, avoid driving.

RESTLESS LEGS SYNDROME

Restless legs syndrome (RLS) is a condition that causes an uncontrollable urge to move the legs, usually because of an uncomfortable sensation. It typically happens in the evening or nighttime hours when you're sitting or lying down. Moving eases the unpleasant feeling temporarily.

Restless legs syndrome, also known as Willis-Ekbom disease, can begin at any age and generally worsens as you age. It can disrupt sleep, which interferes with daily activities.

Simple self-care steps and lifestyle changes may help relieve symptoms. Medications also help many people with RLS.

Symptoms

The chief symptom is an urge to move the legs. Common accompanying characteristics of RLS include:

- **Sensations that begin while resting.** The sensation typically begins after you've been lying down or sitting for an extended time, such as in a car, airplane or movie theater.
- **Relief with movement.** The sensation of RLS lessens with movement, such as stretching, jiggling the legs, pacing or walking.
- **Worsening of symptoms in the evening.** Symptoms occur mainly at night.
- **Nighttime leg twitching.** RLS may be associated with another, more common condition called periodic limb movement of sleep, which causes the legs to twitch and kick, possibly throughout the night, while you sleep.

People typically describe RLS symptoms as compelling, unpleasant sensations in the legs or feet. They usually happen on both sides of the body. Less commonly, the sensations affect the arms.

The sensations, which generally occur within the limb rather than on the skin, are described as:

- Crawling
- Creeping
- Pulling
- Throbbing
- Aching
- Itching
- Electric

Sometimes the sensations are difficult to explain. People with RLS usually don't describe the condition as a muscle cramp or numbness. They do, however, consistently describe the desire to move the legs.

It's common for symptoms to fluctuate in severity. Sometimes, symptoms disappear for periods of time, then come back.

When to see a doctor

Some people with RLS never seek medical attention because they worry they won't be taken seriously. But RLS can interfere with your sleep and cause daytime drowsiness and affect your quality of life. Talk with your health care provider if you think you may have RLS.

Causes

Often, there's no known cause for RLS. Researchers suspect the condition may be caused by an imbalance of the brain chemical dopamine, which sends messages to control muscle movement.

Heredity

Sometimes RLS runs in families, especially if the condition starts before age 40. Researchers have identified sites on the chromosomes where genes for RLS may be present.

Pregnancy

Pregnancy or hormonal changes may temporarily worsen RLS signs and symptoms. Some women get RLS for the first time during pregnancy, especially during their last trimester. However, symptoms usually disappear after delivery.

Risk factors

RLS can develop at any age, even during childhood. The condition is more common with increasing age and more common in women than in men.

RLS usually isn't related to a serious underlying medical problem. However, it sometimes accompanies other conditions, such as:

- **Peripheral neuropathy.** This damage to the nerves in the hands and feet is sometimes due to chronic diseases such as diabetes and alcoholism.
- **Iron deficiency.** Even without anemia, iron deficiency can cause or worsen RLS. If you have a history of bleeding from the stomach or bowels, experience heavy menstrual periods, or repeatedly donate blood, you may have iron deficiency.
- **Kidney failure.** If you have kidney failure, you may also have iron deficiency, often with anemia. When kidneys don't function properly, iron stores in the blood can decrease. This and other changes in body chemistry may cause or worsen RLS.
- **Spinal cord conditions.** Lesions on the spinal cord as a result of damage or injury have been linked to RLS. Having had anesthesia to the spinal cord, such as a spinal block, also increases the risk of

developing RLS.
- **Parkinson's disease.** People who have Parkinson's disease and take certain medications called dopaminergic agonists have an increased risk of developing RLS.

Complications

Although RLS doesn't lead to other serious conditions, symptoms can range from barely bothersome to incapacitating. Many people with RLS find it difficult to fall or stay asleep.

Severe RLS can cause marked impairment in life quality and can result in depression. Insomnia may lead to excessive daytime drowsiness, but RLS may interfere with napping.

Diagnosis

Your provider will take your medical history and ask for a description of your symptoms. A diagnosis of RLS is based on the following criteria, established by the International Restless Legs Syndrome Study Group:

- You have a strong, often irresistible urge to move the legs, usually accompanied by uncomfortable sensations.
- Your symptoms start or get worse when you're resting, such as sitting or lying down.
- Your symptoms are partially or temporarily relieved by activity, such as walking or stretching.
- Your symptoms are worse at night.
- Symptoms can't be explained solely by another medical or behavioral condition.

Your provider may conduct a physical and a neurological exam. Blood tests, particularly for iron deficiency, may be ordered to rule out other possible causes for your symptoms.

In addition, your provider may refer you to a sleep specialist. This may involve an overnight stay and a study at a sleep clinic if another sleep disorder such as sleep apnea is suspected. However, a diagnosis of RLS usually doesn't require a sleep study.

Treatment

Sometimes, treating an underlying condition, such as iron deficiency, greatly relieves symptoms of RLS. Correcting an iron deficiency may involve receiving iron supplementation orally or intravenously. However, take iron supplements only with medical supervision and after your provider has checked your blood-iron level.

If you have RLS without an associated condition, treatment focuses on lifestyle changes. If those aren't effective, your provider might prescribe medications.

Medications

Several prescription medications, most of which were developed to treat other diseases, are available to reduce the restlessness in the legs. These include:

- **Medications that increase dopamine in the brain.** These medications affect levels of the chemical messenger dopamine in the brain. Rotigotine (Neupro) and pramipexole (Mirapex) are approved by the Food and Drug Administration for the treatment of moderate to severe RLS.
  Short-term side effects of these medications are usually mild and include nausea, lightheadedness and fatigue. However, they can also cause impulse control disorders,

such as compulsive gambling, and daytime sleepiness.
- **Drugs affecting calcium channels.** Certain medications, such as gabapentin (Neurontin, Gralise), gabapentin enacarbil (Horizant) and pregabalin (Lyrica), work for some people with RLS.
- **Muscle relaxants and sleep medications.** These drugs help you sleep better at night, but they don't eliminate the leg sensations, and they may cause daytime drowsiness. These medications are generally only used if no other treatment provides relief.
- **Opioids.** Narcotic medications are used mainly to relieve severe symptoms, but they may be addicting if used in high doses. Some examples include tramadol (Ultram, ConZip), codeine, oxycodone (Oxycontin, Roxicodone, others) and hydrocodone (Hysingla ER).

It may take several trials for you and your provider to find the right medication or combination of medications that work best for you.

Caution about medications

Sometimes dopamine medications that have worked for a while to relieve your RLS become ineffective, or you notice your symptoms returning earlier in the day or involving your arms. This is called augmentation. Your provider may substitute another medication to combat the problem. Most drugs prescribed to treat RLS aren't recommended during pregnancy. Instead, your provider may recommend self-care techniques to relieve symptoms. However, if the sensations are particularly bothersome during your last trimester, your provider may approve the use of certain drugs.

Some medications may worsen symptoms of RLS. These include some antidepressants, some antipsychotic medications, some anti-nausea drugs, and some cold and allergy medications. Your provider may recommend that you avoid these drugs, if possible. However, if you need to take these medications, talk to your provider about adding drugs to help manage your RLS.

- NARCOLEPSY

Narcolepsy is a chronic sleep disorder characterized by overwhelming daytime drowsiness and sudden attacks of sleep. People with narcolepsy often find it difficult to stay awake for long periods of time, regardless of the circumstances. Narcolepsy can cause serious disruptions in your daily routine. Sometimes, narcolepsy can be accompanied by a sudden loss of muscle tone (cataplexy), which can be triggered by strong emotion. Narcolepsy that occurs with cataplexy is called type 1 narcolepsy. Narcolepsy that occurs without cataplexy is known as type 2 narcolepsy.

Narcolepsy is a chronic condition for which there's no cure. However, medications and lifestyle changes can help you manage the symptoms. Support from others — family, friends, employers, teachers — can help you cope with narcolepsy.

Symptoms

The signs and symptoms of narcolepsy may worsen for the first few years and then continue for life. They include:

- **Excessive daytime sleepiness.** People with narcolepsy fall asleep without warning, anywhere, anytime. For example, you may be working or talking with friends and suddenly you nod off, sleeping for a few minutes up to a half-hour. When you awaken, you feel refreshed, but eventually you get sleepy again.
- **You may also experience decreased alertness and focus throughout the day.** Excessive daytime sleepiness usually is the first symptom to appear and is often the most troublesome, making it difficult for you to concentrate and fully function.

- **Sudden loss of muscle tone.** This condition, called cataplexy (KAT-uh-plek-see), can cause a number of physical changes, from slurred speech to complete weakness of most muscles, and may last up to a few minutes.

Cataplexy is uncontrollable and is triggered by intense emotions, usually positive ones such as laughter or excitement, but sometimes fear, surprise or anger. For example, when you laugh, your head may droop uncontrollably or your knees may suddenly buckle. Some people with narcolepsy experience only one or two episodes of cataplexy a year, while others have numerous episodes daily. Not everyone with narcolepsy experiences cataplexy.

- **Sleep paralysis.** People with narcolepsy often experience a temporary inability to move or speak while falling asleep or upon waking. These episodes are usually brief — lasting a few seconds or minutes — but can be frightening. You may be aware of the condition and have no difficulty recalling it afterward, even if you had no control over what was happening to you. This sleep paralysis mimics the type of temporary paralysis that normally occurs during a period of sleep called rapid eye movement (REM) sleep. This temporary immobility during REM sleep may prevent your body from acting out dream activity. Not everyone with sleep paralysis has narcolepsy, however. Many people without narcolepsy experience some episodes of sleep paralysis.
- **Changes in rapid eye movement (REM) sleep.** REM sleep is typically when most dreaming happens. REM sleep can occur at any time of the day in people with narcolepsy. People with narcolepsy often transition quickly to REM sleep, usually within 15 minutes of falling asleep.

- **Hallucinations.** These hallucinations are called hypnagogic hallucinations if they happen as you fall asleep and hypnopompic hallucinations if they occur upon waking. An example is feeling as if there is a stranger in your bedroom. These hallucinations may be particularly vivid and frightening because you may not be fully asleep when you begin dreaming and you experience your dreams as reality.

Other characteristics

People with narcolepsy may have other sleep disorders, such as obstructive sleep apnea — a condition in which breathing starts and stops throughout the night — restless legs syndrome and even insomnia.

Some people with narcolepsy experience automatic behavior during brief episodes of narcolepsy. For example, you may fall asleep while performing a task you normally perform, such as writing, typing or driving, and you continue to perform that task while asleep. When you awaken, you can't remember what you did, and you probably didn't do it well.

When to see a doctor

See your doctor if you experience excessive daytime sleepiness that disrupts your personal or professional life.

Causes

The exact cause of narcolepsy is unknown. People with type 1 narcolepsy have low levels of the chemical hypocretin (hi-poe-KREE-tin). Hypocretin is an important neurochemical in your brain that helps regulate wakefulness and REM sleep. Hypocretin levels are particularly low in those who experience cataplexy. Exactly what causes the loss of hypocretin-producing cells in the brain isn't known, but experts suspect it's due to an autoimmune reaction.

It's also likely that genetics play a role in the development of narcolepsy. But the risk of a parent passing this disorder to a child is very low — only about 1%.

Research also indicates a possible association with exposure to the swine flu (H1N1 flu) virus and a certain form of H1N1 vaccine that's currently administered in Europe, though it's not yet clear why.

Normal sleep pattern vs. narcolepsy

The normal process of falling asleep begins with a phase called non-rapid eye movement (NREM) sleep. During this phase, your brain waves slow considerably. After an hour or so of NREM sleep, your brain activity changes, and REM sleep begins. Most dreaming occurs during REM sleep.

In narcolepsy, however, you may suddenly enter into REM sleep without first experiencing NREM sleep, both at night and during the day. Some of the characteristics of narcolepsy — such as cataplexy, sleep paralysis and hallucinations — are similar to changes that occur in REM sleep, but occur during wakefulness or drowsiness.

Risk factors

There are only a few known risk factors for narcolepsy, including:

- **Age.** Narcolepsy typically begins in people between 10 and 30 years old.
- **Family history.** Your risk of narcolepsy is 20 to 40 times higher if you have a family member who has narcolepsy.

Complications

- **Public misunderstanding of the condition.** Narcolepsy may cause serious problems for you professionally and personally. Others might see you as lazy or lethargic. Your performance may suffer at school or work.
- **Interference with intimate relationships.** Intense feelings, such as anger or joy, can trigger signs of narcolepsy such as cataplexy, causing affected people to withdraw from emotional interactions.
- **Physical harm.** Sleep attacks may result in physical harm to people with narcolepsy. You're at increased risk of a car accident if you have an attack while driving. Your risk of cuts and burns is greater if you fall asleep while preparing food.
- **Obesity.** People with narcolepsy are more likely to be overweight. The weight gain may be related to a low metabolism.

Diagnosis

Your doctor may make a preliminary diagnosis of narcolepsy based on your excessive daytime sleepiness and sudden loss of muscle tone (cataplexy). After an initial diagnosis, your doctor may refer you to a sleep specialist for further evaluation.

Formal diagnosis requires staying overnight at a sleep center for an in-depth sleep analysis by sleep specialists. Methods of diagnosing narcolepsy and determining its severity include:

- **Sleep history.** Your doctor will ask you for a detailed sleep history. A part of the history involves filling out the Epworth Sleepiness Scale, which uses a series of short questions to gauge your degree of sleepiness. For instance, you indicate on a numbered scale how likely it is that you would doze off in certain situations, such as sitting down after

lunch.
- **Sleep records.** You may be asked to keep a detailed diary of your sleep pattern for a week or two, so your doctor can compare how your sleep pattern and alertness are related. Often, in addition to this sleep log, the doctor will ask you to wear an actigraph. This device has the look and feel of a wristwatch. It measures periods of activity and rest and provides an indirect measure of how and when you sleep.
- **Polysomnography.** This test measures a variety of signals during sleep using electrodes placed on your scalp. For this test, you must spend a night at a medical facility. The test measures the electrical activity of your brain (electroencephalogram) and heart (electrocardiogram) and the movement of your muscles (electromyogram) and eyes (electrooculogram). It also monitors your breathing.
- **Multiple sleep latency test.** This examination measures how long it takes you to fall asleep during the day. You'll be asked to take four or five naps, each nap two hours apart. Specialists will observe your sleep patterns. People who have narcolepsy fall asleep easily and enter into rapid eye movement (REM) sleep quickly.

These tests can also help doctors rule out other possible causes of your signs and symptoms. Other sleep disorders, such as chronic sleep deprivation, the use of sedating medications and sleep apnea, can cause excessive daytime sleepiness.

Treatment

There is no cure for narcolepsy, but medications and lifestyle modifications can help you manage the symptoms.

Medications

Medications for narcolepsy include:

- **Stimulants.** Drugs that stimulate the central nervous system are the primary treatment to help people with narcolepsy stay awake during the day. Doctors often try modafinil (Provigil) or armodafinil (Nuvigil) first for narcolepsy. Modafinil and armodafinil aren't as addictive as older stimulants and don't produce the highs and lows often associated with older stimulants. Side effects are uncommon, but may include headache, nausea or anxiety. Sunosi (solriamfetol) and pitolisant (Wakix) are newer stimulants used for narcolepsy, headache and anxiety. Pitolisant may also be helpful for cataplexy.

Some people need treatment with methylphenidate (Aptensio XR, Concerta, Ritalin, others) or various amphetamines. These medications are very effective but can be addictive. They may cause side effects such as nervousness and heart palpitations.

- **Selective serotonin reuptake inhibitors (SSRIs) or serotonin and norepinephrine reuptake inhibitors (SNRIs).** Doctors often prescribe these medications, which suppress REM sleep, to help alleviate the symptoms of cataplexy, hypnagogic hallucinations and sleep paralysis. They include fluoxetine (Prozac, Sarafem) and venlafaxine (Effexor XR). Side effects can include weight gain, insomnia and digestive problems.
- **Tricyclic antidepressants.** These older antidepressants, such as protriptyline (Vivactil), imipramine (Tofranil) and clomipramine (Anafranil), are effective for cataplexy, but many people complain of side effects, such as dry mouth

and lightheadedness.
- **Sodium oxybate (Xyrem).** This medication is highly effective for cataplexy. Sodium oxybate helps to improve nighttime sleep, which is often poor in narcolepsy. In high doses it may also help control daytime sleepiness. It must be taken in two doses, one at bedtime and one up to four hours later. Xyrem can have side effects, such as nausea, bed-wetting and worsening of sleepwalking. Taking sodium oxybate together with other sleeping medications, narcotic pain relievers or alcohol can lead to difficulty breathing, coma and death.

If you have other health problems, such as high blood pressure or diabetes, ask your doctor how the medications you take for your other conditions may interact with those taken for narcolepsy.

Certain over-the-counter drugs, such as allergy and cold medications, can cause drowsiness. If you have narcolepsy, your doctor will likely recommend that you avoid taking these medications.

Emerging treatments being investigated for narcolepsy include drugs acting on the histamine chemical system, hypocretin replacement, hypocretin gene therapy and immunotherapy, but further research is needed before any may be available in your doctor's office.

Lifestyle and home remedies

Lifestyle modifications are important in managing the symptoms of narcolepsy. You may benefit from these steps:
- **Stick to a schedule.** Go to sleep and wake up at the same time every day, including weekends.
- **Take naps.** Schedule short naps at regular intervals during the day. Naps of 20 minutes at strategic times during the day may be refreshing and reduce

sleepiness for one to three hours. Some people may need longer naps.
- **Avoid nicotine and alcohol.** Using these substances, especially at night, can worsen your signs and symptoms.
- **Get regular exercise.** Moderate, regular exercise at least four to five hours before bedtime may help you feel more awake during the day and sleep better at night.

Coping and support

Dealing with narcolepsy can be challenging. Making adjustments in your daily schedule may help. Consider these tips:

- **Talk about it.** Tell your employer or teachers about your condition and work with them to find ways to accommodate your needs. This may include taking naps during the day, breaking up monotonous tasks, recording meetings or classes, standing during meetings or lectures, and taking brisk walks at various times throughout the day.
- **Be safe.** If you must drive a long distance, work with your doctor to establish a medication schedule that ensures the greatest likelihood of wakefulness during your drive. Stop for naps and exercise breaks whenever you feel drowsy. Don't drive if you feel too sleepy.

Support groups and counseling can help you and your loved ones cope with narcolepsy. Ask your doctor to help you locate a group or qualified counselor in your area.

Preparing for your appointment

You're likely to start by seeing your family doctor. However, in some cases when you call to set up an appointment, you may be referred to a sleep specialist.

Here's some information to help you prepare for your appointment.

What you can do

- **Be aware of any pre-appointment restrictions.** At the time you make the appointment, be sure to ask if there's anything you need to do in advance.
- **Write down any symptoms you're experiencing,** including any that may seem unrelated to the reason for which you scheduled the appointment.
- **Write down key personal information,** including any major stresses or recent life changes.
- **Make a list of all medications,** vitamins or supplements you're taking.
- **Ask a family member or friend to go with you.** Sometimes it can be difficult to recall all the information you get during an appointment. Someone who accompanies you may remember something that you missed or forgot.
- **Write down questions to ask** your doctor.

Preparing a list of questions for your doctor will help you make the most of your time together. List your questions from most important to least important. For narcolepsy, some basic questions to ask your doctor include:

- What's the most likely cause of my symptoms?
- Are there other possible causes?
- What kinds of tests do I need?
- Do I need a sleep study?
- Is my condition likely temporary or long lasting?
- What treatment do you recommend?
- What are the alternatives to the primary approach you're suggesting?
- I have these other health conditions. How can I best

manage these conditions together?
- Is there a generic alternative to the medicine you're prescribing?
- Are there any brochures or other printed material that I can take home with me? What websites do you recommend?

Don't hesitate to ask other questions anytime during your appointment.

What to expect from your doctor

Your doctor is likely to ask you a number of questions, including:
- When did you begin experiencing symptoms?
- Have your symptoms been continuous or occasional?
- How often do you fall asleep during the day?
- How severe are your symptoms?
- Does anything improve your symptoms?
- What, if anything, appears to worsen your symptoms?
- Does anyone in your family have similar symptoms?

11. Sexual dysfunction

Sexual dysfunction is a problem that can happen during any phase of the sexual response cycle. It prevents you from experiencing satisfaction from sexual activity.

The sexual response cycle traditionally includes excitement, plateau, orgasm and resolution. Desire and arousal are both part of the excitement phase of the sexual response. It's important to know women don't always go through these phases in order.

While research suggests that sexual dysfunction is common, many people don't like talking about it. Because treatment options are available, though, you should share your concerns with your partner and healthcare provider.

Types of sexual dysfunction

Sexual dysfunction generally is classified into four categories:

- **Desire disorders:** lack of sexual desire or interest in sex.
- **Arousal disorders:** inability to become physically aroused or excited during sexual activity.
- **Orgasm disorders:** delay or absence of orgasm (climax).
- **Pain disorders:** pain during intercourse.

Who is affected by sexual dysfunction?

Sexual dysfunction can affect any age, although it is more common in those over 40 because it's often related to a decline in health associated with aging.

Symptoms of sexual dysfunction

In people assigned male at birth:

- Inability to achieve or maintain an erection (hard penis) suitable for intercourse (erectile dysfunction).
- Absent or delayed ejaculation despite enough sexual stimulation (retarded ejaculation).
- Inability to control the timing of ejaculation (early, or premature, ejaculation).

In people assigned female at birth:

- Inability to achieve orgasm.

- Inadequate vaginal lubrication before and during intercourse.
- Inability to relax the vaginal muscles enough to allow intercourse.

In everyone:
- Lack of interest in or desire for sex.
- Inability to become aroused.
- Pain with intercourse.

Causes

Physical causes: Many physical and/or medical conditions can cause problems with sexual function. These conditions include diabetes, heart and vascular (blood vessel) disease, neurological disorders, hormonal imbalances, chronic diseases such as kidney or liver failure, and alcohol use disorder and substance use disorder. In addition, the side effects of some medications, including some antidepressant drugs, can affect sexual function.

Psychological causes: These include work-related stress and anxiety, concern about sexual performance, marital or relationship problems, depression, feelings of guilt, concerns about body image and the effects of a past sexual trauma.

What medications can cause sexual dysfunction?

Some prescription medications and even over-the-counter drugs can have an impact on sexual functioning. Some medicines can affect libido (desire) and others can affect the ability to become aroused or achieve orgasm. The risk of sexual side effects is increased when an individual is taking several medications.

Sexual side effects have been reported with the following medications:

Non-prescription medicines

Some over-the-counter antihistamines and decongestants can cause erectile dysfunction or problems with ejaculation.

Antidepressants

- Tricyclic antidepressants, including amitriptyline (Elavil), doxepin (Sinequan), imipramine (Tofranil), and nortriptyline (Aventyl, Pamelor)
- Monoamine oxidase inhibitors (MAOIs), including phenelzine (Nardil) and tranylcypromine (Parnate)
- Antipsychotic medications, including thioridazine (Mellaril), thiothixene (Navane), and haloperidol (Haldol)
- Anti-mania medications such as lithium carbonate (Eskalith, Lithobid)
- Selective serotonin reuptake inhibitors (SSRIs) such as fluoxetine (Prozac), sertraline (Zoloft), and paroxetine (Paxil).

The following medications may cause erectile dysfunction:

Anti-hypertensive medications (used to treat high blood pressure)

- Diuretics, including spironolactone (Aldactone) and the thiazides (Diuril, Naturetin, and others)
- Centrally acting agents, including methyldopa (Aldomet) and reserpine (Serpasil, Raudixin)
- a-Adrenergic blockers, including prazosin (Minipress) and terazosin (Hytrin)
- b-adrenergic (beta) blockers, including propranolol (Inderal) and metoprolol (Lopressor)

The following medications may decrease sexual desire:

Hormones

- Leuprolide (Lupron)
- Goserelin (Zoladex)

Diagnosis

In most cases, you recognize something's interfering with your enjoyment (or a partner's enjoyment) of a sexual relationship. Your provider usually begins with a complete history of symptoms and a physical. They may order diagnostic tests to rule out medical problems that may be contributing to the dysfunction. Typically, lab testing plays a very limited role in the diagnosis of sexual dysfunction.

An evaluation of attitudes about sex, as well as other possible contributing factors —fear, anxiety, past sexual trauma/abuse, relationship concerns, medications, alcohol or drug abuse, etc. — helps a clinician understand the underlying cause of the problem and recommend the right treatment.

Treatment

Most types of sexual dysfunction can be addressed by treating the underlying physical or psychological problems. Other treatment strategies include:

- **Medication:** When a medication is the cause of the dysfunction, a change in the medication may help. Men and women with hormone deficiencies may benefit from hormone shots, pills or creams. For men, drugs, including sildenafil (Viagra), tadalafil (Cialis), vardenafil (Levitra, Staxyn) and avanafil (Stendra) may help improve sexual function by increasing blood flow to the penis. For women, hormonal options such as estrogen and testosterone can be used (although these medications are not approved for this purpose). In premenopausal women, there are two medications that are approved by the FDA to treat low desire, including flibanserin (Addyi) and bremelanotide

(Vyleesi).
- **Mechanical aids:** Aids such as vacuum devices and penile implants may help men with erectile dysfunction (the inability to achieve or maintain an erection). A vacuum device (EROS-CTD) is also approved for use in women, but can be expensive. Dilators may help women who experience narrowing of the vagina. Devices like vibrators can be helpful to help improve sexual enjoyment and climax.
- **Sex therapy:** Sex therapists can help people experiencing sexual problems that can't be addressed by their primary clinician. Therapists are often good marital counselors, as well. For the couple who wants to begin enjoying their sexual relationship, it's well worth the time and effort to work with a trained professional.
- **Behavioral treatments:** These involve various techniques, including insights into harmful behaviors in the relationship, or techniques such as self-stimulation for treatment of problems with arousal and/or orgasm.
- **Psychotherapy:** Therapy with a trained counselor can help you address sexual trauma from the past, feelings of anxiety, fear, guilt and poor body image. All of these factors may affect sexual function.
- **Education and communication:** Education about sex and sexual behaviors and responses may help you overcome anxieties about sexual function. Open dialogue with your partner about your needs and concerns also helps overcome many barriers to a healthy sex life.

Prognosis

Can sexual dysfunction be cured?

The success of treatment for sexual dysfunction depends on the underlying cause of the problem. The outlook is good for dysfunction that is related to a condition that can be treated or reversed.

12. Gender dysphoria

Gender dysphoria is the feeling of discomfort or distress that might occur in people whose gender identity differs from their sex assigned at birth or sex-related physical characteristics.

Transgender and gender-diverse people might experience gender dysphoria at some point in their lives. However, some transgender and gender-diverse people feel at ease with their bodies, with or without medical intervention.

A diagnosis for gender dysphoria is included in the Diagnostic and Statistical Manual of Mental Disorders (DSM-5), a manual published by the American Psychiatric Association. The diagnosis was created to help people with gender dysphoria get access to necessary health care and effective treatment. The term focuses on discomfort as the problem, rather than identity.

Symptoms

Gender dysphoria might cause adolescents and adults to experience a marked difference between inner gender identity and assigned gender that lasts for at least six months. The difference is shown by at least two of the following:

- A difference between gender identity and genitals or secondary sex characteristics, such as breast size, voice and facial hair. In young adolescents, a difference between gender identity and anticipated secondary sex characteristics.

- A strong desire to be rid of these genitals or secondary sex characteristics, or a desire to prevent the development of secondary sex characteristics.
- A strong desire to have the genitals and secondary sex characteristics of another gender.
- A strong desire to be or to be treated as another gender.
- A strong belief of having the typical feelings and reactions of another gender.

Gender dysphoria may also cause significant distress that affects how you function in social situations, at work or school, and in other areas of life.

Gender dysphoria might start in childhood and continue into adolescence and adulthood. Or you might have periods in which you no longer experience gender dysphoria. You might also experience gender dysphoria around the time of puberty or much later in life.

Complications

Gender dysphoria can affect many aspects of life, including daily activities. People experiencing gender dysphoria might have difficulty in school due to pressure to dress in a way that's associated with their sex assigned at birth or out of fear of being harassed or teased.

If gender dysphoria impairs the ability to function at school or at work, the result may be school dropout or unemployment. Relationship difficulties are common. Anxiety, depression, self-harm, eating disorders, substance misuse and other problems can occur.

People who have gender dysphoria also often experience discrimination, resulting in stress. Accessing health services and mental health services can be difficult due to fear of stigma and a lack of experienced care providers.

Adolescents and adults with gender dysphoria without gender-affirming treatment might be at risk of thinking about or attempting suicide.

Diagnosis

Your health care provider might make a diagnosis of gender dysphoria based on:

- **Behavioral health evaluation.** Your provider will evaluate you to confirm the presence of gender dysphoria and document how prejudice and discrimination due to your gender identity (minority stress factors) impact your mental health. Your provider will also ask about the degree of support you have from family, chosen family and peers.
- **DSM-5.** Your mental health professional may use the criteria for gender dysphoria listed in the Diagnostic and Statistical Manual of Mental Disorders (DSM-5), published by the American Psychiatric Association.

Gender dysphoria is different from simply not conforming to stereotypical gender role behavior. It involves feelings of distress due to a strong, pervasive desire to be another gender.

Some adolescents might express their feelings of gender dysphoria to their parents or a health care provider. Others might instead show symptoms of a mood disorder, anxiety or depression. Or they might experience social or academic problems.

Treatment

Treatment can help people who have gender dysphoria explore their gender identity and find the gender role that feels comfortable for them, easing distress. However, treatment should be individualized. What might help one person might not help another. Treatment options might include changes in gender expression and role, hormone therapy, surgery, and behavioral therapy.

If you have gender dysphoria, seek help from a doctor who has expertise in the care of gender-diverse people.

When coming up with a treatment plan, your provider will screen you for mental health concerns that might need to be addressed, such as depression or anxiety. Failing to treat these concerns can make it more difficult to explore your gender identity and ease gender dysphoria.

Changes in gender expression and role

This might involve living part time or full time in another gender role that is consistent with your gender identity.

Medical treatment

Medical treatment of gender dysphoria might include:

- Hormone therapy, such as feminizing hormone therapy or masculinizing hormone therapy
- Surgery, such as feminizing surgery or masculinizing surgery to change the chest, external genitalia, internal genitalia, facial features and body contour

Some people use hormone therapy to seek maximum feminization or masculinization. Others might find relief from gender dysphoria by using hormones to minimize secondary sex characteristics, such as breasts and facial hair.

Treatments are based on your goals and an evaluation of the risks and benefits of medication use. Treatments may also be based on the presence of any other conditions and consideration of your social and economic issues. Many people also find that surgery is necessary to relieve their gender dysphoria.

The World Professional Association for Transgender Health provides the following criteria for hormonal and surgical treatment of gender dysphoria:

- Persistent, well-documented gender dysphoria.
- Capacity to make a fully informed decision and consent to treatment.
- Legal age in a person's country or, if younger, following the standard of care for children and adolescents.
- If significant medical or mental concerns are present, they must be reasonably well controlled.

Additional criteria apply to some surgical procedures.

A pre-treatment medical evaluation is done by a doctor with experience and expertise in transgender care before hormonal and surgical treatment of gender dysphoria. This can help rule out or address medical conditions that might affect these treatments This evaluation may include:

- A personal and family medical history
- A physical exam
- Lab tests
- Assessment of the need for age- and sex-appropriate screenings
- Identification and management of tobacco use and drug and alcohol misuse
- Testing for HIV and other sexually transmitted infections, along with treatment, if necessary
- Assessment of desire for fertility preservation and referral as needed for sperm, egg, embryo or ovarian tissue cryopreservation
- Documentation of history of potentially harmful treatment approaches, such as unprescribed hormone use, industrial-strength silicone injections or self-surgeries

Behavioral health treatment

This treatment aims to improve your psychological well-being, quality of life and self-fulfillment. Behavioral therapy isn't intended to alter your gender identity. Instead, therapy can help you explore gender concerns and find ways to lessen gender dysphoria. The goal of behavioral health treatment is to help you feel comfortable with how you express your gender identity, enabling success in relationships, education and work. Therapy can also address any other mental health concerns.

Therapy might include individual, couples, family and group counseling to help you:

- Explore and integrate your gender identity
- Accept yourself
- Address the mental and emotional impacts of the stress that results from experiencing prejudice and discrimination because of your gender identity (minority stress)
- Build a support network
- Develop a plan to address social and legal issues related to your transition and coming out to loved ones, friends, colleagues and other close contacts
- Become comfortable expressing your gender identity
- Explore healthy sexuality in the context of gender transition
- Make decisions about your medical treatment options
- Increase your well-being and quality of life

Therapy might be helpful during many stages of your life.

A behavioral health evaluation may not be required before receiving hormonal and surgical treatment of gender dysphoria, but it can play an important role when making decisions about treatment options. This evaluation might assess:

- Gender identity and dysphoria
- Impact of gender identity in work, school, home and social environments, including issues related to discrimination, abuse and minority stress
- Mood or other mental health concerns
- Risk-taking behaviors and self-harm
- Substance misuse
- Sexual health concerns
- Social support from family, friends and peers — a protective factor against developing depression, suicidal thoughts, suicide attempts, anxiety or high-risk behaviors
- Goals, risks and expectations of treatment and trajectory of care

Other steps

Other ways to ease gender dysphoria might include use of:

- Peer support groups
- Voice and communication therapy to develop vocal characteristics matching your experienced or expressed gender
- Hair removal or transplantation
- Genital tucking
- Breast binding
- Breast padding
- Packing
- Aesthetic services, such as makeup application or wardrobe consultation
- Legal services, such as advanced directives, living wills or legal documentation
- Social and community services to deal with workplace issues, minority stress or parenting issues

Coping and support

Gender dysphoria can be lessened by supportive environments and knowledge about treatment to reduce the difference between your inner gender identity and sex assigned at birth.

Social support from family, friends and peers can be a protective factor against developing depression, suicidal thoughts, suicide attempts, anxiety or high-risk behaviors.

Other options for support include:

- **Mental health care.** You might see a mental health professional to explore your gender, talk about relationship issues, or talk about any anxiety or depression you're experiencing.
- **Support groups.** Talking to other transgender or gender-diverse people can help you feel less alone. Some community or LGBTQI centers have support groups. Or you might look online.
- **Prioritizing self-care.** Get plenty of sleep. Eat well and exercise. Make time to relax and do the activities you enjoy.
- **Meditation or prayer.** You might find comfort and support in your spirituality or faith communities.
- **Getting involved.** Give back to your community by volunteering, including at LGBTQI organizations.

Preparing for your appointment

You may start by seeing your primary care provider. Or you may be referred to a behavioral health professional.

Here's some information to help you get ready for your appointment.

What you can do

Before your appointment, make a list of:

- **Your symptoms,** including any that seem unrelated to the reason for your appointment
- **Key personal information,** including major stresses, recent life changes and family medical history
- **All medications, vitamins or other supplements** you take, including the doses
- **Questions to ask** your health care provider

13. Disruptive, impulse-control and conduct disorders:

Disruptive, impulse control and conduct disorders are a group of disorders that are linked by varying difficulties in controlling aggressive behaviors, self-control, and impulses. Typically, the resulting behaviors or actions are considered a threat primarily to others' safety and/or to societal norms. Some examples of these issues include fighting, destroying property, defiance, stealing, lying, and rule breaking. These disorders are:

- Oppositional defiant disorder
- Intermittent explosive disorder
- Conduct disorder
- Pyromania
- Kleptomania

Problematic behaviors and issues with self-control associated with these disorders are typically first observed in childhood and can persist into adulthood. In general, disruptive, impulse-control, and conduct disorders tend to be more common in males than females, with the exception of kleptomania.

OPPOSITIONAL DEFIANT DISORDER

Even the best-behaved children can be difficult and challenging at times. But if your child or teenager has a frequent and persistent pattern of anger, irritability, arguing, defiance or vindictiveness toward you and other authority figures, he or she may have oppositional defiant disorder (ODD). As a parent, you don't have to go it alone in trying to manage a child with ODD. Doctors, mental health professionals and child development experts can help.

Behavioral treatment of ODD involves learning skills to help build positive family interactions and to manage problematic behaviors. Additional therapy, and possibly medications, may be needed to treat related mental health disorders.

Symptoms

Sometimes it's difficult to recognize the difference between a strong-willed or emotional child and one with oppositional defiant disorder. It's normal to exhibit oppositional behavior at certain stages of a child's development. Signs of ODD generally begin during preschool years. Sometimes ODD may develop later, but almost always before the early teen years. These behaviors cause significant impairment with family, social activities, school and work.

The Diagnostic and Statistical Manual of Mental Disorders (DSM-5), published by the American Psychiatric Association, lists criteria for diagnosing ODD. The DSM-5 criteria include emotional and behavioral symptoms that last at least six months.

Angry and irritable mood:
- Often and easily loses temper

- Is frequently touchy and easily annoyed by others
- Is often angry and resentful

Argumentative and defiant behavior:

- Often argues with adults or people in authority
- Often actively defies or refuses to comply with adults' requests or rules
- Often deliberately annoys or upsets people
- Often blames others for his or her mistakes or misbehavior

Vindictiveness:

- Is often spiteful or vindictive
- Has shown spiteful or vindictive behavior at least twice in the past six months

ODD can vary in severity:

- **Mild.** Symptoms occur only in one setting, such as only at home, school, work or with peers.
- **Moderate.** Some symptoms occur in at least two settings.
- **Severe.** Some symptoms occur in three or more settings.

For some children, symptoms may first be seen only at home, but with time extend to other settings, such as school and with friends.

When to see a doctor

Your child isn't likely to see his or her behavior as a problem. Instead, he or she will probably complain about unreasonable demands or blame others for problems. If your child shows signs that may indicate ODD or other disruptive behavior, or you're concerned about your ability to parent a challenging child, seek help from a child psychologist or a child psychiatrist with expertise in disruptive behavior problems.

UNDERSTANDING MENTAL HEALTH

Ask your primary care doctor or your child's pediatrician to refer you to the appropriate professional.

Causes

There's no known clear cause of oppositional defiant disorder. Contributing causes may be a combination of inherited and environmental factors, including:

- **Genetics** — a child's natural disposition or temperament and possibly neurobiological differences in the way nerves and the brain function
- **Environment** — problems with parenting that may involve a lack of supervision, inconsistent or harsh discipline, or abuse or neglect

Risk factors

Oppositional defiant disorder is a complex problem. Possible risk factors for ODD include:

- **Temperament** — a child who has a temperament that includes difficulty regulating emotions, such as being highly emotionally reactive to situations or having trouble tolerating frustration
- **Parenting issues** — a child who experiences abuse or neglect, harsh or inconsistent discipline, or a lack of parental supervision
- **Other family issues** — a child who lives with parent or family discord or has a parent with a mental health or substance use disorder
- **Environment** — oppositional and defiant behaviors can be strengthened and reinforced through attention from peers and inconsistent discipline from other authority figures, such as teachers

Complications

Children and teenagers with oppositional defiant disorder may have trouble at home with parents and siblings, in school with teachers, and at work with supervisors and other authority figures. Children with ODD may struggle to make and keep friends and relationships.

ODD may lead to problems such as:

- Poor school and work performance
- Antisocial behavior
- Impulse control problems
- Substance use disorder
- Suicide

Many children and teens with ODD also have other mental health disorders, such as:

- Attention-deficit/hyperactivity disorder (ADHD)
- Conduct disorder
- Depression
- Anxiety
- Learning and communication disorders

Treating these other mental health disorders may help improve ODD symptoms. And it may be difficult to treat ODD if these other disorders are not evaluated and treated appropriately.

Prevention

There's no guaranteed way to prevent oppositional defiant disorder. However, positive parenting and early treatment can help improve behavior and prevent the situation from getting worse. The earlier that ODD can be managed, the better.

Treatment can help restore your child's self-esteem and

rebuild a positive relationship between you and your child. Your child's relationships with other important adults in his or her life — such as teachers and care providers — also will benefit from early treatment.

Diagnosis

To determine whether your child has oppositional defiant disorder, the mental health professional will likely do a comprehensive psychological evaluation. Because ODD often occurs along with other behavioral or mental health problems, symptoms of ODD may be difficult to distinguish from those related to other problems.

Your child's evaluation will likely include an assessment of:

- Overall health
- Frequency and intensity of behaviors
- Emotions and behavior across multiple settings and relationships
- Family situations and interactions
- Strategies that have been helpful — or not helpful — in managing problem behaviors
- Presence of other mental health, learning or communication disorders

Treatment

Treatment for oppositional defiant disorder primarily involves family-based interventions, but it may include other types of psychotherapy and training for your child — as well as for parents. Treatment often lasts several months or longer. It's important to treat any co-occurring problems, such as a learning disorder, because they can create or worsen ODD symptoms if left untreated.

Medications alone generally aren't used for ODD unless your child also has another mental health disorder. If your child has coexisting disorders, such as ADHD, anxiety or depression, medications may help improve these symptoms. The cornerstones of treatment for ODD usually include:

- **Parent training.** A mental health professional with experience treating ODD may help you develop parenting skills that are more consistent, positive and less frustrating for you and your child. In some cases, your child may participate in this training with you, so everyone in your family develops shared goals for how to handle problems. Involving other authority figures, such as teachers, in the training may be an important part of treatment.
- **Parent-child interaction therapy (PCIT).** During PCIT, a therapist coaches parents while they interact with their child. In one approach, the therapist sits behind a one-way mirror and, using an "ear bug" audio device, guides parents through strategies that reinforce their child's positive behavior. As a result, parents learn more-effective parenting techniques, the quality of the parent-child relationship improves, and problem behaviors decrease.
- **Individual and family therapy.** Individual therapy for your child may help him or her learn to manage anger and express feelings in a healthier way. Family therapy may help improve your communication and relationships and help members of your family learn how to work together.
- **Cognitive problem-solving training.** This type of therapy is aimed at helping your child identify and change thought patterns that lead to behavior problems. Collaborative problem-solving — in which you and your child work together to come up with solutions that work for both of you — can help improve ODD-related problems.

UNDERSTANDING MENTAL HEALTH

- **Social skills training.** Your child may also benefit from therapy that will help him or her be more flexible and learn how to interact more positively and effectively with peers.

As part of parent training, you may learn how to manage your child's behavior by:

- Giving clear instructions and following through with appropriate consequences when needed
- Recognizing and praising your child's good behaviors and positive characteristics to promote desired behaviors

Although some parenting techniques may seem like common sense, learning to use them consistently in the face of opposition isn't easy, especially if there are other stressors at home. Learning these skills will require routine practice and patience.

Most important in treatment is for you to show consistent, unconditional love and acceptance of your child — even during difficult and disruptive situations. Don't be too hard on yourself. This process can be tough for even the most patient parents.\

Lifestyle and home remedies

At home, you can begin chipping away at problem behaviors of oppositional defiant disorder by practicing these strategies:

- **Recognize and praise your child's positive behaviors.** Be as specific as possible, such as, "I really liked the way you helped pick up your toys tonight." Providing rewards for positive behavior also may help, especially with younger children.
- **Model the behavior you want your child to have.** Demonstrating appropriate interactions and

modeling socially appropriate behavior can help your child improve social skills.
- **Pick your battles and avoid power struggles.** Almost everything can turn into a power struggle, if you let it.
- **Set limits** by giving clear and effective instructions and enforcing consistent reasonable consequences. Discuss setting these limits during times when you're not confronting each other.
- **Set up a routine** by developing a consistent daily schedule for your child. Asking your child to help develop that routine may be beneficial.
- **Build in time together** by developing a consistent weekly schedule that involves you and your child spending time together.
- **Work together** with your partner or others in your household to ensure consistent and appropriate discipline procedures. Also enlist support from teachers, coaches and other adults who spend time with your child.
- **Assign a household chore** that's essential and that won't get done unless the child does it. Initially, it's important to set your child up for success with tasks that are relatively easy to achieve and gradually blend in more important and challenging expectations. Give clear, easy-to-follow instructions.
- **Be prepared for challenges early on.** At first, your child probably won't be cooperative or appreciate your changed response to his or her behavior. Expect behavior to temporarily worsen in the face of new expectations. Remaining consistent in the face of increasingly challenging behavior is the key to success at this early stage.

With perseverance and consistency, the initial hard work

often pays off with improved behavior and relationships.

Coping and support

It's challenging to be the parent of a child with oppositional defiant disorder. Ask questions and try to effectively communicate your concerns and needs to the treatment team. Consider getting counseling for yourself and your family to learn coping strategies to help manage your own distress. Also seek and build supportive relationships and learn stress management methods to help get through difficult times.

These coping and support strategies can lead to better outcomes for your child because you'll be more prepared to deal with problem behaviors.

Preparing for your appointment

You may start by seeing your child's doctor. After an initial evaluation, he or she may refer you to a mental health professional who can help make a diagnosis and create the appropriate treatment plan for your child.

When possible, both parents should be present with the child. Or, take a trusted family member or friend along. Someone who accompanies you may remember something that you missed or forgot.

What you can do

Before your appointment, make a list of:

- **Signs and symptoms your child has been experiencing,** and for how long.
- **Your family's key personal information,** including factors that you suspect may have contributed to changes in your child's behavior. Include any stressors and transitions that your child or close

- **Your child's school performance,** including grades and patterns of academic strengths and weaknesses. Include any learning disorder assessments and any special education services.
- **Your child's key medical information,** including other physical or mental health disorders with which your child has been diagnosed.
- **Any medication, vitamins, herbal products and other supplements your child is taking,** including the dosages.
- **Questions to ask** the doctor so that you can make the most of your appointment.

Questions to ask the doctor at your child's initial appointment include:

- What do you believe is causing my child's symptoms?
- Are there any other possible causes?
- How will you determine the diagnosis?
- Should my child see a mental health professional?

Questions to ask if your child is referred to a mental health professional include:

- Does my child have oppositional defiant disorder or another mental health disorder?
- Is this condition likely temporary or long lasting?
- What factors do you think might be contributing to my child's problem?
- What treatment approach do you recommend?
- Does my child need to be screened for any other mental health disorders?
- Is my child at increased risk of any long-term complications from this condition?

- Do you recommend any changes at home or school to improve my child's behavior?
- Should I tell my child's teachers about this diagnosis?
- What else can my family and I do to help my child?
- Do you recommend family therapy?

Don't hesitate to ask additional questions during your appointment.

What to expect from your doctor

Be ready to answer your doctor's questions. That way you'll have more time to go over any points you want to talk about in-depth. Here are examples of questions that your doctor may ask.

- What are your concerns about your child's behavior?
- When did you first notice these problems?
- Have your child's teachers or other caregivers reported similar behaviors in your child?
- How often over the last six months has your child had an angry and irritable mood, shown argumentative and defiant behavior, or been vindictive?
- In what settings does your child demonstrate these behaviors?
- Do any particular situations seem to trigger negative or defiant behavior in your child?
- How have you been handling your child's disruptive behavior?
- How do you typically discipline your child?
- How would you describe your child's home and family life?
- What stressors has the family been dealing with?
- Has your child been diagnosed with any other

medical or mental health conditions?

INTERMITTENT EXPLOSIVE DISORDER

Intermittent explosive disorder involves repeated, sudden episodes of impulsive, aggressive, violent behavior or angry verbal outbursts in which you react grossly out of proportion to the situation. Road rage, domestic abuse, throwing or breaking objects, or other temper tantrums may be signs of intermittent explosive disorder. These intermittent, explosive outbursts cause you significant distress, negatively impact your relationships, work and school, and they can have legal and financial consequences.

Intermittent explosive disorder is a chronic disorder that can continue for years, although the severity of outbursts may decrease with age. Treatment involves medications and psychotherapy to help you control your aggressive impulses.

Symptoms

Explosive eruptions occur suddenly, with little or no warning, and usually last less than 30 minutes. These episodes may occur frequently or be separated by weeks or months of nonaggression. Less severe verbal outbursts may occur in between episodes of physical aggression. You may be irritable, impulsive, aggressive or chronically angry most of the time.

Aggressive episodes may be preceded or accompanied by:
- Rage
- Irritability
- Increased energy
- Racing thoughts
- Tingling
- Tremors
- Palpitations

- Chest tightness

The explosive verbal and behavioral outbursts are out of proportion to the situation, with no thought to consequences, and can include:
- Temper tantrums
- Tirades
- Heated arguments
- Shouting
- Slapping, shoving or pushing
- Physical fights
- Property damage
- Threatening or assaulting people or animals

You may feel a sense of relief and tiredness after the episode. Later, you may feel remorse, regret or embarrassment.

When to see a doctor

If you recognize your own behavior in the description of intermittent explosive disorder, talk with your doctor about treatment options or ask for a referral to a mental health professional.

Causes

Intermittent explosive disorder can begin in childhood — after the age of 6 years — or during the teenage years. It's more common in younger adults than in older adults. The exact cause of the disorder is unknown, but it's probably caused by a number of environmental and biological factors.

- **Environment.** Most people with this disorder grew up in families where explosive behavior and verbal and physical abuse were common. Being exposed to this type of violence at an early age makes it more likely these children will exhibit these same traits as they mature.
- **Genetics.** There may be a genetic component,

causing the disorder to be passed down from parents to children.
- **Differences in how the brain works.** There may be differences in the structure, function and chemistry of the brain in people with intermittent explosive disorder compared to people who don't have the disorder.

Risk factors

These factors increase your risk of developing intermittent explosive disorder:

- **History of physical abuse.** People who were abused as children or experienced multiple traumatic events have an increased risk of intermittent explosive disorder.
- **History of other mental health disorders.** People who have antisocial personality disorder, borderline personality disorder or other disorders that include disruptive behaviors, such as attention-deficit/hyperactivity disorder (ADHD), have an increased risk of also having intermittent explosive disorder.

Complications

People with intermittent explosive disorder have an increased risk of:

- **Impaired interpersonal relationships.** They're often perceived by others as always being angry. They may have frequent verbal fights or there can be physical abuse. These actions can lead to relationship problems, divorce and family stress.

- **Trouble at work, home or school.** Other complications of intermittent explosive disorder may include job loss, school suspension, car accidents, financial problems or trouble with the law.
- **Problems with mood.** Mood disorders such as depression and anxiety often occur with intermittent explosive disorder.
- **Problems with alcohol and other substance use.** Problems with drugs or alcohol often occur along with intermittent explosive disorder.
- **Physical health problems.** Medical conditions are more common and can include, for example, high blood pressure, diabetes, heart disease and stroke, ulcers, and chronic pain.
- **Self-harm.** Intentional injuries or suicide attempts sometimes occur.

Prevention

If you have intermittent explosive disorder, prevention is likely beyond your control unless you get treatment from a professional. Combined with or as part of treatment, these suggestions may help you prevent some incidents from getting out of control:

- **Stick with your treatment.** Attend your therapy sessions, practice your coping skills, and if your doctor has prescribed medication, be sure to take it. Your doctor may suggest maintenance medication to avoid recurrence of explosive episodes.
- **Practice relaxation techniques.** Regular use of deep breathing, relaxing imagery or yoga may help you stay calm.
- **Develop new ways of thinking (cognitive restructuring).** Changing the way you think about a frustrating situation by using rational thoughts,

reasonable expectations and logic may improve how you view and react to an event.
- **Use problem-solving.** Make a plan to find a way to solve a frustrating problem. Even if you can't fix the problem right away, having a plan can refocus your energy.
- **Learn ways to improve your communication.** Listen to the message the other person is trying to share, and then think about your best response rather than saying the first thing that pops into your head.
- **Change your environment.** When possible, leave or avoid situations that upset you. Also, scheduling personal time may enable you to better handle an upcoming stressful or frustrating situation.
- **Avoid mood-altering substances.** Don't use alcohol or recreational or illegal drugs.

Diagnosis

To determine a diagnosis of intermittent explosive disorder and eliminate other physical conditions or mental health disorders that may be causing your symptoms, your doctor will likely:

- **Do a physical exam.** Your doctor will try to rule out physical problems or substance use that could be contributing to your symptoms. Your exam may include lab tests.
- **Do a psychological evaluation.** Your doctor or mental health professional will talk to you about your symptoms, thoughts, feelings and behavior patterns.
- **Use the criteria in the DSM-5.** The Diagnostic and Statistical Manual of Mental Disorders (DSM-5), published by the American Psychiatric Association, is often used by mental health professionals to

diagnose mental conditions.

Treatment

There's no single treatment that's best for everyone with intermittent explosive disorder. Treatment generally includes talk therapy (psychotherapy) and medication.

Psychotherapy

Individual or group therapy sessions that focus on building skills can be helpful. A commonly used type of therapy, cognitive behavioral therapy, helps people with intermittent explosive disorder:

- Identify which situations or behaviors may trigger an aggressive response
- Learn how to manage anger and control inappropriate responses using techniques such as relaxation training, thinking differently about situations (cognitive restructuring), and applying communication and problem-solving skills

Medication

Different types of medications may help in the treatment of intermittent explosive disorder. These may include certain antidepressants — specifically selective serotonin reuptake inhibitors (SSRIs) — anticonvulsant mood stabilizers or other drugs if needed.

Coping and support

Controlling your anger

PART OF YOUR TREATMENT MAY INCLUDE:
- **Unlearning problem behavior.** Coping well with anger is a learned behavior. Practice the techniques you learn in therapy to help you recognize what triggers your outbursts and how to respond in ways that work for you instead of against you.
- **Developing a plan.** Work with your doctor or mental health professional to develop a plan of action for when you feel yourself getting angry. For example, if you think you might lose control, try to remove yourself from that situation. Go for a walk or call a trusted friend to try to calm down.
- **Improving self-care.** Getting a good night's sleep, exercising and practicing general stress management each day can help improve your frustration tolerance.
- **Avoiding alcohol or recreational or illegal drugs.** These substances can increase aggressiveness and the risk of explosive outbursts.

If your loved one won't get help

Unfortunately, many people with intermittent explosive disorder don't seek treatment. If you're involved in a relationship with someone who has intermittent explosive disorder, take steps to protect yourself and your children. The abuse isn't your fault. No one deserves to be abused.

Create an escape plan to stay safe from domestic violence

If you see that a situation is getting worse, and suspect your loved one may be on the verge of an explosive episode, try to safely remove yourself and your children from the scene. However, leaving someone with an explosive temper can be dangerous.

Consider taking these steps before an emergency arises:

- **Call a domestic violence hotline or a women's shelter for advice,** either when the abuser isn't home or from a friend's house. *Domestic violence Helpline: 0800 150 150. Childline: 116. SAPS Emergency Services: 10111.*
- **Keep all firearms locked away or hidden.** Don't give the abuser the key or combination to the lock.
- **Pack an emergency bag** that includes items you'll need when you leave, such as extra clothes, keys, personal papers, medications and money. Hide it or leave the bag with a trusted friend or neighbor.
- **Tell a trusted neighbor or friend about the violence** so that he or she can call for help if concerned.
- **Know where you'll go** and how you'll get there if you feel threatened, even if it means you have to leave in the middle of the night. You may want to practice getting out of your home safely.
- **Come up with a code word or visual signal that means you need the police** and share it with friends, family and your children.

Get help to protect yourself from domestic violence

These resources can help:

- **Police.** In an emergency, call *10111* or your local law enforcement agency.
- **Your doctor or the emergency room.** If you're injured, doctors and nurses can treat and document your injuries and let you know what local resources can help keep you safe.
- **The National Domestic Violence Hotline:** National Shelter Movement of South Africa (NSMSA) –

Helpline for GBV survivors – 0800 001 005, SMS/ WhatsApp/ Please Call me to 082 057 8600/082 058 2215/072 239 7147.

- **A counseling or mental health center.** Many communities offer counseling and support groups for people in abusive relationships.
- **A local court.** Your local court can help you get a restraining order that legally orders the abuser to stay away from you or face arrest. Local advocates may be available to help guide you through the process. You can also file assault or other charges when appropriate.

Preparing for your appointment

If you're concerned because you're having repeated emotional outbursts, talk with your doctor or make an appointment with a mental health professional who specializes in treating emotional disorders, such as a psychiatrist, psychologist or social worker. Here's some information to help make the most of your appointment.

What you can do

Before your appointment, make a list of:

- **Symptoms you're experiencing,** including any that may seem unrelated to the reason for the appointment
- **Key personal information,** including any major stresses, recent life changes and triggers for your outbursts
- **All medications,** vitamins, herbs and other supplements that you're taking, including the dosages
- **Questions to ask** your doctor

Some basic questions to ask your doctor include:

- Why am I having these angry outbursts?
- Do I need any tests? Do these tests require any special preparation?
- Is this condition temporary or long lasting?
- What treatments are available, and which do you recommend?
- Are there any side effects from treatment?
- Are there any alternatives to the primary approach that you're suggesting?
- I have other health conditions. How can I best manage these conditions together?
- Is there a generic alternative to the medicine you're prescribing?
- How long does therapy take to work?
- Do you have any printed material I can have? What websites do you recommend?

Don't hesitate to ask other questions.

What to expect from your doctor

Your doctor is likely to ask you a number of questions, such as:

- How often do you have explosive episodes?
- What triggers your outbursts?
- Have you injured or verbally abused others?
- Have you damaged property when angry?
- Have you ever tried to hurt yourself?
- Have your outbursts negatively affected your family or work life?
- Does anything seem to make these episodes occur more often or less often?
- Is there anything that helps calm you down?
- Has anyone else in your family ever been diagnosed with a mental illness?
- Have you ever had a head injury?

- Are you currently using alcohol, drugs or other substances?

Be ready to answer these questions so you can focus on points you want to spend more time on. Preparing and anticipating questions will help you make the most of your time with the doctor.

- **CONDUCT DISORDER**

Conduct disorder is a group of behavioral and emotional problems that usually begins during childhood or adolescence. Children and adolescents with the disorder have difficulty following rules and behaving in a socially acceptable way. They may display aggressive, destructive, and deceitful behaviors that can violate the rights of others. Adults and other children may perceive them as "bad" or delinquent rather than as having a mental illness.

If your child has conduct disorder, they may appear tough and confident. In reality, however, children who have conduct disorder are often insecure and inaccurately believe that people are aggressive or threatening.

Types of conduct disorder

There are three types of conduct disorder. They're categorized according to the age at which symptoms of the disorder first occur:

- Childhood onset occurs when the signs of conduct disorder appear before age 10.
- Adolescent onset occurs when the signs of conduct disorder appear during the teen years.
- Unspecified onset means the age at which conduct disorder first occurs is unknown.

Some children will be diagnosed with conduct disorder with limited prosocial emotions. Children with this specific conduct disorder are often described as callous and unemotional.

Symptoms

Children who have conduct disorder are often hard to control and unwilling to follow the rules. They act impulsively without considering the consequences of their actions.

They also don't consider other people's feelings. Your child may have conduct disorder if they persistently display one or more of the following behaviors:

- aggressive conduct
- deceitful behavior
- destructive behavior
- violation of rules

Aggressive conduct

Aggressive conduct may include:

- intimidating or bullying others
- aggression to people or animals on purpose
- forcing someone into sexual activity
- using a weapon

Deceitful behavior

Deceitful behavior may include:

- lying
- breaking and entering
- stealing
- forgery

Destructive behavior

Destructive conduct may include arson and other intentional destruction of property.

Violation of rules

Violation of rules may include:

- skipping school
- running away from home

- drug and alcohol use
- sexual behavior at a very young age

Boys who have conduct disorder are more likely to display aggressive and destructive behavior than girls. Girls are more prone to deceitful and rule-violating behavior.

Also, the symptoms of conduct disorder can be mild, moderate, or severe:

Mild

If your child has mild symptoms, it means they display little to no behavior problems above those required to make the diagnosis. Conduct problems cause relatively minor harm to others. Common issues include lying, truancy, and staying out after dark without parental permission.

Moderate

Your child has moderate symptoms if they display numerous behavior problems. These conduct problems may have a mild to severe impact on others. The problems may include vandalism and stealing.

Severe

Your child has severe symptoms if they display behavior problems above those required to make the diagnosis. These conduct problems cause considerable harm to others. The problems may include rape, use of a weapon, or breaking and entering.

Causes

Genetic and environmental factors may contribute to the development of conduct disorder.

Genetic causes

Damage to the brain's frontal lobe has been linked to conduct disorder. The frontal lobe is the part of your brain that regulates essential cognitive skills, such as problem-solving, memory, and emotional expression. It's also home to your personality.

The frontal lobe in a person with conduct disorder may not work correctly, which can cause, among other things:

- a lack of impulse control
- a reduced ability to plan future actions
- a decreased ability to learn from past negative experiences

The impairment of the frontal lobe may be genetic or inherited, or it may be caused by brain damage due to an injury. A child may also inherit personality traits commonly seen in conduct disorder.,

Environmental factors

The environmental factors that are associated with conduct disorder include:

- child abuse
- a dysfunctional family
- parents who abuse drugs or alcohol
- poverty

Who is at risk for conduct disorder?

The following factors may increase your child's risk of developing conduct disorder:

- being male
- living in an urban environment
- living in poverty
- having a family history of conduct disorder
- having a family history of mental illness
- having other psychiatric disorders
- having parents who abuse drugs or alcohol

- having a dysfunctional home environment
- having a history of experiencing traumatic events
- being abused or neglected

How is conduct disorder diagnosed?

If your child shows signs of conduct disorder, they should be evaluated by a mental health professional. The professional will ask you and your child questions about their behavioral patterns to diagnose.

For a conduct disorder diagnosis to be made, your child must have a pattern of displaying at least three behaviors that are common to conduct disorder.

Your child must also have shown at least one of the behaviors within the past 6 months. The behavioral problems must also significantly impair your child socially or at school.

How is conduct disorder treated?

Children with conduct disorder living in abusive homes may be placed into other homes. If abuse isn't present, your child's mental health care professional will use behavior or talk therapy to help your child learn how to express or control their emotions appropriately.

The mental health care professional will also teach you how to manage your child's behavior. If your child has another mental health disorder, such as depression or ADHD, the mental health care professional may prescribe medications to treat that condition as well.

Because it takes time to establish new attitudes and behavior patterns, children with conduct disorder usually require long-term treatment. However, early treatment may slow the disorder's progression or reduce the severity of negative behaviors.

What is the long-term outlook for children with conduct disorder?

The long-term outlook for conduct disorder depends on the severity and frequency of your child's behavioral and emotional problems. Children who continuously display extremely aggressive, deceitful, or destructive behavior tend to have a poorer outlook. The outlook is also worse if other mental illnesses are present. However, getting a prompt diagnosis and receiving comprehensive treatment can significantly improve your child's outlook. Once treatment for conduct disorder and any other underlying conditions are received, your child has a much better chance of considerable improvement and hope for a more successful future. Parents and caregivers must seek treatment as well. Learning how to manage a conduct disordered child can be helpful to the child and adolescent and reduce stress within the family or social environment.

Without treatment, your child could have ongoing problems. They may be unable to adapt to the demands of adulthood, which can result in relationship problems and an inability to hold a job. They're also at an increased risk of substance misuse and problems with law enforcement.

Your child may even develop a personality disorder, such as antisocial personality disorder, when they reach adulthood. This is why early diagnosis and treatment are critical. The earlier your child receives treatment, the better their outlook for the future.

- PYROMANIA

Pyromania is a serious mental health condition characterized by intentionally and repetitively setting fires —and doing so compulsively. People with pyromania feel unable to stop the behavior. Setting a fire releases inner tension or anxiety and gives the person a rush of pleasure or relief.

Symptoms

The latest edition of the Diagnostic and Statistical Manual (DSM-5) files pyromania in the disruptive, impulse-control, and conduct disorders section.

The essential feature of pyromania is the presence of multiple episodes of deliberate and purposeful fire setting.

In addition, individuals with pyromania experience tension and affective arousal before setting a fire. Other symptoms may include:

- A fascination with fire, which may include interest, curiosity, and attraction to fire and fire-setting paraphernalia3
- Watching fires in the neighborhood, setting off false alarms, or gaining pleasure from institutions, equipment, and personnel with fire
- Spending time at a local fire department, setting fires to be affiliated with the fire department, or becoming a firefighter
- Experiencing pleasure, gratification, or relief when starting a fire, witnessing the effects, and participating in the aftermath

People with pyromania do not set fires for monetary gain. They also aren't trying to conceal criminal activity, gain vengeance, or improve their living situation. The symptoms also cannot be in response to delusions or hallucinations.

The fire setting also cannot stem from impaired judgment, such as an intellectual disability. The diagnosis also won't be made if the behavior is better explained by another mental illness, such as conduct disorder or antisocial personality disorder or if it occurs during a manic episode.

Pyromania vs. Arson

A person with pyromania might hoard matches and lighters, burn holes in fabric, rugs, or furniture and set fire to pieces of paper or other flammable materials. They are motivated because of the emotions they experience when they set fires. But they don't have a desire to harm anyone and they aren't looking for monetary gains from the fires they set. Someone committing arson, on the other hand, may burn down someone's house to get revenge or to try to collect insurance money.

Arson is a crime, whereas pyromania is a psychiatric diagnosis. Someone who commits arson does not necessarily have an underlying psychiatric condition; plus, setting fires is only one aspect of the diagnosis for pyromania.

Pyromania has been associated with people who have been sexually or physically abused, or suffer parental neglect or abandonment. People who have a history of crime also tend to display more fire-setting tendencies.

For example, more than 19% of those diagnosed with pyromania has been charged with vandalism at least once, and around 18% have been found guilty of non-violent sexual offenses.

Treatment

Immediate treatment of suspected pyromania is key to avoid

the risk of injury, property damage, jail time or even death. The sole method of treatment for pyromania is cognitive behavioral therapy, which teaches a person to acknowledge the feelings of tension that can lead to setting fires and finding a safer way to release that tension. Family members who are concerned about an individual who seems obsessed with fire might benefit from family counseling. Family therapy can help loved ones understand the disorder while also teaching them how to keep the family safe.

At this point, there haven't been any controlled trials of medication for pyromania, though proposed medical treatments include the use of SSRIs, antiepileptic medications, atypical antipsychotics, lithium, and anti-androgens. Therefore, cognitive behavioral therapy is considered the only viable treatment option at this time.

KLEPTOMANIA

Kleptomania (klep-toe-MAY-nee-uh) is a mental health disorder that involves repeatedly being unable to resist urges to steal items that you generally don't really need. Often the items stolen have little value and you could afford to buy them. Kleptomania is rare but can be a serious condition. It can cause much emotional pain to you and your loved ones — and even legal problems — if not treated. Kleptomania is a type of impulse control disorder — a disorder that involves problems with emotional or behavioral self-control. If you have an impulse control disorder, you have difficulty resisting the temptation or powerful urge to perform an act that's excessive or harmful to you or someone else.

Many people with kleptomania live lives of secret shame because they're afraid to seek mental health treatment. Although there's no cure for kleptomania, treatment with medicine or skill-building therapy that focuses on dealing with urges may help to end the cycle of compulsive stealing.

Symptoms

Kleptomania symptoms may include:

- Inability to resist powerful urges to steal items that you don't need
- Feeling increased tension, anxiety or arousal leading up to the theft
- Feeling pleasure, relief or satisfaction while stealing
- Feeling terrible guilt, remorse, self-loathing, shame or fear of arrest after the theft
- Return of the urges and a repetition of the kleptomania cycle

Features

People with kleptomania usually have these features or characteristics:

- Unlike most shoplifters, people with kleptomania don't compulsively steal for personal gain, on a dare, for revenge or out of rebellion. They steal simply because the urge is so powerful that they can't resist it.
- Episodes of kleptomania generally happen suddenly, without planning and without help from another person.
- Most people with kleptomania steal from public places, such as stores. Some may steal from friends or acquaintances, such as at a party.
- Often, the stolen items have no value to the person with kleptomania, and the person can afford to buy them.
- The stolen items are usually stashed away, never to be used. Items also may be donated, given away to family or friends, or even secretly returned to the place from which they were stolen.
- Urges to steal may come and go or may occur with greater or lesser intensity over the course of time.

When to see a doctor

If you can't stop shoplifting or stealing, seek medical advice. Many people who may have kleptomania don't want to seek treatment because they're afraid they'll be arrested or jailed. However, a mental health provider usually doesn't report your thefts to authorities.

Some people seek medical help because they're afraid they'll get caught and have legal problems. Or they've already been arrested, and they're legally required to seek treatment.

If a loved one has kleptomania

If you suspect a close friend or family member may have kleptomania, gently raise your concerns with that person. Keep in mind that kleptomania is a mental health disorder, not a character flaw, so approach the person without judgment or blame.

It may be helpful to emphasize these points:

- You're concerned because you care about the person's health and well-being.
- You're worried about the risks of compulsive stealing, such as being arrested, losing a job or damaging a valued relationship.
- You understand that, with kleptomania, the urge to steal may be too strong to resist just by "putting your mind to it."
- Treatments are available that may help to minimize the urge to steal and live without addiction and shame.

If you need help preparing for this conversation, talk with your health care provider. Your provider may refer you to a mental health professional who can help you plan a way of raising your concerns without making your friend or relative feel defensive or threatened.

Causes

The causes of kleptomania are not known. Several theories suggest that changes in the brain may be at the root of kleptomania, and that learned patterns of stealing items strengthens the problem

over time. More research is needed to better understand these possible causes, but kleptomania may be linked to:

- **Problems with a naturally occurring brain chemical called serotonin.** Serotonin, a

neurotransmitter, helps regulate moods and emotions. Low levels of serotonin are common in people prone to impulsive behaviors.
- **Addictive disorders.** Stealing may cause the release of dopamine — another neurotransmitter. Dopamine causes pleasurable feelings, and some people seek this rewarding feeling again and again.
- **The brain's opioid system.** Urges are regulated by the brain's opioid system. An imbalance in this system could make it harder to resist urges.
- **Learned habit.** Urges are very uncomfortable. Responding to these urges by stealing causes a temporary decrease in distress and relief from these urges. This creates a strong habit that becomes hard to break.

Risk factors

Kleptomania is not common. But some cases of kleptomania may never be diagnosed. Some people never seek treatment. Other people are jailed after repeated thefts.

Kleptomania often begins during the teen years or in young adulthood, but it can start later. About two-thirds of people with known kleptomania are female.

Kleptomania risk factors may include:

- **Family history.** Having a blood relative, such as a parent or sibling, with kleptomania or addictive disorders may increase the risk of kleptomania.
- **Having another mental illness.** People with kleptomania often have another mental health disorder, such as anxiety, depression or a substance use disorder.

Complications

Left untreated, kleptomania can result in severe emotional,

family, work, legal and financial problems. For example, you know stealing is wrong but you feel powerless to resist the impulse. As a result, you may be filled with guilt, shame, self-loathing and humiliation. And you may be arrested for stealing. You may otherwise lead a law-abiding life and be confused and upset by your compulsive stealing.

Other complications and conditions associated with kleptomania may include:

- Other impulse-control disorders, such as compulsive gambling or shopping
- Alcohol or other substance misuse
- Personality disorders
- Eating disorders
- Depression
- Bipolar disorder
- Anxiety disorders
- Suicidal thoughts and behaviors

Prevention

Because the causes of kleptomania aren't clear, it's not yet known how to prevent it with any certainty. Getting treatment as soon as compulsive stealing begins may help prevent kleptomania from becoming worse and prevent some of the negative consequences.

Diagnosis

Kleptomania is diagnosed based on your symptoms. When you decide to seek treatment for symptoms of possible kleptomania, you may have both a physical exam and psychological evaluation. The physical exam can determine if there are any medical causes triggering your symptoms.

Because kleptomania is a type of impulse control disorder, to help pinpoint a diagnosis, your mental health provider may:

- Ask questions about your impulses and how they make you feel
- Review a list of situations to ask if these situations trigger your kleptomania episodes
- Discuss problems you have had because of this behavior
- Have you fill out questionnaires or self-assessments
- Use the guidelines in the Diagnostic and Statistical Manual of Mental Disorders (DSM-5), published by the American Psychiatric Association

Treatment

Although fear, humiliation or embarrassment may make it hard for you to seek treatment for kleptomania, it's important to get help. Kleptomania is difficult to overcome on your own. Without treatment, kleptomania will likely be an ongoing, long-term condition.

Treatment for kleptomania typically involves medicines and psychotherapy, or both, sometimes along with self-help groups. However, there's no standard kleptomania treatment, and researchers are still trying to understand what may work best. You may have to try several types of treatment to find what works well for you.

Medicines

There's little scientific research about using psychiatric medicines to treat kleptomania. And there is no FDA-approved medicine for kleptomania. However, certain medicines may help, depending on your situation and whether you have other mental health disorders, such as depression or substance misuse.

Your provider may consider prescribing:
- An addiction treatment medicine called naltrexone, which may reduce the urges and pleasure associated

with stealing
- An antidepressant — specifically a selective serotonin reuptake inhibitor (SSRI)
- Other medicines or a combination of medicines

If medicine is prescribed, ask your health care provider or pharmacist about potential side effects or possible interactions with any other medicines.

Psychotherapy

A form of psychotherapy called cognitive behavioral therapy helps you identify unhealthy, negative beliefs and behaviors and replace them with healthy ones that can be used in different situations when needed. Cognitive behavioral therapy may include these skill-building techniques to help you control kleptomania urges:

- **Systematic desensitization and counterconditioning,** in which you practice relaxation techniques and other strategies while in triggering situations to learn how to reduce your urges in a healthy way
- **Covert sensitization,** in which you picture yourself stealing and then facing negative consequences, such as being caught
- **Aversion therapy,** in which you practice mildly painful techniques, such as holding your breath until you become uncomfortable, when you get an urge to steal

Avoiding relapses

It's not unusual to have relapses of kleptomania. To help avoid relapses, be sure to follow your treatment plan. If you feel urges to steal, contact your mental health provider or reach out to a trusted person or support group.

Coping and support

You can take steps to care for yourself with healthy coping skills while getting professional treatment:

- **Follow your treatment plan.** Take medicines as directed and attend scheduled therapy sessions. Remember, it's hard work and you may have occasional setbacks.
- **Educate yourself.** Learn about kleptomania so that you can better understand risk factors, treatments and triggering events.
- **Identify your triggers.** Identify situations, thoughts and feelings that may trigger urges to steal so you can take steps to manage them.
- **Get treatment for substance misuse or other mental health problems.** Your substance use, depression, anxiety and stress can lead to a cycle of emotional pain and unhealthy behavior.
- **Find healthy outlets.** Explore healthy ways to rechannel your urges to steal or shoplift through exercise and recreational activities.
- **Learn relaxation and stress management.** Try stress-reduction techniques such as meditation, yoga or tai chi.
- **Stay focused on your goal.** Recovery from kleptomania can take time. Stay motivated by keeping your recovery goals in mind. Remind yourself that you can work to repair damaged relationships and financial and legal problems.
- **Be honest with loved ones.** You might initially need help with controlling your urges when in higher-risk situations, such as shopping. Let your loved ones know about your struggles and consider using the "buddy system" for a period of time while you're learning more ways to manage your urges.

Support for loved ones

If your close friend or family member is being treated for kleptomania, make sure you understand the details of the treatment plan and actively support its success. It may be helpful to attend one or more therapy sessions with your friend or relative to learn the factors that seem to trigger the urge to steal and the most effective ways to cope.

You also may benefit from talking with a therapist yourself. Recovering from an impulse control disorder is a challenging, long-term undertaking — both for the person with the disorder and close friends and family. Make sure you're taking care of your own needs with the stress-reduction outlets that work best for you, such as exercise, meditation or time with friends.

Self-help groups

People with kleptomania may benefit from participating in self-help groups based on 12-step programs and those designed for addiction problems. Even if you can't find a group specifically for kleptomania, you may benefit from attending Alcoholics Anonymous or other addiction meetings. Such groups don't suit everyone's tastes, so ask your mental health provider about alternatives.

Preparing for your appointment

If you struggle with an irresistible urge to steal, talk to your health care provider. Be honest with your provider about your symptoms. Having that discussion can be scary, but trust that your provider is interested in caring for your health, not in judging you. You may be referred to a mental health provider, such as a psychiatrist or psychologist, with experience diagnosing and treating kleptomania.

You may want to take a trusted family member or friend along to help remember the details. Also, someone who has known you for a long time may be able to ask questions or share information with the mental health provider that you don't remember to bring up.

Here's some information to help you get ready and know what to expect from your provider.

What you can do

To prepare for your appointment, make a list of:

- Any symptoms you're experiencing, and for how long
- **Key personal information,** including traumatic events in your past and any current, major stressors
- **Your medical information,** including other physical or mental health conditions
- **All medicines you're taking,** including any vitamins, herbs or other supplements, and the doses
- **Questions to ask your provider** so that you can make the most of your appointment

Some questions to ask may include:

- Why can't I stop stealing?
- What treatments are available?
- What treatments are most likely to work for me?
- How quickly might I stop stealing?
- Will I still feel the urge to steal?
- How often do I need therapy sessions and for how long?
- Are there medicines that can help?
- What are the possible side effects of these

medicines?
- I have these other health conditions. How can I best manage these conditions together?
- How can my family best support my treatment?
- Are there any brochures or other printed material that I can have? What websites do you recommend?

What to expect from your mental health professional

To better understand your symptoms and how they're affecting your life, your mental health provider may ask:

- At what age did you first experience an irresistible urge to steal?
- How often do you experience the urge to steal?
- Have you ever been caught or arrested for stealing?
- How would you describe your feelings before, during and after you steal something?
- What kinds of items do you steal? Are they things you need?
- In what kinds of situations are you likely to steal?
- What do you do with the items you steal?
- Does anything in particular seem to trigger your urge to steal?
- How is your urge to steal affecting your life, including school, work and personal relationships?
- Have any of your close relatives had a problem with compulsive stealing or with other mental health conditions, such as depression or alcohol or drug misuse?
- Do you use alcohol or recreational drugs? If so, what do you use and how often?
- Have you been treated for any other mental health problems, such as anxiety or depression? If yes, what treatments were most effective?
- Are you currently being treated for any medical conditions?

You may be asked more questions based on your responses, symptoms and needs. Preparing for questions will help you make the most of your appointment.

14. Substance-related and addictive disorders:

- Drug addiction (substance use disorder)

Drug addiction, also called substance use disorder, is a disease that affects a person's brain and behavior and leads to an inability to control the use of a legal or illegal drug or medicine. Substances such as alcohol, marijuana and nicotine also are considered drugs. When you're addicted, you may continue using the drug despite the harm it causes.

Drug addiction can start with experimental use of a recreational drug in social situations, and, for some people, the drug use becomes more frequent. For others, particularly with opioids, drug addiction begins when they take prescribed medicines or receive them from others who have prescriptions.

The risk of addiction and how fast you become addicted varies by drug. Some drugs, such as opioid painkillers, have a higher risk and cause addiction more quickly than others.

As time passes, you may need larger doses of the drug to get high. Soon you may need the drug just to feel good. As your drug use increases, you may find that it's increasingly difficult to go without the drug. Attempts to stop drug use may cause intense cravings and make you feel physically ill. These are called withdrawal symptoms.

Help from your health care provider, family, friends, support groups or an organized treatment program can help you overcome your drug addiction and stay drug-free.

Symptoms

Drug addiction symptoms or behaviors include, among others:

- Feeling that you have to use the drug regularly — daily or even several times a day
- Having intense urges for the drug that block out any other thoughts
- Over time, needing more of the drug to get the same effect
- Taking larger amounts of the drug over a longer period of time than you intended
- Making certain that you maintain a supply of the drug
- Spending money on the drug, even though you can't afford it
- Not meeting obligations and work responsibilities, or cutting back on social or recreational activities because of drug use
- Continuing to use the drug, even though you know it's causing problems in your life or causing you physical or psychological harm
- Doing things to get the drug that you normally wouldn't do, such as stealing
- Driving or doing other risky activities when you're under the influence of the drug
- Spending a good deal of time getting the drug, using the drug or recovering from the effects of the drug
- Failing in your attempts to stop using the drug
- Experiencing withdrawal symptoms when you attempt to stop taking the drug

Recognizing unhealthy drug use in family members

Sometimes it's difficult to distinguish normal teenage moodiness or anxiety from signs of drug use. Possible signs that your teenager or other family member is using drugs include:

- **Problems at school or work** — frequently missing school or work, a sudden disinterest in school activities or work, or a drop in grades or work performance
- **Physical health issues** — lack of energy and motivation, weight loss or gain, or red eyes
- **Neglected appearance** — lack of interest in clothing, grooming or looks
- **Changes in behavior** — major efforts to bar family members from entering the teenager's room or being secretive about going out with friends; or drastic changes in behavior and in relationships with family and friends
- **Money issues** — sudden requests for money without a reasonable explanation; or your discovery that money is missing or has been stolen or that items have disappeared from your home, indicating maybe they're being sold to support drug use

Recognizing signs of drug use or intoxication

Signs and symptoms of drug use or intoxication may vary, depending on the type of drug. Below you'll find several examples.

Marijuana, hashish and other cannabis-containing substances

People use cannabis by smoking, eating or inhaling a vaporized form of the drug. Cannabis often precedes or is used along with other substances, such as alcohol or illegal drugs, and is often the first drug tried.

Signs and symptoms of recent use can include:

- A sense of euphoria or feeling "high"

- A heightened sense of visual, auditory and taste perception
- Increased blood pressure and heart rate
- Red eyes
- Dry mouth
- Decreased coordination
- Difficulty concentrating or remembering
- Slowed reaction time
- Anxiety or paranoid thinking
- Cannabis odor on clothes or yellow fingertips
- Major cravings for certain foods at unusual times

Long-term use is often associated with:

- Decreased mental sharpness
- Poor performance at school or at work
- Ongoing cough and frequent lung infections

K2, Spice and bath salts

Two groups of synthetic drugs — synthetic cannabinoids and substituted or synthetic cathinones — are illegal in most states. The effects of these drugs can be dangerous and unpredictable, as there is no quality control and some ingredients may not be known.

Synthetic cannabinoids, also called K2 or Spice, are sprayed on dried herbs and then smoked, but can be prepared as an herbal tea. A liquid form can be vaporized in electronic cigarettes. Despite manufacturer claims, these are chemical compounds rather than "natural" or harmless products. These drugs can produce a "high" similar to marijuana and have become a popular but dangerous alternative.

Signs and symptoms of recent use can include:

- A sense of euphoria or feeling "high"
- Elevated mood
- An altered sense of visual, auditory and taste perception

- Extreme anxiety or agitation
- Paranoia
- Hallucinations
- Increased heart rate and blood pressure or heart attack
- Vomiting
- Confusion
- Violent behavior

Substituted cathinones, also called "bath salts," are mind-altering (psychoactive) substances similar to amphetamines such as ecstasy (MDMA) and cocaine. Packages are often labeled as other products to avoid detection.

Despite the name, these are not bath products such as Epsom salts. Substituted cathinones can be eaten, snorted, inhaled or injected and are highly addictive. These drugs can cause severe intoxication, which results in dangerous health effects or even death.

Signs and symptoms of recent use can include:

- Feeling "high"
- Increased sociability
- Increased energy and agitation
- Increased sex drive
- Increased heart rate and blood pressure
- Problems thinking clearly
- Loss of muscle control
- Paranoia
- Panic attacks
- Hallucinations
- Delirium
- Psychotic and violent behavior

Barbiturates, benzodiazepines and hypnotics

Barbiturates, benzodiazepines and hypnotics are prescription central nervous system depressants. They're often used and misused in search for a sense of relaxation or a desire to "switch off" or forget stress-related thoughts or feelings.

- **Barbiturates.** An example is phenobarbital.
- **Benzodiazepines.** Examples include sedatives, such as diazepam (Valium), alprazolam (Xanax), lorazepam (Ativan), clonazepam (Klonopin) and chlordiazepoxide (Librium).
- **Hypnotics.** Examples include prescription sleeping medicines such as zolpidem (Ambien) and zaleplon (Sonata).

Signs and symptoms of recent use can include:

- Drowsiness
- Slurred speech
- Lack of coordination
- Irritability or changes in mood
- Problems concentrating or thinking clearly
- Memory problems
- Involuntary eye movements
- Lack of inhibition
- Slowed breathing and reduced blood pressure
- Falls or accidents
- Dizziness

Meth, cocaine and other stimulants

Stimulants include amphetamines, meth (methamphetamine), cocaine, methylphenidate (Ritalin, Concerta, others) and amphetamine-dextroamphetamine (Adderall XR, Mydayis). They're often used and misused in search of a "high," or to boost energy, to improve performance at work or school, or to lose weight or control appetite.

Signs and symptoms of recent use can include:

- Feeling of happy excitement and too much

- confidence
- Increased alertness
- Increased energy and restlessness
- Behavior changes or aggression
- Rapid or rambling speech
- Larger than usual pupils, the black circles in the middle of the eyes
- Confusion, delusions and hallucinations
- Irritability, anxiety or paranoia
- Changes in heart rate, blood pressure and body temperature
- Nausea or vomiting with weight loss
- Poor judgment
- Nasal congestion and damage to the mucous membrane of the nose (if snorting drugs)
- Mouth sores, gum disease and tooth decay from smoking drugs ("meth mouth")
- Insomnia
- Depression as the drug wears off

Club drugs

Club drugs are commonly used at clubs, concerts and parties. Examples include methylenedioxymethamphetamine, also called MDMA, ecstasy or molly, and gamma-hydroxybutyric acid, known as GHB. Other examples include ketamine and flunitrazepam or Rohypnol — also called roofie. These drugs are not all in the same category, but they share some similar effects and dangers, including long-term harmful effects.

Because GHB and flunitrazepam can cause sedation, muscle relaxation, confusion and memory loss, the potential for sexual misconduct or sexual assault is associated with the use of these drugs.

Signs and symptoms of use of club drugs can include:
- Hallucinations

UNDERSTANDING MENTAL HEALTH

- Paranoia
- Larger than usual pupils
- Chills and sweating
- Involuntary shaking (tremors)
- Behavior changes
- Muscle cramping and teeth clenching
- Muscle relaxation, poor coordination or problems moving
- Reduced inhibitions
- Heightened or altered sense of sight, sound and taste
- Poor judgment
- Memory problems or loss of memory
- Reduced consciousness
- Increased or decreased heart rate and blood pressure

Hallucinogens

Use of hallucinogens can produce different signs and symptoms, depending on the drug. The most common hallucinogens are lysergic acid diethylamide (LSD) and phencyclidine (PCP).

LSD use may cause:

- Hallucinations
- Greatly reduced perception of reality, for example, interpreting input from one of your senses as another, such as hearing colors
- Impulsive behavior
- Rapid shifts in emotions
- Permanent mental changes in perception
- Rapid heart rate and high blood pressure
- Tremors
- Flashbacks, a reexperience of the hallucinations — even years later

PCP use may cause:

- A feeling of being separated from your body and surroundings
- Hallucinations
- Problems with coordination and movement
- Aggressive, possibly violent behavior
- Involuntary eye movements
- Lack of pain sensation
- Increase in blood pressure and heart rate
- Problems with thinking and memory
- Problems speaking
- Poor judgment
- Intolerance to loud noise
- Sometimes seizures or coma

Inhalants

Signs and symptoms of inhalant use vary, depending on the substance. Some commonly inhaled substances include glue, paint thinners, correction fluid, felt tip marker fluid, gasoline, cleaning fluids and household aerosol products. Due to the toxic nature of these substances, users may develop brain damage or sudden death.

Signs and symptoms of use can include:

- Possessing an inhalant substance without a reasonable explanation
- Brief happy excitement
- Behaving as if drunk
- Reduced ability to keep impulses under control
- Aggressive behavior or eagerness to fight
- Dizziness
- Nausea or vomiting
- Involuntary eye movements

UNDERSTANDING MENTAL HEALTH

- Appearing under the influence of drugs, with slurred speech, slow movements and poor coordination
- Irregular heartbeats
- Tremors
- Lingering odor of inhalant material
- Rash around the nose and mouth

Opioid painkillers

Opioids are narcotic, painkilling drugs produced from opium or made synthetically. This class of drugs includes, among others, heroin, morphine, codeine, methadone, fentanyl and oxycodone.

Sometimes called the "opioid epidemic," addiction to opioid prescription pain medicines has reached an alarming rate across the United States. Some people who've been using opioids over a long period of time may need physician-prescribed temporary or long-term drug substitution during treatment.

Signs and symptoms of narcotic use and dependence can include:

- A sense of feeling "high"
- Reduced sense of pain
- Agitation, drowsiness or sedation
- Slurred speech
- Problems with attention and memory
- Pupils that are smaller than usual
- Lack of awareness or inattention to surrounding people and things
- Problems with coordination
- Depression
- Confusion
- Constipation
- Runny nose or nose sores (if snorting drugs)

- Needle marks (if injecting drugs)

When to see a doctor

If your drug use is out of control or causing problems, get help. The sooner you seek help, the greater your chances for a long-term recovery. Talk with your health care provider or see a mental health provider, such as a doctor who specializes in addiction medicine or addiction psychiatry, or a licensed alcohol and drug counselor.

Make an appointment to see a provider if:
- You can't stop using a drug
- You continue using the drug despite the harm it causes
- Your drug use has led to unsafe behavior, such as sharing needles or unprotected sex
- You think you may be having withdrawal symptoms after stopping drug use

If you're not ready to approach a health care provider or mental health professional, help lines or hotlines may be a good place to learn about treatment. You can find these lines listed on the internet or in the phone book.

When to seek emergency help

Seek emergency help if you or someone you know has taken a drug and:
- May have overdosed
- Shows changes in consciousness
- Has trouble breathing
- Has seizures or convulsions
- Has signs of a possible heart attack, such as chest pain or pressure
- Has any other troublesome physical or

psychological reaction to use of the drug

Staging an intervention

People struggling with addiction usually deny they have a problem and hesitate to seek treatment. An intervention presents a loved one with a structured opportunity to make changes before things get even worse and can motivate someone to seek or accept help.

It's important to plan an intervention carefully. It may be done by family and friends in consultation with a health care provider or mental health professional such as a licensed alcohol and drug counselor, or directed by an intervention professional. It involves family and friends and sometimes co-workers, clergy or others who care about the person struggling with addiction.

During the intervention, these people gather together to have a direct, heart-to-heart conversation with the person about the consequences of addiction. Then they ask the person to accept treatment.

Causes

Like many mental health disorders, several factors may contribute to development of drug addiction. The main factors are:

- **Environment.** Environmental factors, including your family's beliefs and attitudes and exposure to a peer group that encourages drug use, seem to play a role in initial drug use.
- **Genetics.** Once you've started using a drug, the development into addiction may be influenced by inherited (genetic) traits, which may delay or speed up the disease progression.

Changes in the brain

Physical addiction appears to occur when repeated use of a drug changes the way your brain feels pleasure. The addicting drug causes physical changes to some nerve cells (neurons) in your brain. Neurons use chemicals called neurotransmitters to communicate. These changes can remain long after you stop using the drug.

Risk factors

People of any age, sex or economic status can become addicted to a drug. Certain factors can affect the likelihood and speed of developing an addiction:

- **Family history of addiction.** Drug addiction is more common in some families and likely involves an increased risk based on genes. If you have a blood relative, such as a parent or sibling, with alcohol or drug addiction, you're at greater risk of developing a drug addiction.
- **Mental health disorder.** If you have a mental health disorder such as depression, attention-deficit/hyperactivity disorder (ADHD) or post-traumatic stress disorder, you're more likely to become addicted to drugs. Using drugs can become a way of coping with painful feelings, such as anxiety, depression and loneliness, and can make these problems even worse.
- **Peer pressure.** Peer pressure is a strong factor in starting to use and misuse drugs, particularly for young people.
- **Lack of family involvement.** Difficult family situations or lack of a bond with your parents or siblings may increase the risk of addiction, as can a lack of parental supervision.

- **Early use.** Using drugs at an early age can cause changes in the developing brain and increase the likelihood of progressing to drug addiction.
- **Taking a highly addictive drug.** Some drugs, such as stimulants, cocaine or opioid painkillers, may result in faster development of addiction than other drugs. Smoking or injecting drugs can increase the potential for addiction. Taking drugs considered less addicting — so-called "light drugs" — can start you on a pathway of drug use and addiction.

Complications

Drug use can have significant and damaging short-term and long-term effects. Taking some drugs can be particularly risky, especially if you take high doses or combine them with other drugs or alcohol. Here are some examples.

- Methamphetamine, opiates and cocaine are highly addictive and cause multiple short-term and long-term health consequences, including psychotic behavior, seizures or death due to overdose. Opioid drugs affect the part of the brain that controls breathing, and overdose can result in death. Taking opioids with alcohol increases this risk.
- GHB and flunitrazepam may cause sedation, confusion and memory loss. These so-called "date rape drugs" are known to impair the ability to resist unwanted contact and recollection of the event. At high doses, they can cause seizures, coma and death. The danger increases when these drugs are taken with alcohol.
- MDMA — also known as molly or ecstasy — can interfere with the body's ability to regulate temperature. A severe spike in body temperature can result in liver, kidney or heart failure and death. Other complications can include severe

dehydration, leading to seizures. Long-term, MDMA can damage the brain.
- One particular danger of club drugs is that the liquid, pill or powder forms of these drugs available on the street often contain unknown substances that can be harmful, including other illegally manufactured or pharmaceutical drugs.
- Due to the toxic nature of inhalants, users may develop brain damage of different levels of severity. Sudden death can occur even after a single exposure.

Other life-changing complications

Dependence on drugs can create a number of dangerous and damaging complications, including:

- **Getting an infectious disease.** People who are addicted to a drug are more likely to get an infectious disease, such as HIV, either through unsafe sex or by sharing needles with others.
- **Other health problems.** Drug addiction can lead to a range of both short-term and long-term mental and physical health problems. These depend on what drug is taken.
- **Accidents.** People who are addicted to drugs are more likely to drive or do other dangerous activities while under the influence.
- **Suicide.** People who are addicted to drugs die by suicide more often than people who aren't addicted.
- **Family problems.** Behavioral changes may cause relationship or family conflict and custody issues.
- **Work issues.** Drug use can cause declining performance at work, absenteeism and eventual loss of employment.
- **Problems at school**. Drug use can negatively affect academic performance and motivation to excel in

school.
- **Legal issues.** Legal problems are common for drug users and can stem from buying or possessing illegal drugs, stealing to support the drug addiction, driving while under the influence of drugs or alcohol, or disputes over child custody.
- **Financial problems.** Spending money to support drug use takes away money from other needs, could lead to debt, and can lead to illegal or unethical behaviors.

Prevention

The best way to prevent an addiction to a drug is not to take the drug at all. If your health care provider prescribes a drug with the potential for addiction, use care when taking the drug and follow instructions.

Health care providers should prescribe these medicines at safe doses and amounts and monitor their use so that you're not given too great a dose or for too long a time. If you feel you need to take more than the prescribed dose of a medicine, talk to your health care provider.

Preventing drug misuse in children and teenagers

Take these steps to help prevent drug misuse in your children and teenagers:
- **Communicate.** Talk to your children about the risks of drug use and misuse.
- Listen. Be a good listener when your children talk about peer pressure and be supportive of their efforts to resist it.
- **Set a good example.** Don't misuse alcohol or addictive drugs. Children of parents who misuse drugs are at greater risk of drug addiction.

- **Strengthen the bond.** Work on your relationship with your children. A strong, stable bond between you and your child will reduce your child's risk of using or misusing drugs.

Preventing a relapse

Once you've been addicted to a drug, you're at high risk of falling back into a pattern of addiction. If you do start using the drug, it's likely you'll lose control over its use again — even if you've had treatment and you haven't used the drug for some time.

- **Follow your treatment plan.** Monitor your cravings. It may seem like you've recovered and you don't need to keep taking steps to stay drug-free. But your chances of staying drug-free will be much higher if you continue seeing your therapist or counselor, going to support group meetings and taking prescribed medicine.
- **Avoid high-risk situations.** Don't go back to the neighborhood where you used to get your drugs. And stay away from your old drug crowd.
- **Get help immediately if you use the drug again.** If you start using the drug again, talk to your health care provider, your mental health provider or someone else who can help you right away.

Diagnosis

Diagnosing drug addiction (substance use disorder) requires a thorough evaluation and often includes an assessment by a psychiatrist, a psychologist, or a licensed alcohol and drug counselor. Blood, urine or other lab tests are used to assess drug use, but they're not a diagnostic test for addiction. However, these tests may be used for monitoring treatment and recovery.

For diagnosis of a substance use disorder, most mental health professionals use criteria in the Diagnostic and Statistical Manual of Mental Disorders (DSM-5), published by the American Psychiatric Association.

Treatment

Although there's no cure for drug addiction, treatment options can help you overcome an addiction and stay drug-free. Your treatment depends on the drug used and any related medical or mental health disorders you may have. Long-term follow-up is important to prevent relapse.

Treatment programs

Treatment programs for substance use disorder usually offer:

- Individual, group or family therapy sessions
- A focus on understanding the nature of addiction, becoming drug-free and preventing relapse
- Levels of care and settings that vary depending on your needs, such as outpatient, residential and inpatient programs

Withdrawal therapy

The goal of detoxification, also called "detox" or withdrawal therapy, is to enable you to stop taking the addicting drug as quickly and safely as possible. For some people, it may be safe to undergo withdrawal therapy on an outpatient basis. Others may need admission to a hospital or a residential treatment center.

Withdrawal from different categories of drugs — such as depressants, stimulants or opioids — produces different side effects and requires different approaches. Detox may involve gradually reducing the dose of the drug or temporarily substituting other substances, such as methadone, buprenorphine, or a combination of buprenorphine and naloxone.

Opioid overdose

In an opioid overdose, a medicine called naloxone can be given by emergency responders, or in some states, by anyone who witnesses an overdose. Naloxone temporarily reverses the effects of opioid drugs.

While naloxone has been on the market for years, a nasal spray (Narcan, Kloxxado) and an injectable form are now available, though they can be very expensive. Whatever the method of delivery, seek immediate medical care after using naloxone.

Medicine as part of treatment

After discussion with you, your health care provider may recommend medicine as part of your treatment for opioid addiction. Medicines don't cure your opioid addiction, but they can help in your recovery. These medicines can reduce your craving for opioids and may help you avoid relapse. Medicine treatment options for opioid addiction may include buprenorphine, methadone, naltrexone, and a combination of buprenorphine and naloxone.

Behavior therapy

As part of a drug treatment program, behavior therapy — a form of psychotherapy — can be done by a psychologist or psychiatrist, or you may receive counseling from a licensed alcohol and drug counselor. Therapy and counseling may be done with an individual, a family or a group. The therapist or counselor can:

Help you develop ways to cope with your drug cravings

- Suggest strategies to avoid drugs and prevent relapse
- Offer suggestions on how to deal with a relapse if it occurs
- Talk about issues regarding your job, legal problems, and relationships with family and friends
- Include family members to help them develop better communication skills and be supportive
- Address other mental health conditions

Self-help groups

Many, though not all, self-help support groups use the 12-step model first developed by Alcoholics Anonymous. Self-help support groups, such as Narcotics Anonymous, help people who are addicted to drugs.

The self-help support group message is that addiction is an ongoing disorder with a danger of relapse. Self-help support groups can decrease the sense of shame and isolation that can lead to relapse.

Your therapist or licensed counselor can help you locate a self-help support group. You may also find support groups in your community or on the internet.

Ongoing treatment

Even after you've completed initial treatment, ongoing treatment and support can help prevent a relapse. Follow-up care can include periodic appointments with your counselor, continuing in a self-help program or attending a regular group session. Seek help right away if you relapse.

Coping and support

Overcoming an addiction and staying drug-free require a persistent effort. Learning new coping skills and knowing where to find help are essential. Taking these actions can help:

- **See a licensed therapist or licensed drug and alcohol counselor.** Drug addiction is linked to many problems that may be helped with therapy or counseling, including other underlying mental health concerns or marriage or family problems. Seeing a psychiatrist, psychologist or licensed counselor may help you regain your peace of mind and mend your relationships.
- **Seek treatment for other mental health disorders.** People with other mental health problems, such as depression, are more likely to become addicted to drugs. Seek immediate treatment from a qualified mental health professional if you have any signs or symptoms of mental health problems.
- **Join a support group.** Support groups, such as Narcotics Anonymous or Alcoholics Anonymous, can be very effective in coping with addiction. Compassion, understanding and shared experiences can help you break your addiction and stay drug-free.

Preparing for your appointment

It may help to get an independent perspective from someone you trust and who knows you well. You can start by discussing your substance use with your primary care provider. Or ask for a referral to a specialist in drug addiction, such as a licensed alcohol and drug counselor, or a psychiatrist or psychologist. Take a relative or friend along.

Here's some information to help you get ready for your appointment.

What you can do

Before your appointment, be prepared:

- **Be honest about your drug use.** When you engage in unhealthy drug use, it can be easy to downplay or underestimate how much you use and your level of addiction. To get an accurate idea of which treatment may help, be honest with your health care provider or mental health provider.
- **Make a list of all medicines, vitamins, herbs or other supplements** that you're taking, and the dosages. Tell your health care provider and mental health provider about any legal or illegal drugs you're using.
- **Make a list of questions to ask** your health care provider or mental health provider.

Some questions to ask your provider may include:

- What's the best approach to my drug addiction?
- Should I see a psychiatrist or other mental health professional?
- Will I need to go to the hospital or spend time as an inpatient or outpatient at a recovery clinic?
- What are the alternatives to the primary approach that you're suggesting?
- Are there any brochures or other printed material that I can have? What websites do you recommend?

Don't hesitate to ask other questions during your appointment.

What to expect from your doctor

Your provider is likely to ask you several questions, such as:

- What drugs do you use?
- When did your drug use first start?
- How often do you use drugs?
- When you take a drug, how much do you use?
- Do you ever feel that you might have a problem with drugs?
- Have you tried to quit on your own? What happened when you did?
- If you tried to quit, did you have withdrawal symptoms?
- Have any family members criticized your drug use?
- Are you ready to get the treatment needed for your drug addiction?

Be ready to answer questions so you'll have more time to go over any points you want to focus on.

How common is substance use disorder?

Drug Addiction Statistics in South Africa
The drug problem in South Africa has been on a continual rise, especially in the last few years. Methaqualone (Quaaludes), cocaine, marijuana (known as dagga in South Africa), and heroin are all drugs that are becoming increasingly popular.

Dr. David Bayever from the government drug control organization, known as the CDA, is quoted saying "The drug problem in South Africa remains very serious with drug usage being twice the world norm in most cases...and we are only dealing with what we know about...this is only the tip of the iceberg,". Bayever says that at least 15% of South Africans have a drug problem; this number however is expected to rise. While some drugs are produced directly in South Africa, it is also a major transshipment hub for importing and exporting them.

New Environments Promote Drug Use

South Africa is located in the southernmost part of Africa and has a population of nearly 50 million people. By area, South Africa is one-eighth the size of the United States, just over one-third the size of the European Union, twice as big as France, and nearly four times the size of Germany. Over the past decade, South Africa has become a major country involved in international drug trafficking networks. Experts agree that it is becoming harder and harder to deal with the explosion of the drug trade.

There have been drastic political changes that have been accompanied by social transitioning, rapid modernization, high unemployment rates, and a decline in social, cultural, and family values. As a result, drug use has flourished and new environments, such as night clubs, that promote drug use have been created. These environments appear especially promising for adolescents and young adults looking for an escape. It is in these places that drugs look cool and casual sex is acceptable. Unfortunately, these places are a haven for heavy drug abuse and diseases; such as, HIV and AIDS.

SA drug statistics

- Drug consumption in South Africa is twice the world norm.
- 15% of South Africa's population have a drug problem.
- Drug abuse is costing South Africa R20-billion a year and could pose a bigger threat to the country's future than the Aids pandemic.
- According to SAPS figures, 60 percent of crimes nationally were related to substance abuse. In the

Western Cape, the figure was closer to 80 percent. The perpetrators of these crimes are either under the influence of substances, or trying to secure money for their next fix.
- In 2004, government disbanded the SA Narcotics Bureau (SANAB), a dedicated drug-fighting unit within the SAPS that had achieved some notable successes. Since its closure, drug-related crimes have increased exponentially – in fact by 30 percent.
- The recently-released United Nations World Drug Report had named South Africa as one of the drug capitals of the world.
- The abuse of alcohol and usage of dagga has lead to the country to being one of the top ten narcotics and alcohol abusers in the world.
- One Rand in four in circulation in SA is linked to the substance abuse problem. (CDA-Bayever)
- Drug arrests leapt from 300 in 2006 to 1500 in 2012 in Cape Town. (Times Live)

A Closer Look: Most Abused Drug Statistics

Let's take a closer look at the statistics of the most abused drugs in South Africa. Please note that these statistics are from the World Health Organization or WHO.

Global Drug Stats

The illegal drug trade is a $3 billion global industry. (NatGeo: Drugs Inc, 2010)

Drug Type Statistics:
Cigarettes

- Drug statistics show that 25 000 people die annually of smoking-related illnesses in SA.

According to the Cancer Association of South Africa.
- 2,5 million workdays are lost in SA due to absenteeism from tobacco-related illnesses.
- Worldwide, between 80 000 and 100 000 kids start smoking every day.
- Among young teens (aged 13 to 15), about one in five smoke worldwide.

Alcohol

- Alcohol is the primary drug of abuse in SA.
- It's responsible for nearly half of all motor accidents.
- Over 30% of our population have an alcohol problem or are at risk of having one.
- Alcohol affects 17.5 million South Africans.
- Studies show that people who start drinking before the age of 15 are four times more likely to become alcoholics.
- 10 million of South Africans who consume alcohol drank the equivalent of 196 six-packs of beer or 62 bottles of spirits which is about 20.1 litres of pure alcohol each person per year.
- SA has an estimated 182 000 illegal shebeens.
- 122 out of every 1000 Grade 1 pupils in the Northern Cape town of De Aar have foetal alcohol syndrome – the highest incidence of the syndrome in one population anywhere in the world.
- 18-22 years olds are the group of heaviest alcohol abuse.
- 35% of High schools kids are problem drinkers who drink at least 9 units spirits, 1 liter wine or 2 liters of beer.
- During the CDA study 20% of 14-year-old boys and nearly half of 17-year-old boys drank in the

previous month. Girls was a bit lower with 18% of 14-year-olds and 35% of 17-year-olds in the same period. (CDA)

Dagga

- The use of dagga has increased by 20% in two years.
- In 2006 2.52 million people used dagga and this increased to 3.2 million in 2008. (CDA)
- South Africans use double the amount of Dagga, than the average world-wide figure.
- Over R3,5 billion is spent annually by South Africans to purchase dagga.
- 1500 metric tons of Dagga is used annually.
- South Africans spend an estimated R3560 million on dagga per year.

Mandrax

- Mandrax (Methaqualone) South Africa is the largest user of Mandrax in the world.

Ecstacy

- SA produces approximately one ton of E per year.
- Almost 110 000 people use ecstasy and pay approximately R610 million in one year.

Cocaine

- The use of cocaine has increased by 20% in two years.
- In 2006 there were 250 000 South Africans who consumed cocaine worth about R1 430 million, this increased to 290 000 in 2008. (CDA)
- The number of South Africans in treatment for cocaine addiction increased from 1.5% in 1996 to

17.5%

Crack

- Crack (Rocks) is the drug of choice amongst prostitutes. Some spend up to R30 000 per month. Selling their bodies to between 15 and 25 men per day to be able to finance their addiction.

Methamphetamine (Tik)

- Tik (methamphetamine) is the main drug of choice for 42% of Cape Town drug users.
- Global Meth trade supplies 51 000 000 users worldwide. (NatGeo: Drugs Inc, 2010)
- Worldwide profits of over $ 35 Billion are made from producing and distributing Meth. (NatGeo: Drugs Inc, 2010)

Heroin

- In1996, one percent (1%) of South Africans were in treatment for heroin abuse while in 2008 those in treatment for this addiction increased between 8 – 24%. (CDA)
- "Sugars", a Heroin based drug that affects about 70 percent of households in the Durban south suburb Chatsworth.
- Nyaope, a mixture of dagga and heroin, is causing inestimable damage among Tshwane's township youth.
- Other forms of Heroin is on the increase under names like "Plazana" and "Kwape", this makes the path from Dagga to Heroin much easier.
- More female students than male are using heroin. (UNISA publication "Inspired" Vol 5 2009)

In one year, the percentage of users has doubled in South Africa and is now marketed specifically in townships. Prices have also come down and it is far more affordable to lower income groups.

Rehabilitation

- Between 2% and 6% of those admitted to drug rehabilitation centres are hooked on prescription medications.
- "Most drug rehabilitation centers have a success rate of less than 3%." (Prof. .Malaka / University of Limpopo).
- Teenagers
- School kids who use alcohol or drugs are 3 times more involved with violent crimes. (CDA)
- From 1992 – 95 the use of drugs among teenagers increased by 600%. That figure is still increasing and is now 1100%. (2007)
- The starting age of abuse is twelve and younger, and drug dealers are targeting schools. (CDA – Bayever 2009)
- Studies show that the average age of drug dependency in South Africa to be 12 years old, and dropping.
- One in two schoolchildren admits to having experimented with drugs.
- 1 in 2 kids in the average SA home addicted to drugs or alcohol, or run the risk of becoming. (Die Beeld, 05.03.2010)
- Children who have one alcoholic parent have a 60% chance of becoming one. This percentage rises to 80% if both parents are alcoholics. (Lig, 04.2008)
- 50% of Grade 11 learners admitted that they have used alcohol in the last year. (Lig, 4.2008)
- 31% of school learners drink socially. (CDA, 2008)

- 60% of Grade 8-11 learners in Cape schools that misuse alcohol had to repeat their grade. (CDA, 2008)
- By the age of 18 more than 60% of teenagers has become drunk. 30% had used school time or work time to drink. (The Lancet medical journal, 2009)
- In 2007 there was a clear increase in patients under 20 years, who came for treatment for dagga addiction. (MRC)
- A 2007 report said that Gauteng's youngest drug dealer was a 8 year old boy from Douglasdale. (Gauteng Drug awareness team)
- 35% of High schools kids are problem drinkers who drink at least 9 units spirits, 1 liter wine or 2 liters of beer. (Rapport, 11.05.2008)
- In 2008 it was reported that 12 years before 2% of patients in rehab centers were under 20 years of age. In 2008 the number increased to 20%. Most were addicted to tik (meth), dagga and heroin. (MRC)
- According to research done in May 2008, 20% of 14-year-old boys and nearly half of 17-year-old boys drank in the previous month. Girls was a bit lower with 18% of 14-year-olds and 35% of 17-year-olds in the same period. (CDA)
- Drug syndicates
- In 1995 there were approximately 125 drug syndicates in South Africa, now there are 438. (2007)

What is the most common substance use disorder?

Tobacco use disorder is the most common substance use disorder worldwide.

- COMPULSIVE GAMBLING/ GAMBLING DISORDER

Compulsive gambling, also called gambling disorder, is the uncontrollable urge to keep gambling despite the toll it takes on your life. Gambling means that you're willing to risk something you value in the hope of getting something of even greater value.

Gambling can stimulate the brain's reward system much like drugs or alcohol can, leading to addiction. If you have a problem with compulsive gambling, you may continually chase bets that lead to losses, use up savings and create debt. You may hide your behavior and even turn to theft or fraud to support your addiction.

Compulsive gambling is a serious condition that can destroy lives. Although treating compulsive gambling can be challenging, many people who struggle with compulsive gambling have found help through professional treatment.

Symptoms

Signs and symptoms of compulsive gambling (gambling disorder) can include:

- Being preoccupied with gambling, such as constantly planning gambling activities and how to get more gambling money
- Needing to gamble with increasing amounts of money to get the same thrill
- Trying to control, cut back or stop gambling, without success
- Feeling restless or irritable when you try to cut down on gambling
- Gambling to escape problems or relieve feelings of

helplessness, guilt, anxiety or depression
- Trying to get back lost money by gambling more (chasing losses)
- Lying to family members or others to hide the extent of your gambling
- Risking or losing important relationships, a job, or school or work opportunities because of gambling
- Asking others to bail you out of financial trouble because you gambled money away

Most casual gamblers stop when losing or set a limit on how much they're willing to lose. But people with a compulsive gambling problem are compelled to keep playing to recover their money — a pattern that becomes increasingly destructive over time. Some people may turn to theft or fraud to get gambling money.

Some people with a compulsive gambling problem may have periods of remission — a length of time where they gamble less or not at all. But without treatment, the remission usually isn't permanent.

When to see a doctor or mental health professional

Have family members, friends or co-workers expressed concern about your gambling? If so, listen to their worries. Because denial is almost always a feature of compulsive or addictive behavior, it may be difficult for you to realize that you have a problem.

Causes

Exactly what causes someone to gamble compulsively isn't well understood. Like many problems, compulsive gambling may result from a combination of biological, genetic and environmental factors.

Risk factors

Although most people who play cards or wager never develop a gambling problem, certain factors are more often associated with compulsive gambling:

- **Mental health issues.** People who gamble compulsively often have substance misuse problems, personality disorders, depression or anxiety. Compulsive gambling may also be associated with bipolar disorder, obsessive-compulsive disorder (OCD) or attention-deficit/hyperactivity disorder (ADHD).
- **Age.** Compulsive gambling is more common in younger and middle-aged people. Gambling during childhood or the teenage years increases the risk of developing compulsive gambling. But compulsive gambling in the older adult population can also be a problem.
- **Sex.** Compulsive gambling is more common in men than women. Women who gamble typically start later in life and may become addicted more quickly. But gambling patterns among men and women have become increasingly similar.
- Family or friend influence. If your family members or friends have a gambling problem, the chances are greater that you will, too.
- **Medications used to treat Parkinson's disease and restless legs syndrome.** Drugs called dopamine agonists have a rare side effect that may result in compulsive behaviors, including gambling, in some people.
- **Certain personality characteristics.** Being highly competitive, a workaholic, impulsive, restless or easily bored may increase your risk of compulsive gambling.

UNDERSTANDING MENTAL HEALTH

Complications

Compulsive gambling can have profound and long-lasting consequences for your life, such as:

- Relationship problems
- Financial problems, including bankruptcy
- Legal problems or imprisonment
- Poor work performance or job loss
- Poor general health
- Suicide, suicide attempts or suicidal thoughts

Prevention

Although there's no proven way to prevent a gambling problem, educational programs that target individuals and groups at increased risk may be helpful.

If you have risk factors for compulsive gambling, consider avoiding gambling in any form, people who gamble and places where gambling occurs. Get treatment at the earliest sign of a problem to help prevent gambling from becoming worse.

Diagnosis

If you recognize that you may have a problem with gambling, talk with your health care provider about an evaluation or seek help from a mental health professional.

To evaluate your problem with gambling, your health care provider or mental health provider will likely:

- **Ask questions related to your gambling habits.** Your provider may also ask for permission to speak with family members or friends. However, confidentiality laws prevent your provider from giving out any information about you without your consent.

- **Review your medical information.** Some drugs can have a rare side effect that results in compulsive behaviors, including gambling, in some people. A physical exam may identify problems with your health that are sometimes associated with compulsive gambling.
- **Do a mental health assessment.** This assessment includes questions about your symptoms, thoughts, feelings and behavior patterns related to your gambling. Depending on your signs and symptoms, you may be evaluated for mental health disorders that are sometimes related to excessive gambling.

Treatment

Treating compulsive gambling can be challenging. That's partly because most people have a hard time admitting they have a problem. Yet a major part of treatment is working on acknowledging that you're a compulsive gambler.

If your family or your employer pressured you into therapy, you may find yourself resisting treatment. But treating a gambling problem can help you regain a sense of control — and possibly help heal damaged relationships or finances.

Treatment for compulsive gambling may include these approaches:
- **Therapy.** Behavioral therapy or cognitive behavioral therapy may be helpful. Behavioral therapy uses a process of exposure to the behavior you want to unlearn and teaches you skills to reduce your urge to gamble. Cognitive behavioral therapy focuses on identifying unhealthy, irrational and negative beliefs and replacing them with healthy, positive ones. Family therapy also

may be helpful.
- **Medications.** Antidepressants and mood stabilizers may help treat problems that often go along with compulsive gambling — such as bipolar disorder, depression or anxiety. Some antidepressants may be effective in reducing gambling behavior. Medications called narcotic antagonists, useful in treating substance misuse, may help treat compulsive gambling.
- **Self-help groups.** Some people find that talking with others who have a gambling problem may be a helpful part of treatment. Ask your health care provider or mental health provider for advice on self-help groups, such as Gamblers Anonymous and other resources.

Treatment for compulsive gambling may involve an outpatient program, inpatient program or a residential treatment program, depending on your needs and resources. Self-help treatments such as structured internet-based programs and telephone visits with a mental health professional may be an option for some people.

Treatment for substance misuse, depression, anxiety or any other mental health issue may be part of your treatment plan for compulsive gambling.

Relapse prevention

Even with treatment, you may return to gambling, especially if you spend time with people who gamble or you're in gambling settings. If you feel that you'll start gambling again, contact your mental health provider or sponsor right away to prevent a relapse

Coping and support

These recovery skills may help you to resist the urges of

compulsive gambling

- Stay focused on your No. 1 goal: Not to gamble.
- Tell yourself it's too risky to gamble at all. One bet typically leads to another and another.
- Give yourself permission to ask for help, as sheer willpower isn't enough to overcome compulsive gambling. Ask a family member or friend to encourage you to follow your treatment plan.
- Recognize and then avoid situations that trigger your urge to bet.

Family members of people with a compulsive gambling problem may benefit from counseling, even if the gambler is unwilling to participate in therapy.

Preparing for your appointment

If you've decided to seek help for compulsive gambling, you've taken an important first step.

What you can do

Before your appointment, make a list of:

- **All the feelings you're experiencing,** even if they seem unrelated to your problem. Note what triggers your gambling, whether you've tried to resist the urge to gamble and the effect that gambling has had on your life.
- **Key personal information,** including any major stresses or recent life changes.
- **All medications,** vitamins, herbs or other supplements that you're taking, including the dosages.
- **Other physical or mental health problems** that you have and any treatments.
- **Questions to ask** your provider to make the most of

your appointment time.

Questions to ask may include:

- What's the best approach to my gambling problem?
- What are other options to the primary approach that you're suggesting?
- Should I see a psychiatrist, psychologist, addiction counselor or other mental health professional?
- Will my insurance cover seeing these professionals?
- Can I get help as an outpatient or would I need inpatient treatment?
- Are there any brochures or other printed material that I can have?
- What websites do you recommend?

Don't hesitate to ask any other questions during your appointment.

What to expect from your doctor

Your health care provider or mental health provider will likely ask you several questions, such as:

- When did your gambling first start?
- How often do you gamble?
- How has gambling affected your life?
- Are your friends or family members worried about your gambling?
- When you gamble, how much do you typically put on the line?
- Have you tried to quit on your own? What happened when you did?
- Have you ever been treated for a gambling problem?
- Are you ready to get the treatment needed for your gambling problem?

To make the most of your appointment time, be ready to

answer these questions and to provide an accurate picture of your gambling issues.

15. Neurocognitive disorders:

Neurocognitive disorder is a general term that describes decreased mental function due to a medical disease other than a psychiatric illness.

Neurocognitive disorders are grouped into three subcategories:

- Delirium.
- Mild neurocognitive disorder - some decreased mental function, but able to stay independent and do daily tasks.
- Major neurocognitive disorder - decreased mental function and loss of ability to do daily tasks. Also called dementia.

Causes

Listed below are conditions associated with neurocognitive disorder.

Brain injury caused by trauma

- Bleeding into the brain (intracerebral hemorrhage)
- Bleeding into the space around the brain (subarachnoid hemorrhage)
- Blood clot inside the skull but outside the brain and its covering, which may cause pressure on the brain (subdural or epidural hematoma)
- Concussion

Breathing conditions

- Low oxygen in the body (hypoxia)
- High carbon dioxide level in the body (hypercapnia)

Cardiovascular disorders

- Dementia due to many strokes (multi-infarct dementia)
- Heart infections (endocarditis, myocarditis)
- Stroke
- Transient ischemic attack (TIA)

Degenerative disorders

- Alzheimer disease (also called senile dementia, Alzheimer type)
- Creutzfeldt-Jakob disease
- Diffuse Lewy body disease
- Huntington disease
- Multiple sclerosis
- Normal pressure hydrocephalus
- Parkinson disease
- Pick disease

Dementia due to metabolic causes

- Kidney disease
- Liver disease
- Thyroid disease (hyperthyroidism or hypothyroidism)
- Vitamin deficiency (B1, B12, or folate)

Drug and alcohol-related conditions

- Alcohol withdrawal state
- Intoxication from drug or alcohol use
- Medicine effect, such as corticosteroids, sedative-hypnotics, antihistamines, and antidepressants
- Wernicke-Korsakoff syndrome, a long-term effect of deficiency of thiamine (vitamin B1)
- Withdrawal from drugs, such as sedative-hypnotics

and corticosteroids

Infections

- Any sudden onset (acute) or long-term (chronic) infection
- Blood poisoning (septicemia)
- Brain infection (encephalitis)
- Meningitis (infection of the lining of the brain and spinal cord)
- Prion infections, such as mad cow disease
- Late-stage syphilis

Complications of cancer and cancer treatment with chemotherapy can also lead to neurocognitive disorder.

Other conditions that may mimic organic brain syndrome include:

- Depression
- Neurosis
- Psychosis

- DELIRIUM

Delirium is a serious change in mental abilities. It results in confused thinking and a lack of awareness of someone's surroundings. The disorder usually comes on fast — within hours or a few days. Delirium can often be traced to one or more factors. Factors may include a severe or long illness or an imbalance in the body, such as low sodium. The disorder also may be caused by certain medicines, infection, surgery, or alcohol or drug use or withdrawal.

Symptoms of delirium are sometimes confused with symptoms of dementia. Health care providers may rely on input from a family member or caregiver to diagnose the disorder.

Symptoms

Symptoms of delirium usually begin over a few hours or a few days. They typically occur with a medical problem. Symptoms often come and go during the day. There may be periods of no

symptoms. Symptoms tend to be worse at night when it's dark and things look less familiar. They also tend to be worse in settings that aren't familiar, such as in a hospital.

Primary symptoms include the following.

Reduced awareness of surroundings

This may result in:

- Trouble focusing on a topic or changing topics
- Getting stuck on an idea rather than responding to questions
- Being easily distracted

- Being withdrawn, with little or no activity or little response to surroundings

Poor thinking skills

This may appear as:

- Poor memory, such as forgetting recent events
- Not knowing where they are or who they are
- Trouble with speech or recalling words
- Rambling or nonsense speech
- Trouble understanding speech
- Trouble reading or writing

Behavior and emotional changes

These may include:

- Anxiety, fear or distrust of others
- Depression
- A short temper or anger
- A sense of feeling elated
- Lack of interest and emotion
- Quick changes in mood
- Personality changes
- Seeing things that others don't see
- Being restless, anxious or combative
- Calling out, moaning or making other sounds
- Being quiet and withdrawn — especially in older adults
- Slowed movement or being sluggish
- Changes in sleep habits
- A switched night-day sleep-wake cycle

Types of delirium

Experts have identified three types:

- **Hyperactive delirium.** This may be the easiest type

to recognize. People with this type may be restless and pace the room. They also may be anxious, have rapid mood swings or see things that aren't there. People with this type often resist care.
- **Hypoactive delirium.** People with this type may be inactive or have reduced activity. They tend to be sluggish or drowsy. They might seem to be in a daze. They don't interact with family or others.
- **Mixed delirium.** Symptoms involve both types of delirium. The person may quickly switch back and forth from being restless and sluggish.

DELIRIUM AND DEMENTIA

Delirium and dementia may be hard to tell apart, and a person may have both. Someone with dementia has a gradual decline of memory and other thinking skills due to damage or loss of brain cells. The most common cause of dementia is Alzheimer's disease, which comes on slowly over months or years. Delirium often occurs in people with dementia. However, episodes of delirium don't always mean a person has dementia. Tests for dementia shouldn't be done during a delirium episode because the results could be misleading.

Some differences between the symptoms of delirium and dementia include:

- **Onset.** The onset of delirium occurs within a short time — within a day or two. Dementia usually begins with minor symptoms that get worse over time.
- **Attention.** The ability to stay focused or maintain focus is impaired with delirium. A person in the early stages of dementia remains generally alert. Someone with dementia often isn't sluggish or agitated.
- **Rapid changes in symptoms.** Delirium symptoms can come and go several times during the day. While people with dementia have better and worse times of day, their memory and thinking skills typically stay at a constant level.

When to see a doctor

If a relative, friend or someone in your care shows symptoms of delirium, talk to the person's health care provider. Your input about symptoms, typical thinking and usual abilities will be important for a diagnosis. It also can help the provider find the cause of the disorder.

If you notice symptoms in someone in the hospital or nursing home, report your concerns to the nursing staff or health care provider. The symptoms may not have been observed. Older people who are in the hospital or are living in a long-term care center are at risk of delirium.

Causes

Delirium occurs when signals in the brain aren't sent and received properly.

The disorder may have a single cause or more than one cause. For example, a medical condition combined with the side effects of a medicine could cause delirium. Sometimes no cause can be found. Possible causes include:

- Certain medicines or medicine side effects
- Alcohol or drug use or withdrawal
- A medical condition such as a stroke, heart attack, worsening lung or liver disease, or an injury from a fall
- An imbalance in the body, such as low sodium or low calcium
- Severe, long-lasting illness or an illness that will lead to death
- Fever and a new infection, particularly in children
- Urinary tract infection, pneumonia, the flu or COVID-19, especially in older adults
- Exposure to a toxin, such as carbon monoxide, cyanide or other poisons
- Poor nutrition or a loss of too much body fluid
- Lack of sleep or severe emotional distress
- Pain
- Surgery or another medical procedure that requires being put in a sleep-like state

Some medicines taken alone or taken in combination can trigger delirium. These include medicines that treat:
- Pain
- Sleep problems
- Mood disorders, such as anxiety and depression
- Allergies
- Asthma
- Swelling
- Parkinson's disease
- Spasms or convulsions

Risk factors

Any condition that results in a hospital stay increases the risk of delirium. This is mostly true when someone is recovering from surgery or is put in intensive care. Delirium is more common in older adults and in people who live in nursing homes.

Examples of other conditions that may increase the risk of delirium include:
- Brain disorders such as dementia, stroke or Parkinson's disease
- Past delirium episodes
- Vision or hearing loss
- Multiple medical problems

Complications

Delirium may last only a few hours or as long as several weeks or months. If the causes are addressed, the recovery time is often shorter. Recovery depends to some extent on the health and mental status before symptoms began. People with dementia, for example, may experience an overall decline in memory and thinking skills after a delirium episode. People in better health are more likely to fully recover.

People with other serious, long-lasting or terminal illnesses may not regain the thinking skills or function that they had before the onset of delirium. Delirium in seriously ill people is more likely to lead to:

- A general decline in health
- Poor recovery from surgery
- The need for long-term care
- An increased risk of death

Prevention

The best way to prevent delirium is to target risk factors that might trigger an episode. Hospital settings present a special challenge. Hospital stays often involve room changes, invasive procedures, loud noises and poor lighting. Lack of natural light and lack of sleep can make confusion worse.

Some steps can help prevent or reduce the severity of delirium. To do this, promote good sleep habits, help the person remain calm and well-oriented, and help prevent medical problems or other complications. Also avoid medicines used for sleep, such as diphenhydramine (Benadryl Allergy, Unisom, others).

Diagnosis

A health care provider can diagnose delirium based on medical history and tests of mental status. The provider also will consider factors that may have caused the disorder. An exam may include:

- **Medical history.** The provider will ask what changed in the last few days. Is there a new infection? Did the person begin a new medicine? Was there an injury or new pain such as chest pain? Did headaches or weakness occur? Did the person use alcohol or a legal or illegal drug?
- **Mental status review.** The provider starts by

testing awareness, attention and thinking. This may be done by talking with the person. Or it may be done with tests or screenings. Information from family members or caregivers can be helpful.
- **Physical and neurological exams.** A physical exam checks for signs of health problems or disease. A neurological exam checks vision, balance, coordination and reflexes. This can help determine if a stroke or another disease is causing the delirium.
- **Other tests.** The health care provider may order blood, urine and other tests. Brain-imaging tests may be used when a diagnosis can't be made with other information.

Treatment

The first goal of delirium treatment is to address any causes or triggers. That may include stopping certain medicines, treating an infection or treating an imbalance in the body. Treatment then focuses on creating the best setting for healing the body and calming the brain.

Supportive care

Supportive care aims to prevent complications. Here are steps to take:
- Protect the airway
- Provide fluids and nutrition
- Assist with movement
- Treat pain
- Address a lack of bladder control
- Avoid the use of physical restraints and bladder tubes
- Avoid changes in surroundings and caregivers when possible

- Include family members or familiar people in care

Medications

If you're a family member or caregiver of someone who has delirium, talk with the health care provider about medicines that may trigger the symptoms. The provider may suggest that the person avoid taking those medicines or that a lower dose is given. Certain medicines may be needed to control pain that's causing delirium.

Other types of medicines may help calm a person who is agitated or confused. Or medicines may be needed if the person is showing distrust of others, is fearful or is seeing things that others don't see. These medicines may be needed when symptoms:

- Make it hard to perform a medical exam or provide treatment
- Put the person in danger or threaten the safety of others
- Don't lessen with other treatments

When symptoms resolve, the medicines are usually stopped or are given in lower doses.

Coping and support

If you're a relative or caregiver of someone who is at risk of delirium, you can take steps to prevent an episode. If you take care of someone who is recovering from delirium, these steps can help improve the person's health and prevent another episode.

Promote good sleep habits

To promote good sleep habits:

- Provide a calm, quiet setting
- Use inside lighting that reflects the time of day

- Help the person keep a regular daytime schedule
- Encourage self-care and activity during the day
- Allow for restful sleep at night

Promote calmness and orientation

To help the person remain calm and aware of their surroundings:

- Provide a clock and calendar and refer to them during the day
- Communicate simply about any change in activity, such as time for lunch or time for bed
- Keep familiar and favorite objects and pictures around, but avoid a cluttered space
- Approach the person calmly
- Identify yourself or other people
- Avoid arguments
- Use comfort measures, such as touch, if they help
- Reduce noise levels and other distractions
- Provide eyeglasses and hearing aids

Prevent complicating problems

To help prevent medical problems:

- Give the person the proper medicines on schedule
- Provide plenty of fluids and a healthy diet
- Encourage regular physical activity
- Get prompt treatment for potential problems, such as infections

Caring for the caregiver

Caring for a person with delirium can be scary and exhausting. Take care of yourself too.

- Consider joining a support group for caregivers.
- Learn more about the condition.
- Ask for pamphlets or other resources from a health

care provider, nonprofit organizations, community health services or government agencies.
- Share caregiving with family and friends who are familiar to the person so you get a break.

Preparing for your appointment

If you're the relative or primary caregiver of a person with delirium, you'll likely play a role in making an appointment or providing information to the health care provider. Here's some information to help you get ready for the appointment and know what to expect.

What you can do

Before the appointment, make a list of:
- **All medicines** the person takes. That includes all prescriptions, medicines available without a prescription and supplements. Include the doses and note any recent medicine changes.
- **Names and contact information of any person** who provides care for the person with delirium.
- **The symptoms and when they started**. Describe all symptoms and any changes in behavior that began before the delirium symptoms. They might include pain, fever or coughing.
- **Questions you want to ask** the care provider.

What to expect from the doctor

A health care provider is likely to ask several questions about the person with delirium. These may include:
- What are the symptoms and when did they begin?
- Is there or was there a recent fever, cough, urinary tract infection or sign of pain?
- Was there a recent head injury or other trauma?

- What were the person's memory and other thinking skills like before the symptoms started?
- How well did the person perform everyday activities before the onset of symptoms?
- Can the person usually function independently?
- What other medical conditions have been diagnosed?
- Are prescription medicines taken as directed? When did the person take the most recent dose of each?
- Are there any new medicines?
- Do you know if the person recently used drugs or alcohol? Does the person have a history of alcohol or drug misuse? Is there any change in the pattern of use, such as increasing or stopping use?
- Has the person recently appeared depressed, extremely sad or withdrawn?
- Has the person shown signs of not feeling safe?
- Are there any signs of paranoia?
- Has the person seen or heard things that no one else does?
- Are there any new physical symptoms — for example, chest or stomach pain?

The provider may ask additional questions based on your responses and the person's symptoms and needs. Preparing for these questions helps you make the most of your time with a provider.

- ALZHEIMER'S DISEASE

Alzheimer's disease is a progressive neurologic disorder that causes the brain to shrink (atrophy) and brain cells to die. Alzheimer's disease is the most common cause of dementia — a continuous decline in thinking, behavioral and social skills that affects a person's ability to function independently. The early signs of the disease include forgetting recent events or conversations. As the disease progresses, a person with Alzheimer's disease will develop severe memory impairment and lose the ability to carry out everyday tasks. Medications may temporarily improve or slow progression of symptoms. These treatments can sometimes help people with Alzheimer's disease maximize function and maintain independence for a time. Different programs and services can help support people with Alzheimer's disease and their caregivers.

There is no treatment that cures Alzheimer's disease or alters the disease process in the brain. In advanced stages of the disease, complications from severe loss of brain function — such as dehydration, malnutrition or infection — result in death.

Symptoms

Memory loss is the key symptom of Alzheimer's disease. Early signs include difficulty remembering recent events or conversations. As the disease progresses, memory impairments worsen and other symptoms develop. At first, a person with Alzheimer's disease may be aware of having difficulty remembering things and organizing thoughts. A family member or friend may be more likely to notice how the symptoms worsen.

Brain changes associated with Alzheimer's disease lead to growing trouble with:

Memory

Everyone has occasional memory lapses, but the memory loss associated with Alzheimer's disease persists and worsens, affecting the ability to function at work or at home.

People with Alzheimer's may:

- Repeat statements and questions over and over
- Forget conversations, appointments or events, and not remember them later
- Routinely misplace possessions, often putting them in illogical locations
- Get lost in familiar places
- Eventually forget the names of family members and everyday objects
- Have trouble finding the right words to identify objects, express thoughts or take part in conversations

Thinking and reasoning

Alzheimer's disease causes difficulty concentrating and thinking, especially about abstract concepts such as numbers.

Multitasking is especially difficult, and it may be challenging to manage finances, balance checkbooks and pay bills on time. Eventually, a person with Alzheimer's may be unable to recognize and deal with numbers.

Making judgments and decisions

Alzheimer's causes a decline in the ability to make reasonable decisions and judgments in everyday situations. For example, a person may make poor or uncharacteristic choices in social interactions or wear clothes that are inappropriate for the weather. It may be more difficult to respond effectively to everyday problems, such as food burning on the stove or unexpected driving situations.

Planning and performing familiar tasks

Once-routine activities that require sequential steps, such as planning and cooking a meal or playing a favorite game, become a struggle as the disease progresses. Eventually, people with advanced Alzheimer's often forget how to perform basic tasks such as dressing and bathing.

Changes in personality and behavior

Brain changes that occur in Alzheimer's disease can affect moods and behaviors. Problems may include the following:

- Depression
- Apathy
- Social withdrawal
- Mood swings
- Distrust in others
- Irritability and aggressiveness
- Changes in sleeping habits
- Wandering
- Loss of inhibitions
- Delusions, such as believing something has been stolen

Preserved skills

Many important skills are preserved for longer periods even while symptoms worsen. Preserved skills may include reading or listening to books, telling stories and reminiscing, singing, listening to music, dancing, drawing, or doing crafts.

These skills may be preserved longer because they are controlled by parts of the brain affected later in the course of the disease.

When to see a doctor

A number of conditions, including treatable conditions, can result in memory loss or other dementia symptoms. If you are concerned about your memory or other thinking skills, talk to your doctor for a thorough assessment and diagnosis.

If you are concerned about thinking skills you observe in a family member or friend, talk about your concerns and ask about going together to a doctor's appointment.

Causes

The exact causes of Alzheimer's disease aren't fully understood. But at a basic level, brain proteins fail to function normally, which disrupts the work of brain cells (neurons) and triggers a series of toxic events. Neurons are damaged, lose connections to each other and eventually die. Scientists believe that for most people, Alzheimer's disease is caused by a combination of genetic, lifestyle and environmental factors that affect the brain over time. Less than 1% of the time, Alzheimer's is caused by specific genetic changes that virtually guarantee a person will develop the disease. These rare occurrences usually result in disease onset in middle age.

The damage most often starts in the region of the brain that controls memory, but the process begins years before the first symptoms. The loss of neurons spreads in a somewhat predictable pattern to other regions of the brains. By the late stage of the disease, the brain has shrunk significantly.

Researchers trying to understand the cause of Alzheimer's disease are focused on the role of two proteins:

- **Plaques.** Beta-amyloid is a fragment of a larger protein. When these fragments cluster together,

they appear to have a toxic effect on neurons and to disrupt cell-to-cell communication. These clusters form larger deposits called amyloid plaques, which also include other cellular debris.
- **Tangles.** Tau proteins play a part in a neuron's internal support and transport system to carry nutrients and other essential materials. In Alzheimer's disease, tau proteins change shape and organize themselves into structures called neurofibrillary tangles. The tangles disrupt the transport system and are toxic to cells.

Risk factors

Age

Increasing age is the greatest known risk factor for Alzheimer's disease. Alzheimer's is not a part of normal aging, but as you grow older the likelihood of developing Alzheimer's disease increases. One study, for example, found that annually there were four new diagnoses per 1,000 people ages 65 to 74, 32 new diagnoses per 1,000 people ages 75 to 84, and 76 new diagnoses per 1,000 people aged 85 and older.

Family history and genetics

Your risk of developing Alzheimer's is somewhat higher if a first-degree relative — your parent or sibling — has the disease. Most genetic mechanisms of Alzheimer's among families remain largely unexplained, and the genetic factors are likely complex. One better understood genetic factor is a form of the apolipoprotein E gene (APOE). A variation of the gene, APOE e4, increases the risk of Alzheimer's disease. Approximately 25% to 30% of the population carries an APOE e4 allele, but not everyone with this variation of the gene develops the disease.

Scientists have identified rare changes (mutations) in three genes that virtually guarantee a person who inherits one of them will develop Alzheimer's. But these mutations account for less than 1% of people with Alzheimer's disease.

Down syndrome

Many people with Down syndrome develop Alzheimer's disease. This is likely related to having three copies of chromosome 21 — and subsequently three copies of the gene for the protein that leads to the creation of beta-amyloid. Signs and symptoms of Alzheimer's tend to appear 10 to 20 years earlier in people with Down syndrome than they do for the general population.

Sex

There appears to be little difference in risk between men and women, but, overall, there are more women with the disease because they generally live longer than men.

Mild cognitive impairment

Mild cognitive impairment (MCI) is a decline in memory or other thinking skills that is greater than normal for a person's age, but the decline doesn't prevent a person from functioning in social or work environments.

People who have MCI have a significant risk of developing dementia. When the primary MCI deficit is memory, the condition is more likely to progress to dementia due to Alzheimer's disease. A diagnosis of MCI encourages a greater focus on healthy lifestyle changes, developing strategies to make up for memory loss and scheduling regular doctor appointments to monitor symptoms.

Head trauma

People who've had a severe head trauma have a greater risk of Alzheimer's disease. Several large studies found that in people aged 50 years or older who had a traumatic brain injury (TBI), the risk of dementia and Alzheimer's disease increased. The risk increases in people with more-severe and multiple TBIs. Some studies indicate that the risk may be greatest within the first six months to two years after the TBI.

Air pollution

Studies in animals have indicated that air pollution particulates can speed degeneration of the nervous system. And human studies have found that air pollution exposure — particularly from traffic exhaust and burning wood — is associated with greater dementia risk.

Excessive alcohol consumption

Drinking large amounts of alcohol has long been known to cause brain changes. Several large studies and reviews found that alcohol use disorders were linked to an increased risk of dementia, particularly early-onset dementia.

Poor sleep patterns

Research has shown that poor sleep patterns, such as difficulty falling asleep or staying asleep, are associated with an increased risk of Alzheimer's disease.

Lifestyle and heart health

Research has shown that the same risk factors associated with heart disease may also increase the risk of Alzheimer's disease. These include:
- Lack of exercise
- Obesity
- Smoking or exposure to secondhand smoke

- High blood pressure
- High cholesterol
- Poorly controlled type 2 diabetes

These factors can all be modified. Therefore, changing lifestyle habits can to some degree alter your risk. For example, regular exercise and a healthy low-fat diet rich in fruits and vegetables are associated with a decreased risk of developing Alzheimer's disease.

Lifelong learning and social engagement

Studies have found an association between lifelong involvement in mentally and socially stimulating activities and a reduced risk of Alzheimer's disease. Low education levels — less than a high school education — appear to be a risk factor for Alzheimer's disease.

Complications

Memory and language loss, impaired judgment and other cognitive changes caused by Alzheimer's can complicate treatment for other health conditions. A person with Alzheimer's disease may not be able to:

- Communicate that he or she is experiencing pain
- Explain symptoms of another illness
- Follow a prescribed treatment plan
- Explain medication side effects

As Alzheimer's disease progresses to its last stages, brain changes begin to affect physical functions, such as swallowing, balance, and bowel and bladder control. These effects can increase vulnerability to additional health problems such as:

- Inhaling food or liquid into the lungs (aspiration)
- Flu, pneumonia and other infections
- Falls
- Fractures
- Bedsores
- Malnutrition or dehydration
- Constipation or diarrhea
- Dental problems such as mouth sores or tooth decay

Prevention

Alzheimer's disease is not a preventable condition. However, a number of lifestyle risk factors for Alzheimer's can be modified. Evidence suggests that changes in diet, exercise and habits — steps to reduce the risk of cardiovascular disease — may also lower your risk of developing Alzheimer's disease and other disorders that cause dementia. Heart-healthy lifestyle choices that may reduce the risk of Alzheimer's include the following:

- Exercising regularly
- Eating a diet of fresh produce, healthy oils and foods low in saturated fat such as a Mediterranean diet
- Following treatment guidelines to manage high blood pressure, diabetes and high cholesterol
- Asking your doctor for help to quit smoking if you smoke

Studies have shown that preserved thinking skills later in life and a reduced risk of Alzheimer's disease are associated with participating in social events, reading, dancing, playing board games, creating art, playing an instrument, and other activities that require mental and social engagement.

Diagnosis

An important part of diagnosing Alzheimer's disease

includes being able to explain your symptoms, as well as perspective from a close family member or friend about symptoms and their impact on daily life. Additionally, a diagnosis of Alzheimer's disease is based on tests your doctor administers to assess memory and thinking skills. Laboratory and imaging tests can rule out other potential causes or help the doctor better identify the disease causing dementia symptoms.

Traditionally, Alzheimer's disease was only diagnosed with complete certainty after death, when examining the brain with a microscope revealed the characteristic plaques and tangles. Clinicians and researchers are now able to diagnose Alzheimer's disease during life with more certainty. Biomarkers can detect the presence of plaques and tangles, such as specific types of PET scans or measuring amyloid and tau proteins in plasma and cerebral spinal fluid.

Tests

A diagnostic work-up would likely include the following tests:

Physical and neurological exam

Your doctor will perform a physical exam and likely assess overall neurological health by testing the following:

- Reflexes
- Muscle tone and strength
- Ability to get up from a chair and walk across the room
- Sense of sight and hearing
- Coordination
- Balance

Lab tests

Blood tests may help your doctor rule out other potential

causes of memory loss and confusion, such as a thyroid disorder or vitamin deficiencies.

Mental status and neuropsychological testing

Your doctor may give you a brief mental status test to assess memory and other thinking skills. Longer forms of neuropsychological testing may provide additional details about mental function compared with people of a similar age and education level. These tests can help establish a diagnosis and serve as a starting point to track the progression of symptoms in the future.

Brain imaging

Images of the brain are now used chiefly to pinpoint visible abnormalities related to conditions other than Alzheimer's disease — such as strokes, trauma or tumors — that may cause cognitive change. New imaging applications — currently used primarily in major medical centers or in clinical trials — may enable doctors to detect specific brain changes caused by Alzheimer's.

Imaging of brain structures include the following:

- **Magnetic resonance imaging (MRI).** MRI uses radio waves and a strong magnetic field to produce detailed images of the brain. While they may show brain shrinkage of brain regions associated with Alzheimer's disease, MRI scans also rule out other conditions. An MRI is generally preferred to a CT scan for the evaluation of dementia.
- **Computerized tomography (CT).** A CT scan, a specialized X-ray technology, produces cross-sectional images (slices) of your brain. It's usually used to rule out tumors, strokes and head injuries.

Imaging of disease processes can be performed with positron

emission tomography (PET). During a PET scan, a low-level radioactive tracer is injected into the blood to reveal a particular feature in the brain. PET imaging may include the following:

- Fluorodeoxyglucose (FDG) PET scans show areas of the brain in which nutrients are poorly metabolized. Identifying patterns of degeneration — areas of low metabolism — can help distinguish between Alzheimer's disease and other types of dementia.
- **Amyloid PET imaging** can measure the burden of amyloid deposits in the brain. This imaging is primarily used in research but may be used if a person has unusual or very early onset of dementia symptoms.
- **Tau PET imaging,** which measures the burden of neurofibrillary tangles in the brain, is generally used in the research setting.

In special circumstances, such as rapidly progressive dementia, dementia with atypical features or early-onset dementia, other tests may be used to measure abnormal beta-amyloid and tau in the cerebrospinal fluid.

Future diagnostic tests

Researchers are working to develop tests that can measure biological signs of disease processes in the brain. These tests, including blood tests, may improve the accuracy of diagnoses and enable earlier diagnosis before the onset of symptoms. A blood test for Plasma Aβ is currently available and recently received certification in the U.S. by the Centers for Medicare & Medicaid Services to allow distribution on the market.

Genetic testing generally isn't recommended for a routine Alzheimer's disease evaluation. The exception is people who have a family history of early-onset Alzheimer's disease. Meeting with a genetic counselor to discuss the risks and benefits of genetic testing is recommended before undergoing any tests.

Treatment

Drugs

Current Alzheimer's medications can help for a time with memory symptoms and other cognitive changes. Two types of drugs are currently used to treat cognitive symptoms:

- **Cholinesterase inhibitors.** These drugs work by boosting levels of cell-to-cell communication by preserving a chemical messenger that is depleted in the brain by Alzheimer's disease. These are usually the first medications tried, and most people see modest improvements in symptoms. Cholinesterase inhibitors may also improve neuropsychiatric symptoms, such as agitation or depression. Commonly prescribed cholinesterase inhibitors include donepezil (Aricept), galantamine (Razadyne ER) and rivastigmine (Exelon). The main side effects of these drugs include diarrhea, nausea, loss of appetite and sleep disturbances. In people with certain heart disorders, serious side effects may include cardiac arrhythmia.
- **Memantine (Namenda).** This drug works in another brain cell communication network and slows the progression of symptoms with moderate to severe Alzheimer's disease. It's sometimes used in combination with a cholinesterase inhibitor. Relatively rare side effects include dizziness and confusion.

In June 2021, the Food and Drug Administration (FDA) approved aducanumab (Aduhelm) for the treatment of some cases of Alzheimer's disease. This is the first drug approved in the United States to treat the underlying cause of Alzheimer's by targeting and removing amyloid plaques in the brain. The FDA approved the drug on the condition that further studies be conducted to confirm the drug's benefit. Experts also need to identify which patients may benefit from the drug.

Sometimes other medications such as antidepressants may be prescribed to help control the behavioral symptoms associated with Alzheimer's disease.

Creating a safe and supportive environment

Adapting the living situation to the needs of a person with Alzheimer's disease is an important part of any treatment plan. For someone with Alzheimer's, establishing and strengthening routine habits and minimizing memory-demanding tasks can make life much easier.

You can take these steps to support a person's sense of well-being and continued ability to function:

- Always keep keys, wallets, mobile phones and other valuables in the same place at home, so they don't become lost.
- Keep medications in a secure location. Use a daily checklist to keep track of dosages.
- Arrange for finances to be on automatic payment and automatic deposit.
- Have the person with Alzheimer's carry a mobile phone with location capability so that a caregiver can track its location. Program important phone numbers into the phone.
- Install alarm sensors on doors and windows.
- Make sure regular appointments are on the same day at the same time as much as possible.
- Use a calendar or whiteboard in the home to track

daily schedules. Build the habit of checking off completed items.
- Remove excess furniture, clutter and throw rugs.
- Install sturdy handrails on stairways and in bathrooms.
- Ensure that shoes and slippers are comfortable and provide good traction.
- Reduce the number of mirrors. People with Alzheimer's may find images in mirrors confusing or frightening.
- Make sure that the person with Alzheimer's carries identification or wears a medical alert bracelet.
- Keep photographs and other meaningful objects around the house.

Alternative medicine

Various herbal remedies, vitamins and other supplements are widely promoted as preparations that may support cognitive health or prevent or delay Alzheimer's. Clinical trials have produced mixed results with little evidence to support them as effective treatments.

Some of the treatments that have been studied recently include:

- **Vitamin E.** Although vitamin E doesn't prevent Alzheimer's, taking 2,000 international units daily may help delay the progression in people who already have mild to moderate disease. However, study results have been mixed, with only some showing modest benefits. Further research into the safety of 2,000 international units daily of vitamin E in a dementia population will be needed before it can be routinely recommended. Supplements promoted for cognitive health can interact with medications you're taking for Alzheimer's disease

or other health conditions. Work closely with your health care team to create a safe treatment plan with any prescriptions, over-the-counter medications or dietary supplements.
- **Omega-3 fatty acids.** Omega-3 fatty acids in fish or from supplements may lower the risk of developing dementia, but clinical studies have shown no benefit for treating Alzheimer's disease symptoms.
- **Curcumin.** This herb comes from turmeric and has anti-inflammatory and antioxidant properties that might affect chemical processes in the brain. So far, clinical trials have found no benefit for treating Alzheimer's disease.
- **Ginkgo.** Ginkgo is a plant extract containing several medicinal properties. A large study funded by the National Institutes of Health found no effect in preventing or delaying Alzheimer's disease.
- **Melatonin.** This supplement of a hormone that regulates sleep is being studied to determine if it offers benefits managing sleep in people with dementia. But some research has indicated that melatonin may worsen mood in some people with dementia. More research is needed.

Lifestyle and home remedies

Healthy lifestyle choices promote good overall health and may play a role in maintaining cognitive health.

Exercise

Regular exercise is an important part of a treatment plan. Activities such as a daily walk can help improve mood and maintain the health of joints, muscles and the heart. Exercise can also promote restful sleep and prevent constipation — and it's beneficial for care partners, too.

People with Alzheimer's who develop trouble walking may still be able to use a stationary bike, stretch with elastic bands or participate in chair exercises. You may find exercise programs geared to older adults on TV or on DVDs.

Nutrition

People with Alzheimer's may forget to eat, lose interest in preparing meals or not eat a healthy combination of foods. They may also forget to drink enough, leading to dehydration and constipation.

Offer the following:

- **Healthy options.** Buy favorite healthy food options that are easy to eat.
- **Water and other healthy beverages.** Encourage drinking several glasses of liquids every day. Avoid beverages with caffeine, which can increase restlessness, interfere with sleep and trigger a frequent need to urinate.
- **High-calorie, healthy shakes and smoothies.** Supplement milkshakes with protein powders or make smoothies featuring favorite ingredients, especially when eating becomes more difficult.

Social engagement and activities

Social interactions and activities can support the abilities and skills that are preserved. Doing things that are meaningful and enjoyable are important for the overall well-being of a person with Alzheimer's disease. These might include:

- Listening to music or dancing
- Reading or listening to books
- Gardening or crafts
- Social events at senior or memory care centers
- Planned activities with children

Coping and support

People with Alzheimer's disease experience a mixture of emotions — confusion, frustration, anger, fear, uncertainty, grief and depression. If you're caring for someone with Alzheimer's, you can help them cope with the disease by being there to listen, reassuring the person that life can still be enjoyed, providing support, and doing your best to help the person retain dignity and self-respect.

A calm and stable home environment can help reduce behavior problems. New situations, noise, large groups of people, being rushed or pressed to remember, or being asked to do complicated tasks can cause anxiety. As a person with Alzheimer's becomes upset, the ability to think clearly declines even more.

Caring for the caregiver

Caring for a person with Alzheimer's disease is physically and emotionally demanding. Feelings of anger and guilt, stress and discouragement, worry and grief, and social isolation are common.

Caregiving can even take a toll on the caregiver's physical health. Paying attention to your own needs and well-being is one of the most important things you can do for yourself and for the person with Alzheimer's.

If you're a caregiver for someone with Alzheimer's, you can help yourself by:

- Learning as much about the disease as you can
- Asking questions of doctors, social workers and others involved in the care of your loved one
- Calling on friends or other family members for help when you need it
- Taking a break every day

- Spending time with your friends
- Taking care of your health by seeing your own doctors on schedule, eating healthy meals and getting exercise
- Joining a support group
- Making use of a local adult day center, if possible

Many people with Alzheimer's and their families benefit from counseling or local support services. Contact your local Alzheimer's Association affiliate to connect with support groups, doctors, occupational therapists, resources and referrals, home care agencies, residential care facilities, a telephone help line, and educational seminars.

Preparing for your appointment

Medical care for the loss of memory or other thinking skills usually requires a team or partner strategy. If you're worried about memory loss or related symptoms, ask a close relative or friend to go with you to a doctor's appointment. In addition to providing support, your partner can provide help in answering questions.

If you're going with someone to a doctor's appointment, your role may be to provide some history or your thoughts on changes you have seen. This teamwork is an important part of medical care for initial appointments and throughout a treatment plan.

Your primary care doctor may refer you to a neurologist, psychiatrist, neuropsychologist or other specialist for further evaluation.

What you can do

You can prepare for your appointment by writing down as much information as possible to share. Information may include:

- **Medical history,** including any past or current diagnoses and family medical history
- **Medical team,** including the name and contact information of any current physician, mental health professional or therapist
- **Medications,** including prescriptions, over-the-counter drugs, vitamins, herbal medications or other dietary supplements
- **Symptoms,** including specific examples of changes in memory or thinking skills

What to expect from your doctor

Your doctor will likely ask a number of the following questions to understand changes in memory or other thinking skills. If you are accompanying someone to an appointment, be prepared to provide your perspective as needed. Your doctor may ask:

- What kinds of memory difficulties and mental lapses are you having? When did you first notice them?
- Are they steadily getting worse, or are they sometimes better and sometimes worse?
- Have you stopped doing certain activities, such as managing finances or shopping, because these activities were too mentally challenging?
- How is your mood? Do you feel depressed, sadder or more anxious than usual?
- Have you gotten lost lately on a driving route or in a situation that's usually familiar to you?
- Has anyone expressed unusual concern about your driving?
- Have you noticed any changes in the way you tend to react to people or events?
- Do you have more energy than usual, less than usual or about the same?

- What medications are you taking? Are you taking any vitamins or supplements?
- Do you drink alcohol? How much?
- Have you noticed any trembling or trouble walking?
- Are you having any trouble remembering your medical appointments or when to take your medication?
- Have you had your hearing and vision tested recently?
- Did anyone else in your family ever have memory trouble? Was anyone ever diagnosed with Alzheimer's disease or dementia?
- Do you act out your dreams while sleeping (punch, flail, shout, scream)? Do you snore?

- TRAUMATIC BRAIN INJURY

Traumatic brain injury usually results from a violent blow or jolt to the head or body. An object that goes through brain tissue, such as a bullet or shattered piece of skull, also can cause traumatic brain injury.

Mild traumatic brain injury may affect your brain cells temporarily. More-serious traumatic brain injury can result in bruising, torn tissues, bleeding and other physical damage to the brain. These injuries can result in long-term complications or death.

Symptoms

Traumatic brain injury can have wide-ranging physical and psychological effects. Some signs or symptoms may appear immediately after the traumatic event, while others may appear days or weeks later.

Mild traumatic brain injury

The signs and symptoms of mild traumatic brain injury may include:

Physical symptoms

- Headache
- Nausea or vomiting
- Fatigue or drowsiness
- Problems with speech
- Dizziness or loss of balance

Sensory symptoms

- Sensory problems, such as blurred vision, ringing in the ears, a bad taste in the mouth or changes in the ability to smell

- Sensitivity to light or sound

Cognitive, behavioral or mental symptoms
- Loss of consciousness for a few seconds to a few minutes
- No loss of consciousness, but a state of being dazed, confused or disoriented
- Memory or concentration problems
- Mood changes or mood swings
- Feeling depressed or anxious
- Difficulty sleeping
- Sleeping more than usual

Moderate to severe traumatic brain injuries

Moderate to severe traumatic brain injuries can include any of the signs and symptoms of mild injury, as well as these symptoms that may appear within the first hours to days after a head injury:

Physical symptoms
- Loss of consciousness from several minutes to hours
- Persistent headache or headache that worsens
- Repeated vomiting or nausea
- Convulsions or seizures
- Dilation of one or both pupils of the eyes
- Clear fluids draining from the nose or ears
- Inability to awaken from sleep
- Weakness or numbness in fingers and toes
- Loss of coordination

Cognitive or mental symptoms
- Profound confusion
- Agitation, combativeness or other unusual behavior

- Slurred speech
- Coma and other disorders of consciousness

Children's symptoms

Infants and young children with brain injuries might not be able to communicate headaches, sensory problems, confusion and similar symptoms. In a child with traumatic brain injury, you may observe:

- Change in eating or nursing habits
- Unusual or easy irritability
- Persistent crying and inability to be consoled
- Change in ability to pay attention
- Change in sleep habits
- Seizures
- Sad or depressed mood
- Drowsiness
- Loss of interest in favorite toys or activities

When to see a doctor

Always see your doctor if you or your child has received a blow to the head or body that concerns you or causes behavioral changes. Seek emergency medical care if there are any signs or symptoms of traumatic brain injury following a recent blow or other traumatic injury to the head.

The terms "mild," "moderate" and "severe" are used to describe the effect of the injury on brain function. A mild injury to the brain is still a serious injury that requires prompt attention and an accurate diagnosis.

Causes

Traumatic brain injury is usually caused by a blow or other traumatic injury to the head or body. The degree of damage can depend on several factors, including the nature of the injury and the force of impact.

Common events causing traumatic brain injury include the following:

- **Falls.** Falls from bed or a ladder, down stairs, in the bath, and other falls are the most common cause of traumatic brain injury overall, particularly in older adults and young children.
- **Vehicle-related collisions.** Collisions involving cars, motorcycles or bicycles — and pedestrians involved in such accidents — are a common cause of traumatic brain injury.
- **Violence.** Gunshot wounds, domestic violence, child abuse and other assaults are common causes. Shaken baby syndrome is a traumatic brain injury in infants caused by violent shaking.
- **Sports injuries.** Traumatic brain injuries may be caused by injuries from a number of sports, including soccer, boxing, football, baseball, lacrosse, skateboarding, hockey, and other high-impact or extreme sports. These are particularly common in youth.
- **Explosive blasts and other combat injuries.** Explosive blasts are a common cause of traumatic brain injury in active-duty military personnel. Although how the damage occurs isn't yet well understood, many researchers believe that the pressure wave passing through the brain significantly disrupts brain function. Traumatic brain injury also results from penetrating wounds, severe blows to the head with shrapnel or debris, and falls or bodily collisions with objects following a blast.

Risk factors

The people most at risk of traumatic brain injury include:

- Children, especially newborns to 4-year-olds
- Young adults, especially those between ages 15 and 24
- Adults aged 60 and older
- Males in any age group

Complications

Several complications can occur immediately or soon after a traumatic brain injury. Severe injuries increase the risk of a greater number of and more-severe complications.

Altered consciousness

Moderate to severe traumatic brain injury can result in prolonged or permanent changes in a person's state of consciousness, awareness or responsiveness. Different states of consciousness include:

- **Coma.** A person in a coma is unconscious, unaware of anything and unable to respond to any stimulus. This results from widespread damage to all parts of the brain. After a few days to a few weeks, a person may emerge from a coma or enter a vegetative state.
- **Vegetative state.** Widespread damage to the brain can result in a vegetative state. Although the person is unaware of surroundings, he or she may open his or her eyes, make sounds, respond to reflexes, or move. It's possible that a vegetative state can become permanent, but often individuals progress to a minimally conscious state.
- **Minimally conscious state.** A minimally conscious state is a condition of severely altered consciousness but with some signs of self-awareness or awareness of one's environment. It is sometimes a transitional state from a coma or vegetative condition to greater recovery.

- **Brain death.** When there is no measurable activity in the brain and the brainstem, this is called brain death. In a person who has been declared brain dead, removal of breathing devices will result in cessation of breathing and eventual heart failure. Brain death is considered irreversible.

Physical complications

- **Seizures.** Some people with traumatic brain injury will develop seizures. The seizures may occur only in the early stages, or years after the injury. Recurrent seizures are called post-traumatic epilepsy.
- **Fluid buildup in the brain (hydrocephalus).** Cerebrospinal fluid may build up in the spaces in the brain (cerebral ventricles) of some people who have had traumatic brain injuries, causing increased pressure and swelling in the brain.
- **Infections.** Skull fractures or penetrating wounds can tear the layers of protective tissues (meninges) that surround the brain. This can enable bacteria to enter the brain and cause infections. An infection of the meninges (meningitis) could spread to the rest of the nervous system if not treated.
- **Blood vessel damage.** Several small or large blood vessels in the brain may be damaged in a traumatic brain injury. This damage could lead to a stroke, blood clots or other problems.
- **Headaches.** Frequent headaches are very common after a traumatic brain injury. They may begin within a week after the injury and could persist for as long as several months.
- **Vertigo.** Many people experience vertigo, a condition characterized by dizziness, after a traumatic brain injury.

Sometimes, any or several of these symptoms might linger for a few weeks to a few months after a traumatic brain injury. When a combination of these symptoms lasts for an extended period of time, this is generally referred to as persistent post-concussive symptoms.

Traumatic brain injuries at the base of the skull can cause nerve damage to the nerves that emerge directly from the brain (cranial nerves). Cranial nerve damage may result in:

Paralysis of facial muscles or losing sensation in the face

- Loss of or altered sense of smell or taste
- Loss of vision or double vision
- Swallowing problems
- Dizziness
- Ringing in the ear
- Hearing loss

Intellectual problems

Many people who have had a significant brain injury will experience changes in their thinking (cognitive) skills. It may be more difficult to focus and take longer to process your thoughts. Traumatic brain injury can result in problems with many skills, including:

Cognitive problems

- Memory
- Learning
- Reasoning
- Judgment
- Attention or concentration

Executive functioning problems

- Problem-solving
- Multitasking
- Organization

- Planning
- Decision-making
- Beginning or completing tasks

Communication problems

Language and communications problems are common following traumatic brain injuries. These problems can cause frustration, conflict and misunderstanding for people with a traumatic brain injury, as well as family members, friends and care providers.

Communication problems may include:

- Difficulty understanding speech or writing
- Difficulty speaking or writing
- Inability to organize thoughts and ideas
- Trouble following and participating in conversations

Communication problems that affect social skills may include:

- Trouble with turn taking or topic selection in conversations
- Problems with changes in tone, pitch or emphasis to express emotions, attitudes or subtle differences in meaning
- Difficulty understanding nonverbal signals
- Trouble reading cues from listeners
- Trouble starting or stopping conversations
- Inability to use the muscles needed to form words (dysarthria)

Behavioral changes

People who've experienced brain injury may experience changes in behaviors. These may include:

- Difficulty with self-control
- Lack of awareness of abilities
- Risky behavior
- Difficulty in social situations
- Verbal or physical outbursts

Emotional changes

Emotional changes may include:

- Depression
- Anxiety
- Mood swings
- Irritability
- Lack of empathy for others
- Anger
- Insomnia

Sensory problems

- Problems involving senses may include:
- Persistent ringing in the ears
- Difficulty recognizing objects
- Impaired hand-eye coordination
- Blind spots or double vision
- A bitter taste, a bad smell or difficulty smelling
- Skin tingling, pain or itching
- Trouble with balance or dizziness

Degenerative brain diseases

The relationship between degenerative brain diseases and brain injuries is still unclear. But some research suggests that repeated or severe traumatic brain injuries might increase the risk of degenerative brain diseases. But this risk can't be predicted for an individual — and researchers are still investigating if, why and how traumatic brain injuries might be related to degenerative brain diseases.

A degenerative brain disorder can cause gradual loss of brain functions, including:

- Alzheimer's disease, which primarily causes the progressive loss of memory and other thinking skills
- Parkinson's disease, a progressive condition that causes movement problems, such as tremors, rigidity and slow movements
- Dementia pugilistica — most often associated with repetitive blows to the head in career boxing — which causes symptoms of dementia and movement problems

Prevention

Follow these tips to reduce the risk of brain injury:

- **Seat belts and airbags.** Always wear a seat belt in a motor vehicle. A small child should always sit in the back seat of a car secured in a child safety seat or booster seat that is appropriate for his or her size and weight.
- **Alcohol and drug use.** Don't drive under the influence of alcohol or drugs, including prescription medications that can impair the ability to drive.
- **Helmets.** Wear a helmet while riding a bicycle, skateboard, motorcycle, snowmobile or all-terrain vehicle. Also wear appropriate head protection when playing baseball or contact sports, skiing, skating, snowboarding or riding a horse.
- **Pay attention to your surroundings.** Don't drive, walk or cross the street while using your phone, tablet or any smart device. These distractions can lead to accidents or falls.

Preventing falls

The following tips can help older adults avoid falls around the house:

- Install handrails in bathrooms
- Put a nonslip mat in the bathtub or shower
- Remove area rugs
- Install handrails on both sides of staircases
- Improve lighting in the home, especially around stairs
- Keep stairs and floors clear of clutter
- Get regular vision checkups
- Get regular exercise

Preventing head injuries in children

The following tips can help children avoid head injuries:

- Install safety gates at the top of a stairway
- Keep stairs clear of clutter
- Install window guards to prevent falls
- Put a nonslip mat in the bathtub or shower
- Use playgrounds that have shock-absorbing materials on the ground
- Make sure area rugs are secure
- Don't let children play on fire escapes or balconies

Diagnosis

Traumatic brain injuries may be emergencies. In the case of more-severe TBIs, consequences can worsen rapidly without treatment. Doctors or first responders need to assess the situation quickly.

Glasgow Coma Scale

This 15-point test helps doctor or other emergency medical

personnel assess the initial severity of a brain injury by checking a person's ability to follow directions and move their eyes and limbs. The coherence of speech also provides important clues.

Abilities are scored from three to 15 in the Glasgow Coma Scale. Higher scores mean less severe injuries.

Information about the injury and symptoms

If you saw someone sustain an injury or arrived immediately after an injury, you may be able to provide medical personnel with information that's useful in assessing the injured person's condition.

Answers to the following questions may be beneficial in judging the severity of injury:
- How did the injury occur?
- Did the person lose consciousness?
- How long was the person unconscious?
- Did you observe any other changes in alertness, speaking, coordination or other signs of injury?
- Where was the head or other parts of the body struck?
- Can you provide any information about the force of the injury? For example, what hit the person's head, how far did he or she fall, or was the person thrown from a vehicle?
- Was the person's body whipped around or severely jarred?

Imaging tests
- **Computerized tomography (CT) scan.** This test is usually the first performed in an emergency room for a suspected traumatic brain injury. A CT scan uses a series of X-rays to create a detailed view of

the brain. A CT scan can quickly visualize fractures and uncover evidence of bleeding in the brain (hemorrhage), blood clots (hematomas), bruised brain tissue (contusions), and brain tissue swelling.
- **Magnetic resonance imaging (MRI).** An MRI uses powerful radio waves and magnets to create a detailed view of the brain. This test may be used after the person's condition stabilizes, or if symptoms don't improve soon after the injury.

Intracranial pressure monitor

Tissue swelling from a traumatic brain injury can increase pressure inside the skull and cause additional damage to the brain. Doctors may insert a probe through the skull to monitor this pressure.

Treatment

Treatment is based on the severity of the injury.

Mild injury

Mild traumatic brain injuries usually require no treatment other than rest and over-the-counter pain relievers to treat a headache. However, a person with a mild traumatic brain injury usually needs to be monitored closely at home for any persistent, worsening or new symptoms. He or she may also have follow-up doctor appointments.

The doctor will indicate when a return to work, school or recreational activities is appropriate. Relative rest — which means limiting physical or thinking (cognitive) activities that make things worse — is usually recommended for the first few days or until your doctor advises that it's OK to resume regular activities. It isn't recommended that you rest completely from mental and physical activity. Most people return to normal routines gradually.

Immediate emergency care

Emergency care for moderate to severe traumatic brain injuries focuses on making sure the person has enough oxygen and an adequate blood supply, maintaining blood pressure, and preventing any further injury to the head or neck.

People with severe injuries may also have other injuries that need to be addressed. Additional treatments in the emergency room or intensive care unit of a hospital will focus on minimizing secondary damage due to inflammation, bleeding or reduced oxygen supply to the brain.

Medications

Medications to limit secondary damage to the brain immediately after an injury may include:

- **Anti-seizure drugs.** People who've had a moderate to severe traumatic brain injury are at risk of having seizures during the first week after their injury.

An anti-seizure drug may be given during the first week to avoid any additional brain damage that might be caused by a seizure. Continued anti-seizure treatments are used only if seizures occur.

- **Coma-inducing drugs.** Doctors sometimes use drugs to put people into temporary comas because a comatose brain needs less oxygen to function. This is especially helpful if blood vessels, compressed by increased pressure in the brain, are unable to supply brain cells with normal amounts of nutrients and oxygen.
- **Diuretics.** These drugs reduce the amount of fluid in tissues and increase urine output. Diuretics, given intravenously to people with traumatic brain

injury, help reduce pressure inside the brain.

Surgery

Emergency surgery may be needed to minimize additional damage to brain tissues. Surgery may be used to address the following problems:

- **Removing clotted blood (hematomas).** Bleeding outside or within the brain can result in a collection of clotted blood (hematoma) that puts pressure on the brain and damages brain tissue.
- **Repairing skull fractures.** Surgery may be needed to repair severe skull fractures or to remove pieces of skull in the brain.
- **Bleeding in the brain.** Head injuries that cause bleeding in the brain may need surgery to stop the bleeding.
- **Opening a window in the skull.** Surgery may be used to relieve pressure inside the skull by draining accumulated cerebrospinal fluid or creating a window in the skull that provides more room for swollen tissues.

Rehabilitation

Most people who have had a significant brain injury will require rehabilitation. They may need to relearn basic skills, such as walking or talking. The goal is to improve their abilities to perform daily activities.

Therapy usually begins in the hospital and continues at an inpatient rehabilitation unit, a residential treatment facility or through outpatient services. The type and duration of rehabilitation is different for everyone, depending on the severity of the brain injury and what part of the brain was injured.

Rehabilitation specialists may include:

- **Physiatrist,** a doctor trained in physical medicine and rehabilitation, who oversees the entire rehabilitation process, manages medical rehabilitation problems and prescribes medication as needed
- **Occupational therapist,** who helps the person learn, relearn or improve skills to perform everyday activities
- **Physical therapist,** who helps with mobility and relearning movement patterns, balance and walking
- **Speech and language therapist,** who helps the person improve communication skills and use assistive communication devices if necessary
- **Neuropsychologist,** who assesses cognitive impairment and performance, helps the person manage behaviors or learn coping strategies, and provides psychotherapy as needed for emotional and psychological well-being
- **Social worker or case manager,** who facilitates access to service agencies, assists with care decisions and planning, and facilitates communication among various professionals, care providers and family members
- **Rehabilitation nurse,** who provides ongoing rehabilitation care and services and who helps with discharge planning from the hospital or rehabilitation facility
- **Traumatic brain injury nurse specialist,** who helps coordinate care and educates the family about the injury and recovery process
- **Recreational therapist,** who assists with time

management and leisure activities
- **Vocational counselor,** who assesses the ability to return to work and appropriate vocational opportunities and who provides resources for addressing common challenges in the workplace

Coping and support

A number of strategies can help a person with traumatic brain injury cope with complications that affect everyday activities, communication and interpersonal relationships. Depending on the severity of injury, a family caregiver or friend may need to help implement the following approaches:

- **Join a support group.** Talk to your doctor or rehabilitation therapist about a support group that can help you talk about issues related to your injury, learn new coping strategies and get emotional support.
- **Write things down.** Keep a record of important events, people's names, tasks or other things that are difficult to remember.
- **Follow a routine.** Keep a consistent schedule, keep things in designated places to avoid confusion and take the same routes when going to frequently visited destinations.
- **Take breaks.** Make arrangements at work or school to take breaks as needed.
- **Alter work expectations or tasks.** Appropriate changes at work or school may include having instructions read to you, allowing more time to complete tasks or breaking down tasks into smaller steps.
- **Avoid distractions.** Minimize distractions such as

loud background noise from a television or radio.
- **Stay focused.** Work on one task at a time.

- DEMENTIA

Dementia is a term used to describe a group of symptoms affecting memory, thinking and social abilities severely enough to interfere with your daily life. It isn't a specific disease, but several diseases can cause dementia. Though dementia generally involves memory loss, memory loss has different causes. Having memory loss alone doesn't mean you have dementia, although it's often one of the early signs of the condition.

Alzheimer's disease is the most common cause of a progressive dementia in older adults, but there are a number of other causes of dementia. Depending on the cause, some dementia symptoms might be reversible.

Symptoms

Dementia symptoms vary depending on the cause, but common signs and symptoms include:

Cognitive changes

- Memory loss, which is usually noticed by someone else
- Difficulty communicating or finding words
- Difficulty with visual and spatial abilities, such as getting lost while driving
- Difficulty reasoning or problem-solving
- Difficulty handling complex tasks
- Difficulty with planning and organizing
- Difficulty with coordination and motor functions
- Confusion and disorientation

Psychological changes

- Personality changes

- Depression
- Anxiety
- Inappropriate behavior
- Paranoia
- Agitation
- Hallucinations

When to see a doctor

See a doctor if you or a loved one has memory problems or other dementia symptoms. Some treatable medical conditions can cause dementia symptoms, so it's important to determine the cause.

Causes

Dementia is caused by damage to or loss of nerve cells and their connections in the brain. Depending on the area of the brain that's damaged, dementia can affect people differently and cause different symptoms.

Dementias are often grouped by what they have in common, such as the protein or proteins deposited in the brain or the part of the brain that's affected. Some diseases look like dementias, such as those caused by a reaction to medications or vitamin deficiencies, and they might improve with treatment.

Progressive dementias

Types of dementias that progress and aren't reversible include:

- **Alzheimer's disease.** This is the most common cause of dementia.
  Although not all causes of Alzheimer's disease are known, experts do know that a small percentage are related to mutations of three genes, which can be passed

down from parent to child. While several genes are probably involved in Alzheimer's disease, one important gene that increases risk is apolipoprotein E4 (APOE).

Alzheimer's disease patients have plaques and tangles in their brains. Plaques are clumps of a protein called beta-amyloid, and tangles are fibrous tangles made up of tau protein. It's thought that these clumps damage healthy neurons and the fibers connecting them.

- **Vascular dementia.** This type of dementia is caused by damage to the vessels that supply blood to your brain. Blood vessel problems can cause strokes or affect the brain in other ways, such as by damaging the fibers in the white matter of the brain.

The most common signs of vascular dementia include difficulties with problem-solving, slowed thinking, and loss of focus and organization. These tend to be more noticeable than memory loss.

- **Lewy body dementia.** Lewy bodies are abnormal balloon-like clumps of protein that have been found in the brains of people with Lewy body dementia, Alzheimer's disease and Parkinson's disease. This is one of the more common types of progressive dementia.

Common signs and symptoms include acting out one's dreams in sleep, seeing things that aren't there (visual hallucinations), and problems with focus and attention. Other signs include uncoordinated or slow movement, tremors, and rigidity (parkinsonism).

- **Frontotemporal dementia.** This is a group of diseases characterized by the breakdown of nerve cells and their connections in the frontal and temporal lobes of the brain. These are the areas generally associated with personality, behavior and language. Common symptoms affect behavior, personality, thinking, judgment, and language and movement.

- **Mixed dementia.** Autopsy studies of the brains of people 80 and older who had dementia indicate that many had a combination of several causes, such as Alzheimer's disease, vascular dementia and Lewy body dementia. Studies are ongoing to determine how having mixed dementia affects symptoms and treatments.

OTHER DISORDERS LINKED TO DEMENTIA

- **Huntington's disease.** Caused by a genetic mutation, this disease causes certain nerve cells in your brain and spinal cord to waste away. Signs and symptoms, including a severe decline in thinking (cognitive) skills, usually appear around age 30 or 40.
- **Traumatic brain injury (TBI).** This condition is most often caused by repetitive head trauma. Boxers, football players or soldiers might develop TBI.

Depending on the part of the brain that's injured, this condition can cause dementia signs and symptoms such as depression, explosiveness, memory loss and impaired speech. TBI may also cause parkinsonism. Symptoms might not appear until years after the trauma.

- **Creutzfeldt-Jakob disease.** This rare brain disorder usually occurs in people without known risk factors. This condition might be due to deposits of infectious proteins called prions. Signs and symptoms of this fatal condition usually appear after age 60.

Creutzfeldt-Jakob disease usually has no known cause but can be inherited. It may also be caused by exposure to diseased brain or nervous system tissue, such as from a cornea transplant.

- **Parkinson's disease.** Many people with Parkinson's disease eventually develop dementia symptoms (Parkinson's disease dementia).

DEMENTIA-LIKE CONDITIONS THAT CAN BE REVERSED

Some causes of dementia or dementia-like symptoms can be reversed with treatment. They include:

- **Infections and immune disorders.** Dementia-like symptoms can result from fever or other side effects of your body's attempt to fight off an infection. Multiple sclerosis and other conditions caused by the body's immune system attacking nerve cells also can cause dementia.
- **Metabolic problems and endocrine abnormalities.** People with thyroid problems, low blood sugar (hypoglycemia), too little or too much sodium or calcium, or problems absorbing vitamin B-12 can develop dementia-like symptoms or other personality changes.
- **Nutritional deficiencies.** Not drinking enough liquids (dehydration); not getting enough thiamin (vitamin B-1), which is common in people with chronic alcoholism; and not getting enough vitamins B-6 and B-12 in your diet can cause dementia-like symptoms. Copper and vitamin E deficiencies also can cause dementia symptoms.
- **Medication side effects.** Side effects of medications, a reaction to a medication or an interaction of several medications can cause dementia-like symptoms.
- **Subdural hematomas.** Bleeding between the surface of the brain and the covering over the brain, which is common in the elderly after a fall, can cause symptoms similar to those of dementia.
- **Brain tumors.** Rarely, dementia can result from damage caused by a brain tumor.

- **Normal-pressure hydrocephalus.** This condition, which is caused by enlarged ventricles in the brain, can result in walking problems, urinary difficulty and memory loss.

Risk factors

Many factors can eventually contribute to dementia. Some factors, such as age, can't be changed. Others can be addressed to reduce your risk.

RISK FACTORS THAT CAN'T BE CHANGED

- **Age.** The risk rises as you age, especially after age 65. However, dementia isn't a normal part of aging, and dementia can occur in younger people.
- **Family history.** Having a family history of dementia puts you at greater risk of developing the condition. However, many people with a family history never develop symptoms, and many people without a family history do. There are tests to determine whether you have certain genetic mutations.
- **Down syndrome.** By middle age, many people with Down syndrome develop early-onset Alzheimer's disease.

RISK FACTORS YOU CAN CHANGE

You might be able to control the following risk factors for dementia.

- **Diet and exercise.** Research shows that lack of exercise increases the risk of dementia. And while no specific diet is known to reduce dementia risk, research indicates a greater incidence of dementia in people who eat an unhealthy diet compared with those who follow a Mediterranean-style diet rich in produce, whole grains, nuts and seeds.
- **Excessive alcohol use.** Drinking large amounts of alcohol has long been known to cause brain changes. Several large studies and reviews found that alcohol use disorders were linked to an increased risk of dementia, particularly early-onset dementia.
- **Cardiovascular risk factors.** These include high blood pressure (hypertension), high cholesterol, buildup of fats in your artery walls (atherosclerosis) and obesity.
- **Depression.** Although not yet well-understood, late-life depression might indicate the development of dementia.
- **Diabetes.** Having diabetes may increase your risk of dementia, especially if it's poorly controlled.
- **Smoking.** Smoking might increase your risk of developing dementia and blood vessel diseases.
- **Air pollution.** Studies in animals have indicated that air pollution particulates can speed degeneration of the nervous system. And human studies have found that air pollution exposure — particularly from traffic exhaust and burning wood — is associated with greater dementia risk.

- **Head trauma.** People who've had a severe head trauma have a greater risk of Alzheimer's disease. Several large studies found that in people aged 50 years or older who had a traumatic brain injury (TBI), the risk of dementia and Alzheimer's disease increased. The risk increases in people with more-severe and multiple TBIs. Some studies indicate that the risk may be greatest within the first six months to two years after the TBI.
- **Sleep disturbances.** People who have sleep apnea and other sleep disturbances might be at higher risk of developing dementia.
- **Vitamin and nutritional deficiencies.** Low levels of vitamin D, vitamin B-6, vitamin B-12 and folate can increase your risk of dementia.
- **Medications that can worsen memory.** Try to avoid over-the-counter sleep aids that contain diphenhydramine (Advil PM, Aleve PM) and medications used to treat urinary urgency such as oxybutynin (Ditropan XL).

Also limit sedatives and sleeping tablets and talk to your doctor about whether any of the drugs you take might make your memory worse.

Complications

Dementia can affect many body systems and, therefore, the ability to function. Dementia can lead to:

- **Poor nutrition.** Many people with dementia eventually reduce or stop eating, affecting their nutrient intake. Ultimately, they may be unable to chew and swallow.
- **Pneumonia.** Difficulty swallowing increases the risk of choking or aspirating food into the lungs, which can block breathing and cause pneumonia.

- **Inability to perform self-care tasks.** As dementia progresses, it can interfere with bathing, dressing, brushing hair or teeth, using the toilet independently, and taking medications as directed.
- **Personal safety challenges.** Some day-to-day situations can present safety issues for people with dementia, including driving, cooking, and walking and living alone.
- **Death.** Late-stage dementia results in coma and death, often from infection.

Prevention

There's no sure way to prevent dementia, but there are steps you can take that might help. More research is needed, but it might be beneficial to do the following:

- **Keep your mind active.** Mentally stimulating activities, such as reading, solving puzzles and playing word games, and memory training might delay the onset of dementia and decrease its effects.
- **Be physically and socially active.** Physical activity and social interaction might delay the onset of dementia and reduce its symptoms. Aim for 150 minutes of exercise a week.
- **Quit smoking.** Some studies have shown that smoking in middle age and beyond might increase your risk of dementia and blood vessel conditions. Quitting smoking might reduce your risk and will improve your health.
- **Get enough vitamins.** Some research suggests that people with low levels of vitamin D in their blood are more likely to develop Alzheimer's disease and other forms of dementia. You can get vitamin D through certain foods, supplements and sun exposure.

More study is needed before an increase in vitamin D

intake is recommended for preventing dementia, but it's a good idea to make sure you get adequate vitamin D. Taking a daily B-complex vitamin and vitamin C also might help.

- **Manage cardiovascular risk factors.** Treat high blood pressure, high cholesterol and diabetes. Lose weight if you're overweight.

High blood pressure might lead to a higher risk of some types of dementia. More research is needed to determine whether treating high blood pressure may reduce the risk of dementia.

- **Treat health conditions.** See your doctor for treatment for depression or anxiety.
- **Maintain a healthy diet.** A diet such as the Mediterranean diet — rich in fruits, vegetables, whole grains and omega-3 fatty acids, which are commonly found in certain fish and nuts — might promote health and lower your risk of developing dementia. This type of diet also improves cardiovascular health, which may help lower dementia risk.
- **Get good-quality sleep.** Practice good sleep hygiene, and talk to your doctor if you snore loudly or have periods where you stop breathing or gasp during sleep.
- **Treat hearing problems.** People with hearing loss have a greater chance of developing cognitive decline. Early treatment of hearing loss, such as use of hearing aids, might help decrease the risk.

Diagnosis

Diagnosing dementia and its type can be challenging. To diagnose the cause of the dementia, the doctor must recognize the pattern of the loss of skills and function and determine what a person is still able to do. More recently, biomarkers have become available to make a more accurate diagnosis of Alzheimer's disease.

Your doctor will review your medical history and symptoms and conduct a physical examination. He or she will likely ask someone close to you about your symptoms as well.

No single test can diagnose dementia, so doctors are likely to run a number of tests that can help pinpoint the problem.

Cognitive and neuropsychological tests

Doctors will evaluate your thinking ability. A number of tests measure thinking skills, such as memory, orientation, reasoning and judgment, language skills, and attention.

Neurological evaluation

Doctors evaluate your memory, language, visual perception, attention, problem-solving, movement, senses, balance, reflexes and other areas.

Brain scans

- **CT or MRI.** These scans can check for evidence of stroke or bleeding or tumor or hydrocephalus.
- **PET scans.** These can show patterns of brain activity and whether the amyloid or tau protein, hallmarks of Alzheimer's disease, have been deposited in the brain.

Laboratory tests

Simple blood tests can detect physical problems that can affect brain function, such as vitamin B-12 deficiency or an underactive thyroid gland. Sometimes the spinal fluid is examined for infection, inflammation or markers of some degenerative diseases.

Psychiatric evaluation

A mental health professional can determine whether depression or another mental health condition is contributing to your symptoms.

Treatment

Most types of dementia can't be cured, but there are ways to manage your symptoms.

Medications

The following are used to temporarily improve dementia symptoms.

- **Cholinesterase inhibitors.** These medications — including donepezil (Aricept), rivastigmine (Exelon) and galantamine (Razadyne) — work by boosting levels of a chemical messenger involved in memory and judgment.

  Although primarily used to treat Alzheimer's disease, these medications might also be prescribed for other dementias, including vascular dementia, Parkinson's disease dementia and Lewy body dementia.

  Side effects can include nausea, vomiting and diarrhea. Other possible side effects include slowed heart rate, fainting and sleep disturbances.

- **Memantine.** Memantine (Namenda) works by regulating the activity of glutamate, another chemical messenger involved in brain functions, such as learning and memory. In some cases, memantine is prescribed with a cholinesterase inhibitor.

  A common side effect of memantine is dizziness.

- **Other medications.** Your doctor might prescribe medications to treat other symptoms or conditions, such as depression, sleep disturbances, hallucinations, parkinsonism or agitation.

In 2021, the Food and Drug Administration (FDA) approved aducanumab (Aduhelm) for the treatment of some cases of Alzheimer's disease. The medicine was studied in people living with early Alzheimer's disease, including people with mild cognitive impairment due to Alzheimer's disease. The medicine was approved in the United States because it removes amyloid plaques in the brain. But it hasn't been widely used because studies about its effectiveness at slowing cognitive decline are mixed and coverage is limited. Another Alzheimer's medicine, lecanemab, has shown promise for people with mild Alzheimer's disease and mild cognitive impairment due to Alzheimer's disease. It could become available in 2023.

A phase 3 clinical trial found that the medicine slowed cognitive decline in people with early Alzheimer's disease by 27%. Lecanemab works by preventing amyloid plaques in the brain from clumping. This study was the largest so far to look at whether clearing clumps of amyloid plaques from the brain can slow the disease.

Lecanemab is under review by the FDA. Another study is looking at how effective the medicine may be for people at risk of Alzheimer's disease, including people who have a first-degree relative, such as a parent or sibling, with the disease.

Therapies

Several dementia symptoms and behavior problems might be treated initially using nondrug approaches, such as:

- **Occupational therapy.** An occupational therapist can show you how to make your home safer and teach coping behaviors. The purpose is to prevent accidents, such as falls; manage behavior and prepare you for the dementia progression.

- **Modifying the environment.** Reducing clutter and noise can make it easier for someone with dementia to focus and function. You might need to hide objects that can threaten safety, such as knives and car keys. Monitoring systems can alert you if the person with dementia wanders.
- **Simplifying tasks.** Break tasks into easier steps and focus on success, not failure. Structure and routine also help reduce confusion in people with dementia.

Lifestyle and home remedies

Dementia symptoms and behavior problems will progress over time. Caregivers and care partners might try the following suggestions:

- **Enhance communication.** When talking with your loved one, maintain eye contact. Speak slowly in simple sentences, and don't rush the response. Present one idea or instruction at a time. Use gestures and cues, such as pointing to objects.
- **Encourage exercise.** The main benefits of exercise in people with dementia include improved strength, balance and cardiovascular health. Exercise might also help with symptoms such as restlessness. There is growing evidence that exercise also protects the brain from dementia, especially when combined with a healthy diet and treatment for risk factors for cardiovascular disease.

Some research also shows that physical activity might slow the progression of impaired thinking in people with Alzheimer's disease, and it can lessen symptoms of depression.

- **Engage in activity.** Plan activities the person with dementia enjoys and can do. Dancing, painting,

gardening, cooking, singing and other activities can be fun, can help you connect with your loved one, and can help your loved one focus on what he or she can still do.
- **Establish a nighttime ritual.** Behavior is often worse at night. Try to establish going-to-bed rituals that are calming and away from the noise of television, meal cleanup and active family members. Leave night lights on in the bedroom, hall and bathroom to prevent disorientation.
- **Limiting caffeine,** discouraging napping and offering opportunities for exercise during the day might ease nighttime restlessness.
- **Keep a calendar.** A calendar might help your loved one remember upcoming events, daily activities and medication schedules. Consider sharing a calendar with your loved one.
- **Plan for the future.** Develop a plan with your loved one while he or she is able to participate that identifies goals for future care. Support groups, legal advisers, family members and others might be able to help.

You'll need to consider financial and legal issues, safety and daily living concerns, and long-term care options.

Alternative medicine

Several dietary supplements, herbal remedies and therapies have been studied for people with dementia. But there's no convincing evidence for any of these.

Use caution when considering taking dietary supplements, vitamins or herbal remedies, especially if you're taking other medications. These remedies aren't regulated, and claims about their benefits aren't always based on scientific research.

While some studies suggest that vitamin E supplements may be helpful for Alzheimer's disease, the results have been mixed. Also, high doses of vitamin E can pose risks. Taking vitamin E supplements is generally not recommended, but including foods high in vitamin E, such as nuts, in your diet, is.

Other therapies

The following techniques may help reduce agitation and promote relaxation in people with dementia.

- Music therapy, which involves listening to soothing music
- Light exercise
- Watching videos of family members
- Pet therapy, which involves use of animals, such as visits from dogs, to promote improved moods and behaviors in people with dementia
- Aromatherapy, which uses fragrant plant oils
- Massage therapy
- Art therapy, which involves creating art, focusing on the process rather than the outcome

Coping and support

Receiving a diagnosis of dementia can be devastating. You'll need to consider many details to ensure that you and others are as prepared as possible for dealing with a condition that's unpredictable and progressive.

Care and support for the person with the disease

Here are some suggestions you can try to help yourself cope with the disease:

- Learn about memory loss, dementia and Alzheimer's disease.

- Write about your feelings in a journal.
- Join a local support group.
- Get individual or family counseling.
- Talk to a member of your spiritual community or another person who can help you with your spiritual needs.
- Stay active and involved, volunteer, exercise, and participate in activities for people with memory loss.
- Spend time with friends and family.
- Participate in an online community of people who are having similar experiences.
- Find new ways to express yourself, such as through painting, singing or writing.
- Delegate help with decision-making to someone you trust.

Helping someone with dementia

You can help a person cope with the disease by listening, reassuring the person that he or she still can enjoy life, being supportive and positive, and doing your best to help the person retain dignity and self-respect.

Support for caregivers and care partners

Providing care for someone with dementia is physically and emotionally demanding. Feelings of anger and guilt, frustration and discouragement, worry, grief, and social isolation are common. If you're a caregiver or care partner for someone with dementia:

- Learn about the disease and participate in caregiver education programs
- Find out about supportive services in your community, such as respite care or adult care, which can give you a break from caregiving at

scheduled times during the week
- Ask friends or other family members for help
- Take care of your physical, emotional and spiritual health
- Ask questions of doctors, social workers and others involved in the care of your loved one
- Join a support group

Preparing for your appointment

Most likely, you'll first see your primary care provider if you have concerns about dementia. Or you might be referred to a doctor trained in nervous system conditions (neurologist).

Here's some information to help you get ready for your appointment.

What you can do

When you make the appointment, ask if there's anything that needs to be done in advance, such as fasting before certain tests. Make a list of:

- **Symptoms,** including any that may seem unrelated to the reason for which you scheduled the appointment, and when they began
- **Key personal information,** including any major stresses or recent life changes and family medical history
- **All medications,** vitamins or supplements you take, including the doses
- **Questions to ask** the doctor

Even in the early stages of dementia, it's good to take a family member, friend or caregiver along to help you remember the information you're given.

For dementia, basic questions to ask the doctor include:
- What is likely causing my symptoms?
- Are there other possible causes for my symptoms?
- What tests are necessary?
- Is the condition likely temporary or chronic?
- What's the best course of action?
- What alternatives are there to the primary approach being suggested?
- How can dementia and other health issues be managed together?
- Are there brochures or other printed material I can have? What websites do you recommend?

Don't hesitate to ask other questions.

What to expect from your doctor

The doctor is likely to ask questions, such as:
- When did your symptoms begin?
- Have symptoms been continuous or occasional?
- How severe are symptoms?
- What, if anything, seems to improve symptoms?
- What, if anything, appears to worsen symptoms?
- How have the symptoms interfered with your life?

16. Personality disorders

A personality disorder is a type of mental disorder in which you have a rigid and unhealthy pattern of thinking, functioning and behaving. A person with a personality disorder has trouble perceiving and relating to situations and people. This causes significant problems and limitations in relationships, social activities, work and school. In some cases, you may not realize that you have a personality disorder because your way of thinking and behaving seems natural to you. And you may blame others for the challenges you face.

Personality disorders usually begin in the teenage years or early adulthood. There are many types of personality disorders. Some types may become less obvious throughout middle age.

Symptoms

Types of personality disorders are grouped into three clusters, based on similar characteristics and symptoms. Many people with one personality disorder also have signs and symptoms of at least one additional personality disorder. It's not necessary to exhibit all the signs and symptoms listed for a disorder to be diagnosed.

CLUSTER A PERSONALITY DISORDERS

Cluster A personality disorders are characterized by odd, eccentric thinking or behavior. They include paranoid personality disorder, schizoid personality disorder and schizotypal personality disorder.

Paranoid personality disorder

- Pervasive distrust and suspicion of others and their motives
- Unjustified belief that others are trying to harm or deceive you
- Unjustified suspicion of the loyalty or trustworthiness of others
- Hesitancy to confide in others due to unreasonable fear that others will use the information against you
- Perception of innocent remarks or nonthreatening situations as personal insults or attacks
- Angry or hostile reaction to perceived slights or insults
- Tendency to hold grudges
- Unjustified, recurrent suspicion that spouse or sexual partner is unfaithful

Schizoid personality disorder

- Lack of interest in social or personal relationships, preferring to be alone
- Limited range of emotional expression
- Inability to take pleasure in most activities
- Inability to pick up normal social cues
- Appearance of being cold or indifferent to others

- Little or no interest in having sex with another person

Schizotypal personality disorder
- Peculiar dress, thinking, beliefs, speech or behavior
- Odd perceptual experiences, such as hearing a voice whisper your name
- Flat emotions or inappropriate emotional responses
- Social anxiety and a lack of or discomfort with close relationships
- Indifferent, inappropriate or suspicious response to others
- "Magical thinking" — believing you can influence people and events with your thoughts
- Belief that certain casual incidents or events have hidden messages meant only for you

CLUSTER B PERSONALITY DISORDERS

Cluster B personality disorders are characterized by dramatic, overly emotional or unpredictable thinking or behavior. They include antisocial personality disorder, borderline personality disorder, histrionic personality disorder and narcissistic personality disorder.

Antisocial personality disorder

- Disregard for others' needs or feelings
- Persistent lying, stealing, using aliases, conning others
- Recurring problems with the law
- Repeated violation of the rights of others
- Aggressive, often violent behavior
- Disregard for the safety of self or others
- Impulsive behavior
- Consistently irresponsible
- Lack of remorse for behavior

Borderline personality disorder

- Impulsive and risky behavior, such as having unsafe sex, gambling or binge eating
- Unstable or fragile self-image
- Unstable and intense relationships
- Up and down moods, often as a reaction to interpersonal stress
- Suicidal behavior or threats of self-injury
- Intense fear of being alone or abandoned
- Ongoing feelings of emptiness
- Frequent, intense displays of anger
- Stress-related paranoia that comes and goes

Histrionic personality disorder

- Constantly seeking attention
- Excessively emotional, dramatic or sexually provocative to gain attention
- Speaks dramatically with strong opinions, but few facts or details to back them up
- Easily influenced by others
- Shallow, rapidly changing emotions
- Excessive concern with physical appearance
- Thinks relationships with others are closer than they really are

Narcissistic personality disorder

- Belief that you're special and more important than others
- Fantasies about power, success and attractiveness
- Failure to recognize others' needs and feelings
- Exaggeration of achievements or talents
- Expectation of constant praise and admiration
- Arrogance
- Unreasonable expectations of favors and advantages, often taking advantage of others
- Envy of others or belief that others envy you

CLUSTER C PERSONALITY DISORDERS

Cluster C personality disorders are characterized by anxious, fearful thinking or behavior. They include avoidant personality disorder, dependent personality disorder and obsessive-compulsive personality disorder.

Avoidant personality disorder

- Too sensitive to criticism or rejection
- Feeling inadequate, inferior or unattractive
- Avoidance of work activities that require interpersonal contact
- Socially inhibited, timid and isolated, avoiding new activities or meeting strangers
- Extreme shyness in social situations and personal relationships
- Fear of disapproval, embarrassment or ridicule

Dependent personality disorder

- Excessive dependence on others and feeling the need to be taken care of
- Submissive or clingy behavior toward others
- Fear of having to provide self-care or fend for yourself if left alone
- Lack of self-confidence, requiring excessive advice and reassurance from others to make even small decisions
- Difficulty starting or doing projects on your own due to lack of self-confidence
- Difficulty disagreeing with others, fearing disapproval
- Tolerance of poor or abusive treatment, even when other options are available
- Urgent need to start a new relationship when a

close one has ended

Obsessive-compulsive personality disorder
- Preoccupation with details, orderliness and rules
- Extreme perfectionism, resulting in dysfunction and distress when perfection is not achieved, such as feeling unable to finish a project because you don't meet your own strict standards
- Desire to be in control of people, tasks and situations, and inability to delegate tasks
- Neglect of friends and enjoyable activities because of excessive commitment to work or a project
- Inability to discard broken or worthless objects
- Rigid and stubborn
- Inflexible about morality, ethics or values
- Tight, miserly control over budgeting and spending money
- Obsessive-compulsive personality disorder is not the same as obsessive-compulsive disorder, a type of anxiety disorder.

When to see a doctor

If you have any signs or symptoms of a personality disorder, see your doctor or other primary care professional or a mental health professional. Untreated, personality disorders can cause significant problems in your life that may get worse without treatment.

Causes

Personality is the combination of thoughts, emotions and behaviors that makes you unique. It's the way you view, understand and relate to the outside world, as well as how you see yourself. Personality forms during childhood, shaped through an interaction of:

- **Your genes**. Certain personality traits may be passed on to you by your parents through inherited genes. These traits are sometimes called your temperament.
- **Your environment.** This involves the surroundings you grew up in, events that occurred, and relationships with family members and others.

Personality disorders are thought to be caused by a combination of these genetic and environmental influences. Your genes may make you vulnerable to developing a personality disorder, and a life situation may trigger the actual development.

Risk factors

Although the precise cause of personality disorders is not known, certain factors seem to increase the risk of developing or triggering personality disorders, including:

- Family history of personality disorders or other mental illness
- Abusive, unstable or chaotic family life during childhood
- Being diagnosed with childhood conduct disorder
- Variations in brain chemistry and structure

Complications

Personality disorders can significantly disrupt the lives of both the affected person and those who care about that person. Personality disorders may cause problems with relationships, work or school, and can lead to social isolation or alcohol or drug abuse.

Diagnosis

If your doctor suspects you have a personality disorder, a diagnosis may be determined by:

- **Physical exam.** The doctor may do a physical exam and ask in-depth questions about your health. In some cases, your symptoms may be linked to an underlying physical health problem. Your evaluation may include lab tests and a screening test for alcohol and drugs.
- **Psychiatric evaluation.** This includes a discussion about your thoughts, feelings and behavior and may include a questionnaire to help pinpoint a diagnosis. With your permission, information from family members or others may be helpful.
- **Diagnostic criteria in the DSM-5.** Your doctor may compare your symptoms to the criteria in the Diagnostic and Statistical Manual of Mental Disorders (DSM-5), published by the American Psychiatric Association.

Diagnostic criteria

Each personality disorder has its own set of diagnostic criteria. However, according to the DSM-5, generally the diagnosis of a personality disorder includes long-term marked deviation from cultural expectations that leads to significant distress or impairment in at least two of these areas:

- The way you perceive and interpret yourself, other people and events
- The appropriateness of your emotional responses
- How well you function when dealing with other people and in relationships
- Whether you can control your impulses

Sometimes it can be difficult to determine the type of personality disorder, as some personality disorders share similar symptoms and more than one type may be present. Other disorders such as depression, anxiety or substance abuse may further complicate diagnosis. But it's worth the time and effort to get an accurate diagnosis so that you get appropriate treatment.

Treatment

The treatment that's best for you depends on your particular personality disorder, its severity and your life situation. Often, a team approach is needed to make sure all of your psychiatric, medical and social needs are met. Because personality disorders are long-standing, treatment may require months or years.

Your treatment team may include your primary doctor or other primary care provider as well as a:
- Psychiatrist
- Psychologist or other therapist
- Psychiatric nurse
- Pharmacist
- Social worker

If you have mild symptoms that are well-controlled, you may need treatment from only your primary doctor, a psychiatrist or other therapist. If possible, find a mental health professional with experience in treating personality disorders.

Psychotherapy, also called talk therapy, is the main way to treat personality disorders.

Psychotherapy

During psychotherapy with a mental health professional, you can learn about your condition and talk about your moods, feelings, thoughts and behaviors. You can learn to cope with stress and manage your disorder. Psychotherapy may be provided in individual sessions, group therapy, or sessions that include family or even friends. There are several types of psychotherapy — your mental health professional can determine which one is best for you.

You may also receive social skills training. During this training you can use the insight and knowledge you gain to learn healthy ways to manage your symptoms and reduce behaviors that interfere with your functioning and relationships.

Family therapy provides support and education to families dealing with a family member who has a personality disorder.

Medications

There are no medications specifically approved by the Food and Drug Administration (FDA) to treat personality disorders. However, several types of psychiatric medications may help with various personality disorder symptoms.

- **Antidepressants.** Antidepressants may be useful if you have a depressed mood, anger, impulsivity, irritability or hopelessness, which may be associated with personality disorders.
- **Mood stabilizers.** As their name suggests, mood stabilizers can help even out mood swings or reduce irritability, impulsivity and aggression.
- **Antipsychotic medications.** Also called neuroleptics, these may be helpful if your symptoms include losing touch with reality (psychosis) or in some cases if you have anxiety or anger problems.
- **Anti-anxiety medications.** These may help if you have anxiety, agitation or insomnia. But in some cases, they can increase impulsive behavior, so

they're avoided in certain types of personality disorders.

Hospital and residential treatment programs

In some cases, a personality disorder may be so severe that you need to be admitted to a hospital for psychiatric care. This is generally recommended only when you can't care for yourself properly or when you're in immediate danger of harming yourself or someone else.

After you become stable in the hospital, your doctor may recommend a day hospital program, residential program or outpatient treatment.

Lifestyle and home remedies

Along with your professional treatment plan, consider these lifestyle and self-care strategies:

- **Be an active participant in your care.** This can help your efforts to manage your personality disorder. Don't skip therapy sessions, even if you don't feel like going. Think about your goals for treatment and work toward achieving them.
- **Take your medications as directed.** Even if you're feeling well, don't skip your medications. If you stop, symptoms may come back. You could also experience withdrawal-like symptoms from stopping a medication too suddenly.
- **Learn about your condition.** Education about your condition can empower you and motivate you to stick to your treatment plan.
- **Get active.** Physical activity can help manage many symptoms, such as depression, stress and anxiety. Activity can also counteract the effects of some psychiatric medications that may cause

weight gain. Consider walking, jogging, swimming, gardening or taking up another form of physical activity that you enjoy.
- **Avoid drugs and alcohol.** Alcohol and street drugs can worsen personality disorder symptoms or interact with medications.
- **Get routine medical care.** Don't neglect checkups or skip visits to your primary care professional, especially if you aren't feeling well. You may have a new health problem that needs to be addressed, or you may be experiencing side effects of medication.

Coping and support

Having a personality disorder makes it hard to engage in behavior and activities that may help you feel better. Ask your doctor or therapist how to improve your coping skills and get the support you need.

If your loved one has a personality disorder

If you have a loved one with a personality disorder, work with his or her mental health professional to find out how you can most effectively offer support and encouragement.

You may also benefit from talking with a mental health professional about any distress you experience. A mental health professional can also help you develop boundaries and self-care strategies so that you're able to enjoy and succeed in your own life.

Preparing for your appointment

Because personality disorders often require specialized care, your primary doctor may refer you to a mental health professional, such as a psychiatrist or psychologist, for evaluation and treatment. Taking a family member or friend along can help you remember something that you missed or forgot.

What you can do

Prepare for your appointment by making a list of:

- **Your symptoms,** including any that seem unrelated to the reason for the appointment
- **Key personal information,** including any major stresses or recent life changes
- **All medications,** including over-the-counter medications, vitamins, herbal preparations or other supplements that you're taking, and the doses
- **Questions to ask** your doctor

Basic questions to ask your doctor include:

- What type of personality disorder might I have?
- How do you treat my type of personality disorder?
- Will talk therapy help?
- Are there medications that might help?
- How long will I need to take medication?
- What are the major side effects of the medication you're recommending?
- How long will treatment take?
- What can I do to help myself?
- Are there any brochures or other printed material that I can have?
- What websites do you recommend visiting?

Don't hesitate to ask any other questions during your appointment.

What to expect from your doctor

During your appointment, your doctor or mental health professional will likely ask you a number of questions about your mood, thoughts, behavior and urges, such as:

- What symptoms have you noticed or have others said they notice in you?
- When did you or they first notice symptoms?
- How is your daily life affected by your symptoms?
- What other treatment, if any, have you had?
- What have you tried on your own to feel better or control your symptoms?
- What things make you feel worse?
- Have your family members or friends commented on your mood or behavior?
- Have any relatives had a mental illness?
- What do you hope to gain from treatment?
- What medications, vitamins, herbs or supplements do you take?

17. Paraphilic disorders:

Paraphilias involve sexual arousal to atypical objects, situations, and/or targets (eg, children, corpses, animals). However, some sexual activities that seem unusual to another person or a health care practitioner do not constitute a paraphilic disorder simply because they are unusual. People may have paraphilic interests but not meet the criteria for a paraphilic disorder.

The unconventional sexual arousal patterns in paraphilias are considered pathologic disorders only when both of the following apply:

- They are intense and persistent.
- They cause significant distress or impairment in social, occupational, or other important areas of functioning, or they harm or have the potential to harm others (eg, children, nonconsenting adults).

People with a paraphilic disorder may have an impaired or a nonexistent capacity for affectionate, reciprocal emotional and sexual intimacy with a consenting partner. Other aspects of personal and emotional adjustment may be impaired as well.

The pattern of disturbed erotic arousal is usually fairly well developed before puberty. At least 3 processes are involved:

- Anxiety or early emotional trauma interferes with normal psychosexual development.
- The standard pattern of arousal is replaced by another pattern, sometimes through early exposure to highly charged sexual experiences that reinforce the person's experience of sexual pleasure.
- The pattern of sexual arousal often acquires symbolic and conditioning elements (eg, a fetish symbolizes the object of arousal but may have been chosen because the fetish was accidentally associated with sexual curiosity, desire, and excitement).

Whether all paraphilic development results from these psychodynamic processes is controversial, and some evidence of altered brain functioning and functional anatomy is present in some paraphilias (eg, pedophilia).

In most cultures, paraphilias are far more common among males. Biologic reasons for the unequal distribution may exist but are poorly defined.

Dozens of paraphilias have been described, but most are uncommon or rare. The most common are

- Pedophilia
- Voyeurism
- Transvestic disorder
- Exhibitionism
- Others include sexual masochism disorder and sexual sadism disorder.

Some paraphilias (such as pedophilia) are illegal and may

result in imprisonment and lifetime registration as a sex offender. Some of these offenders also have significant personality disorders (eg, antisocial, narcissistic), which make treatment difficult.

Often, more than one paraphilic disorder is present.

- SEXUAL SADISM DISORDER

Sexual sadism disorder is characterized by taking sexual pleasure from humiliation, fear, or another form of mental harm to a person. Sadistic acts include restraint (such as ropes, chains, or handcuffs), imprisonment, biting, spanking, whipping, or beating. When someone repeatedly practices these sadistic sexual acts without consent from their partner(s), or when sadistic fantasies or behaviors cause social, professional, or other functional problems, sexual sadism disorder may be diagnosed. Extreme sexual sadism can be criminal, and lead to serious harm or even the death of another person.

Sexual sadism disorder falls under the category of paraphilic disorders, which are characterized by sexual interests, preferences, fantasies, urges, and behaviors considered to be "atypical." These interests, preferences, and behaviors are considered symptoms of a disorder only if they are acted upon in ways that have the potential to cause distress or harm to oneself or others, especially others who have not given consent.

Healthy sexual activity can include a wide array of behaviors and activities, which, when fantasized about or experienced between consenting adults can bring people pleasure. The majority of individuals who are active in BDSM (Bondage/Discipline, Dominance/Submission, and Sadism/Masochism) relationships or communities do not express any dissatisfaction with their sexual interests, and their behavior would not meet the criteria for sexual sadism disorder. In fact, many who engage in BDSM, (sometimes referred to as "kink") within the context of romantic relationships report that it brings them closer to their partner(s) due to increased feelings of trust that result from setting and respecting boundaries, as well as the emotional safety that comes from being able to explore less conventional sexual interests without judgment.

Symptoms

According to the DSM-5, to be diagnosed with sexual sadism disorder, a person must experience persistent and intense sexual arousal from causing or fantasizing about the physical or mental suffering of another person, with or without their consent. These symptoms must be present for at least six months and cause severe distress or dysfunction in social, professional, or another significant area of the person's day-to-day life. When combined with traits of antisocial personality disorder—poor impulse control, dishonesty, and lack of empathy and remorse—sexual sadism can be especially dangerous and difficult to treat.

What's the difference between sexual sadism disorder and BDSM, or kink?

BDSM, sometimes referred to as "kink", often involves sexual fantasies and behaviors that may include elements of domination and the infliction of pain upon one's partner. The difference is that relationships involving BDSM can be loving, trusting, and healthy. Studies have found that between 30 and 47 percent of people have tried spanking, dominant/submissive roleplay, or another aspect of BDSM during sexual activity. There is also no reason to believe that BDSM is a recent phenomenon. There is a long history of consensual role-play of domination and submission. For instance, the Kama Sutra, thought to be written more than 2,000 years ago, describes beating techniques that were intended to increase sexual drive.

Sexual sadism disorder is diagnosed when those engaging in the sadistic parts of these behaviors also report dysfunction in social, professional, or other aspects of life as a result, including obsessive thoughts, overwhelming anxiety, shame, or guilt.

How common is sexual sadism?

According to the DSM, the prevalence of sexual sadism disorder is unknown and is largely based on individuals in forensic settings. Depending on the criteria for sexual sadism, prevalence varies widely, from 2 percent to 30 percent of the population. Among individuals who have committed sexually motivated homicides, rates of sexual sadism disorder range from 37 percent to 75 percent.

Causes

While no specific causes have been determined for sexual sadism disorder, there are several theories. These include escapism, or a feeling of power for someone who normally feels powerless in day-to-day life; release of suppressed sexual fantasies; or progressive acting out of sadistic sexual fantasies over time.

Other psychiatric or social disorders may be diagnosed along with sexual sadism disorder, though they are not necessarily the cause.

Why do sexual sadists enjoy the pain of others?

Recent research suggests that engaging in sadistic sexual behaviors is driven by a desire for feelings of power and dominance, in addition to simply sexual pleasure. This is true for those in the general population with a sexually sadistic fetish and for those with a severe enough condition to be diagnosed with sexual sadism disorder.

According to an fMRI brain scan of 15 violent sexual offenders, sadists showed greater amygdala (a part of the brain associated with sexual arousal) activation when viewing images depicting pain. Sadists also rated these images as showing higher levels of pain than did non-sadists in the group. Further, sadists showed more activity in anterior insula (a pain processing part of the brain) than did non-sadists.

Does watching sadistic pornography make someone more likely to be a sexual sadist?

The relationship between sexual sadism and sadistic pornography is unclear. There is evidence that pornography may encourage the conversion of sexual fantasy to sexual offense, while other research suggests that those with sexually sadistic desires seek out sexually sadistic pornography.

A study of 512 men and women in Mozambique showed that men's frequent exposure to pornography was correlated with sadistic behavior by men towards women.

On the whole, it is not clear whether sadistic pornography use is a cause of sexual sadism disorder or a symptom of it.

Treatment

It is uncommon for people with sexual sadism disorder to seek treatment on their own. Instead, those found guilty of a sexual offense are required by law to get professional help from a psychologist or psychiatrist, who may perform an evaluation. Treatment for sexual sadism disorder typically involves psychotherapy and medication.

Cognitive-behavioral therapy can help an individual recognize patterns of sexual arousal and learn new and healthier responses to their urges. A therapeutic technique known as cognitive restructuring can help an individual identify and overcome distorted thinking patterns. Antidepressant medications that reduce impulsive behavior or anti-androgenic drugs that suppress sex drive may also be used to treat sexual sadism disorder.

Can sexual sadism disorder be cured?

Treatment for sexual sadism can be pharmacological or behavioral, or, likely, both. The drugs used most often to treat the condition are antidepressants (SSRIs) and testosterone blockers (anti-androgens and GnRH analogs). Psychotherapies often focus on relationship difficulties and self-regulation. It has also been found that advancing age correlates with a decrease in sexually sadistic desires.

VOYEURISTIC DISORDER

Voyeuristic disorder is a condition that causes a person to act on voyeuristic urges or become so consumed by voyeuristic fantasies that they are unable to function.

Voyeuristic fantasies and urges occur when a person is sexually aroused by watching a person who is unaware that they are being watched engage in sexual activity. This condition typically develops in adolescence or early adulthood and is more common in men than in women.

Voyeurism in itself isn't a disorder. When a person becomes so consumed by voyeuristic thoughts that they become distressed, unable to function or act on the urges with a person who hasn't given their consent, then it becomes a disorder.

Voyeuristic disorder is a type of paraphilic disorder. A paraphilic disorder is a condition that is characterized by strong and persistent sexual interest, urges, and behaviors that are typically focused around inanimate objects or children.

Some people with this condition might also experience thoughts of harming themselves or others during sexual activities.

Symptoms

The most common symptoms of voyeuristic disorder include:

- Persistent and intense sexual arousal from observing people perform sexual activities
- Becoming distressed or unable to function as a result of voyeurism urges and fantasies
- Engaging in voyeurism with a person who doesn't

give their consent

Some people with this condition might also perform sexual acts on themselves while observing others engaging in sexual activities.

This condition often occurs alongside other conditions like depression, anxiety, and substance abuse. In some cases, people with this condition could even develop another paraphilic disorder like exhibitionist disorder.

Causes

No particular cause has been identified for voyeuristic disorder, but certain risk factors could increase a person's likelihood to develop the condition. Factors such as:

- Sexual abuse
- Substance abuse
- Hypersexuality
- Sexual preoccupation

Diagnosis

A medical doctor or a licensed therapist can make a diagnosis of voyeuristic disorder. Upon examining you, if they find that you have voyeuristic urges and fantasies you are unable to overcome and feel distressed or unable to function as a result of these thoughts, a diagnosis of voyeuristic disorder might be made.

Symptoms of the disorder should have also persisted for 6 months or more before a conclusive diagnosis can be given.

A person also has to be at least 18 years old before they can be diagnosed with voyeuristic disorder. This is because it might be difficult to distinguish between the disorder and genuine sexual curiosity in children.

The DSM-5 also specifies the following criteria for a diagnosis of voyeuristic disorder to be made:

- Lasting over a period of 6 months
- Acting on sexual urges with a person who doesn't consent
- Being at least 18 years old

In order to be diagnosed with this condition a person's voyeuristic urges and behaviors must be so severe as to cause harm or distress to themselves or others. The prevalence of this condition is thought to be up to 12% in men and 4% in women. People with this condition are rarely ever diagnosed until they are caught committing sexual offenses as a result of their condition. This is because they are unlikely to share their condition with a medical professional or a loved one.

If you notice symptoms of voyeuristic disorder in a loved one help them get the help they need. Early treatment will prevent the condition from degenerating to a point in which the person living with it might commit a sexual offense.

As already mentioned, it's important to remember that voyeurism by itself isn't a disorder. Many people enjoy engaging in voyeurism which is solely the act of watching and being aroused by another person performing a sexual act.

Voyeurists will typically not engage in sexual activity with the person they are observing.

Treatment

Voyeuristic disorder can be effectively treated with either psychotherapy, medication, or both, depending on the severity of a person's condition.

Medication

Selective serotonin reuptake inhibitors (SSRIs) like Prozac (fluoxetine), Lexapro (scitalopram), and Cipralex are typically used for treating this condition. Although SSRIs are used primarily to treat depression, research shows that they can be effective in the treatment of voyeuristic disorder by helping to suppress impulsive behaviors.

Alternatively, Zoladex (goserelin), Lupron (leuprolide acetate), and drugs that reduce testosterone could also be used to treat this condition. A reduction in your testosterone levels will also cause a reduction in your sex drive which might help suppress voyeuristic urges.

Psychotherapy

Different forms of psychotherapy could help a person with voyeuristic disorder overcome the condition. Cognitive behavior therapy can help them learn to control their impulses and understand why their behavior isn't socially acceptable.

Therapy can also teach them coping mechanisms to help overcome sexual urges that are voyeuristic in nature.

Cognitive therapy can help a person explore the root cause of their behaviors and help them realize that some behavioral changes need to occur.

Coping

The key to coping with voyeuristic disorder is first recognizing that you need help and reaching out for help. You can start with confiding in a parent, friend, or loved one who will be supportive and can help you get the treatment that you need. If you notice that a loved one is exhibiting symptoms of the condition help them, get the help they need. You could do this by referring them to a medical expert or encouraging them to join support groups.

It's often hard for people with this condition to recognize that they have a problem that needs to be treated until they get in trouble.

Just speaking with them and helping them realize the gravity and consequences of their condition is a good start to convincing them to seek treatment.

PEDOPHILIC DISORDER

Pedophilic Disorder is a type of paraphilic disorder that is characterized by recurrent intense sexually arousing fantasies, urges, or behaviors involving prepubescent or young adolescents, usually under the age of thirteen. It is identified by an individual who is five years older or more than the child who is the victim of the fantasies or behavior patterns.

The majority of pedophiles are men. Attraction might be directed toward young males, young girls, or both. However, pedophiles prefer opposite-sex children by a 2 to 1 ratio to the same sex child. The adult is usually someone the child knows, such as a family member, step-parent, neighbor, or someone in a position of authority (e.g., a teacher, a coach). Genital contact appears to be less common than seeing or touching.

Many pedophiles will threaten the child to use force or physically hurt their family or pets if they disclose the abuse.

Causes

It is unknown what causes pedophilia (and other paraphilias). It is possible that pedophilia runs in families, but it's unknown if this is due to genetics or taught behavior. Another possibility with the development of pedophilia is a history of childhood sexual abuse; however, this has not been verified. According to behavioral learning theories, a child who witnesses or is the victim of improper sexual activities may be conditioned to replicate such actions.

There are other studies that indicate that a pedophile is more likely to have suffered childhood head trauma when compared to non-pedophiles.

Symptoms

- Recurrent strong sexually arousing thoughts, sexual impulses, or actions involving sexual interaction with a prepubescent child for at least 6 months (usually age 13 years or younger).
- The individual is at least 16 years old and at least 5 years older than the child.
- A late adolescent participating in an ongoing sexual relationship with a 12- or 13-year-old is not included.

Risk Factors

There are some people who are at a higher risk of developing pedophilia. There appears to be a link between pedophilia and antisocial personality where individuals who share both features being more likely to engage in sexual conduct with children. Second, many adult males with pedophilia report having been sexually assaulted as a child which may or may not be indicative of a causal relationship. Finally, each element that raises the likelihood of pedophilia raises the risk of pedophilic disorder as well.

Diagnosis

To be diagnosed with pedophilic disorder, the following criteria must be met according to the Diagnostic and Statistical Manual of Mental Disorders, Fifth Edition (DSM-5).

- For a period of at least 6 months, recurrent, intense sexual fantasies, urges, or behaviors involving sexual activity with a prepubescent child (generally age 13 or younger). These urges have been acted on or have caused significant distress or impairment in occupational, social, or other important areas of life.

- The individual is at least 16 years old and at least 5 years older than the victim child. This does not, however, include a late adolescent who is engaging in a continuing sexual relationship with a 12- or 13-year-old.
- A pedophilic disorder diagnosis should also describe whether the person is solely attracted to youngsters or not, the gender to whom the person is drawn, and whether the sexual impulses are confined to pedophilia.

Treatment

Psychotherapy

Individuals with pedophilic disorder have been effectively treated using cognitive-behavioral therapy (CBT) methods. Therapy is even more effective if the individual is willing to attend individual and group treatment. Responsibility taking, victim empathy, aversive training, learning about healthy versus unhealthy relationships, and developing a sound relapse prevention plan is key to success. Treatment should be conducted by a qualified therapist who is experienced in sex offender treatment.

Medication

Medication may be used along with psychotherapy if necessary. These include:

- **Antiandrogens,** such as Lupron and Provera are used which can help to lower the hyperactive sex drive.
- **Selective serotonin reuptake inhibitors,** which treat associated compulsive sexual disorders and reduce the symptoms related to stress and anxiety.

CHAPTER VII

The Prevalence Of Mental Health In South Africa

South Africa has a 12-month prevalence estimate of *16.5%* for common mental disorders (anxiety, mood and substance use disorders), with almost a third *(30.3%)* of the population having experienced a common mental disorder in their lifetime. These estimates are relatively high when compared with international prevalence estimates of the WHO (World Health Organization) World Mental Health surveys. As is the case internationally, the treatment gap in South Africa is also high, with only *one in four* people with a common mental disorder receiving treatment of any kind. For those with psychotic disorders, although identification and access to treatment is better, there are insufficient resources at community level for promotion of recovery.

Table 7.1 *The 12-month prevalence of adult mental disorders in South Africa*

Disorder	%
Anxiety	8.1
Mood	4.9
Impulse (personality disorders)	1.8
Substance use	5.8
Schizophrenia	1.0
Bipolar	1.0
Any anxiety, mood, impulsive or substance use	**16.5**

| disorder | |

Source: Williams et al (2007) in Department of Health- (2013: 11)

The 12-month prevalence of child and adolescent mental disorders in the Western Cape was reported to be *17 %* based on a review of local and international epidemiological literature (see Table 8.2)

Table 7.2 *The 12-month prevalence of child and adolescent mental disorders in the Western Cape*

Disorder	%
Attention-deficit/ hyperactivity disorder	5.0
Conduct disorder	4.0
Oppositional defiant disorder	6.0
Enuresis	5.0
Separation anxiety	4.0
Schizophrenia	0.5
Depression & Dysthymia	8.0
Bipolar disorder	1.0
Obsessive compulsive disorder	0.5
Agoraphobia	3.0
Simple phobia	3.0
Social phobia	5.0
Generalized anxiety disorder	11.0
Post-traumatic stress disorder	8.0
Any child and adolescent disorder	**17**

Source: Kleintjes et al (2006) in Department of Health (2013: 12)

Although South Africa is an upper-middle-income country, there are large disparities in wealth and access to resources. Within the health sector, these disparities are reflected in inequities between private and public health provision.

Private healthcare, funded through private health insurance and out of pocket payments, serves approximately *16%* of the population, compared with about *84%* served by public healthcare. Yet gross domestic product spend on each is similar (*4.1% and 4.2%* respectively). To redress these inequities, South Africa is phasing in (over 14 years) a national health insurance system, to ensure universal access to appropriate, efficient and high-quality health services. The introduction of national health insurance involves an overhaul of services as well as systems to support service delivery. Notably, at the district-service level is re-engineering of primary healthcare. This includes the establishment of district specialist clinical teams to provide support to ward-based primary healthcare teams. The latter comprise primary healthcare staff at fixed primary healthcare facilities as well as community outreach teams consisting of a professional nurse and community health workers

Legislative and policy developments specific to mental health include the introduction of a new *Mental Health Care Act (No 17 of 2002)* in 2004, as well as a new national mental health policy framework and strategic plan (2013–2020). Both promote decentralized and integrated care through task sharing. A noteworthy development that will enable implementation is the introduction of specialist district mental health teams expected to play a public mental health role.

Against this background, the South African national Department of Health advised that PRIME (PRogramme for Improving Mental health carE) in South Africa focus on integrating mental health services for depression and alcohol use disorders into the ICDM (Integrated Chronic Disease Management) service delivery platform given departmental priorities to reduce mortality as a result of chronic conditions, including HIV/AIDS. In light of service gaps in community-based psychosocial rehabilitation for patients with schizophrenia, this became a further focus of PRIME in South Africa. Ethical approval for the formative phase of PRIME, including the pilot study, was obtained from the University of KwaZulu-Natal Ethics Committee (HSS/0880/011 and BE 317/13) and the Human Research Ethics Committee of the Faculty of Health Sciences, University of Cape Town (REC Ref: 412/2011). All participants involved in semi-structured interviews consented to participating in the studies using approved informed consent procedures.

CHAPTER VIII

Organization And Structure Of Mental Health Services In South Africa

In line with recommendations from the World Health Organization (WHO) regarding the organization of mental health services, the South African mental health system will include a range of settings and levels of care including PHC, community-based settings, general hospitals and specialized psychiatric hospitals as illustrated in the diagram below.

Figure 8.1

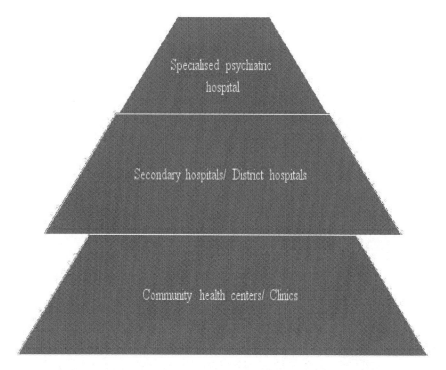

Figure 8.1 Diagram of mental health services in South Africa

Levels of structure and service

This provides information on the structure and services provided by the different levels of the health services. Healthcare in each province is delivered at the community level (CL), at the district level (DL) and the provincial level (PL).

Healthcare at the CL

Community services are delivered from a community health center (CHC), or community clinic (CC) serving a designated community, and are governed by health committee representative of that community. The CC is staffed by nurses, whereas the CHC at most has a basic multidisciplinary team. Most CCs render a 40-hour-per-week daytime service, while CHCs render a full-time service (24 hours, everyday of the week). In terms of mental health care, each clinic should render a comprehensive service, including diagnosing and treating the most common mental health conditions, community-based rehabilitation, and preventative and promotive services. If a condition falls outside the capabilities of clinic staff, or if there is an intractable problem, they consult with support staff at the CHC or the district hospital, who form their support system. The CHC or the district hospital are also the two services to which they may refer patients. Table 8.1 below details the proposed tasks of each level of service.

Table 8.1 Tasks at the various levels of health services

Community level	District level	Provincial level
■ Environmental health ■ Promotive and health education ■ Family planning ■ Antenatal, delivery, post- and neonatal care ■ Comprehensive care for children and school health ■ Comprehe	*All the services in the first column plus:* ■ Planning of health services for the district ■ Development of CL services ■ Provision of essential medicines at CL ■ Transport for the district ■ Environmental health	■ Translate national policy to provinces ■ Monitoring and evaluation of implementation of mental health care ■ Provision of sustainable budget ■ Working with district health

- nsive services for communicable and other diseases, & optometry
- Treatment of common illnesses and injuries
- Community rehabilitation
- Community mental health
- Community geriatric
- Community nursing and home care
- Oral health
- Accident and emergency
- Medical social work
- Basic laboratory and diagnostics, including X-rays
- Health

at DL
- Provision of facilities
- Maintenance of equipment, facilities, etc
- Monitoring and evaluation of health services in the district
- Health information system
- Human resource development
- Training and research
- Cooperation with other districts
- Ensuring cooperation within district

managers
- Consulting with stakeholders for planning and delivery of services
- Facilitating intersectoral collaboration, eg with the department of social development and housing
- Integration of mental health care
- Expanding mental health workforce
- Building capacity for mental health problem
- Establishment of a mental health directorate in each

monitoring ■ Occupational health ■ Basic medico-legal services		province ■ Responsible for provision of psychiatric inpatient and limited outpatient services at hospitals

Healthcare at the DL

Each district has a designated district hospital (level one hospital) for example, Khayelitsha district hospital, at which non-specialist inpatient services are provided, as well as the usual range of community services. As far as mental health care is concerned, in view of the shortage of members of the multidisciplinary team, such as clinical psychologist and occupational therapists, this may be first level at which a team of 'specialists' could be made available for referral and consultation.

Healthcare at the provincial level (PL)

According to the National Heath Act 61 of 2003, the provincial departments of health are responsible for the provision of all hospital services. This includes hospitals at levels one, two, three and four. Provincial hospitals (level three hospitals) provide the final referral service for the whole province, where a wider range of specialties and subspecialties is available. Forensic psychiatry will probably be handled mainly at this level. Level four hospitals are those that supply a service on a national level, for example Groote Schuur Hospital, which supplies a heart transplant service to the whole country. It is envisaged that the various provinces will supply different national services.

Healthcare services and psychotropic medication

Essential psychotropic drugs should be provided and made constantly available all levels of health care. According to the National Mental Health Policy Framework and Strategic Plan 2013-2020 (Department of Health, 2013: 29):

- All psychotropic medicines, as stipulated on the standard treatment guidelines and essential drugs list (EDL), will be available at all levels of care, including at PHC clinics.
- Drug interactions with other medications will be carefully monitored in all treatment of mental disorders.
- Routine screening and treatment of physical illness in all consultations for people with mental illness will be implemented.
- The use of psychotropic medication should be carefully monitored and evaluated, in line with broader quality improvement mechanisms in the Department of Health.

Difference in accessibility of facilities and resources

The following three points outline the wide-ranging differences that exist between the nine provinces in the accessibility of facilities and resources for mental health:

1. In some settings, psychiatric services are still provided by a specialized psychiatric team, which visits primary health clinics on specific days or at specific times. This is mainly in outlying and rural areas. This team consists of psychiatric trained nurses and sometimes a medical doctor and social worker. The team is based at a psychiatric hospital. As soon as a psychiatric patient is classified

as 'chronic stable', they are transferred to the comprehensive service and are no longer seen by specialists (Western Cape Government 2007). In other settings, community health nurses offer the psychiatric service, but at specific times. Not all of these nurses have psychiatric training, and no other special training has been provided to them.

2. In the past, the PHC level service used to be involved with supplying the patient with psychiatric medication, assessing the effectiveness of the medication and organizing admission when necessary. The social worker could assist in obtaining disability grants for the patients. No case finding, rehabilitation or primary prevention activities were involved. The narrow focus on medication without counselling left major needs of patients unattended (Swartz, 2002)

3. When a new patient comes to the clinic, they are referred to a hospital in some instances. From there they may be sent to a psychiatric hospital in the province or put on medication by the local medical doctor. This may involve travelling long distances from an outlying area, or a long period of hospitalization far from home.

Functions of mental health services in different settings

The National Mental Health Policy Framework and Strategic Plan 2013-2020 (Department of Health, 2013: 22) specifies various functions that should be performed by mental health services in different settings. These settings include community mental health services, general hospitals and specialized psychiatric hospitals. The different functions are outlined in the below table.

Table 8.2 Functions of mental health services in different settings

Settings	Functions
1. Community mental health services	■ Community residential care ■ Day-care services ■ General health outpatient services at PHC clinics ■ Specialised mental health support
2. Psychiatric services at general hospitals	■ Inpatient units for admissions of mentally ill persons for all categories ■ Provision of 72-hour assessments ■ Psychiatric wards must be designated in terms of the Mental Health Care Act.
3. Specialised psychiatric hospitals	■ Provision of inpatient and limited outpatient services ■ Functions as centres of excellence in providing training; supervision; support to secondary; and primary health services ■ Provision of subspecialist services like forensic psychiatry and child and adolescent services, for

	example Valkenberg Psychiatric Hospital and Lentegeur Psychiatric Hospital

CHAPTER IX

The Stigma Associated With Mental Illness And Being Mentally Ill

The stigma attached to mental illness is almost universal and greatly increases the suffering of mental health care users (MHCU) and their families. There are other factors mitigating against mental illness being taken seriously. For instance, until recently, psychiatric diagnoses were often vague and unreliable. This led to the conception that mental illness was not a 'real' illness. Newer methods of studying the brain, such as position emission tomography (PET) scans and functional magnetic resonance imaging (MRI) and research-based diagnostic classification (such as DSM-5) are gradually eliminating such misconceptions. Another factor often confusing health care workers used to the 'medical model' is the greater emphasis on the psychosocial context of illness and treatment in mental health care. Cockerham et al (2017:4) explain why the social context of disease is important: 'In emphasizing the social context, we do not imply that social problems are the sole or even the principal cause of mental disorders. However, a brain disorder such as epilepsy may very well be the result of a blow to the head received during civil unrest. Even if the epilepsy is the result of hereditary factors, social factors will determine whether or not the family will be able to obtain anticonvulsive treatment for the child and so avoid complications. Social factors therefore exert an influence on illnesses and healthcare. Psychological factors play an equally important role.

The presentation of any disease, its progress and its outcomes, are profoundly influenced by the person who has the disease. A person suffering from schizophrenia expresses their own personality, life experience and culture in the context of hallucinations, although the hallucinations may be completely biological in nature. Eisenberg (1986) calls mental health care that does not take psychological factors into consideration 'mindless biological psychiatry', and psychological care which underestimates the influence of biological factors 'brainless social psychiatry'

In 2001 the World Health Organization (WHO) dedicated its annual report mental health. In the final chapter of this report, it is said that:

only a few countries have adequate mental health resources. Some have almost none. The already large inequalities between and within countries in terms of overall health care are even greater for mental health care. Urban populations, and in particular the rich, have the greatest access, leaving essential services beyond the reach of vast populations. And for the mentally ill, human rights violations are commonplace.

This report led to the WHO's request to government to scale up their psychiatric services. World leaders recognize the promotion of mental health and well-being, and the prevention and treatment of substance of abuse, as health priorities within the global development agenda. The United Nations General Assembly in September 2015 adopted the Sustainable Development Agenda which includes mental health and substance abuse. Particularly, Goal 3 of the 17 Sustainable Development Goals focuses on ensuring healthy lives and promoting well-being for all at all ages through prevention and treatment of non-communicable diseases, including behavioral, developmental and neurological disorders, which constitute a significant challenge for sustainable development (WHO,2018).

In South Africa, policy such as the National Mental Health Policy Framework and Strategic Plan 2013-2020 (Department of Health, 2013) alludes to the plight mental health consumers face because of their diagnosis. The effects of such a diagnosis include neglect, rejection by family members and peers, social exclusion due to the stigma, abuse and violation of their basic rights which are enshrined in the Constitution of South Africa.

Consumer movement organization have emerged to address the problems that mental health care users (MHCUs) and families face. The influence and strength of these organizations have increased greatly since the dawn of the of the community psychiatric era. Since the change in approach that resulted in MHCUs spending most of their time outside of hospitals – many of them in the care of their families – families have organized themselves to address their common problems. At the same time, MHCU's themselves have become more active participants in the treatment and rehabilitation process, and this has led to groups of MHCU consumers forming support groups. Strictly speaking, only those persons who have been or who are being treated in the mental health system can regarded as consumers. However, families are often so closely involved in this process that they can also be seen as consumers of mental health care.

As a result of the recovery approach as a foundation of the mental health policy in many countries and states, it is now often a legal requirement that consumers should have a greater role in policy, planning and service delivery. In South Africa, the mental health review boards in each province (as stipulated by the *Mental Health Care Act 17 of 2002*), play a key role in advocating for the needs of MHCUs to uphold and protect their human rights. A community person must serve on the board (Mental Health Care Act). There are also a few consumer and family associations in some provinces which are run by non-governmental organizations (NGOs) such as the Mental Health Federation. The involvement of mental health consumers in their care, treatment and rehabilitation necessitates health worker's understanding of the problems that they and their families face as they navigate a health care system in which mental- health care has not been fully integrated.

Consumer's perceptions on recovery from mental illness

South Africa has adopted a recovery model for mental illness. This includes an approach to mental health care and rehabilitation which asserts that hope and the restoration of a meaningful life are possible, despite serious mental illness. Recovery focuses on restoring self-esteem and identity while fostering and attaining meaningful roles in society (South African National Department of Health, 2013). Over the last two decades, MHCU consumers of mental health services have expressed some very definitive views regarding the process of recovery. One such view is about staying in control of their lives (optimal level of functioning) rather than returning to premorbid levels of functioning. This approach focuses on resilience and control over problems that they encounter and how they manage their lives. It is important that health care workers take note of their unique perspective. Dixon et al (2016) conducted a review on various evidence-based, recovery-oriented treatment techniques which improved MHCU outcomes. These emerging techniques have been used by consumers to enhance their experience of mental health treatment and to promote recovery. These include attitudes and interpersonal focus; and emerging innovations towards recovery.

Attitudes and interpersonal focus

This approach involves:

- A therapeutic alliance which focuses on the quality of the relationship between the health care worker and the consumer. Consumers who are able to form good relationships with the health care worker are

- more likely to remain on treatment with a positive recovery outcome.
- Person-centered care which involves a comprehensive approach to understanding and responding to the consumer (MHCU and family), bearing in mind their history, needs, strength, hopes and dreams for recovery, support needed and outcomes with regard to quality of life. The consumer's culture, background and goals are incorporated in the treatment approach towards recovery.

Emerging innovations towards recovery

Technology, such as the internet, smartphone apps and social media, is important in improving engagement with consumers, as information and support from mental health care services can be expanded through the use of this technology. Peer-support networks may assist consumers who stigmatize themselves and have a need for role modelling.

The strategies identified here emphasize the need to remain abreast of technology but one should never forget the role that others (families, communities and stakeholders) play in promoting recovery in people diagnosed with a mental illness. While people with physical illnesses in the form of chronic diseases – like hypertension- are not viewed as being ill, mental illness is viewed differently which gives the impression that recovery is not possible. This in turn leads to a downward spiral of no hope which negatively impacts on recovery. The process of recovery has evolved over the years. Parker (2014) asserts that there is a new understanding of recovery according to which recovery is seen as a journey as opposed to an endpoint. This journey begins when the mental health problem is recognized, followed by the empowering realization that recovery is about the whole person and not just the illness.

The USA's Substance Abuse and Mental Health Services Administration (SAMHSA) has a Recovery Support Strategic Initiative which identifies four dimensions supporting recovery from mental illness (SAMHSA, 2011). These include:

- **Health.** This involves overcoming or managing one's disease or symptoms – for example, abstaining from the use of alcohol, illicit drugs, and non-prescribed medications if the mental illness is related to a substance-abuse problem. When in recovery, informed, healthy choices that support physical and emotional well-being are made.
- **Home.** This means having a stable and safe place in which to live.
- **Purpose.** This has to do with participating in meaningful daily activities, for example being employed, attending school, volunteering at organizations, and taking care of family- thus being independent, having an income and the resources to participate in society.
- **Community.** This involves maintaining relationships and social networks with others that are deemed supportive, provide hope and friendship.

Support groups for consumers

The most effective support groups are grassroots organizations of consumers (families, MHCUs or both) that organize and govern themselves (WHO, 2003). Although professionals may have initiated some of these groups, it is important for consumers to charge to ensure the survival of the group when professionals leave and to make certain that the group addresses the needs of the members. The growth of support groups over the last two decades has its roots in the community psychiatric movement, as well as in the self-help ideology which is part of the primary health care approach. Consumers have come to be recognized as equal partners of health workers in all aspects of care provision. Peer support occurs when people who have shared experiences draw on this experience to offer emotional and practical support to one another to manage their illness (Trachtenberg et al, 2013).

Functions of support groups

In the USA, support groups started small and then grew to formidable organizations. The organization NAMI has over 100 000 members, while other support groups render extensive consumer-run services with enormous budgets. In South Africa, the South African Depression and Anxiety Group (SADAG) is Africa's largest mental health support and advocacy group. SADAG has over 40 000 members and more than 200 support groups in South Africa which include outreach groups in remote rural areas. The activities carried out by the support groups are aimed at people with mental illnesses such as depression, bipolar mood disorders, post-traumatic stress disorder, obsessive compulsive disorder, anxiety, trauma, sleeping disorders, schizophrenia, teen suicide and substance abuse. These support groups are run by MHCUs for MHCUs. Activities include but are not limited to:

- social and recreational activities
- protection or advocacy efforts on behalf of individual consumers
- advocacy efforts on behalf of all persons with psychiatric disability
- assistance with activities of daily living
- provision of information
- therapeutic interventions, for example skills teaching; counselling

- fundraising

Three levels of needs have been identified by NAMI and the organization advises that support groups should try to address all three of these levels at each meeting:

1. *Head out of the sand.* On this level a consumer or family has just begun to accept the mental illness. They are still shocked and grieving and may be denying the reality at times. They need support and education from the group to deal successfully with this stage.
2. *Learning to cope.* The second level refers to families and MHCUs who have lived with mental illness for some time. They have been frustrated by the lack of information and help and disgusted by stigmatization. They are tired of the struggle and angry at the system. They need continued support and further information, as well as assistance and encouragement to work towards independence for the mentally ill person.
3. *Change.* At this level families who have accepted the illness and have learnt to cope; they may now want to do something to improve the services or change the system. They need to be involved in social action, policy making, lobbying and other activities which could bring about change.

Starting a support group

One consumer (family or MHCU) or one professional can start a support group. Asking service providers such as clinics, private practitioners and hospitals to hand out letters of invitation to consumers may prove successful. Social media platforms such as Facebook and WhatsApp can be used to advertise support groups and recruit members. Once a few consumers have been identified, a date, time and place can be set for convenient time. A Saturday or Sunday might be the most appropriate for many people, as long as the venue is accessible by public transport even on a Sunday. A family home might be the best place to meet if the group is small. If people have telephones, it would be a good idea to give them an encouraging call the day before the meeting. Using a bulk cell phone messaging system (WhatsApp message system) for communication is well worth the effort, since most people in South Africa have mobile phones and this system is more economical than phone calls. The group should be run by the consumers themselves; they should begin by structuring themselves by electing a chairperson, secretary and treasurer. A name may also be chosen. NAMI recommends that a group choose a name that does not use a euphemism for mental illness, so as to fight the stigma. The group then decides on goals and a mission and may later develop a complete constitution. Early on, the group members should exchange names, addresses and phone numbers, so that they can form an accessible support network for one another.

It is important that the business part of the meeting be kept short, so that there is enough time for sharing and caring. Consumers are encouraged to share their problems and experiences, while others support and assist with empathy, information and even concrete assistance. Groups usually meet once a month, and deal with business, support and information. Later in the life of the of the group, social action will be included. At that stage more frequent meetings may be necessary. The following factors ensure the growth of a strong support group (Fieldhouse et al, 2017):

- *Give all members a sense of ownership of the group.* Listen to their ideas; use them, involve them in activities, and address their needs.
- *Ensure a rapid turnover of leadership.* A diversity of leaders leads to diverse activities and to the development of people.

- *Create an appropriate structure.* Structures such as membership requirements, a committee, an annual general meeting, a bookkeeping system and a bank account are essential for a fully functioning group.
- *Have regular meetings* with interesting speakers discussing diverse topics.
- *Keep on trying to broaden the membership base and participation.* Recruitment should be an ongoing activity.
- *Try to build continuity on the committees* by staggering the terms of office. In this way, the committee members will never all be new and inexperienced.
- *Establish committees* to work on specific issues such as stigmatization, housing, socialization education and recreation.
- *Hold different kinds of meetings at different times.* These could include general meetings with a speaker, an open house at a new facility, an outdoor meeting, a workshop, or a forum.
- *Produce a brochure* on your group as soon as possible, even if it consists of only one typed page. This can be used in recruitment and in obtaining financial support.
- *Give credit* where and when is due.
- *Hold an annual evaluation and planning meeting,* so that the group stays on track.

Advocacy by consumers

Advocacy means to 'plead in support of' something or somebody. Advocacy has become one of the main tasks of consumer groups worldwide and is usually aimed at legislators (politicians) and top administrators in the services. The National Mental Health Policy Framework and Strategic Plan 2013 – 2020 alludes to the role the Department of Health will play in engaging the consumer and family associations in mental health policy development and implementation, in addition to planning and monitoring of services (South African National Department of Health, 2013). Consumers must be involved in decision making.

The methods of advocacy

A newsletter can be a useful tool for communicating with political representatives and other opinion formers. It need not be long, but there should be a focus on policy issues and on the needs of consumers. Testifying at public hearings, in front of parliamentary committees, and at commissions is another useful method. At first one may not have the required skills, but the first-hand stories of consumers are powerful tools and can have an impact which scientific documents lack. Letters can be written to local newspapers, politicians and administrators. Letters should be short and straight to the point and, even if a whole group decides to write about a single topic, each should use their owns words. Petitions or group letters are not as effective.

The media can play an important role in airing topics that need attention. Groups should get to know health reporters at local papers, and presenters of health programmes on radio. Television is a difficult medium to access but also a powerful one. Serving on boards is an important way of putting consumers in positions of power. Psychiatric hospitals are all required by law to have a hospital boards, and it would be useful for consumer groups to ensure that they are represented on these bodies. In the near future, clinics will also be setting up committees and districts will have health committees. All these bodies could do with a mental health consumer presentative. An interview with a representative or administrator is often a very effective way of dealing with an important issue. Identify and keep to a few important issues, so that the interview does not become a general gripe session. Make sure of the facts about all these issues and decide what the person should do about each one. Select as main spokesperson an articulate member of the consumer group who can speak with confidence. They should, however, involve the other members of the delegation strategically. A diverse group of consumers (for example, parents, siblings, patients, spouses) will have greater impact. Usually delegations number about five people.

Involvement of consumers in policy, planning and evaluation

Service providers should promote the involvement of consumers in the process of decision making in areas of service delivery, service planning and development, training and evaluation of services. Both MHCUs and their families have a unique perspective on care needs and provision, and they should be active partners with adequate power in the process of planning and evaluation. Mechanism for the involvement of consumers are the following:

- Develop empowerment workshops to train consumers in activism and advocacy.
- Make clear policy on the process of consumer involvement, in order to convey transparently to consumers their rights and responsibilities in this matter.
- Involve consumers in planning committees when developing new services, where they should be supported to take part as equal partners.
- Have consultative meetings with consumers at different points during the planning or evaluation process.
- Appoint consumer consultants to facilitate the process of involving consumers. A consumer consultant is a consumer who has been trained

to represent the group and has a network of consumers on whom they can call for input.
- Involve consumers as fieldworkers for needs assessments and service evaluations.
- Conduct in-depth interviews with consumers to explore their experience of using existing services.
- Develop a structure to support consumers in creating their own consumer-participation activities, such as consumer action groups on certain issues like housing (Tambuyzer et al, 2011).

None of these mechanisms will work unless the mental health service creates a supportive environment for consumer participation. The attitudes of health professionals have been seen as a major barrier to consumer involvement – they seem to doubt that consumers add value to the process. Nurses, due to their numbers in the system and their close relationships with consumers, are well placed to change these perceptions. Finally, experience has shown that individual consumers vary in their ability and willingness to become involved. Consumers should not be viewed as a homogeneous population, and opportunities for training and for participation should be individualized.

CHAPTER X

Suicide

Background

Suicide occurs throughout the lifespan, and in 2015 was among the top 20 leading causes of death globally, and the second leading cause of death among persons 15-29 years old (WHO,2017). Globally about 10.7 persons per 100 000 successfully commit suicide, with nearly 800 000 deaths due to suicide in 2016 (WHO, 2018). In South Africa reported suicide mortality rates of 11.6, Swaziland 13.3 and Lesotho 21.2 persons per 100 000 (WHO,2018:32). The reasons for the high suicide rates in Africa are many and include suicide being an escape from legal system with brutal punishments for crimes; a solution to problems linked to poverty and to health issues especially human immunodeficiency virus (HIV)/ acquired immunodeficiency syndrome (AIDS); displacement; homelessness and war. Globally, the success rate is greater for males, particularly in the age group 25-34 years (WHO, 2018). Survivors of suicide have described the experience as something that has links to oppression and to relief, in expressions such as: 'body and mind crushed by life's demands'; 'invisible agony'; and 'death offers a sweet smell'.

Definitions

Suicide behavior includes thinking about suicide, planning for suicide, attempting the suicide and the suicide itself (WHO, 2014). The various terms are defined as follows:

- *Suicide.* Self-inflicted death with evidence (either explicit or implicit) that the MHCU intended to die

- **Suicidal ideation.** Thoughts of engaging in behavior intended to end one's life
- **Suicide plan.** Formulation of a specific method through which one intends to die
- **Suicide attempt.** Engagement in potentially self-injurious behavior in which there is at least some intent to die
- **Suicidal intent.** Subjective expectation and desire for a self-destructive act to end in death
- **Deliberate self-harm.** Willful self-inflicting of painful, destructive, or injurious acts without intent to die

Suicide profile

Suicide profiles differ per geographical setting and between the general population of the specific community. The adoption of a public health model will allow for a structure approach to suicide. It is relevant that each clinical area should develop a profile of suicide, identifying what the problem is, and the population-specific risk, while at the same time not ignoring the outliers to the profile. This should be accompanied by the implementation of specific protective factors to buffer against the risk, followed by evaluation and development of policies and programmes (WHO, 2014). In particular, consideration needs to be given to the fact that MHCUs more frequently use medication as a means for suicide due to its accessibility, and to comorbidities such as chronic pain and substance abuse (Bhatt et al, 2018). However, suicide is prevalent in MHCUs with diagnostic labels of mood disorders, psychotic disorders, substance use disorders (Bhatt et al, 2018) and where impulsivity is evident such as in personality disorders.

Global profile and risk factors

The risk factors need identification for specific regions and encompass biological, psychological, social and economic factors. The risk factors cannot be seen in isolation, but in conjunction with the MHCU's bio-psychological vulnerability, stressors and the strength of protective factors like the availability of social and professional support, willingness to seek support and personal resources to deal with challenges. Below are some risk factors (Dumon, & Portzky,2014; WHO,2014):

- In lower middle-income countries, (LMICs), suicide is 57 per cent higher in men (WHO, 2014)
- Age in LMIC: young adults (15-29 years) and elderly women (>70 years) have higher risk and middle-aged males (WHO,2014)
- IN LMIC, 44 per cent violent deaths in males and 70 per cent violent deaths in females are due to suicide (WHO, 2014)
- In LMICs, pesticide ingestion is most common (WHO, 2014)
- Ethnicity depending on geographical location
- Unemployment
- Relationship steeped in gender-based violence
- Lack of social support
- High-risk profession, e.g., police
- Minority group, for example, lesbian, gay, bisexual, transgender persons
- Social isolation, for example, living alone
- Recent criminal offence
- Substance or alcohol abuse
- Medical conditions causing chronic pain
- Recent loss of a significant person

Suicide prevention

Suicide prevention programmes should incorporate national measures as well as those to be implemented in health care settings.

National measures

National measures that should be put in place include:
- Limiting access to lethal means:
  - changing pack sizes of dispensed medication
  - introducing legislation to limit over-the-counter purchases of analgesics
  - creating blister packs for medication
  - limiting carbon monoxide emissions from cars
  - implementing firearm laws controlling access
  - restricting pedestrian access to bridges, railways or barricade areas of high-rise buildings
  - creating legislation to limit access to alcohol
- Increasing and supporting national surveillance of suicide for a composite data registry
- Raising awareness through education about warning signs for suicide, alcohol and substance-use disorders and bullying (especially cyber-bullying and sexting)
- Recognizing World Suicide Prevention Day on 10 September
- Scaling up treatment of MHCUs attempting suicide
- Providing for accessible 24/7 treatment for crises, relationship issues and mental health disorders
- Controlling insensitive media reporting relating to suicide
- Instituting measures to decrease stigma for health seeking behaviors
- Instituting measures to support MHCUs affected by suicide, inclusive of bereavement
- Providing continued support post-discharge not only for mental health care disorders
- Implementing a national strategy on suicide prevention

Suicide warning signs

The warning signs listed below are general and need to be in context with other behaviors and not in isolation. For example, it might be appropriate for an older person to be writing a will, but this could be questionable for a 10-year-old child. Warning signs can be grouped under the following pointers:

- *Focus of conversation.* Focuses on death, shows despair and openly talks about unbearable pain or hopelessness; verbal suicide threats; enquiring about lethality; talking about being burdensome; guilt statements like 'it's all my fault'; helplessness.
- *Preparation for death.* Updating/writing a will; giving away possessions; saying good-bye to others; cleaning up room/house; writing a suicide note; stockpiling of policies for funeral policy; checking suicide clauses in policies.
- *Signs of depression.* See earlier chapter, under mood disorders (depression).
- *Social withdrawal.* Choosing to be alone and avoiding friends and social activities.
- *Mood change.* Shifting from hopelessness/agitation to sudden calm.
- *Uncharacteristic reckless behavior.* Driving dangerously or increased substance abuse evidencing decreased value for life.
- *Electronic search history.* Showing ways to commit suicide.
- *Display status on social media.* Evidencing death cue statements like 'What's the point?'
- *Self-medication.* Using over-the-counter medication or substances like alcohol or increasing use of prescribed medication in an attempt to ameliorate the feelings of despair/depression.

MISS VUYO NYELI

ABOUT THE AUTHOR

Vuyo Nyeli

MISS VUYO NYELI is a Wellness Coach and a Psychotherapist, she holds a B.Cur degree from the University of the Western Cape, a Psychotherapy Nursing Certificate from Nursing CE, California, USA. She's also been studying law at the University of South Africa and she's due to obtain her LLB degree very soon.

Vuyo is very passionate about mental health awareness. She is the founder and the host of The Mental Health Podcast. She created this podcast in order share her knowledge and experience on mental health as well as reducing the stigma surrounding mental illness and being mentally ill, by educating and creating mental health awareness. The podcast goes live every Thursday at 19:00. She is also a regular guest at a local radio station, Radio Zibonele every Monday at 21:00 where she talks about mental health disorders and other mental health related issues as part of her mental health awareness campaign.

Vuyo Nyeli hails from Cala in the Eastern Cape and currently lives in Boksburg, Johannesburg, South Africa. She has one child, Liwa. She is not married. She has three siblings, two sisters and one brother.

REFERENCES

https://globalwellnessinstitute.org/global-wellness-institute-blog/2021/02/23/industry-research-defining-mental-wellness-vs-mental-health/

https://www.planstreetinc.com/top-ten-reasons-why-mental health-is-so-important/

https://toronto.cmha.ca/documents/benefits-of-good-mental-health/

https://positivepsychology.com/benefits-of-mental-health/

https://www.mind.org.uk/information-support/types-of-mental-health-problems/mental-health-problems-introduction/about-mental-health-problems

https://www.mind.org.uk/information-support/types-of-mental-health-problems/mental-problems-introduction/causes/

https://www.mayoclinic.org/diseases-conditions/mental-illness/symptoms-causes/syc-20374968#:~:text=Certain%20factors%20may%20your,medical%20condition%2C%20such%20as%20diabetes

https://www.mayoclinic.org/diseases-conditions/mental-illness/diagnosis-treatment/drc-20374974

Middleton L. 2020. (Mental Health Nursing, A South African Perspective). Seventh Edition. Juta. Cape Town, South Africa.

NOTE TO READER

Kindly note that the emergency numbers provided in this book are for South Africa and those who reside within the borders of South Africa. Therefore, you are advised to use your own country's 24-hour emergency lines. I used SA emergency numbers only, simply because I am based in South Africa.

CONCLUSION

Mental illness is the instability of one's health, which includes changes in emotion,thinking, and behavior. Mental illness can be caused due to stress or reaction to a certain incident. It could also arise due to genetic factors, chemical imbalances, child abuse or trauma, social disadvantage, poor physical health condition, etc. Mental illness is curable. One can seek help from the experts in this particular area or can overcome this by illness by positive thinking and changing their lifestyle. The way we sometimes fall physically sick, it's the same way we also fall mentally ill. For example, when you have a toothache, you go to a dentist, but when you fall mentally sick you keep to yourself and 'soldier' on. We need to normalize seeking help for psycho-emotional issues too.

To conclude, it is of great importance that awareness is increased in our society so that affected individuals who tend to not seek help due to fear of victimization and stigmatization can feel more welcomed and not see ending their lives as the only option.

ACKNOWLEDGEMENT

To my professional web designer, manager, consultant and a friend, Phumulani Sgudla, thank you for your support and encouragement. I am really honoured to have known you, I learned a lot from you, and I cannot thank you enough for the amazing work you have done for me, starting from the Podcast set up and website design. You are truly the best friend I've ever had in my whole life. I wish you and your Visionary Designs nothing but the best. Keep on being kind, humble, patient and delivering the good work, and take care of yourself.

To Sive Mjanyana of Radio Zibonele, thank you for granting me the opportunity to be a regular guest on your evening show Masifundisane, to raise mental health awareness and other general health issues. I also thank your listeners for their enthusiasm and participation during the show.

Lastly, I would like to thank everyone who showed interest and supported The Mental Health Podcast by listening, subscribing and following our social media pages.

Made in the USA
Columbia, SC
09 February 2023

11333542R00326